the

Stakeholder

CORPORATION

THE BODY SHOP

Blueprint
for maximizing
stakeholder value

David Wheeler
Maria Sillanpää

PITMAN
PUBLISHING

London · Hong Kong · Johannesburg · Melbourne · Singapore · Washington DC

This book is dedicated to Äiti, Isä, Andrea and every one of our personal stakeholders upon whose love and support we depend.

PITMAN PUBLISHING
128 Long Acre, London WC2E 9AN
Tel: +44 (0)171 447 2000
Fax: +44(0)171 240 5771

A Division of Pearson Professional Limited

First published in Great Britain in 1997

The right of David Wheeler and Maria Sillanpää to be identified as
authors of this work has been asserted by them in accordance with the
Copyright, Designs and Patents Act 1988.

All profits to The Body Shop International PLC will be donated
to academic research or investment into stakeholding, after
deduction of publishing and promotional costs.

ISBN 0273 62661 2

British Library Cataloguing in Publication Data
A CIP catalogue record for this book can be obtained from the British Library

10 9 8 7 6 5 4 3 2 1

Typeset by Northern Phototypesetting Co Ltd, Bolton
Printed and bound in Great Britain by Biddles Ltd, Guildford and King's Lynn

The Publishers' policy is to use paper manufactured from sustainable forests.

About the authors

David Wheeler is a senior executive at The Body Shop International and a Visiting Professor at Kingston University. He is a Research Director with the New Academy of Business. He is best known for his work in environmental policy and corporate social responsibility.

Professor Wheeler started his career in the water industry where he specialized in bathing water pollution control. Later, as an academic based at the Robens Institute of the University of Surrey he became a frequent consultant to the World Health Organization, the UK Overseas Development Administration and a wide variety of development agencies working in development projects in Africa and Latin America.

In his five years with The Body Shop, David Wheeler has overseen the publication of a number of independently verified audits of the company's social and environmental performance. Throughout his career, he has published papers and articles in a wide variety of medical, academic and popular journals.

Since 1993 **Maria Sillanpää** has been responsible for the implementation of social auditing within The Body Shop Group and now manages a team of auditors responsible for the production of The Body Shop's public statements on the company's environmental, animal protection and social issues.

She started her career as an academic at Tampere University, Finland, where she initiated a program of business ethics teaching as part of the Business School curriculum in 1990.

Her previous academic work and publications have focussed on the linkages between social responsibility and corporate strategic thinking as well as social auditing. Her current research interests focus on the linkages between the theories of learning organizations, complexity, and a dialogue-based approach to business ethics.

Maria Sillanpää is a member of the Steering Committee of the Institute of Social and Ethical AccountAbility.

ACKNOWLEDGMENTS

Books which are a combination of theory and practical guidance necessarily owe a special debt of gratitude both to those who theorize and to those practitioners who help bring theory to life. In the latter category we are indebted to our colleagues in the Ethical Audit department of The Body Shop who have co-designed and successfully road tested many of the ideas in Part 3: most especially Nicky Amos, Debbie Budden, Rita Godfrey, Red Mills, Sharon Sims, Janet Shepherd, Samantha Towle and Peter Wilson. In 1996 this team was rated as first in the world for environmental and stakeholder reporting in a study conducted for the United Nations and we are very proud of them. Their work, and ours would not have been possible without the constant support of the founders, senior management and employees of The Body Shop over the last five years.

Our external sources of practical inspiration have included numerous external advisers and consultants: but most importantly Dr Simon Zadek and colleagues at the New Economics Foundation. Intellectual and academic stimulation has come from Professor Peter Pruzan of the Copenhagen Business School, Professor Henk van Luijk of Nijenrode University, Professor Tom Cannon of the Management Charter Initiative and Professor Rob Gray of the University of Dundee. Comradeship was a constant from Alan Parker and colleagues at Ben & Jerry's, Richard Evans and colleagues at Traidcraft and the growing network of social and ethical auditors in organizations as diverse as the Cooperative Movement and British Telecom.

Most of the research for this book was done by ourselves and we therefore accept full responsibility for all errors, but we did receive especially valuable inputs from Dr Charles Jackson, Ed Mayo, Alan Parker and Alina Tugend. Thoughtful comments and suggestions for the book were received from Angela Bawtree, Sue Belgrave, Jean Floodgate, Gavin Grant, Iain Lynch, Steve McIvor, Ashley Naylor and Paula Warrell. Rhona Mitchell sourced the illustrations, Sophie Freeman handled contracts and Gemma Lacey secured permissions. Richard Stagg, publisher, and Martin Drewe, project editor, of Pitman Publishing, were most encouraging. Cathy Tingley word processed every word with her customary skill and dedication.

Finally, we would like to thank the Rt Hon Tony Blair MP for putting stakeholding on the political map in 1996. Without this we might not have seen the urgency of writing the book.

Contents

Foreword

After thirty years in business I am still trying to make sense of it all. Some days it seems the most important qualification you need is a degree in semantics or philosophy. Other times it would be useful to have a background is psychology and, on really bad days, in psychotherapy. Standard training in business rarely equips business people with the wisdom and skills to deal with the fundamental challenges let alone the day to day crises which are commonplace in today's ultra-competitive business environment.

As an avid reader and absorber of contemporary business thinking which does try to address some of the deeper questions about the role of enterprise and the responsibilities of leadership, I am regularly refreshed by the sheer good sense of those who argue it is acceptable to be yourself, to debate the issues, to bring your heart to work. Indeed, in the pressure cooker world which business is fast becoming, it is ever more important for individuals to achieve personal balance, to work with colleagues in a noncompetitive and co-creative way and to be able to admit that sometimes we all get things wrong. And if it is important that individuals get the space and spiritual support to reflect on what their work means, it is just as urgent that organizations do the same.

I never cease to be amazed at how much of the "business as usual" approach still pervades company behavior today. Very few chief executives publicly challenge the role of business itself to try to connect their activities to wider social objectives except in a strict economic sense. Some of our best companies still retreat into "shareholder value" justifications for excellent community outreach programmes when they should simply celebrate and say "this is what business should be about". But I detect that things are changing. Large companies around the world are beginning to recognize that legitimacy in society is an active responsibility not a passive one. It takes a little courage to shed the command and control mentality – to see your stakeholders as sources of strength rather than instability. But if fortune favors the brave, then commercial success will increasingly favor the community-based, stakeholder inclusive companies of the twenty-first century.

This book analyzes the history of stakeholding in business and tells a few stories along the way. Some made me laugh, others made me want to weep. Without doubt, business has a lot to answer for and has been responsible for a lot of misery in the world. But business has also contributed hugely to the lives of many people; it has liberated the previously poor and the dispossessed and has generated untold numbers of honorable livelihoods over the generations. The book also contains a few clues along the way as to how the involvement of multitudes of constituencies can be maximized and what benefits it can bring.

I would not pretend that my company is the perfect stakeholder inclusive corporation. We do of course try to continuously improve our relationships and we struggle to make ourselves community-based: multi-local rather than multi-national. And we draw great strength from the growing number of like-minded business people from the cooperative movement and from companies as diverse as Ben & Jerry's and Levi Strauss in the USA, British Telecommunications plc in Europe and Citizens Bank in Japan. Their stories are very different from ours but their aspirations to do the right thing by all their stakeholders are crystal clear. So this book is as much of a beacon for me and my co-workers as I hope it will be for you and yours. It is a business book for a brighter future, when relationships will be more important to successful enterprises than cash flow. I look forward to more reflective, more innovative and more inclusive companies in decades to come, and I hope this book helps them get there.

Anita Roddick OBE

Founder of The Body Shop International Plc

Introduction

The stakeholder corporation

Business people are rarely permitted much time for reflection, still less for daydreaming about the shape of the world to come. But in the final years of a millennium, when business is clearly more influential in the global economy than at any time in history, we must consider whether that influence is always as benign as responsible business people and their stakeholders would wish it to be. And, if it is not, what are the ways of working and standards to which businesses should aspire?

The central proposition of this book is that the long term value of a company rests primarily on: the knowledge, abilities and commitment of its employees; and its relationships with investors, customers and other stakeholders. Loyal relationships are increasingly dependent upon how a company is perceived to create "added value" beyond the commercial transaction. Added value embraces issues like quality, service, care for people and the natural environment and integrity. It is our belief that in the future the development of loyal, inclusive stakeholder relationships will become one of the most important determinants of commercial viability and business success.

> **It is our belief that in the future the development of loyal, inclusive stakeholder relationships will become one of the most important determinants of commercial viability and business success.**

In the book we present examples of best practice from around the world, which we believe demonstrate beyond reasonable doubt that stakeholder inclusion leads to better long term business performance – including increased economic value for shareholders. Evidence for this comes from the USA, from Europe and from the Far East.

In most countries, business is the principal driver of national economic performance. Indeed, since the demise of the planned economies of the Soviet bloc in the 1980s, there is scarcely a debate about the dominance of free enterprise as the main determinant of global economic development. Politicians of the left and the right no longer seriously question the notion of free trade. Nor do they discuss the merits or demerits of state ownership or control of large enterprises. Governments of all persuasions now appear convinced of the superior efficiency of the market in allocating resources and producing goods and services for those who want to buy them. It is only in sectors like education and healthcare that the ideological tussle for control persists.

> **The book is not about right and wrong, good and evil; rather it is a guide to 'best practice' techniques for stakeholder inclusion which aim to deliver optimal business performance.**

It has been estimated by the Worldwatch Institute that the top 500 corporations in the world control 70 percent of world trade and 30 percent of world gross domestic product. This, if nothing else, provides justification for this book. The book is not about right and wrong, good and evil; although examples of stakeholder dilemmas are used to illustrate the extremely challenging nature of managing a socially and environmentally responsible enterprise. Rather, it is a guide to "best practice" techniques for stakeholder inclusion which aim to deliver optimal business performance.

We define stakeholders as individuals and entities who may be affected by business, and who may, in turn, bring influence to bear upon it. Important direct stakeholders include investors, employees, customers, suppliers, and the local community where the firm is based and trades. We refer to these groups as primary "social" stakeholders because their interests are directly linked to the fortunes of the company through social relationships. Secondary social stakeholders might include regulators, civic institutions and pressure groups, media and academic commentators, trade bodies and competitors. The interests of these groups are more indirect, but they nonetheless form part of the social ecology of the free enterprise system.

There are other entities which forward thinking businesses might wish to include in their universe of stakeholder interests: for example the natural environment, nonhuman species and future generations. They have rights which may be impacted by business and the way in which companies behave. These entities also have their "secondary" advocates and defenders – pressure groups and welfare organizations which speak on their behalf.

In the post war era, businesses in well organized, "high trust" or consensual societies (e.g. Japan and Germany) have tended to take a broad view of stakeholder interests – at least as far as owners, employees and customers are concerned. In Scandinavia and the Netherlands business has been especially sensitive to environmental stewardship. In less consensual and more individualistic economies (e.g. America and 1980s Britain) the balance of stakeholder interests has tended to give primacy to owners and shareholders, with mixed results. But as we shall explore, even in the UK and the USA, stakeholder inclusive enterprises have fared better than "shareholder first" companies during most of the twentieth century.

It has been argued by John Plender and others that stakeholding is really a question of balance[1]. If stakeholder interests become unbalanced, for example, if investors secure too low a return on investment and capital becomes too freely available – then rash, uneconomic decisions may be made. Conversely, if shareholder value is maximized too fast with no thought for the long term, then the resilience of the company suffers.

The notion of stakeholding in business is not collectivist, nor is it soft in the non-competitive sense[2]. Rather it is based on a sophisticated view of the company as a social vehicle whose speed and steering are dependent upon careful reading of the road signs and the behavior of other road users. Meanwhile, the route is best determined by involving all passengers with knowledge to contribute to the map reading.

The assumptions underlying this book are:

- that enterprises which are run in the interests of a wide range of stakeholders are more likely to behave responsibly
- that business can successfully create two kinds of value: commercial and social
- that social and commercial value are mutually reinforcing, leading to greater stakeholder loyalty and corporate resilience
- that social and commercial transparency lead to greater organizational identity and efficiency
- that stakeholder inclusive enterprises will outperform stakeholder exclusive enterprises with increasing ease in the twenty-first century.

The first part of the book traces the origins of stakeholder interests in business, starting in most cases with the industrial revolution. We use the metaphor of the game to describe how different economic actors play out their roles. It helps explain why we have some of the dysfunctionalities in business–stakeholder relations today and we conclude that the rules of the game are in need of a little overhaul. Part 2 is a brief resumé of how strategic decisions are taken in business. We use three parables of twentieth century enterprises to illustrate the major influences on business during the last one hundred years. The rest of the book is a manual for stakeholder inclusion which can be dipped into as the reader sees fit. The book takes a stakeholder by stakeholder approach rather than mixing the whole picture into one master plan or prescription. We hope that students and academics, while enjoying the historical, economic and management analyses contained in Parts 1 and 2, may also grit their teeth and force themselves to explore some of the practical implications of those analyses which are described in Part 3. Conversely, we hope that hard pressed business people may take a little time to examine the antecedent causes of some of their problems and dilemmas today, so that they may better appreciate the basis of the subsequent proposals for improved stakeholder inclusion and business performance.

This book has relied heavily on the management theories of R. Edward Freeman, Gareth Morgan and John Kay, the economic analyses of John Kenneth Galbraith and Will Hutton and the corporate critiques of David Korten and Anthony Sampson. Our practical inspiration for a better vision for business was greatly assisted by the thoughts of Tom Cannon, George Goyder, Charles Handy, Thomas Sheridan and Nigel Kendall.

Finally, our historical influences drew a reasonably straight line between the visions of Robert Owen, William Morris, Thomas Watson of IBM, and Anita and Gordon Roddick of The Body Shop – stakeholder advocates all.

From the above, it may be assumed that we are not free marketeers or "shareholder-value" advocates of any purist persuasion. We deplore the false dichotomy created by those who imply that good stakeholder relations undermine the optimization of long-term shareholder value. Indeed we present a good deal of evidence to show that they are mutually reinforcing. We argue for the potential for creative, entrepreneurial businesses to increase economic and social value for all stakeholders, including shareholders and owners. Businesses, large or small, just need to be thoughtful, dedicated to long term prosperity and well organized. This book is designed for the thoughtful, dedicated and well organized manager and comes with our optimism for a brighter future for business people and all those whose livelihoods will depend on them, now and in the future.

Part One

THE RISE OF THE STAKEHOLDER

CHAPTER 1

Does nobody trust us?

The purest treasure mortal times afford is spotless reputation; that way men are but gilded loam or painted clay.
William Shakespeare

Crisis of confidence

There is no doubt that a universal crisis of confidence exists in business as an institution. According to MORI, the majority of the British public disagree with the proposition that "business generally tries to strike a balance between profits and the public interest[1]." Only 15 percent of the British public trust multinational businesses to be "honest and fair" compared with 27 percent who trust their newspapers and 83 percent who trust their medical practitioner. In a 1996 MORI survey 66 percent of those polled said that industry and commerce do not pay enough attention to their social responsibilities. In an ICM poll for *The Guardian* newspaper in November 1996, business leaders came only twelfth out of a list of 20 possible moral role models which people should "try to follow." The only moderately good news was that business leaders scored higher than the royal family, trade union leaders and members of parliament. However, given the press that each of these groups has received in recent years, this is hardly a cause for unrestrained celebration.

In North America, Europe and the Far East, public trust in business and business leaders is no more robust. In 1995, Multinational Monitor in the USA published a list of the ten "Worst Corporations" as a means of re-establishing shame as a driver of good corporate behavior. The list included such august names as Shell, Dow Chemicals, 3M, Du Pont, Johnson & Johnson and Warner-Lambert.

Is this state of affairs peculiar to business? Absolutely not. Religious institutions, political parties, governments, judicial bodies and even educational and medical establishments around the world are all held in increasingly fragile esteem by ordinary citizens. It may be that this new culture of discontent and disrespect arises directly from the replacement of past certainties with new insecurities, particularly about livelihoods and social cohesion[2,3,4].

Perhaps it is the behavior of the press and news media that has changed, bringing to light human frailties and corporate scandals which in former times would have drifted along, pleasantly undisturbed. Contrast the kid glove press treatment of John F. Kennedy's personal behavior in the 1960s[5] with the innuendo and vitriol meted out to Bill and Hillary Clinton in the 1990s[6].

Could it be that innovation in information technology has accelerated the speed with which rumor and lurid speculation spins around the globe[2]. Reputational assaults on business have been no less effectively disseminated, as giant corporations subject to international boycotts like Shell and Nestlé would unhappily attest. One might now say a libel is posted on the internet before a corporate lawyer can say "injunction."

The sheer cumulative impact of two centuries of industrial capitalism may be responsible for declining trust in those responsible for driving economic development. How did our business system permit known occupational health risks like asbestos and coal dust to go unchallenged for so long? Do business-linked political scandals from Turin to Tokyo provide evidence of systemic malaise? Have the environmental disasters of Bhopal, Love Canal and Seveso given business a reputation for spreading poison and pollution from which it is impossible ever fully to recover?

Whatever the social and historical reasons for the crisis of legitimacy faced by business today, there is no doubt that it is a very real phenomenon, and one which adds significantly to the pressures on business executives.

One manifestation of the need to demonstrate greater accountability has been the rise in well-organized stakeholder representatives. Historically, trade unionism was a response to the exploitation of workers by owners, and for many years this was one of the principal constraining forces which governed corporate industrial behavior. But the last thirty years has seen the rise of increasingly well-organized advocates representing consumers, individual shareholders, the environment and the wider community. Some business sectors have nonhuman species as stakeholders and face accountability issues for animal welfare too. Numerous specialist research organizations have emerged to rate and publicly challenge corporate behavior on behalf of these constituencies (see Figure 1.1).

In the USA the Council on Economic Priorities and the Interfaith Center on Corporate Responsibility research and advocate the interests of investors and consumers while the Coalition on Environmentally Responsible Economies presses the environmental case. The Investor Responsibility Research Center tracks companies on behalf of a wide range

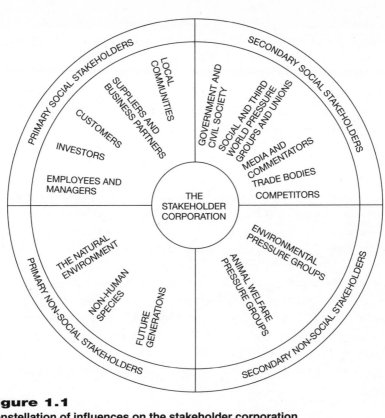

Figure 1.1
Constellation of influences on the stakeholder corporation

of institutional investor interests. In Canada, EthicScan provides a similar service mostly aimed at consumers (see Case Study 1.1).

CASE STUDY 1.1

Ethics on parade

One external rating organization with a very systematic and user-friendly approach to providing information to consumers is Toronto-based Ethic-Scan. The group assesses Canadian-based companies in nine categories scored from A+ to F. They are: gender and family issues, community responsibilities, progressive staff policies, labor relations, environmental performance and management, management practices and consumer relations, sourcing and trading practices and candor. Companies get an A+ rating for scoring 95 percent plus in each category and F for getting 9 percent or less. EthicScan groups companies by sector and lists "Honor Rolls" for the best scoring companies in each category. Everything is then published in a very easy-to-use shoppers' guide.

In Europe, a number of ethical and environmental rating groups exists to advise investors, for example, Ethical Investment Research and Information Service in the UK, Ökom in Germany, Eco-Rating International in Switzerland and Ethibel in Belgium. Consumers have a wide range of executive, governmental, quasi-governmental and non-governmental agencies to protect their well-being. They range from the established to the confrontational, from the regulatory to the hyper-activist.

With these increasing demands for accountability to different stakeholder constituencies comes a need for independent assessment and audit. Consequently, there has been a multiplication of the types of audit which are required of corporations. Again, business is not alone in having to demonstrate its *bona fides* to an increasingly skeptical and demanding set of audiences.

In his book *The Audit Explosion*[7], Michael Power notes "audits are needed when accountability can no longer be sustained by informal relations of trust alone but must be formalised, made visible and subject to independent validation." Auditing and visible public reporting of results provide mechanisms for dealing with the demands of external accountability and stakeholder inclusion. Auditing also provides a powerful and positive tool for increasing legitimacy and organizational efficiency. References to stakeholder audits of various kinds will feature throughout this book.

Free enterprise: the ultimate game

It is not uncommon for business gurus to use game theory to discuss the way in which business success and failure can be explained and justified. Happily, the more sophisticated game theorists have moved on from the crudest forms of jungle law business strategy and now embrace at least some recognition of the importance of cooperative and complementary behavior[8]. We are going to take the broadest possible view of the game theory of business and the players within it.

In its current form, the game of free enterprise is a relatively new phenomenon. The most powerful teams are the transnational corporations (TNCs) with lower league teams comprising many levels of limited liability companies and small–medium size enterprises serving and supplying, and occasionally challenging the TNCs. The principal sponsors are the capital markets, investment funds and lending institutions. The institutions get their cash from many different sources. In English-speaking countries long term vision has not been their strong suit and they do not always watch the game very closely. The international referee is relatively inexperienced and is called the World Trade Organization. On the sidelines are national governments and trading blocs like the European Union, the Association of South East Asian Nations and countries covered by the North American Free Trade Agreement.

The team managers are a mixed bunch of entrepreneurs, autocrats and paternalists whose rewards have grown rather well over the years. Sadly, the playing field is not in good shape and some of the teams are so strong that occasionally they deploy rather too much influence both on the referee and the line judges. Nevertheless, the ball is in play and it is worthwhile examining the various elements of the game to see whether the main supporters, the workers and the consumers, are going to be satisfied with the result or whether a revolt is to be expected before too long.

CHAPTER 2

Free enterprise

the rules of the game

Practical men, who believe themselves to be quite exempt from any intellectual influences are usually the slaves of some defunct economist.
John Maynard Keynes

Free enterprise is a game which has been played out over two centuries: first in Britain, Europe and the Americas, later spreading to Asia, and ultimately becoming a global phenomenon. During this period, the principal participants have experienced spectacular successes and miserable failures. But broadly speaking, free enterprise has grown to a position of undisputed dominance as a system of global wealth creation. From its earliest manifestations to the present day, politicians, economists, business people and their stakeholders have debated the nature and merits of free enterprise and the necessity, or otherwise, for rules to govern or constrain its impacts. Monumental struggles have occurred between owners, workers and consumers within competing political systems and economic frameworks.

For us to understand why and how present-day rules and frameworks have developed, it is essential to explore the history of business endeavor and how competing interests have struggled to assert their influence. We start this exploration at the dawn of the free enterprise system in late eighteenth century Britain.

The rules of free enterprise have long been dictated by practitioners of that most "dismal" of sciences: economics. Undoubtedly, the most influential of these practitioners was Adam Smith. This Scottish moral philosopher, turned university scholar and independent tutor is credited with establishing the earliest and most enduring guidelines for wealth creation in a competitive market economy.

Smith formed his theories during a period of major transition in British, European and American history. The Spanish and Ottoman empires were beginning to crumble and British imperial influence was approaching its zenith. The agriculturally based economies of Northern Europe were

Adam Smith – the founding father of free enterprise

beginning to experience the first impacts of the scientific discoveries of the Age of Enlightenment. The dominance of merchant trading, backed by the force of imperial navies and armies, was still strong. But there were also the stirrings of the machine age: the physical laws explored and explained by scientists such as Isaac Newton and Robert Boyle in the late seventeenth and early eighteenth centuries were already being applied in the fields of "scientific agriculture," medicine and navigation. Increasingly they were finding expression in industrial and engineering endeavor[1].

The industrial revolution

As ever, technical progress was proving something of a mixed blessing. Very much on the positive side of the balance sheet, the Age of Enlightenment provided the means by which the medical profession moved from superstition to surgery and science. In 1712 the first steam engine was developed to pump water from coal mines, thereby improving both efficiency and safety. In contrast, the success of new distilling processes was so great, and the consumption of cheap gin by the poor so prodigious, that for a short time around 1740 the death rate in London superseded the birth rate by a factor of two.

English agriculture had started to embrace machines at the beginning of the 18th century with Jethro Tull's seed drill, but it was in textiles that the greatest impetus was to be given to industrial production with inventions such as Hargreaves' "spinning jenny" (1763), Arkwright's water frame (1769) and Compton's "mule" (1775). The transfer of cotton weaving and wool spinning from the home to the factory together with the development of the steam engine patented by James Watt in 1769 marked the real beginnings of the industrial revolution. Smelting of iron and the use of steam engines fueled by coal and coke would provide most of the raw materials and energy for that revolution in the following century. The first country to embrace this revolution was Britain.

Wealth of Nations

So this was the context for Adam Smith's theories of the free market. In 1765 he had travelled to France, meeting luminaries such as the philosopher Voltaire, the physician Francois Quesnay and the physiocrat Anne Robert Jacques Turgot[2]. The physiocrats believed that all wealth derived from agriculture. Smith was to come to a different conclusion. He saw the awesome potential for industrialization and the gains in efficiency of output which could be generated by a "division of labor" whereby individual workers were segregated into different specialisms. Smith used the example of a pin factory to explain the point. Most importantly he was convinced that wealth would best be generated by removing all inhibitions to international trade: so that individual enterprises and nations could best pursue their comparative advantages unhindered.

Smith published his views in 1776 in *An Inquiry into the Nature and Causes of the Wealth of Nations*. The book had a significant impact on the British political scene. At a time when domestic revolution was fomenting in America and France, Britain controlled the majority of its empire with relative ease. But Smith saw that imperial subjugation and domination of markets by mercantile interests was not an optimal means of securing wealth for the long term. Indeed Britain was about to undergo a series of foreign policy disasters which would destroy forever the dream of the merchant adventurers. Whether it was the morally outrageous shipping of slave labor to the sugar and tobacco plantations of the Caribbean and North America, or the plundering of timber from Scandinavia and sugar and spices from the colonies, military and naval supremacy were not going to be the long-term guarantors of wealth. Manufacturing and free trade were the clear prescriptions of Adam Smith.

The attitude of Smith and his political contemporaries to the emerging independence of America is especially enlightening in this respect. The American Declaration of Independence was proclaimed in the same year as the publication of *Wealth of Nations*. It was a revolutionary statement of principles and rights inspired by the strong antipathy of most Americans to economic exploitation by Britain (see Case Study 2.1).

CASE STUDY 2.1

Tom Paine: advocate of freedom, revolution and regulation

Tom Paine[3] was an English exciseman who developed most of his political ideas in the sleepy Sussex town of Lewes. Today, Paine is best known as an enthusiastic advocate of republican revolution in America and France, vitriolic polemicist and pamphleteer, and author of *The Rights of Man* and *The Age of Reason*. He was a close friend of Thomas Jefferson and a bitter enemy of George Washington. For someone so influential in

Chapter 2: free enterprise

the cause of American independence and freedom, his thoughts on the free market are quite instructive. While believing in the vitality of free enterprise as a counter-balance to the power of the state, he had no faith in self-regulating free markets. Like Adam Smith, he railed against monopolists and self-enriching merchants. But unlike Smith he argued for civil society to shape political and legal instruments to optimize the functioning of the market and for banks and governments to invest actively in wealth creating enterprise.

While George III hung on to the hopeless notion that the American colonies could be forced into submission, others, including Smith and a number of British politicians of the day, saw an alternative option[4,5]. Leading opinion was mortified by the idea of continuing an unsustainable war against America and her allies France and Spain. Significantly, one of Britain's most successful manufacturers and exporters, the potter Josiah Wedgwood was an enthusiastic supporter of American independence. He also had much to lose from a fracturing of trade with key European markets. As Smith had noted, France had a market far larger than the American colonies and, due to its geographical proximity, it was able to trade several times as fast.

The dawn of free markets

By November 1779, matters had deteriorated still further with war declared on Holland for supporting American independence and significant danger of insurrection in Ireland and India. In June 1780, a Member of Parliament, William Pitt the Younger, described war with America as "a most accursed, wicked, barbarous, cruel, unnatural, unjust and diabolical war." It was no surprise then, when Pitt became Chancellor of the Exchequer at the age of 23 in 1782, that he supported the new Prime Minister Sir William Petty Shelburne in seeking peace. Shelburne and Pitt wanted to establish commercial treaties with America and the European powers which represented nothing less than "a revision of our whole trading system."

The treaty with America was concluded eventually by the succeeding administration, though not before the new Secretary of State Charles James Fox had reviewed the free trade dimension and re-inserted some protection for the merchants[6]. But when Pitt returned to office as Prime Minister in December 1783, strengthened by a general election in the spring of 1784, he set about the dismantling of trade barriers and tariffs, expansion of trade with America and Ireland, and establishment of com-

William Pitt the Younger

mercial treaties with Spain, Portugal, France and Russia. In particular, the treaty with France, ably concluded in 1786 by William Eden (a "man of business") was described by Pitt's ally, Henry Dundas, as "the greatest boon the Manufacturers ever received."

Pitt's measures, together with the steady expansion of trade which he sought to secure, led to a significant recovery in Britain's economic fortunes by the end of the eighteenth century. Exports almost doubled between 1783 and 1792. In the same period a trade deficit of £2.5 million was converted to a surplus of nearly £2 million. Inevitably, the transition to a free trade agenda was not a totally smooth one. One severe irritation to the young prime minister was the coalition of opposition politicians and business people which conspired to frustrate his desire to establish more equitable trade conditions with Ireland. This coalition was led by the first chairman of the Great Chamber of the Manufacturers of Great Britain, Josiah Wedgwood. Wedgwood and his colleagues, who included engineers and scientists of the calibre of James Watt and Joseph Priestley, were all keen to protect their own interests.

Another frustration to the free traders was the territorial and imperial ambition of one Napoleon Buonaparte. In the closing years of the 18th century this resulted in Britain attempting to block trade between France and neutral territories by force. Not surprisingly this ended up with Russia, Sweden, Prussia and Denmark forming an armed alliance to protect their own trading interests.

Free trade and the nineteenth century

Despite the setbacks, as the nineteenth century dawned the ideal of free trade had become established as one of the tenets of economic orthodoxy – in theory if not always in practice. There were still to be many examples of industrial or agricultural special interests seeking to maintain monopoly power or persuading governments to protect them through the imposition of tariffs, price support and trade barriers.

The early years of the nineteenth century witnessed the final collapse of Buonaparte's ambition and the establishment of reasonably normal trade relations between Britain and France. In the Congress of Vienna (1814–15) which marked the end of the Napoleonic Wars, trading stability was formally re-established between the major European powers. Indeed Europe was to enjoy a period of relative peace and stability for much of the next one hundred years.

A brief war between Britain and America in 1812 again interrupted trade between the world's two most powerful maritime nations. This gave way in 1816 to a brief period of protectionism in America, with tariffs imposed to protect new manufacturing industries such as textiles and iron smelting. Slowly, US tariffs began to be recognized as internally divisive, for although they protected the largely northern based manufacturers, they caused increasingly severe difficulties for the poorer southern states. Thus, in 1833, a tariff bill was passed in Congress designed to return all duties in excess of 20 percent to the more moderate levels imposed in 1816.

Meanwhile, following two centuries of government granted monopoly to the joint stock companies, Indian trade was opened to all British subjects in 1813. This was followed twenty years later by freeing of trade with China.

Heavily backed by Britain's increasingly dominant industrial interests, and supported by the economic theories of David Ricardo MP, the 1820s witnessed the implementation of a formalized policy of economic *laissez-faire* predicated on the principles of free trade. In 1821 tariffs on timber were reduced. In 1824, duties on silk and wool were removed, the duty on manufactured goods was lowered from 50 to 20 percent and on raw materials from 20 to 10 percent[7].

Wine excises were abolished in 1825, tea in 1833 and tobacco in 1840. Machinery import duty was set at a maximum of 20 percent by British Prime Minister Robert Peel, but exports completely freed in 1843. By the time of William Gladstone's budgets in 1853 and 1860, Britain was virtually a free trade country[7].

By the middle of the nineteenth century, the industrial revolution was in full swing in Britain and many of its most damaging social side-effects were already manifest. We shall return to these when we consider the lot of workers and communities in the free enterprise system. But for now, let us summarize the economic principles which were established in the half century following the publication of Adam Smith's *Wealth of Nations*. It was a period which witnessed the demise of mercantilism (merchant trading backed by force of arms) and the birth of industrialization. It was also a period which saw momentous political transformations: revolutions in America and Europe, successful wars of independence in North and South America, the weakening of the Spanish and Ottoman empires and the consolidation of American, British and Russian spheres of influence.

The iron rules

The iron rules of the game of free enterprise, forged in the tumultuous years of the late seventeenth and early eighteenth centuries, and still advocated by most economists and business people today, are as follows:

■ Decisions in a free market should be guided by self-interest. Owners should act in the interest of owners and consumers should act in the interest of consumers; if all actors in the economy make rational decisions on their own behalf, benefits and wealth should flow as though from a cornucopia. Meanwhile, an "invisible hand" of moral restraint will prevent the abuse of self-interest.

■ There should be true competition on the basis of price. This means no rigging of the market through price fixing or externalizing costs, e.g. making other people pay for the social and environmental damage you cause. Businesses must not connive at monopolistic control or market domination; there should be free entry to markets by new participants.

■ Economies and companies must be free to exploit their comparative advantages, e.g. intellectual or raw material resources, without the hindrances of import duties or covert protectionism. The main exception to this, acknowledged by Adam Smith, is when nations are at war and self-determination is threatened.

■ Information concerning transactions must be complete for rational decisions to be taken. If participants in a transaction have imperfect knowledge about that transaction, deep misunderstanding and mistrust may follow.

■ Owners of firms (i.e. shareholders) and consumers must retain their sovereignty. It becomes terribly confusing when managers, workers or suppliers start behaving in ways which undermine this sovereignty, e.g. by following their own interests or demanding rights which have nothing to do with the creation or exchange of monetary value.

■ Efficiency, and thus maximized wealth creation, flows through division of labor. Separating functions on a factory line so that everyone sticks to what they do best (and most often) may challenge people's sanity, but it is absolutely the way to maximize production.

The rules today

The orthodoxies of free enterprise remain largely intact, despite challenges posed to capitalist economics by the communist Karl Marx in the late nineteenth century and the social liberal John Maynard Keynes in the mid-twentieth century. Both Marx and Keynes rejected the *laissez-faire*, non-interventionist doctrines of Adam Smith and David Ricardo. They believed that untrammeled free trade would lead to crisis and hardship for ordinary citizens unless either the proletariat (Marx) or the government (Keynes) intervened to take control of, or manage the economy more effectively. Today, the theories of Marx and Keynes have been pretty well buried. Control of a modern industrial economy, either by a revolutionary working class or an interventionist state is no longer considered by the majority of governments to be a viable option.

Of course it is simple to spot the flaws in the iron rules of free enterprise. It does not require skeptics or environmentalists to point out that the majority of businesses does not adhere slavishly to these dogmas. For years supermarket soap and detergent makers and soft drink manufacturers have sought to protect their interests through dominating market share in direct contravention of the spirit of true competition. Aggressive branding backed by almost unlimited advertising budgets has relatively little to do with providing "perfect information" to the consumer about product performance and attributes. By 1990, the advertising budget of Procter & Gamble was estimated to have topped $1.5 billion[8]. Today the McDonald's hamburger chain is estimated to spend nearly $2 billion per annum projecting its images, most especially to the young for whom they employ a rather dubious-looking character named Ronald.

Since the beginning of the industrial revolution businessmen have pressed governments for special protection through imposition of standards or direct levies which impact negatively on their foreign-based competitors. In this context, recent disagreements between European and US governments with Japan over technical inhibitions to foreign imports were no more than a distant echo of the protests of American and Irish producers at the beginning of the nineteenth century who watched their British counterparts cultivating free trade in Europe and the East while ensuring price discrimination against them. In 1995 the European Union Commissioner for Competition policy fined companies operating in Europe nearly £400 million for operating cartels and price fixing.

These examples of rule flouting are not cited to make a political point. They simply serve to illustrate that simplistic interpretation of the rules ignores the fact that human beings in a market economy behave in a more complex way than might be allowed by any purist prescription. What the iron rules of free enterprise miss is the human element. It is not possible to isolate economic behavior from social pressures or normal human psychology. Adam Smith's "invisible hand" of ethical behavior which should ensure that even when following selfish interests, economic actors do not cause moral decline has not always materialized. Indeed, in the last two hundred years the invisible hand has proven so random in its moral effects that some have likened it more to an invisible elbow[9].

As for the ideal of true free market competition, which business with a small share in a highly competitive market would cheer the entry of a new, cash-rich rival with a strong brand? Yet under a simple application of Adam Smith's rules, new entrants should automatically be welcomed. Which business leader striving hard to ensure the highest possible benefits for his workers and the highest standards of environmental protection for his firm does not squirm at the prospect of competition from companies based in Southeast Asia which exploit the business benefits of the tiger economies? And yet, as recent governments in Britain have argued in respect of European legislation, each country should be sovereign in its social standards. If economic globalization was cricket, English manufacturers would all now be applauding politely from the pavilion as the high tech exporters of Malaysia, Indonesia and the Philippines ruthlessly exploit their competitive advantages of low wages and minimalist regulation.

Lessons for the stakeholder corporation

- Adam Smith's rules of free enterprise are not applied in their pure form in any market economy on earth.
- Corporations may tend towards market domination via brand reinforcement rather than competing simply on the basis of price and product characteristics.
- The rules of free enterprise completely understate the human and social dimensions of economic decision-making.
- The moral, technological and trading climate in Adam Smith's time was a little different to that of the late twentieth century; consequently the early practical constraints may not provide the safety net they once did.

The following chapters are devoted to the main participants in the game and how historically they have tried and often failed to compensate for the inability of free enterprise to regulate itself to optimal outcomes for all stakeholders. We start with the referees and line judges who are supposed to impose and enforce the rules.

CHAPTER 3

The referees and line judges

who enforces the rules?

No nation was ever ruined by trade
Benjamin Franklin

If one shares the outlook of conventional economic theorists, one should welcome the advent of the global marketplace with open arms. No longer do the planned economies of the communist bloc or the social democracies of Europe stand in the way of the inexorable logic of economic globalization. No longer will elected politicians interfere with the iron rules of free enterprise. Since the collapse of communism the shrill challenge of the new free marketeers has become: "compete or die." It is repeated with ever increasing triumphalism[1]. In comparison, the pessimism of the protectionists, social activists and environmentalists only occasionally registers with politicians or the media; even less often with those captains of industry in the English-speaking world who need to satisfy the short-term demands of today's capital markets.

In Europe, North America and the East, political perspectives are converging. Left of center parties are learning the language of economic competitiveness and the free trade zeal of their more conservative opponents. In the European Union, countries preparing for monetary union recognize that a social price may have to be paid for political and economic convergence but they are proceeding anyway. Political agitation in France and even in the private sector in Germany marked the beginnings of popular unrest at this prospect (see Case Study 3.1).

CASE STUDY 3.1

The German social market economy under strain

In October 1996, the world's largest trade union I G Metall called out on strike 400,000 of Germany's engineering workers in defense of sick pay. Car plants and steel works were shut down for a day. This followed a change in German federal law lowering the legal

▶ minimum payments for sickness from 100 percent to 80 percent of normal salary and benefits. The German engineering employers federation Gesamtmetall was appalled by the losses to production and observed that the action "demonstrates to domestic and foreign investors that the preservation of social entitlements counts more than competitiveness."

Both sides of the political spectrum in Europe seem prepared to face down the nationalists, social welfare activists and trade unions in order to secure what they believe to be the main prize: a cohesive and competitive European economy. So in coming years the burden of welfare provision in Europe's social democracies will shift steadily from the state to the individual. Private insurance policies and personal pension arrangements will replace those universal benefits previously associated with state provision. Of course this process is already well advanced in North America. So, in the brave new ultra-competitive world of the early twenty-first century, who will maintain the balance between economic and social development? Who will be policing the rules, and what will those rules be?

Growth of world trade

For most of the twentieth century, governments were pretty well in control of national economic performance and social provision. Through direct control of the banking system and key industries they could precipitate overproduction, underproduction, currency crises, stock market crashes, growth, stagnation, spending booms, deflation or inflation. They would manipulate industrial policy and national economic cycles in order to maximize their own chances of re-election, attempting to conjure social benefits and economic recovery whenever electoral necessity demanded it. Intervention was often done for absolutely the right reasons. Franklin D. Roosevelt's New Deal in the 1930s probably marked the moral high point of US governmental interventionism.

In Europe, state welfare institutions, public health provision and social security arrangements were part of the architecture of the post-war democratic consensus. In Britain Sir William Beveridge designed an entire welfare state which would banish forever the five giant evils of want, disease, ignorance, squalor and idleness. Adjustments in interest rates and taxation, monetary policy and price controls were all deployed by post-war governments in search of the holy grail of low inflation, low unemployment, social welfare, increasing industrial production and stable economic growth.

In these endeavors, governments were assisted by international economic agreements, designed at least in part to prevent the wildly fluctuating economic conditions which led to crippling unemployment, the rise of fascism and eventually global conflict in the 1930s. Immediately after World War II, in 1947, the General Agreement on Tariffs and Trade (GATT) sought to establish rules aimed at progressively removing export and import barriers, thereby maximizing the potential for free trade. Supported by the Bretton Woods institutions, the International Monetary Fund and the World Bank, the GATT was to become the principal mechanism for promoting the liberalization of trade and maintenance of peace and prosperity in the non-communist world. It did this largely by seeking to impose constraints on exchange rates and monetary flows. As a result of the GATT, world trade blossomed (see Figure 3.1).

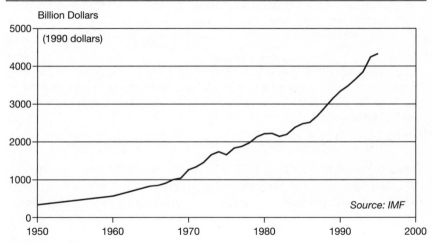

Figure 3.1
Growth of world trade 1950-95 (total dollar exports expressed in billions at 1990 value)[2]

World Trade Organization (WTO)

Between 1950 and 1995 world trade increased twelvefold – twice the increase in industrial output. Each round of GATT negotiations embraced more and more nations keen to benefit from the opportunities afforded by free trade. By 1994, well over one hundred countries were part of the GATT system, accounting for approximately 90 percent of world trade. The eighth round of negotiations, concluded in 1994 (the Uruguay Round) resulted in the setting up of the premier policing and enforcement agency for global trade: the World Trade Organization (see Exhibit 3.1).

The rules and scope of the World Trade Organization

Roger Bennett[3] has summarized the three main principles which the WTO is designed to police:

- Non-discrimination, meaning that each member country must apply the same rates of tariff to imports from all member nations, although customs unions and free trade areas are permitted and special arrangements apply to underdeveloped countries. This principle is sometimes referred to as the application of "most favoured nation" treatment to all WTO members.

- Resolution of disputes via consultation, though note that the "dumping" of exports at less than their cost of production may be counteracted by retaliatory measures targeted at the offending country.

- Non-legality of quantitative restrictions on imports, unless a country is economically underdeveloped, is experiencing severe balance of payments difficulties, or if an agricultural or fisheries product is involved.

In addition, the Uruguay Round of GATT established special provisions for protecting intellectual property by prohibiting trade in counterfeit goods; it introduced trade in services (e.g. telecommunications and banking) within the remit of the WTO, and limits were proposed for subsidies to agriculture and inefficient industries.

Many commentators have pointed out that the WTO was brought into being with no rules for protecting the environment or promoting social cohesion. Consumer activists and environmentalists on the left like Ralph Nader in the USA, together with his counterparts in Europe and Asia were loud in their criticism of an international free trade club without rules. Populist protectionists like Ross Perot and nationalists on the right like Pat Buchanan in the USA and James Goldsmith in Europe launched fierce critiques of regional free trade initiatives like NAFTA and the European Union. But together these disparate voices of concern were as nothing against the leviathan forces of the International Chamber of Commerce and those large business interests with their shoulders to the wheel of the WTO bandwagon.

The global economy

Deregulation of trade, freeing up capital flows and true globalization of the economy now appear unstoppable. And all of it will happen whether nationally elected politicians decide to intervene or not. The simple truth is that when it comes to issues of economic and social destiny, individual nation states are no longer the main actors. So, nearly all have accepted the inevitable and embraced the need for global industrial competitiveness. They vary only in their prescriptions for investment in research and development, education and skills development in the workforce. They appear united in their desire to pull government out of social welfare provision except for the grindingly impoverished or the permanently sick. The implications for business of this shift in policy are enormous.

Free market super-enthusiasts Lowell Bryan and Diana Farrell estimate that to avoid a debt crisis, countries with high existing levels of social provision (e.g. Sweden, Germany, Italy and Canada) will have either to raise taxes or cut social provision by 25 to 30 percent[1]. The global capital market will simply not tolerate the sort of debt/GDP ratios which would emerge otherwise. They are hopeful that "we will not let petty politics get in the way of pursuing rational policies", but are sanguine enough to concede that the revolution which is about to occur in the global economy will not be "bloodless." So, as governments around the world back away from intervention in basic industries and relinquish control over exchange rates, interest rates and the banking system, and as they minimize their exposure to social welfare costs, it is not surprising that politics are becoming quite uniform. Politicians of every persuasion are simply recognizing the inevitable. Of course, the referee is there in the shape of the World Trade Organization. The only irony is that the rules which the WTO is there to enforce are remarkably few – and they have almost nothing to do with looking after the long-term interests of stakeholders, the natural environment or those who will inherit the planet in future generations.

Where does this leave the socially responsible business person? We believe that the global picture painted above will most certainly emerge. But it will not happen overnight. Also, we believe that whatever the momentum of the free market argument, social factors will intervene to temper the most negative impacts of accelerating global trade. Some of this will play through the multilateral regional trading blocs like the European Union, the North American Free Trade Agreement, the Association of South East Asia Nations, the Andean and Central American Common Markets, and the Mercado Cono Sur (South America). And some of the burden will pass direct to business.

There will be no return to the Bretton Woods settlement which guaranteed some measure of exchange rate stability and virtually complete national control of economies, banking systems and capital flows. But there will undoubtedly be many opportunities for nations within trading areas to establish collective political and social instruments aimed at mitigating the worst vicissitudes of globalization. The subrules which result will simply operate at regional rather than national levels.

We also believe that improved access to information and communications in the industrialized world (as well as wealth) will allow consumers and workers alike to exert ever more pressure on business and industry to behave in a responsible way. It will not matter whether businesses are based in Shanghai or Chicago: stakeholders will not welcome an economic relationship based on naked exploitation. We may see rather more pressure for the type of health and welfare insurance for workers which has grown in the USA in recent decades. We may see more consumer activism, more environmental pressures on business.

There is also a distinct though small possibility that the WTO will eventually be forced to accept the need for some basic rules on workplace rights and environmental protection which will have the effect of raising the level of the global economic playing field rather than tilting it still further in the direction of the low wage, low standards economies of parts of Asia and Latin America. So in the future, there will be a referee (the WTO) and there will be line judges (the regional trading blocs). And they will receive increasing pressure from consumers, workers and activists for imposing social and environmental rules as well as the principles of free trade.

Happily there are institutions, apart from the WTO, that can facilitate the discussion about the rules and objects of the game. For example, the Organization for Economic Co-operation and Development tries to coordinate and inform economic policy-making among its members. Subsets of its most powerful members, G10 and G7, focus respectively on monetary and political dimensions of global economic policy. The Forum on Asia–Pacific Economic Co-operation is increasingly influential for Far Eastern, Australasian and North American countries. In addition, the United Nations also provides opportunities for discussing international trade policy and its social and political implications. In particular, the UN Conference on Trade and Development (UNCTAD), and the International Labour Organization (ILO) seek respectively to establish issues of Third World development and workplace conditions as essential components of the global economic debate (see Exhibit 3.2).

Other UN bodies like The World Bank (International Bank for Reconstruction and Development) and the International Monetary Fund were set up in 1946 and 1947 respectively after the Bretton Woods conference in 1944. They now function in a much less strategic way than originally envisaged. Their decline as UN institutions mirrors the unshackling of the global economy from exchange rate controls and direct economic intervention in the last twenty years.

EXHIBIT 3.2

The priorities of the International Labour Organization

Roger Bennett has summarized some of the key principles which the ILO seeks to establish through voluntary codes and encouraging UN members to enact worker protection into national law[3]. The ILO constitution requires it to:

- encourage the improvement of the conditions of workers;
- discourage particular countries from failing to adopt humane conditions of labor;
- promote the principle that labor not be regarded as a mere "commodity or article of commerce";
- support the view that the price of labor be determined by human need and that workers are entitled to a reasonable standard of living.

In line with the principles of the UN Declaration on Human Rights (1948), the ILO Conference has adopted specific policies in favor of freedom of association, protection against dismissal for trade union membership, health and safety at work and the right to withdraw labor.

The future

What kind of social and environmental rules may be expected at regional bloc or WTO level in coming years?

Clearly, member states of the European Union, most of whom are classic social democracies with strong commitments to the environment and quality of life, will not wish to see existing standards of workplace safety and environmental protection eroded – whatever the international competitive pressures. Minimum wages and maximum working hours will be harmonized across the community, as will mechanisms for safeguarding the natural environment. There may be a slow-down in the number of prescriptive social and environmental legal instruments emerging from Brussels, but there will undoubtedly be increasing convergence of basic standards.

In North America we may see less generous public welfare programs in the USA and Canada in order to help balance budgets, but we should not expect engineering workers in the Midwest to lower their standard of living to that which might be expected by maquilladora workers in Mexico. We should not expect the Canadian public to accept clear-felling of Ontario timber on quite the same scale as the rape of Indonesian and

Malaysian forests. Once social and environmental protection are established as basic rights in the public consciousness, they are not easy to remove.

British Labour Member of Parliament, Denis MacShane, has described the case for a social clause as part of the WTO's obligations in order to protect workers' rights, eliminate discrimination, establish equality of opportunity and rewards, and outlaw child and forced labor[4]. MacShane argues against pressing the case too strongly for "material" rights which may be seen as especially contrary to the interests of developing countries, it being culturally and economically impossible to equalize wages and living conditions between the USA, Europe, Africa and Asia in the immediate future. Instead, he argues for "enabling rights" which allow workers in newly industrializing countries, and the developing world generally, to argue for better conditions through trade union activity and collective bargaining. It remains to be seen whether social activists, trade unionists and environmentalists make much headway with the WTO in pressing the case for social or environmental obligations on companies at international level. This battle is only just beginning. If MacShane's prescription succeeds it will be because of a combination of stakeholder pressures: workers, consumers and activist groups, assisted by free access to information about the production standards of multinational companies around the world.

The lower league referees and rules

There is no great value in detailing here the specific national regulatory agencies, laws, codes of practice and standards which constrain and guide businesses around the world. Nevertheless, some general reflections may be useful. Jonathon Charkham has described legal and governance practices in five countries: Germany, Japan, France, the USA and UK[5]. A former advisor to the Governor of the Bank of England and member of the UK Cadbury Committee on Corporate Governance, Charkham was able to draw parallels, expose idiosyncrasies and point out key influences in these five jurisdictions. In every case, the historic, political and cultural influences of the five countries were more influential in determining corporate behavior than the specifics of company law and regulation.

Charkham identified some especially interesting factors which would intrigue any student of stakeholding. For example, in Germany, Article 14(2) of the constitution ensures that the concept of duty attaches to property ownership. In practical terms this plays through into special concerns for consumers and workers dependent on German business. For example, the Works Constitution Act of 1972 enshrines the rights of workers' representatives to participate in works councils which negotiate and in some cases "codetermine" conditions of work. There are also statutory rights to information on economic, investment and organizational questions.

The consensus rather than confrontational model of industrial management in Japan is similar to that practised in Germany, although with less legal compulsion and even more reliance on cultural factors. Here, long-termism and stakeholder inclusivity is driven by a Commercial Code and the vital cultural dimension of mutual security delivered by:

- the high level of direct involvement of the banking system;
- the power of industrial groupings (*Kairetsu*);
- a belief in family honor.

The Japanese Commercial Code deals with company conduct, for example, with respect to obligations to shareholders, the role of directors and boards and the period of tenure of directors.

Whatever the relevance of the Commercial Code, the cultural influences are most important. As Charkham notes, Japanese companies would consider distasteful aggressive takeovers and the commodification or exploitation of workers. The Japanese believe "an employee who devotes his life to a business has morally a bigger stake in it than a shareholder." Charkham quotes Yamamoto as confirming that "Japanese management puts employees miles before shareholders." There is nothing in Japanese law which asserts the primacy of shareholders and owners (including the banks and institutions). Investor interest in Japanese company ownership is everything to do with stability, growth and security and almost nothing to do with maximizing short-term profits on investment.

Unlike Germany and Japan where the consensual approach is reinforced by both legal and cultural factors, in the USA and UK the dominant rights of investors are enshrined both by regulatory and cultural factors.

Since the introduction of limited liability in the UK in 1862, the odds have been well stacked in favor of investors in the English-speaking economies. Banks and institutions exert very little direct influence on company affairs. Instead, the London Stock Exchange and the US Securities and Exchange Commission and various US stock exchanges are extremely powerful agencies for the protection of investors' rights by virtue of their rules for corporate access to capital markets. Interestingly, there is no federal legislation on corporate governance in the USA; instead a regulatory framework is provided which has been variously described as a question not of "diligence but of laxity" and "a race for the bottom[5]." The division of powers between Congress and the states means quite simply that US local company law is weighted as much as possible in the interests of owners in order to attract inward investment. By way of compensation, the federal government has developed some of the most prescriptive and draconian consumer and environmental protection laws on the planet, enforced by powerful agencies with a real taste for litigation and the pursuit of liabilities. Based on its experience of the nineteenth century robber barons, the USA also has a vibrant anti-trust tradition aimed at preventing present day would-be monopolists from price fixing and dominating markets to the detriment of ordinary citizens.

Britain too has its Monopolies and Mergers Commission, Office of Fair Trading, consumer law and environmental and safety laws and regulations to ensure the basic responsibility of companies. While such regulatory regimes are increasingly driven from the European Union and are significantly less prescriptive than their equivalents in the USA, nevertheless they serve to temper the tendency of companies to abuse the rights of stakeholders in pursuit of shareholder value and maximization of profit. Britain also maintains an intricate web of formal law (Companies Acts and employment law), best practice codes (e.g. on Governance: Cadbury and Greenbury), national professional management standards (e.g. in accounting, environmental management, quality and employee training) and a rather touching belief in "fairness." But undoubtedly, in Britain as in the USA, the main obligations of a company, in law and in practice, are to the owners.

Lessons for the stakeholder corporation

■ Economic globalization will result in further retreat of nation states from important aspects of industrial, economic and social policy.

■ In an increasingly competitive world, there will be greater emphasis on individual self-reliance for workers and the rights of consumers. This may significantly increase pressures on the private sector for social responsibility.

■ Regional trading blocs may become more influential in setting minimum social and environmental standards for industry.

■ The WTO may be persuaded to adopt minimum standards for workers' rights. But ...

■ The only important rule in an increasingly aggressive global economy seems to be eliminate tariffs, compete or die. The WTO and the regional trading blocs will enforce this rule above all others with ruthless single-mindedness.

CHAPTER 4

The teams

companies and corporations

The diffusion of manufacturers throughout a country generates a new character in its inhabitants; and as this character is formed upon a principle quite unfavourable to individual or general happiness, it will produce the most lamentable and permanent evils ...
Jeremy Bentham

At the beginning of the British industrial revolution, the most powerful companies were either family owned or the products of mercantile adventure. Into the latter category we may place the joint stock companies: monoliths like the Hudson's Bay Company, the Royal African Company and the East India Company. These organizations were designed specifically to extract the maximum wealth for the minimum expense from Britain's colonies and trading partners from Canada to China and all points south. Their ostensible purpose was to further the (British) public good. The joint stock companies were granted by (British) royal charter a geographical sphere of influence which excluded all other (British) traders.

In the time of Elizabeth I this monopoly was deemed justifiable because of the expense of the military and naval establishments which had to be maintained to protect the interests of these London-based corporations. The owners of the companies included the aristocracy and great land owners and consequently had almost infinite political leverage. But as we have already seen, monopolistic joint stock trading companies dependent on private armies and navies were not well suited to the demands of the industrial revolution and free trade, however profitable they may have been for their aristocratic owners over the preceding two centuries.

Industrial growth in Britain

Economic liberalization was both a spur and a necessary outcome for the development of new forms of industrial enterprise in the first half of the nineteenth century. Historians of the start of the industrial revolution in Britain invariably describe the growth of the textile industry, in particular the cotton mills of Lancashire, as the principal manifestation of early industrialization. Eric Hobsbawm describes how in the space of two generations a family of yeoman farmers and domestic weavers, the Peels, established a very large industrial textile business[1]. Robert Peel (1750–1830), perhaps the leading industrialist of his time, harnessed the newly available technologies and with his own entrepreneurial flair became dazzlingly rich. In due course, his son became Prime Minister.

In the first decades of the nineteenth century, cotton products comprised about one half of all British exports. The rates of growth of industrial production in the UK in the first half of the century were little short of spectacular[2]. British exports of railroad iron and steel multiplied threefold between 1845 and 1875; machinery exports increased fivefold between 1850 and 1875. The new model industrial enterprises were certainly working.

Not all of the new industrialists and business people were as fortunate as the Peels. Because at that time there was no concept of limited liability, fortunes could be lost as well as won. The author Sir Walter Scott was unfortunate enough to underwrite a friend's publishing business which went bankrupt. In 1825 Scott was saddled with a debt of £130,000 – a fortune at that time[3].

The risks of investing in new industrial endeavors tended to limit the size of the early British industrial companies, as did the rudimentary nature of the British transportation system. But by the middle of the nineteenth century, a number of significant changes had occurred which removed forever the limits to growth of the industrial firm in Europe and America.

First, bridge building and the growth of steamships and railways allowed much more rapid and efficient transportation and trade of raw materials and finished goods[1,2]. Between 1840 and 1850, around 6,000 miles of railways were opened in Britain. This compared with around 7,000 miles in the rest of Europe combined and 7,000 in the USA. Second, the investment options created by the increased variety of industries employing mechanization and factory labor multiplied to an enormous extent. In Britain the growth of the iron and steel industry, transport and capital goods manufacture led to a doubling of the industrial working class between 1851 and 1881. Third, and most importantly, was the invention of the limited liability company. The notion was first enacted in Britain in 1855. It was subsequently consolidated in the Companies Act of 1862 which established for the first time that directors of a company should have principal regard to the interests of shareholders and that the shareholders or owners are in turn legally separate from the corporation itself so cannot be liable for all of the debts of that entity[3].

By the middle of the nineteenth century, Britain produced two-thirds of the world's coal, around half of its iron and steel, approximately half of its cotton manufactures and 40 percent of its hardware. But even by this time, leadership of technological innovation was already slipping from Britain's grasp. From about this period American companies started to pioneer much of the innovation for small-scale modern machinery. Meanwhile, German enterprises had already embarked on a technological path which would rapidly propel them to the forefront of chemical manufacturing worldwide.

Industrial growth in the USA

Bill Bryson has cataloged the explosion of American inventiveness and productivity in the second half of the nineteenth century[4]. During that time coal production increased from 14 million tons to more than 100 million; steel production increased twenty-five-fold, paper ninefold, and pig iron sevenfold. During a period when the US population increased threefold, national wealth increased thirteenfold to nearly $100 billion. Meanwhile factory output was buoyed by a string of gadgets and inventions: elevators, escalators, the telephone, the cash register, electric lights, box cameras, pneumatic tires, adding machines and typewriters.

By 1909, the top three corporations in America were US Steel, Standard Oil and American Tobacco[5], demonstrating the early ascendancy of those two vital drivers of the US industrial economy: steel and oil. The age of the conglomerate and mega-corporation was dawning. US Steel was the product of one of the most successful robber barons of all times: Andrew Carnegie.

A former bobbin-boy in a cotton factory, Carnegie had formed the United States Steel Corporation in 1901. It was amalgamated from Carnegie's wide range of iron- and steel-related industries. The express purpose was to consolidate and dominate production and market share. The huge capital resources of US Steel provided immense opportunities for expansion as well as significant power over dependent industries like the railroads. Standard Oil was another corporation or "combination" established to secure market domination. A 1904 survey in the USA showed that more than 5,000 previously independent businesses had been combined into just 300 industrial trusts[6].

The growth of these all-powerful trusts and corporations occurred against a background of growing public and political concern. Various measures were enacted, starting with the Sherman Antitrust Act of 1890. A decade later, implementation of this Act led to President Theodore

Roosevelt gaining the nickname "trust buster." Following his re-election in 1904, the Hepburn Act extended the jurisdiction of the Interstate Commerce Commission in regulating trade and forced the divestment of shipping and coal interests by railroad owners. Meanwhile the Department of Commerce and Labor was pursuing corporations for tax evasion and secret deals: Standard Oil ended up with fines totalling $29,240,000 for infringements on 1,462 contracts.

The behavior of US industrial concerns in the late nineteenth and early twentieth centuries was keenly criticized at the time by the popular press and by contemporary authors such as Mark Twain and Upton Sinclair. The behavior of US corporations since has been savagely attacked by eminent economists like John Kenneth Galbraith, by consumer activists like Ralph Nader and by commentators like Ralph Estes, author of *The Tyranny of the Bottom Line*[7] and David Korten, who wrote *When Corporations Rule the World*[8]. However, the power of the US corporate sector remains largely undisturbed after one hundred years and limited liability remains the most powerful force for the continued expansion of large-scale business corporations worldwide.

The rise of the transnational corporation

According to the US-based Institute for Policy Studies, of the 100 largest "economies" in the world today, 51 are global corporations[9]. There are now 40,000 corporations whose activities transcend national boundaries; the top 200 of these have sales equivalent to more than a quarter of the world's total economic activity.

On a strictly financial basis, Mitsubishi has a sales turnover bigger than Indonesia (the country with the 22nd biggest economy in the world). General Motors outweighs Denmark (number 23 in the list of national economies). Ford is bigger than Hong Kong and Turkey (the 25th and 26th largest economies). Toyota and Royal Dutch Shell outrank Norway (29th). IPS also calculates that between 1982 and 1995 the revenues of the top 200 corporations rose as a percentage of world gross domestic product from 24.2 to 28.3 percent. Table 4.1 lists the world's top twenty corporations; eleven are Japanese.

Given the size of some of the corporations listed in Table 4.1, it is easy to overlook the fact that the majority of people are still employed in small business and family owned concerns (see Case Study 4.1). Indeed, the top 200 companies employ less than one percent of the world's working population (18.8 million out of 2.6 billion)[9]. But as Jeremy Rifkin argues,

Table 4.1
The world's top twenty global corporations ranked by 1995 sales[9]

Rank	Company	Business	Country	Sales ($ million)	Employees (thousands)
1	Mitsubishi	Trading	Japan	184,510	13.9
2	Mitsui and Co.	Trading	Japan	181,661	11.7
3	Itochu	Trading	Japan	169,300	7.2
4	General Motors	Automobiles and trucks	USA	168,829	709.0
5	Sumitomo	Trading	Japan	167,662	25.3
6	Marubeni	Trading	Japan	161,184	9.9
7	Ford Motor	Automobiles and trucks	USA	137,137	347.0
8	Toyota	Automobiles	Japan	111,139	142.6
9	Royal Dutch Shell Group	Energy	Nether-lands/UK	109,853	104.0
10	Exxon	International oil	USA	197,893	84.0
11	Nissho Iwai	Trading	Japan	97,963	17.0
12	Wal-Mart	Drug and discount stores	USA	93,627	648.5
13	Hitachi	Electricity and electronics	Japan	84,233	331.9
14	Nippon Telephone & Telegraph	Telecommuni-cations	Japan	82,002	231.4
15	AT & T	Telecommuni-cations	USA	79,609	301.9
16	Daimler-Benz	Automobiles	Germany	72,253	321.2
17	IBM	Computer systems	USA	71,940	222.6
18	Matsushita Electric/Industrial	Appliances	Japan	70,454	265.4
19	General Electric	Electrical equipment	USA	70,028	219.0
20	Tomen	Trading	Japan	67,809	2.9

that does not let the major companies off the hook[10]. Only 1 percent of US companies employ more than 500 people, but these firms still employ two-fifths of all American workers.

We may compare the top corporations to the equivalent of Champions' league status – teams competing for the Super Bowls and World Cups of corporate leadership. Family-run enterprises and private firms (some of which are very large indeed) compete in the lower divisions but are nevertheless capable of giving the top teams a good run for their money in straight competition.

CASE STUDY 4.1

Keeping it in the family

The influence of family control and stability in Japanese business is legendary. The Hoshi hotel is reputed to have been founded in the year 718 and to have passed through 46 generations. In the West, family owned and dominated firms are still very common. According to the Swiss-based Family Business Network, US family firms represent 40 percent of GDP and employ 60 percent of the workforce. In Germany, two-thirds of GDP and three-quarters of the workforce are employed in family owned firms. In Britain both figures are around 50 percent. The results can be both good and bad: often a contributory factor to long-termism and stability, family interests can also introduce monumental and explosive tensions. Of family firms 90 percent do not make it to the third generation. Very occasionally a family will bounce back and retake control after a period of public flotation, e.g. Levi Strauss in the USA.

Lessons for the stakeholder corporation

- Limited liability creates a license to take risks which is important for entrepreneurial behavior. It also creates opportunities for fraud and abuse. This needs to be countered by reinforcing formal and informal mechanisms to ensure accountability.

- Businesses may say they believe in free trade and competition, but historically they have had a tendency to aim for market dominance and monopoly via merger.

- Large corporations are among the most powerful economic influences on the planet. They have immense capacity for creating wealth and doing good; equally they have unlimited ability to abuse their economic power. As we have already seen, this phenomenon persists in something of a policy vacuum.

CHAPTER 5

The sponsors

investors and bankers

There is one and only one responsibility of business – to use its resources and engage in activities designed to increase its profits so long as it stays within the rules of the game.
Milton Friedman

It has been the central belief of American academic Milton Friedman and his more uncritical supporters that increasing shareholder value is the over-riding moral obligation for the corporation. Indeed exercising any other act of social responsibility is in effect a tax on the wealth of the owners and is therefore akin to a socialist doctrine[1]. Where did this pre-occupation with the rights of owners or shareholders come from?

It is at least arguable that Adam Smith's iron rules lie at the heart of Friedman's argument and the so-called Chicago school of neoclassical economics. If one believes (as did the European aristocracy for many years) that property and wealth are God-given or alternatively the just rewards of Christian virtues of hard work and endeavor, then it is a very small step to believing in the sanctity of money and the wealth it represents. As we have seen, Smith's theories took hold at a time when wealth and power were being transferred from older aristocratic and landed families to the energetic industrial and manufacturing entrepreneurs of the industrial revolution. The new industrial aristocracy was just as keen on divine justification as the landed gentry.

In the 1980s, belief in the essential morality of Smith–Friedmanite economics led first Margaret Thatcher, and then Ronald Reagan, to articulate extremely compelling, populist, political doctrines which virtually laid to rest the notion of interventionist economics as far as business and wealth creation in the English-speaking countries were concerned. Reagan and Thatcher were not embarrassed to cite Christian ethics as part of their political doctrines. Significantly, Reaganomics did not kill the arguments over business ethics – if anything these arguments intensified. The seemingly seductive arguments in favor of relying on increased profits and shareholder value to generate public virtue leaves two key questions of stakeholder ethics to be resolved.

First, we are not living in a time when ethical dilemmas can be governed by a single philosophical or moral code, i.e. Christianity. There is a wide variety of codes on offer, not all of them religious or indeed enlightened. It usually comes down to how people believe power, property, wealth and happiness should be shared out. Readers who wish to explore this subject in more detail are referred to the voluminous and erudite literature on business ethics and philosophy.[2,3,4,5,6,7,8,9,10]

Second, today's individual and institutional owners of wealth have numerous mechanisms for insulating themselves from the moral implications of their investments which the early family-owned industrial ventures did not. Sources of wealth and investment are notoriously difficult to track. A bank generates "wealth" through lending other people's money whether that cash derives from a deacon or a drug baron, a cook in the Salvation Army or a crook in the Nigerian Army. This problem applies as much to venture capitalists, investment trusts and pension funds. But there is no doubt that the most effective way of disguising the source of wealth is to pass it through a bank. Dictators and despots have had little difficulty salting away their blood money in foreign banks. During the twentieth century, hundreds of billions of dollars have been hidden by the Swiss banking system. From the Nazis to President Ferdinand Marcos of the Philippines and President Mobuto of Zaire, Swiss banks have happily tended the cash of the world's tyrants.

Banks as investors

John Kenneth Galbraith has had much fun lampooning the bankers and shufflers of wealth. In *The Age of Uncertainty*[11] he describes how banks in the Middle Ages were originally repositories of gold and silver coinage. They reached quite powerful and sophisticated heights in Venice, Florence and Genoa. Then, in the early seventeenth century the merchants of Amsterdam created a bank that loaned wealth at a rate of interest which created yet more wealth for depositors and, of course, the bank itself. This simple innovation has proven remarkably resilient over the last four hundred years.

The progress of the banking profession has not always been smooth. Even betting shops sometimes go bust. This happened to the Bank of Amsterdam in 1819, largely as a result of excessive lending to Dutch merchant adventurers whose ships were being sunk rather too frequently by the navies of British merchant adventurers. Galbraith describes the tendency of bankers through the ages to gamble on pet causes and sometimes their own pecuniary interests. One of the best mechanisms invented to facilitate this temptation was the issuing of banknotes or paper money.

In several infamous cases the issue of paper money proved disastrous. The Banque Royale was created in France in 1716 by John Law to bail out the bankrupt French Treasury. One year later Law created a company, later known as the Mississippi Company, to exploit the riches of French-owned Louisiana. The silver and gold wealth (and the notes) went round and round in ever-decreasing circles until both the bank and the company imploded, leaving investors and depositors clutching a confetti of worthless banknotes.

The Bank of England proved more resilient and innovative than Banque France, making sure that paper money maintained a somewhat closer relationship to the gold and silver coinage on which it was supposedly based. Until 1914 it was still possible to demand gold for paper money from a British bank. The Bank of England also regulated rates of interest and the lending of smaller commercial banks, deploying its reserves when necessary.

In the USA, the First and then Second National Banks came and went, not because they were ill disciplined, more because they got a little too influential for the taste of early nineteenth century US presidents. As a result, a plethora of state banks emerged so that by the time of the American Civil War there were more than 7,000 legitimate banknotes competing for currency and a further 5,000 counterfeit ones. In 1865, the right of state banks to issue money was abolished, partly because of the confusion of notes, and partly because of the frequency of crashes.

Finally, in 1914, the USA set up a central institution, the Federal Reserve System to act as a supposedly conservative influence in banking. But in the 15 years following its creation, America was to be hit twice by unsustainable booms, the first in farm commodities and real estate in 1919–20, the second in 1927–9 in stocks and shares. This later boom culminated in the stock market crash of 24 October 1929 and the Great Depression which was to have repercussions well beyond the fevered environs of Wall Street. Clearly, something was not quite working with the central bank; indeed Galbraith argues that the Federal Reserve was almost fated to make the wrong decisions and exaggerate the economic and social impacts of every turn of the economic cycle on those least able to cope with its effects. As the USA soon discovered, even private banks could suffer. In the first half of 1929, no fewer than 346 US banks failed[12].

It was this inability of banks to take the broader social view which eventually led to state intervention to improve the flow of money through the real economy – the New Deal in America, pre-war reconstruction in Nazi Germany and post-war reconstruction throughout the rest of Europe.

This was the approach advocated by John Maynard Keynes, whose theories were published in 1936 as *The General Theory of Employment Interest and Money*. In this book, Keynes argued that government could boost investment by borrowing and thereby correct an unfortunate tendency in capitalism to come to rest in a low investment – high unemployment equilibrium, i.e. in a slump like the Great Depression.

Even today, banks are not immune from undermining economic development, poor commercial judgement and even collapse. Lending policies of Western banks in Latin America in the 1960s and 1970s proved disastrous all round. Nevertheless the sophistication of controls ensuring interdependence mean that total failure of the global banking system is now a virtual impossibility. Specialist banks have collapsed – usually as a result of fraud or incompetence. The failure of the Bank of Credit and Commerce International in 1991 was ascribed by many to the fact that the Bank of England did not react promptly to warning signals. The demise of Barings, many believed, was caused as much by supervisory failure as by the gambling instincts of a young trader in futures. But the untimely coincidence of two human frailties: greed and reckless error remain the main danger for any bank. No amount of regulatory oversight can prevent chunks of investors' money going to exciting, if unsound, ventures in far-off lands. No amount of management supervision can prevent an individual in a position of trust from abusing that trust in the interests of self-enrichment if that person is determinedly dishonest.

In recent years there has been increasing interest in the differences of behavior of banks in the UK and USA compared with that of their counterparts in continental Europe and the Far East. Will Hutton has mobilized a devastating attack on the short-termism and non-engagement of UK banks in British industry[13]. He contrasts the situation in Britain and the USA where stock markets require far higher returns from banks than in Germany, Japan and even Switzerland. He notes the major influence of the availability of long-term finance to home industry via the Industrial Bank of Japan, the Kreditanstalt für Wiederaufban (KFW) or reconstruction bank in Germany and their equivalents in Korea and France. Hutton is in no doubt that the inflexibility of the British banking system has been a major contributor to the downward spiral of productive British industry and its failure to exploit new technological opportunities. In Germany and Scandinavia it is common for local and state banks to be deeply involved with their local economies, providing long term loans and sharing directorships with companies and people whose activities they know and to whose success they can cheerfully contribute.

In Japan, in 1985 banks held 18 percent of corporate equity[14]. This formed a key element of the *kairetsu*, or networks of cross-shareholding. Indeed it is commonplace for Japanese banks to have directors on the boards of companies they sponsor. In 1990, ten of the largest shareholdings in Nissan were held by banks, funds and insurance companies. They ranged from 2.0 percent for Meiji Mutual Life, to 5.7 percent for the Dai-Ichi Mutual Life Assurance Company.

These relationships matter. It is not simply a question of access to long-term capital investment at lower rates of interest, vitally important though this is. Constructive relationships between industrial firms and bankers in non-English-speaking countries provide networks of support and trust which really count when the exploitation of technological advances requires rapid integration and collaboration across industrial sectors.

Of course, the banks are not the only backers in the game of free enterprise. And this is only one reason why simplistic application of the theory of shareholder value becomes a little problematic. The reality is that today it is very difficult to connect the notion of ownership directly to the decision-making processes of the firm, still less to secure any direct accountability to a multiplicity of investors for the economic value of the business. Among the complicating factors are: the complex and diffuse nature of accountability to individual investors through investment intermediaries; the role of local or national governments as investors; and the role of corporations themselves as investors. We will examine each of these confounding factors in turn.

Individuals as investors

As we have already seen, banks are intermediaries for other people's wealth. They do not typically poll their investors on how their cash should be lent. And only in rare cases do banks have overt lending policies which stipulate anything other than commercial criteria. The Co-operative Bank in Britain and the Netherlands-based Triodos Bank are honourable exceptions to this rule. There are alternatives to conventional banking, for example, large credit unions like the Citizens Bank in Tokyo, and VanCity in Vancouver, as well as the friendly societies. But these alternative sources of finance rarely invest in anything larger than a small – medium sized enterprise.

Similarly, investment trusts and pension funds only rarely take a broad view of the social and environmental responsibility of their investments. In the USA, the Social Investors Group estimates that "socially screened" investments increased sevenfold between 1985 and 1992 – much of this related to the concern over apartheid in South Africa. In 1990, around $500 billion was screened to some extent. But overtly marketed ethical funds remain a small proportion.

So far, so good, for the shareholder value theory since it may be argued that the only contract which exists between the conventional individual investor and the bank, investment portfolio or pension fund manager is to maximize the return and security of the original investment. Indeed, in the case of pension funds it may be illegal for trustees to act in any other way. It may also be argued that there is a chain of accountability from the management of the corporation to the board of directors to the banks, institutional investors and thus to individual investors and shareholders which ensures that management always acts in such a way as to improve profits, market capitalization and thus shareholder value. So theoretically, what is good (or bad) for an individual direct investor should also be good (or bad) for an individual investor who uses an intermediary like a bank or fund manager.

Sadly, this is where the theory breaks down, as anyone who has attended the recent turbulent annual general meetings of British Gas or Hanson plc will testify. These are the occasions when individual shareholders complain and when institutions and banks (supposedly acting as proxies for other individual investors) close ranks, opt for a quiet life and pray that continuity will bring its own reward. In reality, individual shareholder activism in the USA has struggled to make a major impact since the head of the Episcopal Church in America, John Hines intervened in General Motors' 1971 AGM and asked the company to withdraw from South Africa. Although the Investor Responsibility Research Center in the USA is able to point to increasing numbers of shareholder resolutions to US annual general meetings, the Securities and Exchange Commission has recently ruled that companies could legitimately exclude resolutions on equal opportunities and workplace issues. And in Britain Margaret Thatcher's dream of a vibrant shareholding democracy (or "popular capitalism" in her words) has yet to materialize.

Institutions as investors

In the USA pension funds own two-fifths of the equity and debt of the largest companies. It is estimated that UK financial institutions own around two-thirds of the London stock market. According to Neville Bain, Chief Executive of Coats Viyella, and David Band, just 50 institutions own 45 percent of all British shares[15]. They argue that this might allow the institutions to build up larger stakes, i.e. in excess of 10 percent, in return for closer, longer term relationships with a handful of top companies. But it is unlikely that the Bain–Band prescription will be taken up. It would require a revolution in attitudes of the institutions.

Indeed it is relatively rare for the institutions in Britain and the USA to demand any direct accountability for their investors. They usually prefer quietly to sell under-performing shares and thereby insulate their portfolios from the worst examples of boardroom failure and incompetence. There are exceptions, as Thomas Sheridan and Nigel Kendall have pointed out[14]. In 1991 The California Public Employees' pension fund Calpers voted against the re-election of ITT's directors because of the excessive remuneration of Chairman Rand Araskog. Ethical investment vehicles like the Calvert social investment funds (US) and Friends Provident Stewardship Trust (UK) tend to keep a closer watch on corporate governance as well as performance. Groups like Franklin Research and Development (US) and Pension Investment Research Consultants (UK) are not averse to recommending individual and institutional shareholders to drop shares or vote against boards of directors whose behavior they disfavor.

Just occasionally, institutional investors succeed in ousting the most incompetent, autocratic or secretive chief executives. Sir Ralph Halpern of Burton and Professor Sir Roland Smith of British Aerospace discovered this in 1990 and 1991 respectively. In neither case did institutional investors balk at wielding a rather sharper sword than was used at the time of their investitures as knights of the realm. In 1993, the heads of American Express, Westinghouse and IBM suffered a similar fate – all in the space of a week.

But these examples do remain the exception rather than the rule. In high profile sackings, as indeed in other celebrated cases of corporate mis-

CASE STUDY 5.1

Eastman Kodak: a snapshot triumph of shareholder value over employee security

David Korten relates the experience of Eastman Kodak in 1992–3. In 1992 Chairman Kay R. Whitmore announced the redundancies of 3,000 of Kodak's 132,000 employees. Unfortunately, institutional investors were hoping for an order of higher magnitude. So despite profits of $1.14 billion for the year, Whitmore was removed by outside directors on what was described by one investment manager as "a great day for the American shareholder." The day was so great that Kodak stock ended $3.25 higher by close of trading.

demeanors in Britain and the USA, the main objective of the institutional investors is not to establish good overall governance, rather it is to restore short-term trading performance. It is not about establishing the long-term security of the firm, its stakeholders and their livelihoods; it is about bringing in new management who will give the kiss of life to the share price and pump up next year's dividends (see Case Study 5.1).

Will Hutton quotes the work of two economists at the Federal Reserve Bank of New York[13]. They calculate that over the last thirty years the British stock market has required an average of 9.8 percent returns from British banks. This compares with the 3.1 percent required by capital investors in Japanese banks, and 6.9 percent in the case of German banks. It is no surprise, therefore, that the rates of interest which are offered to British companies by British banks are rather less favorable than may be obtained in Germany and Japan.

Interestingly, there are signs that now even the German social market economy (Sozial Marktwirtschaft) is beginning to feel the pressure of international institutions for higher returns on investment. Chief Executive of Siemens, Heinrich von Pierer, estimated that low levels of foreign inward investment cost Germany more than 300,000 jobs in 1996. In 1995 outward investment from Germany was DM47.9 billion compared with inward investment of only DM13.9 billion. It remains to be seen whether the forces of economic globalization will eventually establish the concept of "shareholder value" as strongly in Germany as it currently prevails in the UK and the US.

The state or municipality as investor

These days, following the demise of communism and the wholesale retreat of state capitalism (nationalization) in favour of privatization, it seems almost inconceivable that there was once a time when the take-over of private enterprise by governments was both politically popular and economically expedient. In the first part of the twentieth century, collectivization and state ownership were not confined to the Soviet Union and its satellites.

In 1933, Herbert Morrison signaled the intentions of a British Labour government when it came to power. "We are seeking a combination of public ownership, public accountability and business management for public ends[16]." Consequently, when Labour formed the post-war government in 1945, it was no surprise that nationalization of the Bank of England, civil aviation, coal mining, gas, electricity, iron and steel and transport were high on the agenda for public ownership. Taking over the "commanding heights" of the economy for reasons of socialist doctrine, economic efficiency and public accountability was the culmination of half a century of socialist dreams. It is a testament to the power of the vision that these measures took another fifty years for Conservative governments to disentangle (the Bank of England remaining the sole exception to the de-nationalization imperative). Contrast Morrison's words in 1933 with those of Labour leader Tony Blair in a speech to Rupert Murdoch's News Corporation management in July 1995: "The old left solutions of rigid economic planning and state control won't work."

In the rest of Western Europe and elsewhere, the lure of nationalization was just as strong. Post-war reconstruction in Europe demanded levels of investment far beyond the capacity of the Marshall Plan and private capital to finance. The Keynesian prescription of government intervention to stimulate economic growth and full employment was widely accepted as justification for governments throughout Western Europe to take significant financial stakes in key industries. It was a model followed in large measure by newly independent and industrializing countries in the developing world.

Today, economic orthodoxy demands that governments in industrialized countries divest themselves of state enterprises while governments of Third World countries are threatened with foreclosure by the international banks if they fail to privatize key sectors of their economies. This may not be a wholly bad thing; state-run enterprises have rarely exhibited entrepreneurial dynamism or excellence in stakeholder relations. Many of the bureaucratic, non-participative state enterprises which resulted from nationalization generally failed to secure the best return possible for their investors, i.e. the state on behalf of the people, still less to inspire any real stakeholder loyalty.

But it would be a mistake to believe that all forms of public ownership are discredited or indeed inefficient. A more stakeholder friendly and vibrant form of public ownership has persisted for more than a century at local and municipal level. Utilities and other enterprises accountable to local communities through their elected local representatives have proven remarkably resilient in Europe and North America. Provided they stay localized and subject to genuine forms of accountability, small water and sewerage companies and municipal power companies owned or financed by their local governments can be both efficient and popular.

Following the devastating cholera and typhoid epidemics of the mid-nineteenth century, it was largely municipal intervention which secured the huge investments necessary to build sanitary infrastructures providing safe water and efficient sewerage to the townspeople of Europe. London's

Metropolitan Water Board became a world leader in water treatment technology and wastewater processing as well as ensuring value for money and accountability to stakeholders. Its successor, the privatized Thames Water, has struggled to maintain this reputation. Indeed, most of the private water companies in Britain are charged with failing miserably to maintain adequate rates of investment in their crumbling sanitary infrastructures even though they are now free from government imposed borrowing constraints. Happily for those at the helm, most still manage to find the resources to pay their executives fabulous remuneration packages.

The community as investor

Today, in many industrialized countries, investment of public funds by municipal and regional governments in order to stimulate local economies is an increasingly popular and effective means of economic regeneration. An extremely powerful vehicle for directing such funds is the community development bank (see Case Study 5.2).

CASE STUDY 5.2

Los Angeles riots lead to a new banking initiative

The Los Angeles Community Development Bank (LACDB) was set up in 1995 with public sector finance to provide non-traditional loans to new or growing businesses within the Los Angeles Supplemental Empowerment Zone (LASEZ). The empowerment zone was created by the Clinton administration following the riots of 1994. Unlike commercial banks, the LACDB is a lending institution only, with the overriding goal of promoting a positive investment environment and sustainable jobs for residents and others within the designated zone. The LASEZ encompasses a 19 sq mile area with a population of 213,000 of which 40 percent are classified as living in poverty (in receipt of less than $16,000 per annum per household) and includes 49 percent single parent households. Commercial banks have "redlined" the zone, i.e. they have pulled out entirely. While it has attracted public funding, the bank is very much community driven and operates under the ethos that local people are those who best understand the needs of a community. Community based organizations cooperate with the bank to identify projects and businesses that fit the criteria to receive finance. The LACDB acts as a channel for special economic development funding, sourced via the Los Angeles City and County Economic Development Initiative (EDI) Funds ($115 million) and a special loan guarantee program funded through the Department of Housing and Urban Development ($315 million). Commercial banks have also committed up to $310 million.

Ed Mayo of London-based think tank the New Economics Foundation describes five alternative models to conventional banking. Community development banks operate largely as commercial banks offering a wide variety of financial services to local communities and socially or environmentally benign enterprise. The Los Angeles CDB, the South Shore Bank in Chicago (US), Caja Laboral in Spain and Triodos Bank in Europe are all examples of community development banks which have invested hundreds of millions of dollars since their inception in the 1970s. Credit unions are cooperative savings and lending institutions: there are more than 37,000 of these worldwide with assets exceeding $400 billion, serving 88 million members. VanCity Credit Union in Vancouver is an excellent example (see Cast Study 5.3).

CASE STUDY 5.3

A co-operative approach to credit

VanCity's 1995 Annual Report details a number of community economic development lending initiatives. Community Investment Deposits are loaned to environmental and affordable housing programs which receive loans at 1 percent discount. This is matched by investors accepting 1 percent lower rates too. Between 1993 and 1995 $1 million was loaned from $4.6 million receipts. Self-reliance loans and Community Loan Funds provide funds of up to $15,000 and $5,000 respectively to micro enterprises and other community initiatives.

Community exchange schemes or local exchange trading systems (LETS) use local (non-monetary) currency which allows people to exchange skills, services and goods without conventional cash. There are around 300 LETS schemes operational in Britain. Community development loan funds and micro-loan funds provide small loans for low to moderate income people needing cash for housing or micro enterprises. Examples of the latter include Working Assets (US) and ADIE (France). Funds of this type have loaned nearly $150 million in the USA in the last twenty years. In 1995, the Citicorp Foundation established a $10 million initiative to provide seed money of around $50,000 each to "microlenders" mostly in Latin America, Africa and Asia.

It seems that in a mixed economy there will always be a place for economic investment of public and community funds, i.e. citizens' cash, especially at local level. Is this any more or less accountable to the individual creator or owner of wealth than investment by a conventional bank or other financial institution? It is at least arguable that individuals' well-being and prosperity will be best secured by living and working in a dynamic local economy with an efficient infrastructure and diverse sources of capital investment. If part of that investment comes from community taxes and individual savings, is that less accountable to local people and local businesses than funding from a distant bank? Almost certainly not; indeed the investment is more likely to be long term and therefore more secure.

The corporation as investor

As we noted in the Introduction, the world's top 500 companies are responsible for 70 percent of direct foreign investment. One-third of all world trade simply involves transactions between the leading transnational companies. Through their procurement policies, ability to "outsource" and freedom to transfer production from one sector to another, one country to another, corporations exercise immense power of investment and disinvestment. Indeed, because of the twin thrusts of privatization and globalization in recent years, this power is now greater than ever.

If one believes in the Friedmanite notion of accountability, perhaps this is not an issue. But there is an increasing level of unease about the non-accountability of corporations for investment decisions. This could turn into a rather nasty backlash.

When a car manufacturer switches production to another country or region because costs there are lower and the workforce more compliant, it may be argued that the corporation is acting in the clear interests of its shareholders: maximizing efficiency of investment and enhancing profits. The same manufacturer will also hope to maintain its home market and see sales of its cars continue in the country where production was originally located. This is a simple playing out of the iron rules of free enterprise. The CEO who has laid off thousands of workers back home hopes that someone else will employ them so that they will still be able to afford the cars they used to make and which are now imported and distributed by local dealers (see Case Study 5.4).

At this point, another flaw in the theory starts to become apparent. It is not possible for the CEO as investor to predict whether someone else will step in to create the economic opportunities he has removed. The social implications of the original decision could, if compounded by similar decisions by fellow industrialists, actually become cataclysmic for a local community. Michael Shuman has argued that the Uruguay Round of GATT "thwarts local economic development" and has described the dilemma of local communities faced with the flight of inward investment "either cut wages, eviscerate environmental standards, and offer tax

CASE STUDY 5.4

Exporting textile jobs from West to East

Advocates of free trade often question whether jobs are really exported to the low wage economies of Asia and the Far East. The evidence of the textile industry proves otherwise. In 1996, well-established British firms like Dewhurst, Coats Viyella, Courtaulds Textiles, Claremont and William Baird were all contemplating factory closures and job losses in the UK and the expansion of overseas manufacture. With wage rates in Bangladesh, Vietnam and China around 3 percent of those in Britain, significant cost savings can be made in garment manufacture. And with major retailers like Marks and Spencer adopting a more global outlook to their sourcing the implications for the British textile industry are clear. The GMB General Union secretary for the textile industry summed up the gloomy prospects: "Since 1979 we've lost 400,000 jobs, and if you look at the statements [from the textile manufacturers] about moving production overseas, by the end of the decade there could be 50,000 more jobs at risk."

breaks to induce corporations to build new factories or offices, or prepare to become an economic ghost town[17]." There are numerous examples of single industry towns which have collapsed socially after the demise of that industry (see Case Study 5.5).

CASE STUDY 5.5

Death of a steel town

Birthplace of pop superstar Michael Jackson, Gary was once a booming steel town on the Indiana shore of Lake Michigan. Its heyday was in the 1950s and early 1960s. In 1970, the steelworks still employed 30,000; today it employs less than a third of that number. In 1996, Gary had unemployment at three times the national average, 40 percent child poverty and a thriving underworld specializing in narcotics. The town also boasted the highest murder rate in the USA, at just over one murder per 1,000 members of the population – four times that of Chicago. One 21-year-old crack dealer explained: "There ain't nothing to do in this fucked up place. If you ain't got money, you ain't got shit."

It is quite possible to envisage a reducing capacity to generate economic wealth within a nation or region leading to a decline in social cohesion and demands for a different sort of economic order altogether. Industrial workers are not stupid. It is this fear which has prompted revived political interest in the idea of protectionism. Several authors have analyzed the lack of accountability of corporations for investment decisions and have drawn attention to the dangers this represents, either to democracy, to the natural environment or to economic well-being[18].

Populist politicians from the center to the far right have seized on these dangers to begin articulating the need to protect workers' jobs against the icy winds of international competition. Ross Perot and Pat Buchanan tapped a good deal of public support for protectionist ideas in the US presidential races of 1992 and 1996. The forces which may be unleashed if these ideas take full hold may not be very pleasant. In Europe, there are strong links between protectionist ideas and vile political philosophies based on fear of foreigners or even outright racism (see Case Study 5.6).

CASE STUDY 5.6

The rise of the new right in France

The far right National Front polled 15 percent of the popular vote in the French presidential elections of 1995. A year later the party was aggressively recruiting French workers for its new trade unions in the police, prison and transport sectors. Campaigning against political corruption and for the "rights" of workers displaced by foreign competition, the National Front provides sinister echoes of a darker past in Europe. The blame for worsening conditions and cutbacks in France's manufacturing and defense industries is laid squarely at the door of economic globalization. This sits quite comfortably, if simplistically, with the overt racism of National Front leader, Jean-Marie Le Pen, as repugnant and as dangerous an influence as could be imagined in late twentieth century European politics.

So we have the specter of apparently politically neutral corporate investment policies today providing the future intellectual and political space for a backlash of a most unpleasant kind. This looks suspiciously like yet another example of Adam Smith's invisible hand failing to materialize.

Another form of corporate "investment" is the company takeover. Virtually all of the "friendly" takeovers and mergers in recent years have involved American and British companies. And most have been about securing bigger shares of the same market; for example, the various media acquisitions of Walt Disney, the $13 billion takeover of Gulf by Chevron, or the £9 billion takeover of Wellcome by Glaxo. In telecommunications, the mergers between McCaw Cellular and AT&T, and British Telecommunications plc (BT) and MCI left no one betting against a global market dominated by just a handful of international operators by the first years of the twenty-first century.

Both in the USA and Britain, it is relatively common for companies to merge or to take each other over in an aggressive and predatory way, "investing" huge sums of cash to win over the current owners – institutional and individual. This behavior, often aimed at securing market dominance or asset stripping, is almost unknown in Germany. In that country there have been only four contested takeovers since 1945. In Britain there have been an average of forty per annum[13]. Mergers may well be in the long-term interests of all stakeholders – particularly where industries are undergoing significant structural change. But there is little evidence that predatory "investments" lead to greater management efficiency, although they can certainly boost returns at the expense of longer term investments in research and development, plant or people.

It is not only in the USA and Britain that companies may fall prey to get-rich-quick temptations. This particular anglophone behavior also affects Australians. Hostile takeovers, asset stripping and breathtaking profiteering found free rein in the deregulating Australia of the 1980s (see Case Study 5.7). We will return to this issue in Chapter 6.

CASE STUDY 5.7

Rogue trader down under

In 1987–8, the Bond Corporation and the News Corporation made profits of $A673 million in tax havens, quite legally. In 1989, the Bond empire had debts of between $A8 billion and $A14 billion – comprising more than 10 percent of the Australian national debt. Meanwhile, in just four years Alan Bond's personal fortune rose from $A25 to $A400 million. In August 1996, Alan Bond was committed to prison for his dishonest handling of Van Gogh's *Irises* – a painting purchased by Bond for $A58 million. Doubtless Van Gogh, who died penniless by his own hand, would have appreciated the irony.

Lessons for the stakeholder corporation

- Banks can be contributors to industrial resilience and innovation or they can throttle it.

- Individual investors have virtually no power over companies in whom they invest.

- Institutional investors in English-speaking countries rarely exercise any other accountability requirement than for the maximization of short-term returns.

- Nationalization is dead and buried, but local public ownership is still thriving and popular with stakeholders.

- Corporations can create massive swings in investment and disinvestment and thereby incur significant social impacts.

CHAPTER 6

The team captains

business leaders and CEOs

*I have never known much good done by those who affected to trade for
the public good.*
Adam Smith

The early Victorian industrialists were not all bad. That there was
much suffering and hardship in the factories, mills and mines of
early nineteenth century Britain is not in doubt. But many of the Victorian industrialists had a strong sense of their personal moral obligations.
Indeed it was the principal assumption of Adam Smith that wealth cre-
ators would be guided by the invisible moral hand which allowed him to
argue so forcefully for the minimization of state interference in trade and
the pressing necessity for individuals to act in their own self-interest.
Indeed Smith firmly believed that this was all part of a "natural order"
which ensured that wealth would automati-
cally be circulated between rich and poor via
consumption and investment[1]. This was all part
of the will of God enshrined in the notion that
"thou shalt love thy neighbor as thyself."

John D. Rockefeller

We will see later how this belief in human
and social mutuality was given a somewhat different spin by the cooperative movement. But
for now it is simply enough to note that there
exists a moral justification based on Christian
ethics which allows the free market business
case to be argued. Indeed Victorian industrial
families like the Pilkingtons (glass making),
Whitbreads and Trumans (brewing), Cadburys
and Rowntrees (confectionery) and Wills and
Players (tobacco) were all bound by a religious
world view which accepted profit-making and
individual wealth creation as absolutely consistent with God's work[2].
Later, American industrialists took wealth creation, self-help and self-

improvement to spectacular heights, generating fabulous profits, some of which eventually trickled into good works and philanthropy.

John Kenneth Galbraith has described the tendency of American captains of industry to use moral laws and even scientific theories like Darwinism to justify ruthless business practices[3]. He notes how the cut-throat business empires of "robber barons" like Rockefeller and Carnegie were dependent on the principle of cheap production, suppression of competition and selling expensive goods and services to a captive public. And yet John D. Rockefeller once justified the "sacrifices" which must occur in the course of business thus: "This is not an evil tendency in business. It is merely the working-out of a law of nature and a law of God."

There are ways in which the apparent exercise of good stewardship of shareholders' money can be argued to be compatible with arrogant and acquisitive behavior on the part of individual senior executives. But it is important to understand the psychology here. Galbraith argued for many years that the "technostructure" of giant corporations acted first to secure its own power and security and second to look after the interest of its owners: "At the highest level of development – that exemplified by the General Motors Corporation, General Electric, Shell, Unilever, IBM – the power of the technostructure, so long as the firm is making money, is plenary. That of the owners of capital, i.e. the stockholders, is nil[4]."

Scientific management

The twentieth century has witnessed a number of key trends in corporate management style. World War I was infamous for its carnage; but it was also very good for business. Industrialization in the USA, Britain and continental Europe accelerated throughout the early years of the twentieth century, and not just in the oil, steel and armaments industries.

The invention of the production line and breakthroughs in chemical manufacturing required a new form of industrial management to emerge. Associated originally with the ideas of Frederick Winslow Taylor and carried to extreme conclusion by Henry Ford and his counterparts at General Motors, the notion of "scientific management" took hold in the first two decades of the twentieth century. Between 1908 and 1927, more than 16 million Model T Fords were built in 20 factories around the world. In essence, scientific management was a logical working out of the original division of labor prescriptions of Adam Smith – with the added impetus of technologies of which Smith could only have dreamed. Industrial manufactures, from cars to synthetic chemicals, required a command structure and a discipline unseen before in the history of business. Massive new assembly lines provided both the tools of war and consumer benefits of peace. We shall return to this story in Part 2.

The entrepreneurs who thrived on the tenets of Taylorism were usually autocratic executives with unlimited personal ambition. Foremost among these, Henry Ford included, were individuals whose appreciation of stakeholder needs was at best quirky. As with the Victorian pioneers of the industrial revolution, there were the enlightened, stakeholder-friendly philanthropist types. Thomas Watson of IBM was described by management guru Peter Drucker as creating in the 1930s "the social organization and the work community of the post-industrial society." Watson was every bit as individualistic as his paternalistic forebear Robert Owen had been one hundred years earlier. Most of his contemporaries in oil, chemicals and motor cars just made do with autocracy and worried somewhat less about paternalism and the rights of consumers, workers or the communities where they lived.

Scientific management and mass production became the subject of artistic satire; Charlie Chaplin, Fritz Lang, George Orwell, Aldous Huxley and George Bernard Shaw all savaged the de-humanizing tendency of industrially driven enterprise in the 1930s and 1940s.

In his excellent book *Company Man*[5], Anthony Sampson traces the massive shifts in managerial culture which have occurred since the first major corporations developed one hundred years ago. He describes how in the 1930s a new class of manager emerged to supplant the power previously wielded by the industrial magnates and owners. He cites a former vice-president of General Electric, T. K. Quinn, writing in 1953: "We had then, in effect, a huge economic state governed by non-elected, self perpetuating officers and directors in the direct opposite of the democratic method."

The emergence of "company man", in the middle of the twentieth century, particularly in large corporations was about asserting conformity, control and personal power and security. It had everything to do with structure and rationality (Galbraith's "technostrucure") and relatively little to do with the promotion of accountability to stakeholders or the development of the individual. Large bureaucracies grew in companies like Shell, Unilever and Du Pont. In some cases the managerial systems of the private sector overlapped neatly with that of government. In the USA the relationship between the Pentagon and the arms manufacturers, companies like General Dynamics, General Electric and General Motors, famously led President Dwight Eisenhower to warn in 1961 of the creeping power of the "military industrial complex."

It was not until the 1960s that the scientific approach to management softened a little. Fear of sacking or sidelining for nonconformity began to be understood as a sub-optimal way of motivating people. Starting in the USA, and later in Europe, new emphasis was placed on balancing team playing behavior with opportunities for enhanced personal identity. The birth of organizational development and industrial relations were as much a response to the dehumanizing impact of the technocratic corporation of previous decades as the realization that new forms of management were essential to recruit the brightest young executives and retain their loyalty. Of course the major corporations in Japan had long understood that.

Sadly, the ideal of united, creative, fulfilled, super-performing, secure and well-paid corporate management cadres was to prove somewhat short-lived. Just as the dream seemed within the grasp of the more enlightened major corporations, disaster struck. The days of plenty gave way to the era of downsizing, delayering, decentralization, outsourcing and re-engineering.

The corporate raiders

Sampson describes how in the 1980s a belief in the jungle law of business, survival of the fittest, was given a new twist in the USA, Britain and Australia. Echoing the political and moral philosophies of Carnegie and Rockefeller and armed with a virulent antipathy towards corporate bureaucrats, a new breed of corporate predator emerged. The corporate raiders borrowed massive sums of capital in order to take over, slim down and asset strip undervalued and (in their terms) underperforming corporations. Flamboyant and egotistical financiers like Sir James Goldsmith, Ross Johnson, Ivan Boesky, Michael Milken, James (Lord) Hanson and Alan Bond stalked well-established, often stakeholder-friendly companies with a view to acquisition or merger. The impact of their activities was immense personal enrichment for all and, in a few cases, imprisonment.

For a while, these corporate sharks hunted in the waters of political *laissez-faire* and easy finance. It was certainly a glamorous life surfing with the sharks. But the glamor wore a little thin for those communities and employees whose economic prospects suffered as a direct result of the asset stripping which followed. More insidiously, the psychological impact of the raids on senior executives throughout the English-speaking world was profound. The message of the 1980s was clear: "Don't invest too much in capital assets, research and development, plant or people, it only makes the company ripe for takeover; keep the shareholders sweet and the dividends high if you want to survive." The direct result was less

room for social responsibility, more centralization of power; less investment for the long term, and more attention to the short term demands of
the capital markets.

The raiders also unleashed a new corporate leadership style, the tough
talking, ruthless downsizer; only this time they were on the inside. From
the anti-bureaucratic Jack Welch at General Electric to the bombastic and
much loathed Bob Horton at British Petroleum and countless characters
in between, the tone of the 1980s was set. In the 1990s, corporations
achieved downsizing and delayering with less revolutionary fervor and a
little more humanity but the pain was still real for the managers and
workers of IBM, BT and a host of other companies struggling to compete with the new commercial pressures of maximizing shareholder value
and global competitiveness. As if to recapture the language of caring
in the early 1990s one IBM community relations officer added
"metamorphosis" to the growing list of euphemisms for mass redundancy. Later, after further restructuring which resulted in a 20 percent
decrease in corporate headquarters staff a colleague was more can-
did. One senior vice president for human resources at IBM said, "Our
view of corporate headquarters is that there should be as little of it as
possible."

Between 1980 and 1993, companies in the US Fortune 500 list shed
more than four million jobs. General Motors alone cut 100,000 jobs
during the 1980s. The company saved $2 billion by axing 40,000 salaried
staff[6]. According to *Business Week*, worker layoffs increased by 39 percent in the USA between 1990 and 1995. Interestingly, in the same five
year period average CEO remuneration almost doubled to nearly $4 mil-
lion per annum. We shall return to this phenomenon.

An entire lexicon was developed to explain to an increasingly troubled
and skeptical middle management salariat that while their immediate loyalty was valued and their self-denying commitment appreciated, the job-
for-life contract was over. An explosion of popular management
literature developed to explain the phenomenon and how to cope with it.
And while middle managers in major corporations the world over quaked
in their corporate boots, they were offered scant comfort by the gurus.
Liberation Management[7] is not much fun when you are the person who
used to fill *The Empty Raincoat*[8].

The primary cause of all this uncertainty – the need to slash management costs in the face of cutthroat competition in the global marketplace
– is not going to go away. The danger is that all too often the result in
management terms will not be a quest for better team playing or a kinder
style of leadership, it will be a return to the tough, autocratic tendency

which characterized the early years of the industrial revolution. A customer-focused entrepreneur like Richard Branson of Virgin can become an icon for the young with his relaxed dress, daring stunts and his David and Goliath reputation for taking on the bad guys; but that should not disguise his very hard-nosed approach to business, with no-frills management and vigorous exploitation of his Virgin brand. Bill Gates may encourage informality and meritocracy at Microsoft, but none of his managers and staff are in any doubt about the implications of failing to deliver. Branson and Gates are not robber barons like Carnegie or Rockefeller, and doubtless they have a lot more heart than a Hanson or a Bond. But their success in recent years has depended to a great extent on the rebirth of management by heroism. Theirs are the acceptable faces which disguise the rise and rise of the less well-known business leaders – the ruthless downsizers and outsourcers who generate value for the corporation while employees and suppliers sweat or go under.

Virgin is no longer publicly listed, so there is no pressure for instant returns to shareholders for Branson to consider. But for most large British and American corporations, driven as they are by the urgent demands of the institutional investors, there has been little room for wider issues of employee and middle manager well-being. All too often, the question has been simply who is going to keep the customer and, most importantly, the investors satisfied. And in many cases this required an autocrat at the helm.

The behavior of autocratic corporate executives has led to much public debate. At best we may describe individual business leaders as having a mixed record when it comes to corporate social responsibility. In their book *Corporate Governance*[9], Thomas Sheridan and Nigel Kendall catalog failures of leadership and even illegality in business empires as diverse as Salomon Brothers, the august American securities firm, and Maxwell Communications Corporation, the media fiefdom of super-rogue Robert Maxwell. Secretive and complex conglomerates led by aggressive tycoons seem to be able to thumb their noses at calls for greater nonexecutive involvement and accountability. This issue was one of the main causes of the bust-up between arch autocrat Lord Hanson and his erstwhile protégé Dieter Bock.

Executive pay

In the last few years much of the discussion of company management style in Britain and the USA has centered on the issue of executive pay and benefits. In Britain, greatest interest has been excited by the "fat cat" bosses of privatized utilities – many of whom control virtual monopolies and can award themselves huge pay rises and share options with virtual impunity. Total directors' remuneration in the nationalized industries (water, electricity, gas and telecommunications) increased from around £5 million to more than £30 million in 1996 after privatization (excluding share options). The salary bill at British Gas leaped nearly sevenfold. Occasionally the regulators, shareholders, workers and even politicians object, but the gravy train rolls on, fueled by exciting opportunities for resale, acquisition and merger with other utilities (see Case Study 6.1).

CASE STUDY 6.1

Plugging in to fat cat profits

According to analysis done by *The Guardian* newspaper in the UK, pay-offs to electricity executives leaving the industry because of five major mergers and acquisitions in 1995–6 totalled £26.9 million. Top recipient of the golden handshake treatment was Norweb's Chairman, Ken Harvey. When Norweb was taken over by North West Water to create United Utilities, Harvey received £407,000 compensation for loss of office and a £378,000 contribution to his pension. This was on top of his salary of £610,248 for eight months' work (up from £233,589 for the previous 12 months) and his share options, netting Mr Harvey nearly £3 million in total.

In the USA, executive pay has exploded in the last three decades. According to the US Bureau of Labor Statistics a typical factory worker received the equivalent of 2.5 percent of his chief executives' salary in 1960. In 1990 this had slipped to just 1.2 percent. Whereas US CEOs earn 85 times more than their employees, the differential in Germany is just 21 times and Japan just 16 times more than the average wage. According to *Business Week*, average CEO pay increased by 92 percent between 1990 and 1995 when it reached $3.75 million. It is not uncommon for US CEOs to make more than $10 million per annum.

What is going on here? Simple human greed is one answer; but a deeper explanation of managerial behavior requires an examination of what actually happens in board rooms and how executive decision-making actually plays out in practice.

There is no doubt about the theory. Under the iron rules of free enterprise, corporate executives are custodians of the wealth of their investors and should be directly accountable for their stewardship of that wealth. In most jurisdictions this notion has the force of the law behind it, as

Henry Ford unwittingly helped establish in the USA in 1916 (see Case Study 6.2).

The strange case of Henry Ford and the Dodge brothers

An interesting landmark in defining what responsibility captains of industry have towards shareholders is the strange legal case of Horace and John Dodge versus Henry Ford. The Dodge brothers were decidedly unhappy as minority shareholders when, in 1916, the motor magnate withheld their special dividends. Ford made clear that he thought the 60 percent normal dividend was quite adequate for investors who had already had their initial investment more than reimbursed. He declared, "My ambition is to employ still more men, to spread the benefits of the industrial system to the greatest possible number, to help them build up their lives and their homes. To do this we are putting the greatest share of our profits back into the business." If Ford had argued that by looking after his workers this would have been in the long term interests of the shareholders, he would have won the case. This is because "the business judgement rule" ensures judicial restraint in stopping US courts interfering in the day-to-day decision-making of corporations. However, in blithely challenging the notion that the *primary* responsibility of senior executives is to look after the interests of shareholders, Ford was inviting trouble. Ironically, by losing the case, Ford helped establish the principle that corporate altruism for its own sake is unacceptable, even fraudulent, in US law.

The one route out of trouble and the best way to keep both the shareholders and the executive elite happy is to grow the firm. Growth can disguise all but the most horrendous excesses.

"Growth" asserts Galbraith, "both enhances power over prices, costs, consumers, suppliers, the community and the state, and also rewards in a very personal way those who bring it about[4]." So the real game is about growth, increasing shareholder value, and power. Executive pay and boardroom excess are merely the slightly sordid public manifestations of the underlying motivation of many of the new breed team managers.

Senior executives in Britain and America usually justify their remuneration packages on the basis of competition for their services and the notional insecurity of their positions. What is interesting to note, however, is that there appears to be relatively little correlation between the size of the rewards and the performance of the company as judged by its investors. So, ultra free marketeers have invented performance-based schemes for senior executives which have attempted to rectify this dis-connect. Economic Value Added (EVA) is one such product of the free market Chicago school. But such schemes do not usually take into account the wider responsibilities of executives to generate genuine eco-nomic activity, secure the livelihoods of all stakeholders and build the long-term viability of their enterprises. Other performance measures are needed for this. Indeed, there is a number of prescriptions for corporate leadership for more enlightened CEOs[10,11,12,13]. We shall return to these in Parts 2 and 3.

Lessons for the stakeholder corporation

- Business people are not necessarily bad; they just work within an eco-nomic framework which increasingly rewards short-termist and auto-cratic behavior.

- In the last one hundred years, leading team managers have trans-formed themselves from the autocratic to the corporatist and back again to the autocratic. Meanwhile their direct reports still have to use the language of euphemism and team playing.

- Investing too much in people, plant and other long-term assets is not rewarded by those who provide capital to major corporations in Britain and the USA.

- In English-speaking countries there is an increasing gap between the rewards of the team managers and their ordinary employees.

- All is not lost.

CHAPTER 7

The supporters

employees and customers

The public be damned.
Cornelius Vanderbilt

Then the game of free enterprise has two sorts of supporter without which the game simply could not continue. There are the long-term supporters who may usually be relied upon to turn out week after week giving their all for their team: the workers and their local communities. Then there are the supporters who come and go and who exercise a much greater level of choice as to who they reward with their affections: the customers. In practical terms there are limits to the loyalty which companies can demand from their workers and the amount of choice which can be exercised by customers. In both cases a market exists: the worker sells his or her labor and skills and if insufficiently rewarded is theoretically free to move on; the customer chooses the product from the supplier he wants provided price and quality are optimal from his perspective.

But what if the worker does not have the option to move on because he or she does not possess the skills for a change in job direction? What if their ties to the local community, through schools, dependent relatives and friendships are too strong to sever? What if there are no local employers who are offering work, i.e. no one is competing for their labor? What if the choice is to accept low paid work or starve – will the labor–pay transaction be fair?

What if a customer has a high level of dependency on a specialist product, e.g. a life saving drug which comes only from one source – will the price always be fair? What if the customer is educated into believing in wants and desires as much as needs – will this lead to the payment of price premia which serve to reinforce desire rather than generate social benefit?

These questions lie at the heart of the relationship between workers and their communities, customers and the modern corporation. Getting the balance right between value for labor and value for money is one of the most difficult challenges in business. But if the balance is struck well, the rewards can be enormous (see Case Study 7.1). The Royal Society of Arts' *Tomorrow's Company Inquiry* in the UK quoted numerous indicators which demonstrated how an employee and customer inclusive approach to business was closely correlated with commercial success. For example, the Inquiry cited unequivocal conclusions from research on 3,000 businesses in North America and Europe which confirmed that "intangible" factors like intellectual property, innovation and quality were the strongest drivers of competitive performance. It is only free market ideologues who now seriously question conclusions like these.

CASE STUDY 7.1

Maintaining a balance between consumers, employees and shareholders

In a study conducted by two Harvard researchers, John P Kotter and James L Heskett, the benefits of a stakeholder approach to business were compared with those of a "shareholder first" philosophy. Over an eleven-year period, large established companies which gave equal priority to employees, customers and shareholders demonstrated sales growth of four times, and employment growth of eight times, that of the shareholder-first companies. In a study of British firms following stakeholder inclusive principles, Kleinwort Benson found that a portfolio of 32 quoted stocks rose 90 percent over a three and a half year period compared with an all share average rise of only 38 percent.

The worker

If we return for a moment to the beginnings of the industrial revolution, it is relatively easy to find examples of where the value for labor equation failed. Technology fundamentally challenged the independence of the home-working, hand-looming, textile producing family of the late eighteenth century. Textile workers were increasingly presented with a new dependency: factory work or penury. The new availability of unskilled work for women and children further weakened the bargaining power of the homeworkers.

These developments did not go unchallenged. Some homeworkers seeing their craft standards and markets undermined by the emergence of master traders took direct action. Machine-breaking gangs in the English Midlands were formed by stocking-makers who issued letters signed by "King Lud" or "Ned Lud." These gangs smashed around 1,000 textile frames rented out by the textile masters between 1811 and 1812 and coined the term Luddism. Luddites in Lancashire and Yorkshire attacked factory machines and many were hanged or transported to the colonies for their activities[1].

During a period of war and burgeoning industrialization, repression was frequently the response of choice when British workers complained about their lot. In 1799 and 1800 Combination Acts had been passed to prevent workers organizing to better their conditions. As minor insurrection and organized public protest became more common, military and legislative responses grew cruder still.

Following two years of depression and strikes, in August 1819 80,000 people gathered in St Peter's Fields, Manchester, England, to demonstrate for political and economic reform. They were scattered by mounted cavalry attempting to arrest the main speaker "Orator" Hunt. More than 400 protesters were wounded and eleven died in the "Peterloo Massacre," including two women and a child. Despite the vigorous complaints of reformers, the government moved to enact the Six Acts aimed at cracking down on public meetings, "seditious libels" and general agitation by the workers.

At this time working conditions in factories, mills and mines were in many cases nothing short of appalling. The Protestant work ethic was not necessarily perceived to lack consistency either with slavery in the colonies or child labor in the Lancashire Mills. And while slow but inexorable progress was made towards the abolition of slavery through the efforts of Thomas Clarkson and William Wilberforce MP, the rights of British workers in the first fifty years of the industrial revolution were to be hard won.

Children under the age of ten were forced to work in unsafe, insanitary conditions; working time frequently exceeded twelve hours per day for adults and children alike. Beatings and loss of earnings were the penalties for arriving late or for committing other minor misdemeanors.

In 1819, the first Factory Act was passed limiting the hours of cotton mill work for under-16s to twelve hours per day and prohibiting the use of children under the age of nine altogether. The Factory Act of 1833 extended the 1819 Act from cotton to other textiles and for the first time made provision for a paid government inspectorate (a total of four persons) to oversee implementation. Agitation for a ten hour maximum working day for women and children was led by working class leaders and reforming politicians like Lord Ashley. A Ten Hours Bill was first introduced by Ashley in 1832 but was not to be passed for another fifteen years.

In 1824, the Combination Acts had been repealed and it became possible for workers once more to organize legally to protect their interests. Among the first groups of workers to organize collectively were the miners. Working conditions in the coal mines were even less safe and more exploitative than in the textile mills.

The dangers of mining were established well before the start of the industrial revolution. An explosion in Chester-le-Street in 1708 led to the deaths of 100 miners: "One man was blown quite out of the mouth of the shaft, which is full fifty fathom, and found at a prodigious distance from the place[2]." A pit disaster in Silkstone, Yorkshire, in 1838 claimed the lives of twenty six children between the ages of seven and seventeen.

In 1842 a government report noted the extensive use of children as young as four years old in the mines. Ill-treatment of children was rife and accidents common. One commissioner noted that in the mines of Lancashire and Cheshire, accidents were a "daily occurrence in almost every mine where numbers are employed, and so common that a record of them is seldom kept."

Trade unions

These conditions, including the obligatory long hours led to the formation of one of the earliest trade unions in Northumberland and Durham in 1825. In 1831, the Pitmans' Union of the Tyne and Wear went on strike in protest at working conditions and secured a number of concessions from mine owners. But one year later the owners retaliated by refusing to employ trade unionists – a tactic reinforced by the use of police and black leg (non-union) labor which eventually broke the union[1].

In 1842 the Mines Act provided a belated governmental response to the problems of the miners, forbidding the underground employment of women and children below the age of ten[2]. And in 1850 a Mines Inspectorate was established to improve attention to safety in the coal mines.

While miners were starting to establish their rights and protect their interests through trade unionism and (eventually) governmental regulation, other workers were also beginning to organize. A number of industry specific unions had sprung up after the repeal of the Combination Acts, including the Grand General Union of all the Operative Spinners of the United Kingdom and the Operative Builders' Union. In addition, there were attempts to form national general unions like the National Association for the Protection of Labor which attracted many affiliations and more than 100,000 members before folding in 1831. In

1834, the Grand National Consolidated Trades Union was formed and via affiliations of numerous and varied sorts, rapidly reached a membership of half a million people. The GNCTU supported strikes in a variety of industries by applying levies of one shilling or one shilling and sixpence per head per week on its working members.

One of the most celebrated cases of early trade union activism supported by the GNCTU was that of six agricultural workers living in Tolpuddle in Dorset. George Loveless, his brother James and four others formed a union but committed the unfortunate error of binding their membership with an oath of secrecy (still unlawful under the Six Acts of 1819). Following their arrest and sentencing in 1833, the two brothers were transported to Hobart, Tasmania, and their four colleagues to Botany Bay. Despite vigorous public protests they did not return until 1838.

In 1834, the GNCTU collapsed. The causes it had supported had failed. The industrial owners had set their faces against a fairer settlement with their workers and the forces of the state had been mobilized in violence and repression. Laws designed to improve conditions and eliminate the worst abuses of the owners came late and then only grudgingly. The tone for the next century and a half of British industrial relations had been set. In their greed and short-sightedness, the early Victorian indus-

Trade Union protests against the deportation of the Tolpuddle Martyrs, Copenhagen Fields, 1834

trialists bequeathed a legacy of conflict and mutual distrust between employers and employees that persists to this day. Those who had argued for better conditions for workers threw their energies into political causes like Chartism and in due course socialism and communism.

Political activism on behalf of the oppressed worker was to become a pattern throughout the industrialized world – largely driven by the intellectual vigour of continental revolutionaries like Karl Marx, Friedrich Engels and Giuseppe Mazzini. The manifestation of their theories in Russia and China in the twentieth century has not been especially enlightening from a stakeholder perspective. Violence and repression undertaken on behalf of a revolutionary working class (never, of course, a bureaucratic elite) is no less despicable than if it is exercised by an emperor or czar. The vision and idealism of the early revolutionaries[3,4] all too quickly turned to brutality. Repression reigned from Berlin to Beijing. Thus the failure of early industrialists to establish an effective model for treating workers fairly may justifiably be considered the root cause of much political strife in the last one hundred years. It is the business–stakeholder failure *par excellence*.

It is interesting to examine the history of the trade union movement since 1850: idealistic and courageous in so many cases[5,6], bureaucratic and politically corrupt in a few others[7]. Trade unions started as the essential counter-weight to greedy and uncaring bosses in industrialized countries. Now they are frequently reduced to facilitating communication and providing legal and financial insurance in the event of individual grievance. Indeed, it is argued by some that this is what they should stick to. A survey of trade unions in Britain in 1996 reported in *The Guardian* newspaper showed that while 57 percent of activities related to legal services, only 32 percent involved representation and negotiation and 7 percent health and safety at work. In contrast there was a rising trend in insurance and financial services.

Trade unions in the industrialized world desperately need to reinvent themselves if they are to avoid continuing marginalization. As leading modernizers like John Monks of the British Trades Union Congress have concluded, there is no future in perpetuating the outmoded conflicts and miscommunications which were set in train at the beginning of the industrial revolution. Like business, they need to reflect on the failures which brought them into being and work out what will be their role when stakeholder inclusive corporations become the norm rather than the exception.

If trade unions and effective labor activism are struggling to reinvent themselves in industrialized countries today, their traditional skills are still urgently required in many parts of Asia, Africa and Latin America. As Denis MacShane has noted: every year 5,000 miners are killed in industrial accidents in China; 16 million prisoners are working in Chinese factories and gulags; in Pakistan 20 million people are working is some form of "debt bondage" slavery; in 1992 nearly 1,000 labor activists were murdered in Colombia; in 1993 there were between 200 and 300 million children working worldwide – more than 18 percent between the ages of 10 and 14[8].

According to the International Labor Organization 120 million children below the age of 14 are in full time work around the world. Another 130 million are part-timers. The worst of the work is in the sex industry, and in high risk jobs like mining and agriculture. In countries like Uganda, Ethiopia and Nepal, more than 40 percent of 10 to 14 year olds are economically active. One million children in Asia are involved in prostitution. The ILO lays much of the blame for these figures on the rapid transition of many developing countries to market economies, and cuts in social welfare forced by the "structural adjustment" programs of the International Monetary Fund.

Industrialization and market economies do not have to create so much exploitation and conflict between owners, managers and workers. Indeed there were alternative models on offer as early as 1800 which, if they had been replicated, could have led to altogether more harmonious and participative forms of industrial organization, while retaining some level of consumer sovereignty.

The worker–consumer alliance

Robert Owen was an enlightened entrepreneur whose main contribution to management theory was his belief that the character of individual workers is shaped by their environment. Owen believed that by improving the working environment, workers could be empowered to become self-reliant and responsible citizens. Owen took over his father-in-law's textile mill in New Lanark, Scotland in 1799. He made a huge success of the business; to such an extent that by 1807 he was able to buy out his partners for £84,000 in cash[9]. Owen employed around 2000 people in New Lanark, many from the poorer areas of Glasgow and Edinburgh. He stopped the employment of children below the age of 12 and reduced working hours for older children from 13 to 10½ hours per day. Moreover, he provided educational opportunities both for the adult workers and their children; indeed the first British infant school was established at New Lanark[2]. It may have been an early manifestation of the "learning organization." Owen was something of a social engineer, an evangelist who ensured temperance by banning alcohol and public houses in New Lanark, and a utopian who was convinced that proper application of rational principles would bring about a new and more enlightened economic order.

In the end, Owen was to be disillusioned. In later life he searched in vain for the key to unlock the secret of establishing and replicating co-operative and moral industrial communities. His attempt to establish such a model community in New Harmony, Indiana failed in argument and recrimination[9]. On his return to England in 1829 he threw himself into the nascent trade union movement and various strategies "to render the employer superfluous[1]." It was to be a less confrontational approach which would provide a more lasting and effective vehicle for some of Owen's earlier ideas: the co-operative movement.

The cooperative movement

William King was a contemporary of Robert Owen but while he shared much of Owen's basic philosophy, he was altogether a more pragmatic character. As a political economist and physician, King was well placed to analyze the problems of industrial capitalism and in particular its effects on the working classes. He helped set up a friendly society to provide mutual insurance for the poor but believed very firmly that insurance was not enough; the poor also had to work and trade their way out of poverty[10]. One way for the working classes to retain the value of their endeavors would be to exercise control over the places where they bought their necessities, especially food and clothes. Another would be to accumulate capital via cooperative societies and through the profits of trading. In due course land and machinery could be purchased, food and other goods could be produced by members, education and pensions could be provided and the community would become wholly self-sufficient.

King's early experiments and his practical extension of Owen's vision inspired a group of Lancashire artisans and idealists to set up a cooperative venture in 1844 which has endured to this day. The venture was founded on retailing; a single shop in Toad Lane, Rochdale, funded by forty subscribers investing three pence per week.

Today, the Rochdale Pioneers are generally credited with establishing the principle ground rules for efficient co-operative enterprise, with participation based on ownership. The principles were:

The Rochdale Pioneers – founders of the modern cooperative movement

- open membership;
- democratic control;
- distribution of surplus in proportion to trade;
- payment of limited interest on capital;
- political and religious neutrality;
- cash trading;
- promotion of education.

Above all, these retailing co-operators were able to mobilize a sense of common purpose and pragmatism via democratic participation which their more industrially based contemporaries never had a chance of enjoying.

The cooperative movement is now truly international[11]. It is no longer dominated by consumer cooperatives like the one originally pioneered in Rochdale; there are other equally robust and well-established forms. The credit co-op or cooperative savings bank traces its roots to Germany in the late 1840s. The agricultural co-op, which emerged from the credit co-op, first became established in Germany around 1860; spreading rapidly to Italy, France, Belgium, Switzerland and, most successfully of all, Denmark. Finally there is the worker cooperative. Experiments in France in the early nineteenth century and the USA inspired by Charles Fourier and Philippe Buchez nearly all failed. But the idea was kept alive in Italy and Bulgaria.

By 1895, the International Co-operative Alliance (ICA) was established to promote all forms of co-operation; its first congress in London received delegates from Belgium, Denmark, France, Holland, Hungary, Italy, Russia, Serbia, Australia, India, Argentine Republic, USA and Britain.

In 1992, financial co-operatives represented 33 percent of the ICA international membership, agricultural coops 21 percent and multi-purpose coops 27 percent. Consumer coops represented 14 percent, housing coops 3 percent and worker coops 1 percent. All of these represent a participative and stakeholder-friendly approach to enterprise. Some of the more innovative enterprises are in the worker co-operative area. They have grown strongly in the last forty years. The Mondragon coops were set up in 1956 in Spain by a Basque priest. Within 20 years there were 59 industrial enterprises with a combined turnover of £200 million and a labor force of 13,000. In response to business failures in Italy, Spain and France, worker takeovers backed by state investment have resulted in the formation of thousands of new businesses based on participation and co-operation. In Britain and North America, worker co-operatives mushroomed as part of the movement to develop local self reliance and economic regeneration, in the UK backed by local government and Co-operative Development Agencies, and in the USA by the Co-operative League and the Community Services Administration.

In Southeast and Northeast Asia, worker co-operatives are deeply involved with the challenge of sustainable development: managing ecological resources and economic demands in a sensitive way. Forestry, fisheries and agricultural coops are thriving in Asia because they are recognized as more trustworthy and more committed to long-term development than conventional forms of enterprise.

Participation is the key

What are the lessons of the co-operative or common ownership model for ordinary businesses? Clearly, co-operatives can work, but where they mingle ownership with executive responsibility they are not necessarily known for their dynamism, entrepreneurial flair or customer service. Democratic decision-making can be a laborious affair. While they have proven increasingly successful in areas like banking, credit and housing provision, there is no doubt that in retailing and wholesaling they have struggled to turn participation into enduring competitive advantage.

However, there is something compelling in the idea that an enterprise can be run for the direct benefit of its workers and customers. And there is something especially attractive in the notion that a business can unite around a set of common values and ideas which are not just to do with making money. Moreover, when these values are properly articulated and understood through a process of continuing education they seem to result both in increased empowerment and enhanced loyalty. So if we are to set aside the idea that industrial giants can be converted into worker co-operatives, what lessons might they learn from the successes of the co-operative movement in the last two centuries?

The ideal of genuine worker participation has been something of a holy grail for management theorists over the last two hundred years. From the idealism and paternalism of Robert Owen the co-operative tradition emerged. Since 1896, the Karl Zeiss Foundation in Germany has proven commercially successful as an employee-owned concern producing specialist optical equipment[12]. Later, experiments like the John Lewis Partnership and Scott Bader in the UK showed how majority or full ownership of a company could be successfully transferred to its workers in enterprises as diverse as retailing and chemicals. These transfers occurred in 1929 and 1951 respectively. In the USA, Procter & Gamble introduced a stock purchase program for employees as early as 1889. Today employees and retirees own around 25 percent of the company. In 1916, retailer Sears, Roebuck (US) established an employee trust fund which involved setting aside 10 percent of gross profits per annum and placing it in an employee share trust to purchase the company's shares on the open market. Over the years this created a significant holding and each month employees received a statement of their financial stake in the company.

Whether it is direct co-operation, full or shared ownership, there is no doubt that employee commitment is enhanced by such arrangements. They represent "stakeholding" in a literal, financial sense (see Case Study 7.2).

CASE STUDY 7.2

Employees behaving like owners: a fable of ESOPs

One company which has transformed its internal culture through employee participation in share ownership is Reflexite – a high technology firm based in Connecticut. In 1984 company founders Hugh and Bill Rowland rejected a sellout to 3M, instead backing the judgement of senior executive Cecil Ursprung that an employee stock ownership program (ESOP) was the answer. Combining growing ownership with a quality improvement plan in 1989 proved to be a winner for Reflexite – ▶

▶ efficiencies flowed without threats to job security and workers got votes as well as shares in their business. Between 1984 and 1994 the value of the ESOP increased from $150,000 to $19 million – equivalent to 42 per-cent of the company. Reflecting on the implications for structure and res-ponsibility, Ursprung noted, "To get the maximum amount of participation in decision making, you have to have the flattest organiza-tion possible, because the main purpose of managers and supervisors is to tell people what to do. And so the growth in managerial and supervisory jobs in this company hasn't matched the company's growth overall. There are people at Reflexite who in a very traditional sense have diffi-culty seeing their next step up the ladder and their perception is accu-rate."

In order to capture some of this spirit, many companies now run share option and share savings schemes for ordinary workers which they hope will generate greater loyalty and dedication. According to Britain's Inland Revenue there are more than 5,000 discretionary share schemes operat-ing in Britain today. In addition, there are more than 1,000 profit share schemes and a similar number of savings related schemes. However, such schemes do not usually engender the type of fundamental shift in the psy-chological contract between workers and their company which is achieved by a cooperative or common ownership model of participation.

In Japan, paternalism and cultural conformity generated another form of workplace participation which has had a more significant impact on management–worker relations in Europe and America. According to Eammon Fingleton, permanent employment is still regarded as a key competitive advantage in Japan[13]. It contributes to accountability in the workforce as well as securing the firm's long term investment in training, safe in the knowledge that a competitor will not benefit from the invest-ment by poaching the best trained workers. In the Japanese industrial cul-ture participative involvement has little to do with ownership. It is much more concerned with the common bond of mutual commitment (and security) which flows from a recognition of interdependency of owners, managers, workers and customers.

One of the advantages which flows from inclusive and participative models of industrial organization is a more collaborative approach to problem solving. In Japan, the benefits to product quality from a com-mitment to continuous improvement involving all workers are legendary. On product quality an active partnership between the worker and the firm undoubtedly leads to greater commercial effectiveness.

Taking a lead from Japan, particularly with respect to the quality management, "zero defects" and "just in time" techniques which a participative workforce can deliver, American and British businesses started to explore the potential for self-management and devolution of decision-making during the 1970s and 1980s. The idea was that by concentrating on team work, quality, customer focus, minimizing obstacles and continuous improvement, any company could match the high performance of Japanese companies.

This is also where the notion of empowerment came from. It involved pushing authority down through the organization with managers ceasing to be directors and controllers and instead becoming leaders, mentors and facilitators. Centralization was to be replaced by decentralization to strategic business units and everyone was to have a say.

A study on Employee Direct Participation in Organizational Change in Europe backed by the European Commission and the UN International Labor Organization (ILO) found that both employers and unions recognized the potential benefits of participation[14]. For the employers participation meant better economic performance, good personnel practice, improved quality, greater cohesion and enhanced motivation. In the 1970s, the fashion was for establishing autonomous work groups; this approach was pioneered by companies like Volvo (Sweden), Philips (Netherlands) and Olivetti (Italy). In the 1980s there was a transition to a "quality circles" approach. By the beginning of the 1990s, participation was manifested widely through total quality management, lean production, team working and continuous improvement. Whereas the original motivation for greater participation had been to improve worker recruitment and retention, the objectives of the 1990s were enhanced productivity, business performance and quality. In short, globalization, competition and ever-increasing pressures for shareholder value makes high performance through participation, devolution and cost cutting an essential prerequisite for survival. In 1996, the UK employers federation, the Confederation of British Industry was even talking about promoting a voluntary British standard on employee involvement and German automotive companies were openly defending the notion of "workholder value" (see Case Study 7.3).

CASE STUDY 7.3

Workholders with equal value

Major corporations in Germany have started to demonstrate in practical ways their belief that maximizing short-term financial returns for shareholders is not reconcilable with consensus based industrial relations. ▶

> ▶ Volkswagen has emerged as one of the most outspoken skeptics of over-reliance on "shareholder value", saying openly that "workholder value" should carry equal weight. As a way of demonstrating this philosophy in practice, employees now receive part of their wages in "time" shares. These are not denominated in money but in working hours. The monetary equivalent of the time shares, plus interest, is to be reinvested in the company, so that employees become quasi-shareholders. The scheme can be used to finance early retirement, buy extra holiday, or even as protection against redundancy. Daimler-Benz, Germany's largest industrial group, is also keen to limit the influence of shareholderism. As chairman Jürgen Schrempp put it, "Shareholder value must not be pushed at the expense of future viability and future earnings potential. Our future lies not only in chips, machinery, buildings and concepts but also in the heads and hearts of our employees."

Before we get carried away with the vision of a New Deal for all based on principles of inclusion and participation, let us take a reality check. Whatever the management theorists may argue, it is safety and security that most workers want above all else and which Japanese companies have provided better than any others (at least for their male workers). And the sad fact is, the New Deal may not always be on offer. In his disturbing study *The End of Work*[15], Jeremy Rifkin cites a 1994 survey conducted by *The New York Times* which showed just how insecure US workers feel. Two-fifths of American workers expressed concerns that "they might be laid off, required to work reduced hours, or be forced to take pay cuts" during the next two years. Two-thirds said that joblessness was having "a substantial effect" on their communities.

Things look no brighter in Europe. Rifkin quotes Percy Barnevik, CEO of Asea Brown Boveri, a successful European-based engineering firm, who predicts that the number of people employed in manufacturing and business services in Europe will decline from 35 percent of the workforce now to just 15 percent by 2015: "If anybody tells me, wait two or three years and there will be a hell of a demand for labor, I say, tell me where? What jobs? In what cities? Which companies? When I add it all together, I find a clear risk that the 10 percent unemployed or underemployed today could easily become 20 to 25 percent." Indeed we are already beginning to witness significant weakening of the employer–employee bond and a clear upward trend in outsourcing and temporary and fixed term contract working in companies which face the greatest international competitive pressures. When this happens, real participation and trust fly out of the window. As we have seen, free market addicts like Lowell

Bryan and Diana Farrell make no bones about what "unleashing global capitalism" will mean in coming decades. Rather chillingly, they predict "We should expect significant social, labor, and political turbulence as nations grapple with cutting entitlements and liberalizing product and markets restrictions." There are no quick fixes but we shall revisit these issues in some detail in Parts 2 and 3.

The consumer

The concept of consumerism can be traced back to biblical times; the Old Testament and the ancient laws of India spell out prohibitions against adulterated food and false weights and measures. For as Proverbs XI states, "A false balance is abomination to the Lord: but a just weight is his delight."

General European consumer protection laws began appearing in the fifteenth and sixteenth centuries. These statutes carried with them some unique sanctions: for instance in Austria, the seller of poor quality or adulterated milk had to drink it himself. French consumers were allowed to throw rotten eggs at vendors who were guilty of sharp practice. But, as Eirlys Roberts, long-time British consumer activist and author of *Consumers* points out, "The frequency with which the laws had to be passed showed how little they were kept[16]."

The modern-day consumer movement really began in the late nineteenth century in the USA, which predated the organized European consumer movement by a good twenty years. According to Robert Mayer[17], the American consumer movement has been characterized by three distinct eras.

The first era commenced in the late ninetenth century, with the beginning of mass production and bulk distribution over long distances. The emergence of brand named, advertised goods also spurred a new consumer awareness. The 1870s saw the first Heinz bottle of ketchup and the first bar of Ivory soap. It was in 1906 that Upton Sinclair wrote *The Jungle*, focusing on the horrors of the meat packing industry, a book which Mayer labels "the first consumer exposé."

The second era began in the 1920s. Life became more complicated with the emergence of electrical goods, new convenience products such as packaged desserts and personal hygiene products, such as mouthwash. Consumers in general had more income and more choices, but they also needed more information.

The year 1927 is considered a high-water mark in the consumer movement, with the publication in the USA of *Your Money's Worth*, by Stuart

Chase and Frederick J. Schlink. In a portrayal of the modern consumer society that would ring true some seventy years later, Chase and Schlink depicted American consumers as operating in a world of "conflicting claims, bright promises, fancy packages, soaring words and almost impenetrable ignorance." The book showed consumers how the government, universities, armed services and other large bodies tested products in order to purchase the best and least costly product. Why should consumers be denied equivalent access to such information? *Your Money's Worth* spawned the Consumer's Club Commodity List, which later became a magazine called *Consumer's Research Bulletin*. It grew from 565 subscribers in 1927 to 42,000 five years later.

Labor disputes led to the establishment of a breakaway organization in 1932, the Consumers Union. It published its first magazine, *Consumers Union Reports*, in 1936. Today, the (now shortened) title of *Consumers Reports* is the largest circulation consumer magazine in the world. The creation of the Consumers Union was a key event for the US consumer movement, and indeed for the international movement as a whole, which initially emulated the structure – especially in the area of product testing – of the American organization.

The third important consumer wave took place in the 1960s, when several key events occurred in rapid succession. In a speech that reinforced the important role which the consumer plays in society, US President John F. Kennedy outlined his Consumer Bill of Rights. "Consumers by definition, include us all," Kennedy told Congress on March 15, 1962. "They are the largest economic group, affecting and affected by almost every public and private economic decision. Yet they are the only important group ... whose views are often not heard." Kennedy's Consumer Bill of Rights included rights to safety, information, choice among a variety of products and services at competitive prices and a fair hearing by governments in the formulation of consumer policy. Every March 15, consumer organizations around the world commemorate World Consumer Rights Day, focussing on a different key consumer issue each year.

Consumer movements

Three years after Kennedy's speech, consumer crusader Ralph Nader published his seminal work, *Unsafe at Any Speed*, which was both an exposé of the safety defects in General Motors' Chevrolet Corvair and a condemnation of giant corporations in general who seek profit at the expense of consumer good[18].

The success of that book led to the establishment in 1969 of the Center for Study of Responsive Law. College students eager to take on big business signed up in droves to work for little money but a great deal of psychological satisfaction in such areas as corruption in government agencies, documenting the hazards of air pollution, and exposing the Food and Drug Administration's lax oversight of the food industry. It was through this work that they earned the nickname Nader's Raiders.

Despite the growth of consumer co-operatives in the nineteenth century, only after World War II did consumer organizations begin to appear in Europe. They grew, at least in part, as a reaction to the scarcity of the war years and the sense that the "take it or leave it" attitude of some suppliers and retailers was no longer good enough.

In the UK, consumer groups were the offshoot of government formed committees aimed at women, such as Women's Voluntary Services, Business and Professional Women and Townswomen's Guilds. As Eirlys Roberts noted[16], consumers in Britain in the late 1940s and early 1950s were in the same position as American consumers had been in 1936 – they needed to learn about the products they were buying. *The Shopper's Guide*, initially started by a journalist and later sponsored by the government's Consumer Advisory Council, came out in 1957. It contained basic information about standard marks and a mild comparison of gas cookers. But even this gentle product survey made manufacturers uneasy.

The first issue of *Which?* was published a few months after the initial *Shopper's Guide*. It was the magazine of the Consumers' Association, an organization started in 1957 by a group of economists, solicitors, barristers and engineers. The first issue reported on electric kettles and published an analysis of aspirin brands. It also reproduced the American Consumers Union report on small cars. *Which?* proved immediately successful, with several thousand members joining up in the first month. More importantly, it marked a new legal era in Britain. Articles in *The Shopper's Guide* and *Which?* were the first time in British history when anyone had published criticisms of products by name and with impunity. *Which?* was independent and proved remarkably successful. At the end of 1996 the magazine had about 650,000 subscribers. *The Shopper's Guide*, which was tied to government, failed.

The timing of *Which?* and the Consumers' Association could not have been better. As Peter Goldman, director of the Consumers' Association from 1965 to 1987, said, "rationing and control had just ended ... shops were beginning to fill with all sorts of different merchandise and people clustered for all information like hungry paupers round a soup kitchen."

By the end of 1959, the Netherlands, Belgium and France had all founded consumer organizations and begun publishing information for

consumers. A year later, the Australians followed suit. The early emphasis – and for most Western consumer movements still the major emphasis – was independent product testing. Pioneered on washing machines
and kettles, product testing has broken social taboos by testing condoms
and tackling monopolies and major services from transport to banking.
As consumer organizations became stronger, the realization among most
of the major representatives of the more powerful groups was that they
could have even more influence if they joined across national borders. In
1960, the International Organization of Consumers Unions, now called
Consumers International, was started by the American, Australian,
British, Dutch and Belgian consumer organizations. Its goal was to support and strengthen member organizations and the consumer movement
in general to fight for policies at the international level that respect consumer concerns[19].

UN Guidelines on Consumer Protection

One of Consumer International's greatest successes was the passage in
1985 of the UN Guidelines on Consumer Protection. They were the culmination of some ten years of persistent lobbying by Consumers International's representatives. The Guidelines are the single most important
document aimed at protecting consumers' rights around the world. They
address key aspects of consumer protection such as health and safety,
access to goods and services and measures for redress. The Guidelines are
important to all nations, but particularly serve as a blueprint for consumer protection laws in developing countries, where such legislation is
still in its infancy. In 1995 the UN agreed for the first time to make significant changes to its Guidelines for Consumer Protection, to include areas
such as environmentally responsible consumption.

Although the list of consumer laws and organizations fills whole books,
the success of the consumer movement over the years is still the subject
of heated debate. Some argue that the service and product deficiencies
uncovered and addressed by consumer groups would eventually have
been resolved through the workings of the free market, with or without
the input of consumer groups.

Others, such as John Beishon, former director of the UK Consumers'
Association, claim that the consumer movement has never been as successful as other political movements – such as trade unionism – because
consumerism is such a broad term that "there is no commonality of
interest among consumers. Consumers have in common their role as consumers of products and services, which includes every member of society.

For an interest group or organization to be successful, it needs a strong defining characteristic that separates and identifies the members from the mass of society[20]."

There are those who argue to the contrary that consumerism has been a powerful force for change throughout the decades. Peter Goldman, Beishon's predecessor as Consumers' Association director from 1965 to 1987 and president of IOCU from 1970 to 1975, described the consumer movement: "It is first and foremost a protest movement – or rather an action movement – with specific economic and social ills to challenge, specific market abuses to change and specific improvements to secure in the law and its enforcement, both national and international."

The importance of the consumer movement is not simply its immediate impact on products, but its psychological effect on citizens. Eirlys Roberts[16] argued: "The really, really important thing is that it made people realize in this country that they could stand up to manufacturers – they knew the facts behind the products." This healthy skepticism, derived from a "moral self-confidence" spread to government, politicians and the general public.

One lesson for the stakeholder corporation:

■ **You have to listen.**

CHAPTER 8

The playing field

protecting the environment

Our factory must make no sordid litter, befoul no water, nor poison the air with smoke.
William Morris

Environmental protection means different things to different people. For some stakeholders, the environment is their immediate locality. They may be concerned about the visual impact of the new building which is being planned or the implications of the visible airborne emissions from the local factory on the health of their children. Pressure groups may get involved in these issues, but are just as likely to question the company on its overall strategy on waste minimization and recycling, toxic emissions, energy efficiency or transport policy. Consumers may draw no distinction between environmental issues and questions of animal welfare and human rights in developing countries. Investors, business partners and customers are more likely to be interested in environmental management systems and a company's auditing and reporting record. Regulators want to know if companies comply with local, national (and in some cases) international laws and permits.

Indeed there are few areas of management where the stakeholders come from so many different directions at once. This can be daunting for a large corporation, let alone a small or medium sized enterprise.

Another challenge faced by business organizations trying to deal with their environmental responsibilities seriously is the problem of agenda-bending. The magnitude of some ecological risks is so imponderable that their saliency to politicians and the news media veers wildly according to the latest fragment of scientific evidence or instance of direct action campaigning. Many companies cry foul when bounced from global warming to toxic waste, or from acid rain to industrial effluent. Corporations in the energy and chemicals sectors are sitting ducks for agenda-bending.

Meanwhile, smaller companies may be forgiven for keeping their heads down when the issues are so complex and the debates so bloody. The jargon does not help; neither does the proliferation of management system standards (e.g. EMAS, BS 7750, CSA 7750, IS 310, ISO 14001) and voluntary codes (e.g. ICC Business Charter on Sustainable Development, CERES Principles, Keidanran Charter, CCPA, and CIA Responsible Care). According to a 1996 survey conducted for Business in the Environment, nearly nine out of ten UK FTSE 100 companies have now produced an environmental policy statement and eight out of ten have given a board member specific responsibility for the issue. However, less than half had a formalized environmental management system or an established internal audit program. Less than 10 percent of the oil, gas, chemicals and minerals sector had companywide audit programs with external verification.

Some commentators have described corporate responses to the environmental agenda as graduating from "why me?", through "smart movers" to "enthusiasts" (three point scale). Others have recognised four levels: resistant, passive, reactive, innovative, and yet others five levels (resistance to transcendence), and even ten levels (ostriches to innovators)[1]. This book is most definitely not for ostriches, but it is only fair to acknowledge that for most business people care for the natural environment only recently became a strategic issue.

Nevertheless, it would be wrong to believe that it has only been in the last two or three decades that environmental damage caused by industrial development has become evident. Equally, it would be a mistake to assume that the potential for business to manage its affairs in an environmentally sensitive and even beneficial way is a new phenomenon. The history of water and wastewater treatment provides numerous examples of how private enterprise can get environmental protection spectacularly right as well as devastatingly wrong.

Pollution of water and air

The first ever piped, filtered and safe public water supply in Britain was provided in the early nineteenth century to the community of Greenock, Scotland, when the local dyeing works discovered it had installed too much water treatment capacity for its own purposes. Conversely, it was after the failure of private water companies to provide wholesome sources of water that led to major epidemics of cholera in the crowded, insanitary slums of Europe in the early years of the industrial revolution. In the last quarter of 1849, 13,000 people died from cholera in London alone. John Snow, a London physician was able to prove the waterborne nature of the epidemic by comparing the quality of source water of two competing private water companies.

In 1856, the source of most of London's water supplies, the River Thames, received so much untreated industrial and domestic sewage that it began to ferment. The resulting Great Stink was so bad that the windows of the Houses of Parliament were draped with sheets soaked in chloride of lime to counteract the smell.

Most people can conjure images of the industrial revolution by reference to the industrial chimneys, smokeladen skies and cities featured in the soot-encrusted art and literature of the period. Many artists, authors and agitators used the grime and squalor of the industrial cities to add weight to their calls for political reform. In Britain, novelists Charles Dickens and

Charles Kingsley (author of *The Water Babies*) were prominent advocates of a better deal for the working men, women and children living and toiling in the choking filth of the industrial towns. The Chartist orator Reverend J. R. Stephens summed up his perception of the evils of factory production in the 1830s: "You see yonder factory, with its towering chimney: every brick in that chimney is cemented with the blood of women and little children." In France, Claude Monet made his contribution to critiques of environmental degradation with paintings depicting innocent walkers and bathers against a background of polluting factories and the evil slime of the River Seine.

William Morris

Perhaps the greatest nineteenth century advocate of environmentally responsible manufacturing was William Morris who was a poet, author, arts and crafts designer, retailer and revolutionary socialist. Morris's classic Utopian novel *News from Nowhere* depicted a post-industrial society of the future where dehumanizing, polluting factory work was abolished and everyone worked on a small scale on the basis of need and cooperation (see Case Study 8.1).

CASE STUDY 8.1

Business in the environment: an early pioneer

"Why must Yorkshire and Lancashire rivers run mere filth and dye," bemoaned William Morris in 1879. Four years later, Morris opened his own textile factory which included weaving and dyeing at Merton Abbey, south London. The plans of the local water company to expropriate most of the flow of the river Wandle would, Morris feared, reduce it to a "muddy ditch." Morris confirmed his environmental credentials in a letter to his local MP: "I think you will believe me when I say that such a loss of a beautiful stream would grieve me more on public than on private grounds." In an essay written in 1893, William Morris made clear his views on his preference for natural rather than aniline chemical dyes: "Of these dyes it must be enough said that their discovery, while conferring the greatest honour on the abstract science of chemistry, and while doing great service to capitalists in their hunt after profits, has terribly injured the art of dyeing, and for the general public has nearly destroyed it as an art."

In the same way that abuse of working people led eventually to the introduction of protective legislation and government inspectorates, so too did factory pollution lead to governmental intervention. Large municipalities around Europe started to act on water and wastewater pollution in the latter part of the nineteenth century – usually by taking full responsibility for infrastructural investment and service provision. In Britain, central government introduced acts of parliament designed to curb the worst offending factory and power station emissions.

Regulation

Controls continued to be added, often belatedly, during the twentieth century. In Britain, the post-war smogs of London led to alarming increases in deaths from asthma and related bronchial disorders. This in turn led to the appointment of a governmental Air Pollution Committee in 1954 and the eventual introduction of the Clean Air Act of 1956 strengthening controls on grit, smoke and harmful gases from factories. In the USA a powerful federal Environmental Protection Agency was set up to drive national legislation and standards for the protection of air, land and water quality[2]. Between 1972 and 1992 the amount of money spent on environmental protection in the USA tripled; more than $100 billion per annum is now spent on environmental protection.

Throughout the twentieth century environmental laws and regulations have been enacted in every jurisdiction, and with increasing urgency. National laws protecting the quality of urban and rural environments, air, land and water have been supplemented by international treaties and protocols dealing with issues of global significance, for example, safeguarding the marine environment, protecting biodiversity and the world's threatened planet and animal species, combating ozone depletion and arresting global warming. Simultaneously, inspectorates, regulators and environmental protection agencies have grown in scope and authority at local, national and international levels.

The initial business response to this rising tide of environmental regula-

tion and enforcement was at best grudging, and all too frequently obstruc-
tive. The notion that environmental resources are essentially free goods provided by the Almighty has proven remarkably resilient in business circles.
Dilution and dispersion were considered adequate solutions for most forms
of industrial discharge and industrialists frequently lobbied against strict
emission standards or environmental quality objectives. Investment in pollution abatement technologies often needed to be encouraged by threats of
prosecution, to which industrialists and factory managers would respond
with threats of relocation, closure and local job losses. Workers and trade
unionists would then normally side with the managers in an unholy alliance
of direct stakeholders against the environment and the wider community.

Public concern

All of that started to change in the 1980s. A string of warning signals had
impacted on public opinion in the previous two decades, starting with the
publication of Rachel Carson's seminal book *Silent Spring* which gave
apocalyptic warnings of the cumulative effects of intensive use of agrochemicals in the countryside. Industrial environmental disasters like Love
Canal in 1976 (USA), Seveso in 1976 (Italy), Three Mile Island in 1979
(USA), Bhopal in 1984 (India) and Chernobyl in 1986 (USSR) directly
affected human health and well-being and had an even greater impact on
the public psyche. Each of these accidents cost hundreds of millions of
dollars to clean up, but it was the threat of direct health impacts which
were most frightening to ordinary people. (See Case Study 8.2)

CASE STUDY 8.2

The legacy of the US chemical industry

The Love Canal disaster in New York State had a particularly sobering
impact on the US public. Following excavation and redevelopment above
an old waste dump in 1976 it became apparent that huge quantities of
toxic waste had leached from storage drums contaminating soil and
drinking water sources for the local community. This led to the introduction of the draconian Comprehensive Environmental Response Compensation and Liability Act (CERCLA or Superfund) which established
joint, strict and several liability for polluters and taxed the chemicals and
petrochemicals industries in order to establish a rapid response clean-up
fund for environmental disasters. Between 1980 and 1995 approximately $30 billion dollars were committed to cleaning up Superfund
sites. Of 2,000 sites on the priority list, only 100 were considered totally
clean by 1996.

Public concern about discharges and emissions of toxic materials by US industry led to the setting up of a mandatory disclosure scheme – the Toxics Release Inventory. The inventory requires US companies to publish details of any releases of 308 toxic compounds in 20 categories. The public nature of the TRI has been a major driver for US corporations to reduce their production and release of toxics. The first inventory was compiled for 1987, when 74,000 reports were submitted by 19,000 manufacturing plants. Under public scrutiny as never before Monsanto pledged a 90 percent reduction in air emissions by 1992[3].

Public distrust of industry was confirmed by the emergence of real problems and the burgeoning environmental movement capitalized on this disquiet to real effect. As the stunts of the environmental organizations became ever more daring and their memberships soared it became crystal clear to ordinary people who was on their side when it came to controlling environmental risks. And it was not industry or politicians.

Rio conference

Further urgency was given to the environmental agenda with the 1987 publication of a report from the World Commission on Environment and Development convened by Norwegian Prime Minister Gro Harlem Brundtland. *Our Common Future*[4] popularized the term "sustainable development" and for the first time in international fora made explicit the linkages between environmental protection, social equity and economic development in developing countries. For the World Commission, sustainable development was that which met the needs of the present without compromising the rights of future generations to meet their own needs.

Our Common Future prepared the ground for the UN Conference on Environment and Development in Rio de Janeiro in June 1992[5]. Finally, environmental protection had come center stage and was put in its proper political and socio-economic context. Business had no choice but to embrace the new agenda and start to respond pro-actively to the challenge.

Foremost among business leaders in rising to the challenge were Stephan Schmidheiny of ABB and Maurice Strong, organizer of the Rio Conference. Together with the World Business Council on Sustainable Development, set up in 1990, Schmidheiny produced a hard-hitting agenda for business in the run-up to the Rio Conference in the form of a book called *Changing Course*[6]. It was a clarion call for business leaders to place environmental and social responsibility at the heart of their business strategies. The price to be paid by business for failure, warned Schmid-heiny, would be grave indeed.

Suddenly, corporate leaders recognized that environmental protection and sustainable development were not issues that could be ignored, and they joined a stampede to get involved. Some commentators were suspicious of this new found interest of business leaders in the environmental agenda[7]. Surely this was a rearguard action aimed at coopting the debate and avoiding too many concessions? Others were more charitable. The Prince of Wales set up Business in the Environment to promote best practice in environmental management in industry, including small–medium sized enterprises. The Swedish Royal family backed the Natural Step as a scientifically rational methodology for greening industry. Meanwhile, in the USA, Vice Presidential candidate Al Gore published *Earth in the Balance*[8] – another radical prescription for environmental and economic reform with wide-ranging implications for business and industry.

Business and environment networks started to spring up in Europe, North America and the Far East. Between 1992 and 1996 British, European Union and International Standards Organization standards emerged for environmental management systems which could be independently audited and certified. Textbooks, blueprints and guides aimed at business emerged in huge numbers. Environmental auditing and public reporting became standard practice for many companies and captured the imagination of the accounting profession, particularly in Britain, the USA and Canada.

Agenda 21

Of course, pressure for providing more information on environmental performance did not just come from the professions, pressure groups or academics. The Fifth Environmental Action Programme of the European Union and Agenda 21, the blueprint for action which emerged from the Rio Conference (endorsed by 178 governments) both recommended environmental transparency in business. As a result of these clearly articulated exhortations to provide more information, many industries started to move. Companies as disparate as Norsk Hydro, Dow Chemicals, BT and The Body Shop produced independently verified statements of environmental performance in order to demonstrate their belief in transparency. The UN Environment Programme and SustainAbility produced a five-stage model for environmental and sustainable development reporting (see Figure 8.1).

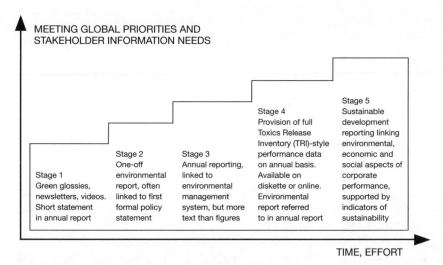

Figure 8.1
The evolution of environmental and sustainable development reporting[9]

As a result of all this activity, mainstream business associations like the International Chamber of Commerce (ICC) and the Chemical Industries Association produced detailed charters and guidelines for their members.

Today, the sheer momentum of the environmental debate has forced engagement by senior industrialists in a way that would have been thought impossible even ten years ago. The role of the International Chamber of Commerce has been especially interesting. In the run-up to the Rio Conference it prided itself on how it was able to neutralize action on global climate change. And following the conference it lost no time in setting up the necessary committees and initiatives to position business in the middle of the environment and development debate. The World Industry Council on the Environment was one such vehicle, later taking over Schmidheiny's more visionary grouping the Business Council on Sustainable Development to form the World Business Council for Sustainable Development in 1995. Some commentators have argued that ICC's dogged advocacy of further trade liberalization via the eighth (Uruguay) round of the General Agreement on Tariffs and Trade was a direct means of transnational corporations "striking back at global demands for legislation to tackle ecological concerns and the third world's demands for global economic justice[10]." Others have cataloged the engagement of transnational companies in multiple layers of ICC committees and other business fora.

It would be good to believe that those industries and industrial leaders spending so much time on the sustainable development agenda today are doing so from a sense of responsibility towards stakeholders and genuine care for the environment, and not, as some commentators aver in order to co-opt and neutralize the agenda. However, this is a debate which is just heating up. If the larger corporations are inspired by more than opportunistic or defensive motives, then there may yet be some hope for reform and the development of industrial practices which tread lighter on the planet. The evidence for this will not be the cruder forms of lobbying which have emerged in recent years. Equally it will not just be found in technical solutions like "eco-efficiency," "life cycle assessment" and "risk management," helpful though these may be in reducing pollution and waste in the shorter term.

A genuine commitment to environmental sustainability will be manifest only when large corporations embrace the full sustainable development agenda of environmental protection and social fairness. Sustainable businesses will need to exhibit a long-term vision if future generations are to inhabit a more environmentally secure planet. The starting point for this is full transparency on environmental and social impacts and absolutely honest engagement with stakeholders.

Lessons for the stakeholder corporation

- Business and industry have long had an impact on the environment – sometimes positive, usually negative.

- For 200 years, the characteristic response of industry to environmental regulation and reform was unenthusiastic or hostile.

- Prompted by pressure groups and wider governmental and public concern in the last two decades, industry has been forced into more active and sophisticated responses, but is still reluctant to embrace the social and economic implications of sustainable development.

- Distrust of business and industry and its management of the playing field of free enterprise will only be diminished by an absolute commitment to transparency and accountability to stakeholders on environmental and social impacts of industrial activity.

Part Two

CORPORATE STRATEGY

Three parables of twentieth century management

Without doubt, the challenge of embracing stakeholders is a key strategic issue for twenty-first century business. The response of a company to this strategic challenge, whether implicitly or explicitly expressed, defines the very essence of the organization. The response of a company to its individual stakeholders reflects the way the business sees itself as an entity, how it sees itself in relation to its environment (whether competitive, political or social) and how it sees people and groups both inside and outside the formal organizational boundaries.

The following three chapters tell the story of how stakeholders have been embraced – or not – by management theorists and corporations during the twentieth century. Despite its very recent emergence as a political and economic issue[1,2], the basic logic of stakeholding has been around as long as business itself – most obviously since the advent of the consumer cooperative movement in the 1840s. As a term, stakeholding may only have been coined in the early 1960s[3,4], but the word "constituency" was a commonly used predecessor, placing stakeholding firmly within the age-old philosophical discourse about the nature of society, governance and the distribution of wealth.

In recent years there has been intense debate between the advocates of traditional shareholder value models of industrial enterprise and those who believe in a more stakeholder inclusive approach. This debate has been largely an academic one, as all the evidence suggests that stakeholder inclusive enterprises also deliver greatest long-term value for investors and owners. So the discussion has really been about competing philosophical motives for running companies.

It was only the impact of excessively short-term realization of "shareholder value" by the corporate raiders of the 1980s which gave the debate immediate practical relevance. But, as we have seen, the implications of management by short-termism were enormous: millions of job losses in Europe and North America and erosion of social standards and workers' security worldwide. Downsizing and delayering were the most obvious manifestations of short-termism. They were set in train by the corporate raiders, but they are now driven by technological advance, increased competition in the global economy and the ever-increasing demands of investors. So re-engineering, which started out as a process optimization technique, has also now been co-opted as yet another way for companies to lose workers.

Therefore it is important that we understand how the different business models operate: how they are designed and what are the strengths and weaknesses which characterize each. We are going to tell the story in three parables of archetypal corporations: fictional caricatures which we hope the reader will recognize. Our companies are: Freemarket Motor Parts Inc, Responsive Systems and Technology Inc and the Inclusive Magazine Company.

CHAPTER 9

Freemarket Motor Parts Inc

Over the last two hundred years, some people (we may decide to call them capitalists, owners or shareholders) have risked their money by investing in corporations. They have entered into voluntary contractual relationships with people called "managers" to direct the affairs of companies, to act as agents or custodians of their cash. The manager's job has been to transform capital, raw materials, and labor into products that customers will buy in order to ensure that shareholders receive a return on their capital investment.

It has always been assumed that shareholders are entitled to the maximum possible return on their investment since they have borne the risk. The minimum return has been defined by available alternatives, but should always be greater than the risk-free rate that an investor could obtain by buying treasury bills or gilts. The maximum return available has been limited by the rules of the game which usually means obtained through open and free competition without deception or fraud. Since the shareholders own the company they are entitled to govern it by electing representatives to its governance process, and they are liable only for the value of their investment under conditions of limited liability.

Managers have been entitled to be compensated for their decision-making ability. Other stakeholders have been considered factors of production or members of the supply or product markets and could negotiate bilateral agreements according to the worth of their inputs in an open and free market system. All other activities in which the company engages have at best been considered purely instrumental, or at worst "theft" of corporate resources and therefore shareholders' money, or "subversive" behavior and unauthorized "taxation." That is, they have been important only insofar as they directly assist in earning returns for shareholders[1,2,3].

We all know the story. Most of us live variations of it on a daily basis. As we described in Part 1, it is the mantra of many in the English-speaking free market economies and has been repeated by captains of industry for most of the last two centuries. Like any mantra, it represents a highly condensed description of the world of business and how it ought to be. The following parable of Freemarket Motor Parts Inc aims to explore some of the realities which lie behind the mantra. We draw special attention to what may follow for true believers if they wish to keep the mantra sacred and continue to implement it in its purest form.

In search of the rule book

Let us assume that our story begins in the 1920s. Our CEO is the tough talking, hard working John Nilsson, son of a Swedish immigrant metalworker. Freemarket Motor Parts Inc has already secured a foothold in the automotive industry, supplying metal parts for vehicle engines and gearboxes.

For John, the deal was very clear. Since the market had been established, and looked set to grow on the back of the rapidly expanding automobile industry, the job for John and his senior colleagues was to make it happen. John's role as custodian of the resources entrusted to his care by his investors was to make sure that maximum outputs were created from minimum inputs. His challenge was one of technical efficiency:

- to find the most efficient way to get resources into the company from his suppliers;
- to allocate those resources within the organization in the most efficient way possible;
- to organize the overall company structure and especially the process of production in the most efficient way possible;
- to find the most efficient way to get the finished products to his customers.

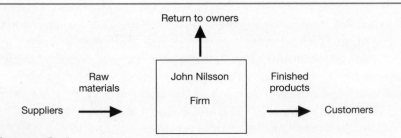

Figure 9.1
John Nilsson's conceptual picture of Freemarket Motor Parts Inc

In 1921, John's conceptual picture of Freemarket Motor Parts Inc looked something like Figure 9.1. John was a straightforward guy and drew several rational conclusions. Since his overall goal had been determined (maximum profit) and his task within the organization was clear, his attention focussed on two key questions:

■ How do I structure the organization?
■ What type of process do I need for maximum efficiency?

Both the structure and the process needed to be designed to deliver maximum returns for minimum costs. His formula began to emerge. It was almost scientific, certainly rational, and at this point John realized he was not alone any more. He could turn to management theorists for assistance and seek their prescriptions to address his problems. Some management theories were already being applied within the automotive industry.

The first nostrum that John found useful for his structural and process questions was the need for division of labor. This opened up a whole world of options that he could tap into. While browsing in a local bookstore, he picked up a handbook for industrial managers translated from the original French. He learned that if he treated his organization like a machine, he could reach the highest levels of efficiency. Second, to create the ideal organizational machine, there were clear formulae that he could follow. He learned that all activities which firms take on can be divided into six groups:

1 Technical activities (production, manufacture).
2 Commercial activities (buying, selling, exchange).
3 Financial activities (optimum use of capital).
4 Security activities (protection of property and persons).
5 Accounting activities (stocktaking, balance sheet, costs, statistics).
6 Managerial activities (planning, coordinating, controlling).

John read his handbook with an increasing sense of excitement. Apparently, according to the writer, Henri Fayol, to manage was to forecast and plan, to organize, to command, and to control. Amazingly, it was just like in the army which John had left only three years before. To organize meant building up a dual structure for the firm: material and human. This dual structure would bind together, unify and harmonize all activity and efforts. To manage meant seeing that everything occurred in conformity with established rules. All he needed from his workers was obedience[4].

He found the handbook incredibly helpful for understanding the process of his own work. Suddenly, it was all very clear. He copied the list of principles and pinned them on his office wall. Frederick the Great of Prussia, whose principles of the "military machine" lay at the heart of John's new list, would have glowed with pride (see Exhibit 9.1).

EXHIBIT 9.1

Fayol's general principles of management[5]

(as adapted by John Nilsson and Freemarket Motor Parts Inc)

1 **Division of work:** tasks should be divided up and employees should specialize in a limited set of tasks so that expertise is developed and productivity increased.

2 **Authority and responsibility:** authority is the right to give orders and entails the responsibility for enforcing them with rewards and penalties; authority should be matched with corresponding responsibility.

3 **Discipline:** is essential for the smooth running of business and is dependent on good leadership, clear and fair agreements, and the judicious application of penalties.

4 **Unity of command:** for any action whatsoever, an employee should receive orders from one superior only; otherwise authority, discipline, order and stability are threatened.

5 **Unity of direction:** a group of activities concerned with a single objective should be co-ordinated by a single plan under one head.

6 **Subordination of individual interest to general interest:** individual or group goals must not be allowed to override those of the business; this is achieved through firmness, example, and constant supervision.

7 **Centralization:** the extent to which orders should be issued only from the top of the organization is a problem which should take into account its characteristics, such as size and the capabilities of the personnel.

8 **Line of authority:** communications should normally flow up and down the line of authority running from the top to the bottom of the organization, but sideways communication between those of equivalent rank in different departments can be desirable so long as superiors are kept informed.

9 **Span of control:** the number of people reporting to one superior must not be so large that it creates problems of communication and co-ordination.

10 **Staff and line:** staff personnel can provide valuable advisory services, but must be careful not to violate line authority.

11 **Discipline:** both materials and personnel must always be in their proper place; people must be suited to their posts so there must be careful organization of work and selection of personnel; obedience and outward marks of respect in accordance with agreed rules and customs.

12 **Equity:** personnel must be treated with kindliness and justice; remuneration should be fair, encourage effort, and not lead to overpayment.

13 **Stability of tenure of personnel:** rapid turnover of personnel should be avoided because of the time required for the development of expertise.

14 **Initiative:** all employees should be encouraged to exercise initiative within the limits imposed by the requirements of authority and discipline.

15 **Esprit de corps:** efforts must be made to promote harmony within the organization and prevent dissension and divisiveness.

After these revelations, John felt very confident about how the structure of FMP should look. He started to draw. He drew boxes and lines forming a pattern of precisely defined jobs organized in a hierarchical manner and reflecting precise lines of communication and command (see Figure 9.2).

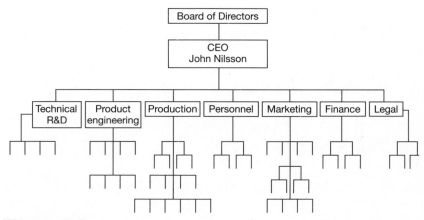

Figure 9.2
FMP's first topline organizational chart (circa 1924)

Some of the detail John put into the chart for the production division was beautiful. It could not have been more precise (see Figure 9.3). John was a quick learner and nothing if not methodical. His chart reflected all the dictums he had learned. He had divided the organization based on the principle of functional specialization. Each division and department had its own independent hierarchy. The chain of command was clear. From any place at the bottom of the organization there was only one route to the top, reflecting the principle of "one man, one boss." The lines of authority had been considered and no "staff" divisions (e.g. legal and personnel) had authority over "line" divisions (e.g. production).

Now that John had his big picture sorted, he could start thinking about how to design individual jobs. A friend of his from the Chamber of Commerce recommended a great new book by an American engineer Frederick Winslow Taylor for this task[6]. He immediately went back to the bookstore, obtained a copy of Winslow Taylor's book and again found himself deeply impressed. Another neatly typed list of principles appeared next to the General Principles of Management on John's notice board. The spirit of Frederick the Great swelled again with pride. (see Exhibit 9.2.)

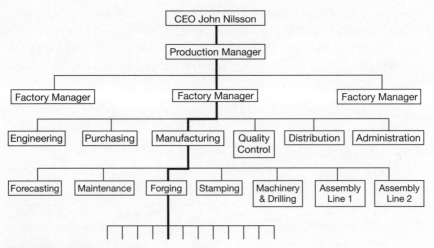

Figure 9.3
FMP's production division (circa 1925)

Taylor's principles of scientific management[7]
(as adapted by John Nilsson and FMP)

1 **Shift all responsibility for the organization of work from the worker to the manager:** managers should do all the thinking relating to the planning and design of work, leaving the workers with the task of implementation.

2 **Use scientific methods** to determine the most efficient way of doing work; design the worker's task accordingly, specifying the precise way in which the work is to be done; eliminate all false movements, slow movements, and useless movements.

3 **Select** the best person to perform the job thus designed.

4 **Train** the worker to do the work efficiently.

5 **Monitor** worker performance to ensure that appropriate work procedures are followed and that appropriate results are achieved.

To bring the above principles to life, Winslow Taylor strongly advocated time-and-motion studies as a way of analyzing and standardizing activities. So, to find the optimum mode of performance for FMP, John and his senior colleagues decided to observe and measure even the most routine activities in minute detail and translate the observations into clear work instructions and procedures.

John could easily see the benefits of doing such a huge job. He would gain total control of the organization and it would enable him to implement his Ultimate Principle of Management – Division of Labor – to its perfection. He could see that the notion could be applied to office staff and to assembly line workers alike. It would make his company run like clockwork.

A couple of years later, when everyone's jobs had been designed, proceduralized and co-ordinated with each other, the effects were enormous. The productivity of the company skyrocketed and reached levels of true mass production. Unit costs went down dramatically. The company did suffer a bit from high turnover of staff, but the overall benefits in profit far outweighed this inconvenience. And most importantly, the owners were ecstatic, and awarded John a handsome pay increase.

Things went swimmingly well for ten years or so. Even during the Depression, the company went from strength to strength. But then something strange started to happen. FMP's sales people started to relay disquieting messages from their customers, the large automobile and truck companies and their distributors. Suggestions came in about using lighter and more durable materials. This was a bit cheeky, thought John, after all FMP's products were the cheapest on the market. But John was ever the forward-looking CEO.

He realized that the automotive industry was changing. People had started to talk about a new discipline called marketing. Apparently, this was the order of the day – you needed to listen to what your customers wanted. Some automobile companies had even gone as far as introducing new models on a regular basis. As FMP's sales staff explained, not every customer wanted to have the same car. This had potentially enormous implications for the automotive parts industry. In 1939, just as John started to implement his response to the challenge of multiplying automobile models, FMP got caught up in the war effort. Reflections on changing customer needs went out of the window. The assembly lines were converted to serve the pressing demands of military customers and FMP started to produce engine parts for fighter airplanes, armored cars and tanks. Before the war was over, more than half of FMP's output was in defense.

As FMP entered the 1950s, the changes that John had started to adjust to before the war re-emerged. Customer demand started to saturate for some products. The massive R&D facilities set up by the big defense corporations during the war spewed out new technology and new demands almost on a daily basis. The war had brought new customers to FMP; the government had emerged as a major buyer. Most importantly, people's attitudes had changed fundamentally.

John figured it was time to quit. A grateful board of directors sent John into retirement with a very comfortable pension. The workforce clubbed together to buy "Old Jack" an antique grandfather clock with the most precise and reliable mechanism they could find.

The planning machine

The new Chief Executive Officer, George Wilson, had been a pre-war high flyer at FMP. During the war he signed up for active service and distinguished himself in the Pacific theater – on one occasion saving an entire platoon through his individual bravery. As a reward for his exploits (and his promise), George was sent by FMP to Harvard to get a formal business qualification. After graduation and a couple of meteoric years in sales, George was handed the top job at FMP. He was just 44 years old.

At Harvard, George had been privy to the very latest thinking in what was really important in managing businesses in the dramatically changed post-war world. He had especially enjoyed a course he had attended on business policy[8]. Business policy taught him about an important "big idea" for modern management – corporate strategy. Although the concept of strategy was familiar to him from his military service during the war, the application of it to business management was something new[9]. George's professors had described three main reasons for a new approach to management[10,11,12].

■ A company needs well-defined scope and direction. In the absence of direction, the firm faces the danger of not recognizing opportunities for growth.

■ Profit objectives do not provide sufficient direction on their own.

■ New rules are required if the company is to have orderly and profitable growth.

The key to success, according to one of the professors, was to acknowledge that the traditional way of identifying the firm with a particular industry had become too narrow. "Today," he said, "a great many firms find themselves in a number of different industries. … the boundaries of business are continually changing, and new ones are being born. For example, radio, television, transistors, home appliances, and atomic energy are all industries which did not exist fifty years ago. The need is for a concept of business which on the one hand will give specific guidance for the firm and on the other hand will provide room for growth[10]." He then proceeded to describe such a model.

First the company should identify its **product-market scope**. This specifies the particular industries within which the firm confines its product-market position. This has the advantage of focusing on well-defined areas for which common statistics and economic forecasts are generally available.

Second, a firm should identify its **growth vector**, which indicates the direction in which the firm is moving with respect to its current product-market posture.

Then, the professor argued, companies needed a unique approach that kept the company on course. This would give the firm its **competitive advantage**.

Finally, he talked about **synergy**. Companies should seek a "2 + 2 = 5" effect in their search for product-market positions. He talked about "sales synergy," "operating synergy," "investment synergy," "management synergy," and so on.

He ended the lecture by summarizing that together, the four complementary elements he had outlined formed the key **components of corporate strategy**.

The following week, in his second lecture on strategy, the professor introduced a model of what strategic decision making should look like in a company (see Figure 9.4).

The basic message was that strategy is the pattern of purposes and policies that defines a company and the businesses in which that company is engaged. The aim of the framework was to allow managers to match resources and capabilities to opportunities and risks present in the business environment. There were two key problems connected with strategy: "formulation" (decisions about what to do); and "implementation" (decisions about how to execute decisions for business success).

Formulation and implementation activities needed to be further subdivided into seven categories. In deciding what to do a manager must perform four formulation tasks:

- Identify opportunities where his company may be successful and identify the business risks that are associated with these opportunities;
- Determine the capabilities of the company in terms of material, technical, financial, and managerial resources;
- Assess the personal values and aspirations of the senior executive team;
- Decide how to fulfill the company's noneconomic responsibilities to society.

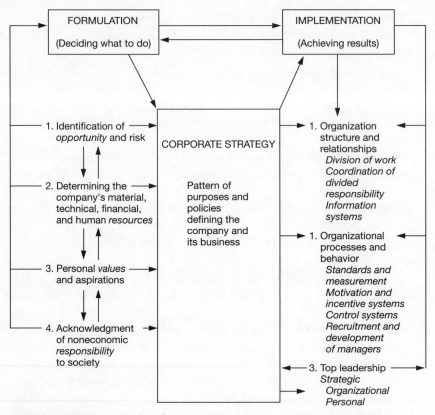

Figure 9.4
The Harvard Policy Framework
Reprinted from Andrews, K. (1987) *The Concept of Corporate Strategy*. Homewood, Ill:
Richard D. Irwin. Reproduced with the permission of the McGraw-Hill Companies.

In completing these tasks, managers articulate a set of decisions and a pattern of policies that need to be implemented. In sum, strategy formulation was about establishing the product mission of the corporation, its purpose and goals, and then defining a set of appropriate business ventures, methods of competition, and relationships with the company's constituencies.

In order to achieve results with a strategy formulated in this way, managers must then perform three implementation tasks:

■ Decide how to structure the organization and coordinate the division of labor;

■ Design and implement systems and procedures to accomplish what the organization is going to do;

■ Focus on leadership necessary to bring about the desired results.

A pattern of purposes and policies would then emerge from executives' efforts to address these seven tasks. At this point in the lecture, George had drifted away. Somehow what he had heard sounded familiar, as if he had read or seen something similar before. Maybe it was something Old Jack had said when he had spoken to George the first day he started at FMP.

George drifted back from his daydream and heard the professor emphasizing that managers can secure the desired results for their businesses if they follow a deliberate program of thinking about their companies' strategies. He went on: "A business enterprise guided by a clear sense of purpose rationally arrived at and emotionally ratified by commitment is more likely to have a successful outcome, in terms of profit and social good, than a company whose future is left to guesswork and chance[13]."

When George took charge of FMP, he made sure that all the ideas he had learned at Harvard were implemented. Later on in the 1960s he and his colleagues learned more about strategic planning. Managing by objectives was one useful tool which emerged for putting their strategy into action. They worked out that they needed a detailed and formal plan for the implementation of their corporate strategy. Corporate strategy needed to be broken down into divisional programs, objectives and action plans for every eventuality. Only then could they rest assured that budget allocation was efficient and that things would actually happen. They reflected on what their own annual strategic planning cycle would look like and came up with the process shown in Figure 9.5.

After a few more years in the hot seat at FMP, George decided with his executive colleagues that it was time to look again at diversifying the business. The 1950s had been tough and change was needed badly. George had bought into the Harvard message but it was becoming clear in the increasingly consumer-driven, post-war years that there was still something missing. Companies needed to understand their markets better. George still subscribed to the *Harvard Business Review* and was most impressed by an article he read in 1960 entitled "Marketing Myopia[17]." The author was Theodore Levitt.

Levitt's message that "industry is a customer-satisfying process, not a goods-producing process" – seems obvious enough for managers educated in business schools in the 1980s. But it was not necessarily so in the 1960s, when industry was at its apogee of post-war growth. Levitt was prescient enough in 1960 to see that Detroit's automobile industry was heading for a fall. The industry had never properly researched the customer's wants, only "the kind of things which it had already decided to offer him."

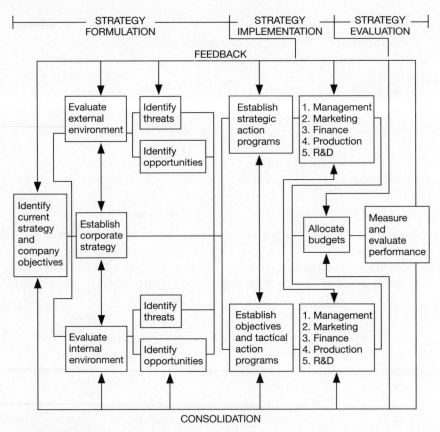

Figure 9.5
A formal strategic planning cycle[14,15,16]

In every case, Levitt argued, where growth in an industry is slowed or stopped, it is not because the market itself is saturated, "it is because there has been a failure in management". Taking the US railroads as an example, his article pointed out that the railway companies let the car, truck and aircraft industries take the business away from them because they saw themselves as in the railroad business rather than the transportation business. A thoroughly customer oriented management could keep a vibrant company growing even after the first obvious opportunities had been exhausted, wrote Levitt. While no amount of improvement could save a product whose time of obsolescence had come, sensitivity to customers' needs would always suggest a diversification.

The mists cleared from George's eyes. He realized that to make his new strategy really work for the company, he needed to identify what his end customers wanted. He needed to build up the marketing function and find ways of systematically assessing what new businesses FMP should diversify into. In any case, they had grown a bit tired of going through the annual rigmarole of creating dozens of plans, subplans, and sub-subplans, spending huge amounts of time and energy in gathering all the necessary information and having dozens of goal-setting meetings. It seemed to George that however much time was spent on this, something always changed and prevented FMP from reaching its goals.

The arrival of strategic business units

By the end of the 1960s, George was committed to a new, market-oriented approach for FMP. He invited in management consultants for the first time. They were well-known experts on strategy and they came with lots of ideas. Their first presentation was impressive. It included the following pearls of wisdom:

- The ultimate aim is to reduce corporate risks and increase returns. Diversify as a way of avoiding undue risk; don't put all your eggs in one basket, and take advantage of opportunities for growth.

- Think of your business as a portfolio of businesses in the same way as an investor does.

- The real action takes place within and across components of a diversified organization that serve particular markets. These components should be called strategic business units (SBUs).

- SBUs should sell a distinct set of products or services to an identifiable group of customers against competition from a well-defined group of competitors.

- An SBU must be meaningfully separate from the rest of the organization's businesses – at least in accounting sense (easier to assess profitability and to sell the SBU if necessary).

George went for SBUs in a big way. They provided FMP with the ideal organizational response to the demands of diversification. The SBU concept helped FMP to define strategy market by market: aviation, automotive and military. Everything became more concrete and manageable, easier to implement.

As the consultants asserted: "No market is free from competition any more. For the business strategist, as for the military one, the key to victory is to bring superior resources to bear where your competitor is vulnerable. The way to do that is to find markets in which your particular position and resources make you stronger and to fight your biggest battles there[8]."

Using this "portfolio" approach[18,19], the attractiveness of each of FMP's three new SBUs became a function of expected market conditions and competitive pressures.

Market conditions and competitive pressures allowed George to decide how to allocate finite corporate resources among his three SBUs and how they should be managed. His strongest SBU was serving the growing market of aviation. This was to be the greatest long-term producer of wealth. FMP Aviation was what the consultants had called a "star." So he made sure that it was given the resources necessary for rapid growth. His other relatively strong SBU which served a less favorable market (FMP Defense) was seen as a "cash cow" that could provide cash needed for nurturing his "star." FMP Defense would be allowed to grow and develop but only slowly.

His weakest SBU, Autoparts, which served a declining automotive market was a "dog" which should be allowed to shrink or – if it was not producing cash – to be eliminated to avoid draining resources that might be better used elsewhere. As the consultants had advised, FMP should also have a few "wild cats" stewing up as potential new "stars." So, George set up five small ventures in aerospace and agriculture.

According to George's advisors, the faster the growth of the market in which an SBU competes and the greater its share of that market relative to the share of its largest competitor, the stronger the SBU. The goal for a manager was simple – gain more market share to ensure optimum cash flow. By managing the corporate portfolio in this way, the company should be self-sufficient in cash and thus be protected from the vagaries of the financial markets.

With these strategic tools and techniques, FMP struggled through the rest of the 1960s and just about coped with the 1970s, before entering the mayhem of the 1980s.

The early 1980s were a period of growing angst over Japan's rising power in increasingly competitive global manufacturing markets[20,21]. The portfolio models failed to offer satisfactory answers to what exactly was driving competition in different industries, how to analyze what competitors were likely to do, and how any given industry was going to evolve. As George prepared for a well-earned retirement, he was recommended a new book by another highly rated Harvard man, Michael Porter[22]. George's heart sank. He realized that he no longer had the energy to meet the challenge of a wholly new analysis. But he passed Porter's book to his successor, Frank Baron, with his best wishes.

Survival of the fittest

The basic idea of Porter's *Competitive Strategy* was that a company will be more or less successful depending on forces at work in the company's industry. These forces could be understood in terms of the underlying structure of the industry.

According to Porter, the concept of competition needed to be understood much more widely than the economists, marketeers or portfolio managers recognized. The real nature and dynamics of competition could only be understood when the suppliers, potential market entrants, buyers and potential substitutes had been thoroughly analyzed. This analysis needed to happen at the industry level. A company could only succeed if it really understood its industry. The level of long-term financial returns available to a company was a function of the strength of these forces in the industry and the actions taken by management to position the company among and against these forces (see Figure 9.6).

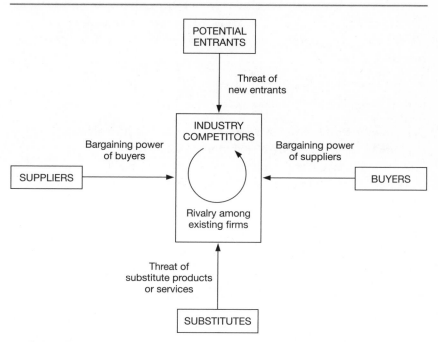

Figure 9.6
Five forces of industry structure
Reprinted with permission of The Free Press, a Division of Simon & Schuster, from *Competitive Strategy: Techniques for Analysing Industries and Competitors* by Michael E. Porter. Copyright © 1980 by The Free Press.

Each industry had its own set of alternatives for formulating competitive strategies depending on whether it was growing, declining, local or global.

Porter spoke of a "strategic window" which helped a company to make some basic choices about its strategy. These choices needed to be made in relation to the company's strategic advantage and strategic target. Thus, three competitive strategies emerged:

- **differentiation** (where the aim was to be unique in some way that customers will value)
- **cost leadership** (where the aim was to become the low-cost leader in the chosen industry)
- **focus** (where specific niche markets within an industry were targeted).

A choice had to be made. There was no justification or time to be wasted "being stuck in the middle."

Just when FMP had absorbed Porter's first message and scrambled to a slightly better competitive position (and having reduced its workforce by 30 percent under the new CEO, Frank Baron) out came another 600 page blockbuster: *Competitive Advantage*[23]. Porter's next epic concentrated on two basic ideas:

- cost leadership;
- differentiation.

Before competitive advantage could be systematically analyzed, let alone exploited, its connection to something called a value chain must be understood. Linked to a company's value chain were the supplier's distribution channel and customers' value chains. Together these formed a system of values. A company could find a competitive advantage if, in addition to understanding its own value chain, it could also adapt this to the larger system of values (see Figure 9.7).

Following the logic of portfolio management, by chopping the company into small pieces and paying careful attention to the linkage of these pieces with each other and the outside world, we arrive at the company's value core. Understanding and improving the value chain was thus the key to everything: cost advantage and differentiation, segmentation and behavior in substituting products, in launching an offensive or in adopting a defensive strategy. Frederick the Great would have had no problem with that one.

Finally, Porter went political. His next book was an extrapolation of his previous work. What was good for industrial competitiveness was good for

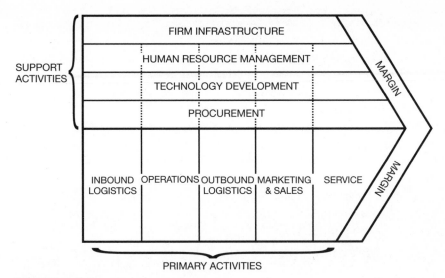

Figure 9.7
The value chain in competitive strategy
Reprinted with the permission of The Free Press, a Division of Simon & Schuster, from
Competitive Advantage: Creating and Sustaining Superior Performance by Michael E. Porter.
Copyright © 1980 by The Free Press.

the nation[24]. It was now Adam Smith's turn to smile down benignly from above. The book was a result of Porter's appointment in the mid-1980s to President Ronald Reagan's Commission on Industrial Competitiveness. Porter found himself among a group of business and labor leaders, academics and government officials, none of whom could agree on a definition of competitiveness. To business, competitiveness meant the ability to compete in world markets; to politicians, it meant a favorable balance of trade; to union leaders it meant job security and adequate wages.

By now an avid disciple, Frank Baron had his own ideas about competitiveness, but Porter certainly helped him articulate them to his friends at the golf club. Porter argued that competitors in an industry could strengthen rather than weaken a firm's competitive advantage. "Tough domestic rivalry breeds international success," he claimed. Full marks again from Adam Smith.

In the 1980s Frank went for it. With Porter as his guide he reinforced the role of FMP Defense as his cash cow. No one could touch FMP on their quality of service and reliability on contracts with the big military hardware providers. The competition did not come even close. FMP Aviation continued to suck in most of the spare cash, growing somewhat erratically but nevertheless giving cause for long-term optimism.

The really radical decision which Frank based on his competitive analysis was to get out of automobile parts. No way, he argued, would the US motor industry out-compete the Japanese. And he was damned if he was going to develop new alliances with non-American car producers. It was all too dangerous. Many at FMP had misgivings. The whole company had been built on supplying automobile parts. That was their tradition, their heritage. There were wrangles and a few resignations. The Nilsson family sold their shares in a fit of pique. But Frank got his way. He was supported almost 100 percent by the Board. FMP Autoparts was sold off to its management (who promptly secured some major new contracts with US-based Japanese car firms together with a good deal of technical help on quality management). Frank's strategy of concentrating on defense and aviation won the day.

A couple of bad years at FMP Aviation in 1989–90 led to group losses for the first time. Frank blamed bureaucracy and inefficiency and took the opportunity to axe another third of the workforce. He became convinced that maintaining market share was all down to speed and efficiency. He was inspired by two management consultants, George Stalk Jr and Thomas M. Hout, who wrote *Competing Against Time*[25]. They argued that the ways in which leading companies managed and compressed time in all their activities – whether R&D, production, distribution, marketing – were the most powerful sources of competitive advantage.

Responsiveness, giving customers what they wanted when they wanted it, was the key to success. Stalk and Hout claimed that time compression was the fundamental advantage behind Japanese success in a number of highly competitive markets, enabling them to increase the variety and technological sophistication of their products and services. "Providing the most value for the lowest cost in the least amount of time is the new pattern for corporate success."

As time cycles were compressed, productivity increased, costs were lowered, risks were reduced and market share would increase. Most importantly, new products and services could be brought to market much more quickly, establishing a valuable lead over competition and raising the innovative company's margins.

In order to compress the time cycles throughout an organization, it was first necessary to understand organizational systems and to analyze where time delays were incurred. This was, of course, an integral part of business process redesign or re-engineering. It provided Frank with justification for more job cuts at FMP.

Competing Against Time outlined three key areas for managerial attention: how work was structured; how information was created and shared;

and how performance was measured. These were all familiar managerial tasks to Frank. And then, in 1993 disaster struck. The Cold War had never really struck Frank as a key part of his competitive strategy. Porter never told him to worry about those kind of politics. So when the Cold War ended and defense equipment contracts started to be cancelled, FMP did not see it coming. In a matter of two years the FMP Defense "cash cow" had become a *de facto* "dog." It was hemorrhaging money. FMP Aviation was insufficiently profitable to float the group and FMP Autoparts had gone. The game was up.

In 1994, FMP was declared insolvent. It was broken up with 70 percent job losses, one of which, of course, was that of Frank Baron, a freemarket strategist if ever there was one. What had he missed?

CHAPTER 10

Responsive Systems and Technology Inc

Our parable of Freemarket Motor Parts Inc started when Western industry was maturing into a new age – the era of mass production. Most managerial energies went into creating, developing and consolidating industrial technology, the surrounding organizational structures and staking out market shares. The focus of managerial attention was almost entirely on internal efficiency and on the question of how progressively to decrease the unit cost of products. The result was a set managerial perceptions and preferences which later came to be known as a production mentality.

Industry borders were well defined. The inducement to diversify into brand new environments appealed only to the most adventurous firms. A majority was satisfied with their own growth prospects. Steel companies were in the steel industry, and automobile companies in the automotive industry.

On the political front, the business sector was well protected from outside interference. Political and social controls were minimal. In North America, Europe and the Far East government interference with free enterprise was relatively infrequent. In post-war Europe a number of basic industries were taken into public ownership for a few decades, but by 1990 this experiment was virtually over. When companies flagrantly transgressed social norms, government reacted by limiting freedoms of business action, such as anti-trust and anti-price collusion legislation. But these were occasional events; most of the time the boundaries of the business environment remained inviolate. The booms and recessions that came and went with varying frequency before and after World War II were accepted by business people as the price to be paid for competitive freedom[1].

For the first thirty years of the century, success went to firms like FMP provided they delivered to the lowest price. Products were largely undifferentiated and the ability to produce at the lowest unit cost was the secret of success. But toward the end of the 1930s the demand for very basic consumer goods was reaching saturation. With "a car in every garage and a chicken in every pot" the increasingly affluent consumer began to look for more than basic performance. Demand for products like the Model T Ford began to flag.

The human problems resulting from scientific approaches to management eventually became glaringly obvious, especially when built into assembly line technology. For example, when Henry Ford established his first assembly line to produce the Model T, employee turnover rose to approximately 380 percent per annum. Only by doubling wages to his famous $5 a day was he able to stabilize the situation and persuade workers to accept the new technology. In the 1970s when employment was still plentiful in the American car industry, workers shunned the assembly line, again resulting in high turnover figures. At Ford's Wixom plants, for instance, turnover was constantly running at almost 100 percent per annum[2,3].

The first and most famous assault on Taylorism and other classical management approaches came from the so-called Hawthorne Studies conducted in the 1920s and 1930s under the leadership of Elton Mayo[4]. The studies were conducted at the Hawthorne Plant of the Western Electric Company in Chicago. Initially the studies were concerned with investigating the relationship between conditions of work and the incidence of fatigue and boredom among employees.

As the study progressed, interesting things started to happen, and Mayo soon realized that the narrow scientific perspective had to be abandoned to understand what was going on. The intriguing thing was that productivity increased among the test groups after they had discussed working conditions with the researchers – irrespective of whether or not conditions actually improved. The really baffling thing was that in some experiments productivity increased even when conditions were worsened, for example, when the lighting was dimmed.

From these experiments Mayo drew revolutionary conclusions that later gave birth to a whole new field of research – human relations or industrial sociology. His basic conclusion was that productivity increased if employees had the opportunity to discuss their working conditions with managers. Further, Mayo was the first to identify that an informal organization existed alongside the designed formal organization. In other words friendships mattered and managing organizational teams could be just as important in achieving success as designing individual jobs.

The psychology of consumers as well as workers started to be recognized as vital components of competitive success. Signs of changing times in the 1930s were innovations such as General Motors' introduction of annual model changes and Ford's reluctant introduction of a multimodel suite of automobiles after the unsuccessful Model A. Promotion, advertising, selling and other forms of consumer influence became priority concerns for management.

Along with the increased orientation towards markets, the managerial focus shifted from an introverted perspective to a more open, extroverted one. This also meant a transfer of power from production-minded to marketing-minded managers. The era of internal power struggles had dawned in the executive suite. Beyond the power struggles, many managers resisted the shift to a more consumer-driven approach. It required costly, time-consuming and psychologically threatening acquisition of new skills and facilities, development of new problem-solving approaches, changes in structure, in systems, and acceptance of new levels of uncertainty about the future.

But the post-World War II world saw accelerating and cumulative changes that began to impact significantly on industrial boundaries, structures and market dynamics[5]. Companies were increasingly confronted with new and unexpected challenges which were so far-reaching that Peter Drucker – the guru of all management gurus – called the new era the *Age of Discontinuity*[6]. Growing governmental regulation, consumer dissatisfaction, increased international competition, technological breakthroughs, changing work attitudes, increased affluence – all these factors contributed to major shifts in attitudes – at least among successful businesses. The outside world could no longer be treated just like the weather. Tools for longer term planning processes were needed to tackle these challenges.

Acknowledging environments

Responsive Systems and Technology Inc was a child of the 1940s. RST started out as a supplier of switches and electromechanical gadgets to telephone companies. But in the 1950s the company realized that the hardware and technology of storing and transmitting information was the place to be. There seemed to be no limit to the demand of industries and ordinary individuals to communicate information. RST's first CEO, Joe Walters, was a thoughtful guy. He was bright, articulate and knew how to get the best out of his workers. He was also a strong believer in giving people a chance. And he had absorbed the post-war message from Harvard in a big way. Marketing was everything.

Joe was not afraid of change. Indeed, as a graduate of MIT he saw every technological development as a market opportunity. He did not mind if it came from his own R&D people or his competitors. Responding to the ever-changing needs of his customers was Joe's philosophy. So he was very pleased when the suggested answer to increased uncertainty in the marketplace was the concept of business policy and strategy. As we have seen, the first such framework offered by the business schools was the Harvard Policy Framework.

The main thing about the Harvard Policy Framework was that it acknowledged the importance of additional "environments" as well as the purely economic one. The Harvard Policy Framework model opened companies to other sources of opportunity and, more importantly, threats. For a thinker like Joe, this was a major step forward from the rationalist, linear equations of meeting market demand with calculated equations of efficiency.

In order to respond to the demands of increasing competition and to establish "what business should we be in?" the Harvard Policy Framework made it necessary to move on from previous management thinking based on "closed system" assumptions toward more openness by acknowledging the need to factor in noneconomic responsibilities.

The Harvard Policy Framework also added the question: "What program of civic contribution is consistent with both the company's strategic opportunities and its social responsibility?" The Harvard Policy Framework allowed CEOs to behave like decent citizens. Joe liked that. It suggested that executives might gain from a reasonable program of "enlightened self-interest," although it did not offer any clear guidance how this "self-interest" might relate to the company's day-to-day business decisions.

The Harvard Policy Framework did not contradict portfolio approaches or competitive strategy. Each was based on an assumption that one of the tasks of strategy was to match internal dimensions of the corporation to the external environment. However, in all cases strategy formulation and implementation took place within a single company. They did not necessarily take into account what other companies were formulating and implementing. Competitors might, indeed, be formulating and implementing something very similar. This assumption of self-sufficiency was commonplace in post-war strategic models and had major implications for how the company perceived its competitive arena and its role in society. Porter's strategy model with its extended external analysis aimed to alleviate this pitfall, but arguably his analysis did not extend anywhere near broad enough.

The self-sufficiency syndrome was largely a product of the assumed over-riding importance of the firm. At best, other players were categorized generically. The catalog of external forces tended to be a fixed set, including customers, suppliers and competitors. Government and other social and political forces were acknowledged, but they were assumed to manifest themselves via more traditional business forces: commonly as a threat or a factor decreasing market attractiveness. The unsophistication in the level of differentiation between stakeholders is understandable if one bears in mind that at that time the external environment was a very novel concept for management theorists.

All this left companies like RST largely to their own devices with respect to the outside world. Guidance on how to cope with pollution problems, the consumer movement or the changing demographics of the workforce would be hard to identify using the frameworks. Nevertheless, they gave Joe Walters all the justification he needed to stick with his market research, nurture his key suppliers and other business partners, look after his workforce and give 3 percent of pretax profits to good causes in the local community.

Happily, in the 1950s a group of thinkers influenced by Elton Mayo's earlier work started to emerge. For the emerging Human Relations School the whole issue of work motivation became an important area of interest and a point of departure for those wishing to criticize the mechanistic assumptions of mainstream research and corporate practice. Important work was done by researchers such as Abraham Maslow, Frederick Herzberg and Douglas McGregor. Their work started to gain recognition in the 1960s and early 1970s. Joe was a philanthropist at heart and lapped this up.

Abraham Maslow had pioneered the theory of motivation in 1950s[7]. He presented a hierarchy of needs that human beings were driven to fulfil which included:

- physiological needs (e.g. wages, health and safety)
- security needs (e.g. job tenure, pension and health care insurance)
- social needs (e.g. work organization conducive to interaction with colleagues)
- ego needs (e.g. feedback and recognition on performance, scope for achievement and responsibility)
- self-actualizing needs (e.g. a job as an expressive dimension of an employee's life).

Maslow's theory had powerful implications, for it suggested that machine organizations which sought to motivate through money, or by merely providing job security, confined human development to the lower levels of the need hierarchy. Management theorists were quick to see that jobs could be redesigned to create conditions for personal growth which would simultaneously help organizations to achieve their objectives.

Maslow's work was reinforced by Douglas McGregor, a social psychologist who produced one of the most influential and enduring contributions to people management and motivation with his Theory X and Theory Y[8]. Theory X was based on the traditional view that control in organizations was necessary: people were inherently lazy, work was a necessary evil and therefore people needed to be supervised with carrots and sticks. Theory Y, by contrast, viewed people as welcoming work and responsibility, believed that commitment to objectives is a function of the rewards associated with their achievement, and stated that under the Theory X conditions of modern organizational life "the intellectual potentials of the average human being are only partially utilized."

Finally, Frederick Herzberg came along[9,10]. He was a clinical psychologist who was greatly influenced by Maslow and turned into a passionate humanist after his wartime experience. Herzberg coined two concepts that every human resource manager today has in their vocabulary:

- hygiene factors which meet basic economic needs (e.g. salary, company policies, supervision, status and working conditions)
- motivation factors which meet deeper aspirations (e.g. achievement, recognition, progress and personal development).

Herzberg also devised a theory of job enrichment, which is now built into management theory and practice at levels ranging from flexible working, flexible benefits, all the way up to empowerment.

The idea of integrating the needs of individuals and organizations grew to become a powerful influence. It formed the basis of what is now known as human resource management. The idea that bureaucratic machine organizations could be made both more productive and humane by modifying structures and leadership styles and by creating enriched, motivating jobs that would encourage people to exercise their capabilities had a natural appeal. Employees were to be seen as a valuable resource for the success of the enterprise, not merely interchangeable cogs in the big wheel of commercial activity. The added benefit quickly worked out by some less than scrupulous managers was that all this offered the possibility of motivating staff through higher-level needs without paying them any more money[10].

But this was not Joe's motivation. He just wanted a happy and creative workforce. During the 1960s and 1970s he invested heavily in his people. His personnel and training department grew massively in size. He even recommended to his son Patrick that he should specialize in the new field of industrial psychology when he started his studies at business school.

Survival of the fitting

The 1960s were interesting times for RST. The arrival of real consumer affluence allowed people to question economic growth as the main instrument of social progress. People's aspirations started to shift towards quality of life. They started to question the increasing influence of industry as a threat both to economic efficiency (through monopolistic practices) and to peace and democracy. The growth ethic, which had provided a clear guiding light to business behavior, was rejected by increasing numbers of citizens both inside and outside the corporation. The "flower power" generation became increasingly suspicious of the wisdom of business and its values. Some of this generation, including Joe's son Patrick, found their way into the universities and embarked on crusades for increased corporate social responsibility.

Once more, complexity and uncertainty became the name of the game. But this time complexity was cumulative rather than sequential. In the 1960s and 1970s new managerial imperatives did not replace the earlier ones – they simply added to them. The new sociopolitical concerns came on top of the traditional preoccupations of competition and production.

The optimism of post-war mainstream strategic thinking had been based on the assumption that the company could choose what environmental pressures to respond to. It had been assumed that changes in the competitive environment were predictable enough to enable the company to plan its response. This was consistent with the experience of the previous fifty years, but according to critics, (including Patrick and his new academic colleagues), no longer sufficient. Patrick was now working in a very liberal business school.

According to Patrick's research, growth strategies needed to be accompanied by defensive survival or legitimacy strategies. The traditional preoccupation with product/market/technology strategies had to be broadened. The model built on the idea of a single critical contact point with the environment needed to be enlarged to handle multiple and distinctive critical contact points. The traditional sources of legitimacy were no more sufficient. The license to operate needed endorsement from a wider set of stakeholders[11,12,13].

The message that started to emerge was that individuals and groups as well as organizations had a wider set of needs than purely economic ones. The consequence for business was that it needed to recognize its dependence on a wider environment for various kinds of sustenance. It was this kind of thinking that started to underpin the so-called systems approach to organizations, which took its main inspiration from the work of theoretical biologists like Ludwig von Bertalanffy[14]. Developed simultaneously on both sides of the Atlantic, the systems approach built on the principle that organizations, like organisms, are open to their environment and must develop an appropriate relationship with that environment if they are to survive, let alone prosper[15].

Patrick's work in the business school was shared with his father. He explained to his old man that an open-systems approach to organizations needed to focus on a number of key issues.

First, companies need to understand the environment in which they existed. The early theories of management, Patrick explained, devoted very little attention to the environment. For them the organization was a closed mechanical system and the key management problem was that of internal design. The subsequent models of strategic management, including the Harvard Policy Framework, all tried to open up the organization a bit, but their basic assumptions about the nature of the environment–organization interface were inadequate. Patrick showed a book on systems thinking to his father. It included a diagram which struck a chord with Joe[16] (see Figure 10.1).

The early systems thinkers advocated that much more attention needed to be devoted to understanding the immediate "task environment" (defined by the organization's interactions with customers, suppliers, competitors, government agencies, etc), as well as the broader "contextual" or "general environment." All this was argued to have important consequences for organizational management. Business needed to be able to scan and sense changes in both task and contextual environments. It needed to be able to bridge and manage critical boundaries and areas of interdependence, and to develop appropriate strategic responses. Simply put, the key message was that business needed to build up its ability to be much more sensitive to what was going on in the world.

A second feature of the open systems approach defined the organization in terms of interrelated subsystems. Organizations consisted of individuals. They, in turn belonged to departments, which belonged to divisions etc. The same logic applied to both intra- and inter-organizational relations.

The third area of focus in organizational systems thinking was the

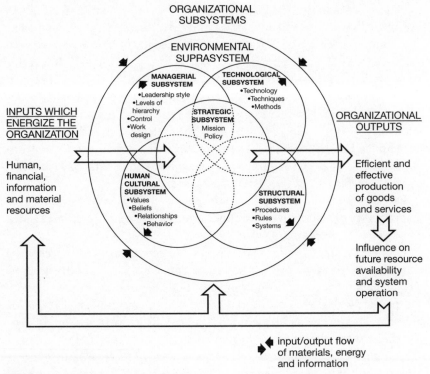

Figure 10.1
The responsive organization[16]

attempt to establish "congruencies" between different systems, and to identify and eliminate potential dysfunctionalities. So matching different subsystem requirements was central. This could be achieved by applying techniques of differentiation and integration and ensuring requisite variety was present. For example, variety was important in designing control systems for the management of internal and external boundaries – for these had to embrace the complexity of the phenomena being controlled.

Together, these ideas pointed the way to theories of organization and management that allowed managers finally to break free from scientific and mechanistic ways of working. At last organizations would be managed in a way that met the wider requirements of their environment.

From Joe's perspective he had always been a systems person. He just did not know that it could be applied so effectively to organizations. So with Patrick's help he started to overhaul RST. He was going to make sure that all his people felt part of a team-based, flexible outfit, fully aware of what was going on within and outside the business.

Joe accepted the message of systems thinkers that there was probably no single best way of organizing. The most appropriate structure and style of management depended on the kind of task environment which people were dealing with and that these, above all, should reflect a "good fit" with the environment. Effective organization was about ensuring compatibility between strategy, structure, technology, the commitments and needs of people and the external environment.

Joe was quite comfortable as his company grew within an expanding industry in the 1970s. RST looked at the external environment as a source of information and feedback that needed intelligent interpretation by the company and its business units (statistics, trends, inflation, interest rates, etc.). Everyone seemed to need IT hardware and Joe had some of the most creative and dynamic people in the business. Relations with customers and suppliers were important but in Joe's mind they were still separate entities.

In the 1980s, like everyone else, RST got heavily into competitive strategy. Joe liked the fact that Michael Porter emphasized thorough analysis of external players. Patrick, however, had murmured something about Porter's analysis being something of a one-way street. He had said that companies should listen to a wider set of influences than Porter recommended. "There are other voices out there that are important for RST's strategy," he had said. He reminded Joe about the systems models they had talked about earlier. "You should look into your other stakeholders too[17,18,19,20]."

Joe was not quite sure what Patrick was talking about. You could take the systems thing too far. He was pretty content the way things were going. Like most CEOs in the 1970s and 1980s he was seeking a safe harbor amid a sea of inhospitable forces. He believed that, like himself, his company was the master of its own destiny; that not only the company's environment but its future could be planned and to a certain extent predicted. Things were under control. He humored Patrick's academic enthusiasm for so-called stakeholder models.

In 1985 RST's sales growth started to dip for the first time in the company's history. It was happening to all of the company's US-based competitors, so Joe did not feel too fearful for RST's future. But he recognized that times were changing and decided the time was approaching when he might need to make way for younger blood. If there was going to be a fight with the manufacturers of the tiger economies, then better someone young and fit was at the helm.

One evening when he was discussing his thoughts about retirement with Patrick, he mentioned the issue of increased competition from the

Far East as one of the factors contributing to his decision. "We just need to work out how they get so damned efficient and beat them at their own game", said Joe. A few days later Joe received in the mail a photocopy of a mid-1970s article from Patrick. It had been written by a Canadian academic Henry Mintzberg[21,22].

Mintzberg was in disagreement with the science of "programmed game playing." He argued that technological analysis could never be seen in the same uncritical light after the Vietnam War when, in his words, "America's finest analytic talent, drawn from the centres of liberal intelligentsia, applied the modern [decision making] techniques to the White House's non-programmed decisions, and the result was a war effort both ill-conceived and fundamentally immoral."

What went wrong, according to Mintzberg, was the inability of the hard-line analysts to handle soft data – the will of the enemy, for example – as opposed to hard data such as the number of bombs needed to lay waste a jungle:

> Facts become impregnated with value when they consistently line up behind a single set of goals. In Vietnam they supported the military goals; the humanitarian goals, supported only by soft data, were driven out of the analysis. We see the same thing in corporations when the hard data line up behind the economic goals – cost reduction, profit increase, growth in market share – leaving the social goals – product quality, employee satisfaction, protection of the environment – to fend for themselves.

It started to dawn on Joe that there were two fundamental problems in his own assumptions: first, that the company was the sole master of its own destiny; second, that the environment was sufficiently predictable to enable the company to plan its response to change in advance. Who could have predicted the amazing success of the high-tech exporters of Southeast Asia?

Joe did not feel that strategic planning per se should be abandoned. Planning as well as planners had an important role to play in organizations. But he recognized that the main flaw in planning-based models was the belief that strategy could be formulated formally, that the hard analytical procedures of planning could generate the full synthesis required in strategy. The danger was that planning took you straight back to the machine assumptions: assemble all the parts (goals, structure, process, techniques, checklists, etc.) and you have an operating whole. But machines are first designed somewhere else, whereas the planning machine itself is supposed to produce the blueprint – the strategy. According to Mintzberg, that is why the phrase "strategic planning" – like

progressive conservative or civil engineering – has proven to be an oxy-
moron. The problem lay in the misconceived idea that planning constituted decision-making, or future thinking. Planning was not a means to
create strategy but one to operationalize strategies already created by
other means.

From Joe's perspective none of what he had learned over the years was
completely wrong. The Harvard Policy Framework clearly had its merits.
It had acknowledged early on that the values people held were important
in how decisions were made[23]. The model had astutely observed that the
values of key executives must be consistent with a strategy or else these
persons will not be able to exercise the leadership needed to carry it out.

But he felt a bit let down by how the game had played out. Where were
the global issues in Porterism? Where were the people? Where were the
managers in portfolio approaches? It seemed to Joe that somewhere a
thread had been lost. The business environment had changed. Unexpected competitors had emerged. Customers had changed. And somehow
RST had missed it regardless of all the external analysis they had done.
Perhaps they had not been responsive enough? Perhaps there was something in those stakeholder models Patrick had talked about.

Joe was now ready to throw in the towel. The 1980s were most definitely very rocky years, and the shareholders were getting impatient.
There were even rumors of takeover. Joe decided to step down in 1988.
Against Patrick's advice, but with the full support of his Board, he handed
over to Bob Scott. Bob was of a new breed entirely: his personal creed was
a mixture of "survival of the fittest" and "you have to be cruel to be kind."
As a graduate of Chicago University, Bob was a bit of a freemarketeer. But
more than that, he believed that a responsive organization should also be
a lean and fit one. Otherwise its internal comfort levels would drag it
down – particularly when there was such cutthroat competition from the
Far East. Bob believed in people, but he wanted fit, flexible, high performing people. The rest would have to go.

Like Patrick, Bob was a bit of a systems persons but his thinking had
been influenced more by a rather hardline version which started to
emerge in the 1970s. Bob believed in a "population-ecology" view of
organizations which placed Darwin's theory of evolution right at the
centre of organizational strategy[24]. In essence, the argument was that
organizations, like organisms in nature, depend for survival on their ability to acquire an adequate supply of the resources necessary to sustain
existence. In this effort they have to face competition from other organizations. Since there is usually a resource scarcity, only the fittest survive.
The environment is thus the critical factor in determining which organi-

zations succeed and which fail, selecting the most robust competitors through elimination of the weaker ones.

Within five years, Bob downsized RST twice: by about 20 percent in 1989 – just one year into the job – and by another 25 percent in 1992. Most of the jobs which went were middle management and administrative. The business embraced quality in a big way, got its costs down and entered the 1990s with a domestic market share more or less intact and a share price about double what it had been in 1985.

Joe's much loved HR department had been cut back to about a third of its former size. Now they too had to deliver value for money. Morale was lower than anyone could remember, and people were stressed. But at least most were still working. Re-engineering came along in 1994, and with it went another tranch of jobs. Morale did not pick up.

Something had been lost along the way. The soul of the organization which Joe had nurtured for thirty years had gone. His words were still there in company literature and he still attended company events. But the sparkle had gone out of his eyes. Those of his former employees who still remembered how it used to be were mostly looking to move on.

CHAPTER 11

The Inclusive Magazine Company

The story of Responsive Systems and Technology Inc was a parable of post-war high technology enterprise. For three decades it seemed that companies like RST could do no wrong. RST was in a growing industry and able to give full rein to some of the "softer" elements of business strategy. It was relatively simple for them to embrace new techniques of customer responsiveness – from the sales and marketing prescriptions of the 1950s and 1960s to the customization and quality demands of the 1970s and 1980s. Companies like RST were able to respond to the needs of their employees and the local community with the full blessing of models like the Harvard Policy Framework. This was further reinforced by the rise of human resource management techniques which emphasized the need for emotional and intellectual engagement of employees: a happy workforce was a productive one.

Even when individual stakeholders like customers and employees became quite insistent on their rights, there was usually enough wealth around for corporations to respond and embrace these concerns. The demands of consumer activists, trade unions and the early environmentalists were to a large extent assimilated and life continued fairly comfortably.

Then, in the late 1970s the landscape started to change. Competition from Japan in cars, motorcycles and electronic consumer goods started to impact on Western markets. The portfolio models and the later prescriptions of Michael Porter's *Competitive Strategy* did not quite meet the challenge. For while companies like Toyota, Honda and Mitsubishi were developing a quite vibrant and interactive set of relationships with their stakeholders (manifested most notably by their quality management approach), the mindset of most Western corporations was still very top down.

Later, when more high tech exporters started to emerge in Korea,

Singapore and the tiger economies of Southeast Asia in the 1980s, they had the twin advantage of high quality and even lower overheads.

For the most part, these Asian-based companies were not going in for some kind of grand military-style strategy. It was based more on knowledge creation, a belief in experimentation, stable finance and hard work. It took quite a while for this message to sink in.

William Ouchi was one of the first management theorists to explore the differences in Western and Eastern management styles[1]. In his book *Theory Z* he described a number of powerful experiences based on his research. In one case Ouchi interviewed senior managers in the US headquarters of a Japanese bank. He first interviewed two American vice-presidents and asked how they felt about working for the bank. "They treat us well, let us in on the decision making, and pay us well. We're satisfied." Ouchi went on to probe whether there was anything they would like to change about the way things were done. The response was quick and clearly one that was very much on their minds: "These Japanese just don't understand objectives, and it drives us nuts!"

Next he interviewed the president of the bank, an expatriate Japanese. Ouchi asked the same question about the American vice-presidents. "They are hard-working, loyal, and professional. We think they're terrific." When asked whether he would like to change anything about them, the reply was: "These Americans just don't seem to be able to understand objectives."

It was clear to Ouchi that the issue of objectives needed to be further investigated. The second round of interviews sought clarification. First, the American vice-presidents: "We have all the necessary reports and numbers, but we can't get specific targets from him. He won't tell us how large a dollar increase in loan volume or what percentage in operating costs he expects us to achieve over the next month, quarter, or even year. How can we know whether we're performing well without specific targets to shoot for?"

Ouchi then returned to re-interview the Japanese president. He explained, "If only I could get these Americans to understand our philosophy of banking. To understand what the business means to us – how we feel we should deal with our customers and our employees. What our relationship should be to the local communities we serve. How we should deal with our competitors, and what our role should be in the world at large. If they could get that under their skin, then they could figure out for themselves what an appropriate objective would be for any situation, no matter how unusual or new, and I would never have to tell them, never have to give them a target."

In the mid-1980s, panic gripped many major corporations in the English-speaking world. Corporate raiders and merger mania accelerated the move towards greater emphasis on short-termism. Threats to market share and competitiveness led to massive downsizing and delayering. Much of the real knowledge and wisdom of large corporations was thrown to the four winds. So just when Western companies needed stakeholder loyalty most, they set about dismantling it on the altar of short-term shareholder value.

In the 1990s, re-engineering came along, only to exacerbate the problem: it seemed that for every process and technology gain, there was a further price to be paid in the morale and commitment of the workforce.

Towards shared futures

Meg Taylor was a child of the 1960s. At the age of seven, she marched with her parents for civil rights. At the age of eleven she protested against the Vietnam War. Meg graduated from college with a bachelor's degree in modern literature and journalism in 1974. Her marriage to a musician collapsed in 1980 and she was left with Janice, a daughter she would die for. In the mid-1970s she got around to reading Rachel Carson's *Silent Spring* and was disturbed by the way the environment and the food chain were being threatened by agrochemicals. Most of all, she was worried about the kind of world Janice would grow up in.

Meg was also active in the feminist movement and at college blamed male corporate America for many of the world's ills. In the late 1970s, while she was raising Janice, Meg did freelance writing for environmental and arts magazines. But by the time Janice went to junior high, Meg knew she would soon need to make a proper living to get her daughter through university. So while there was still time, Meg borrowed a few thousand dollars from her parents and went back to college. She thought that she would go into business – but a different kind of business to provide for herself and Janice. First she needed a business degree.

In her first year at business school in 1981, Meg's greatest interest was organizational behavior and psychology. She was captivated by ideas of business organization which were based on emerging principles of organizational ecology and systems thinking. She was already concerned about the natural environment and industrial threats to planetary ecosystems. So the idea that business could be based on harmonious coexistence and collaboration rather than outright competition really appealed to her ideals. She genuinely believed that business should be sensitive, nonex-ploitative and successful at the same time.

In her second year Meg researched the work of the Tavistock Institute which developed concepts of industrial democracy well advanced for their time. Their work established the so-called socio-technical school which aimed to capture the interdependent qualities of social and technical aspects of work. In their view, these aspects of work were inseparable, because the nature of one element always has important consequences for the other. Their philosophy was based on promoting work systems that used skills, intelligence and technology in an integrated and effective way to achieve an efficient and content workforce.

The work of the Tavistock Institute had started in the 1950s with research in the British coal industry. A new technology, the long-wall method of mining, was causing low morale and stress disorders among miners. The Tavistock group introduced multiskilling, team working and decision-making by the work team. The result was higher productivity and a happier workforce. The socio-technical school then moved to Scandinavia, where it was adopted by several companies including Norsk Hydro and Volvo.

The socio-technical approach had a humanistic as well as an efficiency objective. It was similar to W. Edwards Deming's quality movement, believing that everyone in an organization could be trained to optimize the whole system. With Deming, this was achieved by training workers in process control; in the case of socio-technical restructuring, it involved making the worker responsible for decisions. Everyone from shop floor upwards was expected to experiment in organizing their work, to meet their colleagues regularly to discuss changes and to monitor the effects of these changes[2].

Meg was less than impressed by the more traditional theorists who saw business in constant tension with the external world, in some kind of macho, survival of the fittest struggle. But she was captivated by the idea that organizations and their environments were engaged in patterns of "co-creation," where each impacted upon and helped sustain the other. For just as in nature an ecosystem is composed of networks of complementary populations of diverse organisms, so organizational environments are in large measure composed of mixtures of different organizations and their stakeholders. So business environments are in some measure always "negotiated environments," rather than a soup of hostile external forces. With this interpretation, the notion of collaboration became much more significant.

This thinking led Meg to see how patterns of organizational relationships could help shape the future for businesses in a more positive way.

Co-creative relationships are a natural response to increased complexity and turbulence in any environment. Groups gain protection and resilience from cohabitation. If applied to business, this allowed firms to transcend the conflictual polarity of "them" and "us" to a way of working that encouraged collaborative action. It could facilitate the emergence of common values and norms, and thus new solutions to shared problems[3,4]. True, Meg thought, but it would be naive to think that harmonious collaboration was the only way organizations could be managed. In nature organisms compete, kill and eat each other. But they do not compete, kill and eat each other for someone else's profit.

Meg saw that some of the hugely popular books based on so-called corporate culture arguments emerging in the 1980s strongly echoed the ideas of the systems thinkers. It all fitted together very neatly. The corporate culture school based their arguments on the observation that national cultures clearly affected the way companies operated in different countries. Organizations also consisted of different subcultures just as different individuals have different personalities. Companies should not merely be seen as micro-economies but also as mini-societies.

More importantly, writers on corporate culture added an extra dimension to the management equation. In contrast to the traditional models based on rational and objective decision-making, corporate "anthropologists" built on the work of the human relations school and emphasized that people's commitment to their employer and the level of their motivation was directly linked to a "psychological contract" between the firm and its employees. An employee's "moral" commitment to the employer meant that the person intrinsically valued the mission of the organization and his or her job, and was personally involved and identified with the company[5].

Meg could easily see how this had major implications for a variety of management issues: leadership, work design, company values and its sense of ethics. In a nutshell, corporate anthropologists seemed to be saying in the words of the biblical proverb: "Where there is no vision, people will perish." Their research was pointing out that companies which consistently performed well were usually notable for powerfully rooted *shared values* and a steadfast vision or purpose beyond the purely commercial.

Meg liked the sometimes journalistic, catchy style of many of the corporate culture books. She found them both entertaining and informative. She learned a lot from them about empowerment, job enrichment, team dynamics, leadership styles etc. They were good stories with human faces[6,7,8,9,10]. They introduced her to the notion of the "social architecture" of the firm.

When it came to studying business strategy, Meg was especially intrigued by the idea of cybernetics. The term cybernetics was coined in the 1940s by an MIT mathematician Norbert Wiener as a metaphorical application of the Greek *kubernetes*, meaning steersman. The Greeks had developed the concept of steersmanship, probably from their understanding of the processes involved in the control and navigation of vessels, and extended its use to the process of government and statecraft. Wiener used this imagery to characterize processes of information exchange through which machines and organisms engage in self-regulating behavior that maintain "steady states[11]."

Learning to learn – the art of steersmanship

Cybernetics established some unconventional ways of looking at how systems engage in self-regulating behavior. According to cybernetics, the ability of a system to engage in self-regulating behavior depends on processes of information exchange involving *negative feedback*. If we shift a boat off course by taking the rudder too far in one direction, we can get back on course again only by moving it in the opposite direction. Simple systems of negative feedback engage in this kind of error detection and correction automatically, so that movements beyond specified limits in one direction initiate movements in the opposite direction to maintain a desired course of action.

Meg saw how cybernetics could revolutionize the way communication and learning could be viewed in strategic management. It led to a number of key principles:

■ Systems (or organizations) must have the capacity to sense, monitor, and scan significant aspects of their external environment.

■ They must be able to relate this information to the operating norms that guide internal system behavior.

■ They must be able to detect significant deviations from these norms.

■ They must be able to initiate corrective action when discrepancies are detected.

All these are characteristics that any sensible CEO would wish their organization to have. If these four conditions are satisfied, a continuous process of information exchange is created between a system and its environment, allowing the system to monitor changes and initiate appropriate responses. In this way the system can operate in an intelligent, self-regulating manner.

When Meg graduated in 1985 she was brimming with ideas and confidence. She was going to start out as she meant to go on. Meg's business was going to be highly creative and entrepreneurial, it would be in tune with its commercial environment and it would have ways of constantly checking its position within its sphere of trading. It was also going to be fabulously successful.

With Meg's first degree and continued interest in journalism, her chosen business venture was publishing. She was aware that people's interests in a wide range of new leisure activities were developing rapidly. She had a strong gut feeling that there was a growing demand for more specialist magazines and periodicals. Meg started small, but things developed quickly. A title aimed at green consumers was rapidly followed by one on women's health. Within five years The Inclusive Magazine Company was employing 70 journalists and advertising sales people running five specialist titles. By 1993, there were ten titles (all printed on chlorine-free paper) with a combined readership of 3 million. Turnover was $50 million based mostly on very loyal subscribers.

Meg's formula was simple but devastatingly effective. Each title was built around a deep understanding of the needs and interests of its readership. Each was produced by a small team of "creatives" (journalists, editors, and designers), advertising sales people and administrators. The biggest team had just twelve members; the bulk of the writing was done by freelance specialists not on the payroll. Printing was all outsourced; the only thing the teams specified was the source of the paper and inks (in deference to IMC's environmental policy).

Meg arranged things so that each team was pretty well autonomous, but they recognized the value of being part of a wider IMC group which gave them longer term strength and support. Each publishing team was actively involved in a number of networks. They paid as much attention to the needs of their main "suppliers" – the freelance journalists – as to their readers and to the company. They also saw themselves as collaborating in the publishing environment with other titles. They never tried to compete head on with an established magazine. Instead they always found a particular niche. So IMC people were always known as the "eco-friendlies": socially conscious, non-threatening, creative and fun to be around. They always seemed to know that was going on in publishing; their socializing and networking knew no bounds. Meg's conceptual picture of IMC looked something like Figure 11.1.

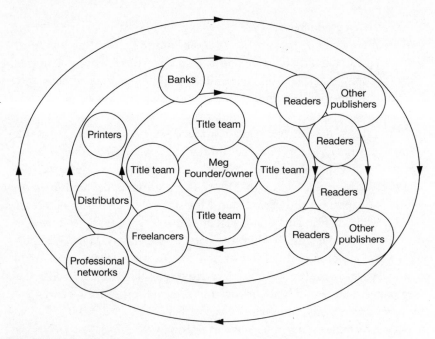

Figure 11.1
Meg Taylor's conceptual picture of IMC

Most of the IMC structure was based on Meg's application of the principles of organizational ecology, culture and cybernetics which she had learned at business school. But in the early 1990s she was to discover another insight consistent with her personal philosophy. One of the IMC titles was a professional journal aimed at human resource consultants and practitioners. Throughout the late 1980s, contributors to this magazine were becoming increasingly interested in Japanese and Eastern approaches to organizational development. Much of this linked to well understood systems of continuous improvement or *kaizen*.

Meg was especially interested to learn how cybernetics was now being applied to organizational development. Increasingly, contributors to the magazine were drawing a distinction between simple feedback systems and more complex ones. They argued there was a difference between the process of responding to the outside world and adapting to it (single loop learning) and responding in such a way as to impact on the outside world, challenging and engaging with it (double loop learning)[12,13].

Contributors to the journal argued that many organizations had become very proficient at single-loop learning, developing their ability to scan the environment, to set objectives, and to monitor the general performance of the system in relation to these objectives. This basic skill was often institutionalized in the form of management information systems designed to keep the organization on course (e.g. management by objectives, budgeting, indeed anything where the future could be built on the experience of the past).

The ability to achieve proficiency at double-loop learning proved more elusive[14,15]. Chris Argyris maintained that while some companies had been

---

Single-loop learning rests in the ability to detect and correct error in relation to a given set of operating norms:

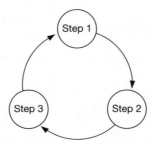

Double-loop learning depends on being able to take a double look at the situation by questioning the relevance of operating norms:

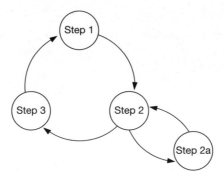

Step 1 =	The process of sensing, scanning and monitoring the environment.
Step 2 =	The comparison of this information against operating norms.
Step 2a =	The process of questioning whether operating norms are appropriate.
Step 3 =	The process of initiating appropriate action.

Figure 11.2
Single-loop learning and double-loop learning[16]

---

successful in institutionalizing systems that review and challenge basic norms, policies and operating procedures in relation to changes occurring in their environment – by encouraging ongoing dialogue, debate and innovation – many fail to do so. This failure was especially true of bureaucratic organizations, since their management principles and defense mechanisms often operated in a way that actually obstructed learning rather than encouraged it.

Following up on some of the earlier references, Meg came across a book which was published in 1986, *Images of Organization*[16]. In it Gareth Morgan had pointed to a number of problems with non-systems based companies that needed to be challenged:

1 Bureaucratic approaches impose fragmented structures of thought on their members, encouraging piecemeal views of the organizational whole and thus creating false boundaries, encourage politicking and prevent the free flow of information. This leads to a situation where questioning of policies and standards by members tends to be exceptional rather than the rule. This may keep the organization following the wrong course, but very efficiently.

2 Bureaucratic notions of accountability reward narrowly defined criteria of success and punish failure; they encourage various forms of deception rather than innovative challenges to "this is how we do things here."

3 The gap between what organizations and managers say and what they actually do often prevents them from understanding and dealing with problems.

In order to overcome these barriers to learning, Morgan proposed four guidelines. First, organizations should encourage and value an openness and reflectivity that accepts error and uncertainty as an inevitable feature of life in complex and changing environments. A philosophy that "it is admissible to write off legitimate error against experience," and that "negative events and discoveries can serve as a source of knowledge and wisdom of great practical value" are examples of the kind of stance required.

Second, businesses should encourage an exploratory approach to analyzing complex problems that recognizes the importance of different viewpoints. Given the fact that the issues faced by organizations in complex environments are unclear and multidimensional, one of the major problems is that of defining the nature of the problems with which one is faced. Recognizing the importance of probing the various dimensions of a situation, allowing constructive conflict and debate between those who have a stake in the solution is the best way to facilitate good decision making. In this way issues can be fully explored, and perhaps redefined so that they can be approached and resolved in new ways. This kind of inquiry helps an organization absorb and deal with the uncertainty of its environment rather than trying to avoid or eliminate it. The key job for senior managers is to facilitate this type of exploratory learning and to ensure that required resources are allowed to make it happen.

Third, Morgan urged business to avoid imposing structures of action upon organized settings. This principle relates to the importance of inquiry-driven action. In contrast with traditional approaches to planning, which tend to impose goals, objectives, and targets, it is important to devise means where intelligence and direction can emerge from ongoing organizational processes. When goals and objectives have a pre-determined, top-down character they tend to provide a framework for single-loop learning but discourage double-loop learning. More double-loop learning can be generated by encouraging bottom-up or participative approaches to the planning process. But cybernetics also emphasizes the central role played by norms and standards (e.g. policies, procedures, indicators, etc.) as guidelines for action. It shows us that these guidelines are of significance as limits to be placed on system behavior, rather than as specific targets to be achieved. Double-loop learning is thus best understood as a process which questions the limits that are to be placed on action.

Meg recognized that this third principle provided a radically new perspective on strategic thinking and organizational development. Whereas the traditional models emphasized the importance of creating a master plan with clear-cut hierarchies of targets, cybernetics suggested that it may be systemically wiser to focus on defining and challenging constraints. Intelligent strategy making involved a choice of limits – the negative feedback problems one wishes to avoid – rather than just a choice of ends. The implication of this approach for business strategy was to define an evolving space of possible actions that satisfy critical limits. So the type of strategic questions we ask, the type of measures we use to define our performance and the measurement processes we use all have implications for the organization's ability to renew itself.

IMC reflected this in a number of ways, for example, by their environmental policy. The policy itself did not mention specific targets, rather it outlined the type of behaviors IMC wished to avoid and specified that continuous improvement in the avoidance of these behaviors was the overall aim of the company. The more specific procedures and guidelines underpinning the policy defined the type of indicators that should be used in measuring progress. Meg was quite pleased that intuitively they had established a cybernetic environmental management system. The annual review made sure that the company was on the right course, but she realized that this did not yet make the system double loop learning. Somehow they had to make sure that the policy and the indicators they used were the right ones. Maybe it was time to start thinking about publishing a environmental report. In that way they could invite feedback from all their stakeholders to ensure that IMC was doing the right thing.

The final principle, espoused by Morgan, in facilitating the development of "learning to learn" related to the need to make interventions and create organizational structures and processes that helped implement the first three principles. The key to such structures and processes was the inbuilt capacity to self-organize. For unless an organization was able to change itself to accommodate the ideas it produced and its evolving values, it was likely eventually to block its own innovations.

The double-loop learning perspective to management required a degree of openness and self-criticism that was foreign to traditional Western modes of management. It ran counter to the inclination of many corporate managers who stressed secrecy, exclusion, and the need to keep a tight rein on operations. Learning to learn required a cultural change that emphasized the importance of activeness over passiveness at every level of the organization, including its multiple stakeholders. Double loop learning emphasized autonomy over dependence, flexibility over rigidity, collaboration over authoritarian belief.

After reading this, Meg was convinced that public reporting on their environmental performance coupled with a dialogue process with key stakeholders was the thing to do. But she could see much wider possibilities.

A great many well-established management theories are preoccupied with understanding the environment as a kind of world out there that has an existence of its own. In contrast, the ideas of the new systems thinking suggested that the best way of thinking strategically may not be the development of techniques that help companies to look at their environment. A richer and more constructive picture may well emerge from engaging in systematic dialogue with the networks of stakeholder relationships in and around the firm.

Traditional organizations draw boundaries around a narrow definition of themselves, and attempt to advance the self-interest of this narrow domain. In the process, they truncate and distort their understanding of the wider context and surrender their future to the way the world evolves. So their fate often rests in seeing what happens rather than in actively engaging stakeholder views on how to create the basis for a shared future.

When we recognize that the environment is not separate from "us" and that we do not necessarily have to compete or struggle against the environment, a completely new set of relationships becomes possible. Organizations committed to this kind of self-discovery are able to develop a kind of systemic wisdom[17]. They become more aware of their role and significance within the business and social environment, and of their ability to facilitate change and development that will allow their identity to evolve along with that of the wider system. In the long run, survival can only be survival with, never survival against the business environment in which the company is operating. In seeing how one's suppliers, one's customers, one's employees, one's local, national, and worldwide community, and even one's competitors are really parts of the same system, it becomes possible to move towards an appreciation of systemic interdependence.

All of this was very exciting for Meg. She was always a great networker and intuitively she knew that was best for her company too. So she was delighted that her natural instincts were being reinforced by the work of leading edge academics. The concept of learning organizations[18,19] appealed to her strongly and she knew that it would fit hand in glove with the type of organization IMC had become. They were first and foremost a knowledge-creating company and this, according to some current writers, had major implications for how companies should be managed[20,21,22]. Meg's vision for the long-term future started to emerge. She was ready for some changes and she called a meeting with her team leaders to sound them out.

First of all, she was keen to make sure that the new ideas around "learning organizations" were further embedded in the ways IMC worked. Taking their environmental management system a step further could provide the first opportunity to trial some systems. Everyone immediately agreed that it was a logical thing to do, not least because of the nature of their readership.

But before launching into learning strategies, Meg decided that it was time to propose major changes in the ownership structure of IMC. It was 1993 and the company was doing brilliantly. It had grown into its niche and there were plenty of developments going on within the market to provide opportunities for the future. It was clear that IMC had reached a point where it could be successfully listed on one of the securities markets. Meg's thinking behind this was that she wanted to transform her employees into owners. She proposed to the ten leaders of each "title team" that half of IMC should be listed. She would keep 25 percent of the shares and 25 percent should be transferred to employees over the next five years. Her proposal was debated and eventually agreed with much enthusiasm.

Meg did not see that being a full-time CEO was the best way for her to serve the company's interests any longer. IMC needed a "Chief Learning Officer," a constant provider of new ideas and someone whose behavior encouraged people to challenge established ways of working. One way she thought she could do that was to start devoting more time to her writing again. By publicly challenging conventional ideas of management she could inject new ideas into the company. There were plenty of arenas where she could air her thoughts.

Next the membership of the IMC Board had to be considered – everyone agreed it needed to reflect a wide range of stakeholder interests. The management structure and style of IMC was pretty well established along the right principles already with autonomous teams and lots of active networking. But it was agreed that in order to facilitate continuous learning, new initiatives should be brainstormed and implemented. New initiatives that were proposed included:

■ Weekly "circles of knowledge" within the title teams. These were to be informal lunchtime brainstorming and debating sessions around issues relating to current projects.

■ Monthly one day "circles of knowledge" attended by the leaders of the ten title teams. This was effectively the new executive team and the monthly session was to be in addition to their regular executive team meetings.

■ Membership rotation between the different title teams to promote diversity of ways of working, and to challenge "groupthink."

■ Individual learning projects (always to involve networking and benchmarking with other companies).

■ Encouragement of multiskilling within teams.

■ Access to information across the company, basically everything except personal files: i.e. benchmarking reports, reports on "circles of knowledge," team reports on key performance indicators, etc.

■ A menu of annual training events based on comprehensive training needs analysis (the first menu to include project evaluation skills for team leaders).

■ Annual "circles of knowledge" to be organized by each title team with their key stakeholders; initially with readers, contributors, other relevant suppliers and key networking partners. This would give feedback on products and services and help establish how well they were performing.

A blast from the past

Just as IMC started to put some of these ideas into place along came the traditionalist backlash. It had started to influence the articles of IMC's human resources journal in the early 1990s and Meg was not very impressed by what she read. The new model was called re-engineering and it was obviously a response to technological change and the new competitive challenges faced by many industries. But it usually resulted in massive job losses.

The 1980s seemed to be back all over again. There were four primary elements in the re-engineering arguments: fundamental, radical, processes, and dramatic. Each characteristic implied a particular managerial approach. Meg was perplexed by what she read because each of these elements seemed to take managers in different directions with respect to the empathy they were required to feel toward their employees and other stakeholders. While the need for more efficiency was undeniable, the prescription seemed like a real mishmash of different philosophies.

At the outset, the fundamentals of re-engineering did not appear too bad. The logic went like this: senior management is a custodian of the corporate entity in the face of stakeholder demands and technical and economic developments which necessitate a re-engineering response. As custodians, managers must attend to the "fundamental" task of determining "what a company must do and on what should be." This task meant that senior managers need to ensure that the values of employees and customers and other stakeholders were in tune with what senior managers needed to accomplish.

Of employees, the main advocates of re-engineering, Hammer and Champy[23] wrote: "An organization's management systems – the ways in which people are paid, the measures by which their performance is evaluated, and so forth are the primary shapers of employees' values and beliefs." Of customers, they wrote: "Understanding customers' needs doesn't mean asking customers what those needs are. They'll say only what they think they want ... they will tend to answer from their own unexpanded mindset."

Meg was stunned by the implications of what she was reading. They were completely opposite to the IMC philosophy. She knew that the success of IMC was based on the way they constantly sought feedback from their readers. She knew that her staff, like everyone else, appreciated a fair and competitive salary but they also valued the strong communal spirit of IMC. In fact all of them chose to come to the office at least for a couple days a week regardless of the homeworking options they enjoyed precisely because they appreciated the buzz of creating things together and being part of something they believed in. However, she was well aware of the different nature of companies like IMC compared to more traditional manufacturing industries.

But the sinister side of re-engineering became apparent to Meg when she read about its radical mode. The implied managerial approach here was that the senior manager comes down from the executive suite and steps into the role of "new affiliate" with others in the company. Hammer and Champy charged these managers with a duty to ask what seemed like a brilliant question: "If I were re-creating this company today, given what I know and given the current technology, what would it look like?" This could be an excellent question from an ethical point of view, because it deals with the very purpose of the company.

But the brilliance became an illusion when Meg considered its potential impact on employees. The question wipes clean any reference to the history of the relationships that got employees, including managers, to where they were before re-engineering. There is no "we" in the question. There is no "given the history that we carry with us" in the question. The employees do not fit neatly into either "what I know" or "current technology." With this question, the history that managers and employees have lived in the company until re-engineering is tossed out the window.

Just when Meg thought it could not get much worse, along came the dramatic phase of the process. The implied managerial approach here was sheer heroics. A senior manager becomes the daring leader, a Lone Ranger who rescues the organization by adapting it to an environment of threatening stakeholders. If there are casualties in this war, so be it.

"Re-engineering isn't to everyone's advantage," Hammer and Champy wrote. "Some employees do have a vested interest in current operations, some people will lose their jobs, and some workers may be uncomfortable with their jobs post-re-engineering. Trying to please everyone is a hopeless ambition that will either devalue re-engineering to a programme of incremental change or delay its implementation into the future."

Evidently, Meg thought, the threat to the organization in which re-engineering rides to the rescue makes empathy with the existing work-force a hopeless ambition. If there was a place for long-term employees after re-engineering, it was by pure luck[24].

In her new role as external ambassador for IMC, Meg sought an early opportunity to write for a popular business magazine. Her first article was called "The science, art and spirit of management". It was a not so subtle rebuke of re-engineering. She wanted to make its tacit assumptions clear and make the point that the world had moved on. It was about time that a more holistic view was adopted and that business managers learned to separate simplistic fads from some simple but fundamental principles. Good management called for a combination of solid scientific techniques and tools; the creative skills of an artist; as well as for the acknowledg-ment and engagement of the human spirit. A good theory helps managers to embrace all these aspects; a piecemeal one does nothing else than sus-tain the fragmentation of humans and human communities.

In the next few years she was proven right about re-engineering. What-ever its original intentions its implementation proved to be a total failure. It was simply hijacked as another excuse for downsizing[25]. Even its origi-nal proponents seemed to be backtracking.

By 1996, if there was one thing that was becoming clear to Meg, it was that there were no simple answers. She remained committed to her beliefs and encouraged the formalization of "stakeholder dialogue" at IMC through focus groups and surveys. But as for management theory she found it hard to disagree with the view that: "The basic truths of good management are not complex – understanding management theory is important, but the faddism it generates should be approached with a good deal of scepticism[26]."

Part Three

THE GUIDE

We now move from twentieth century parables to twenty-first century reality. Our contention, based on knowledge of the first two hundred years of free enterprise, is that intelligent, stakeholder inclusive companies are the ones that flourish in the long term. The days when companies could rely solely on command and control, military-style management techniques have long disappeared. Technological and efficiency gains are still possible, but today they are only incremental and, as re-engineering has demonstrated, sometimes counter-productive. Western corporate strategy, based mostly on top-down models have proved to be less than optimal when compared with the double-loop learning, knowledge-creating, collaborative strategies emphasized by Far East corporations.

In our third parable, IMC stumbled on some of these insights and found a way of articulating the belief that Western based companies could also be vibrant, empowered, and in harmony with their environment. Companies can become more resilient through networking and double-loop approaches to continuous improvement. Commercial success and long-term value can be generated if companies see themselves as part of their environment and embrace all their stakeholders in a systematic and genuinely inclusive way.

The rest of this book is a do-it-yourself guide to techniques which help institutionalize double-loop learning and stakeholder inclusion. In every case we advocate cyclical techniques which will be familiar to anyone who has been touched by total quality or environmental management. It is our belief that any company, large or small, that can do quality management can also do stakeholder inclusion. Stakeholder inclusion does not involve techniques that companies do not already have, nor does it require hugely expensive consultants to be engaged.

Part 1 was a political and economic history of stakeholders. In Part 2 we related three stories which concluded that stakeholders need to be embraced in management style and corporate strategy. We would like Part 3 to be more of a conversation. So we will start referring to you, the reader, as though you are experiencing real life situations, as indeed you undoubtedly are. Consider yourself to be one of our stakeholders.

CHAPTER 12

Governance and stakeholding

a broad definition of governance

The term governance is used most frequently by politicians and business leaders. This is no coincidence, because debates around governance are essentially about power and accountability. We have already seen how, throughout the twentieth century, executives of large corporations established significant power bases for themselves. Today, whatever might happen to politicians, provided companies continue to deliver acceptable returns to institutional and individual shareholders, corporate leaders are unlikely to be replaced (see Case Study 12.1).

CASE STUDY 12.1

You can be sure of Shell's directors

Royal Dutch Shell suffered two appalling public relations disasters in 1995 – first over the Brent Spar oil rig dumping fiasco, and later over charges of culpability for the executions of Nigerian environmental and human rights activist Ken Saro-Wiwa and eight colleagues. There were consumer boycotts in Europe and calls for Shell to disinvest in Nigeria by South African President Nelson Mandela. The US administration proposed sanctions against Nigeria which would have severely damaged both the military dictatorship and Shell. Nevertheless, the Shell International Board of Directors remained unmoved and seemingly unthreatened. The key to Shell's executive resilience, and indeed the onward march of its share price after these reputational setbacks, was its reliability from the perspective of its major investors.

Amazingly, even when share prices plummet, there is no automatic request from investors for the heads of corporations on a silver platter. Following a number of celebrated liability claims on tobacco companies in 1996, there were some spectacular collapses in share price. The decline in share value of major tobacco companies ran into billions of dollars –

£3 billion for British American Tobacco alone. But sure enough, the executives in charge were not held culpable. It was as though they were dealing with an Act of God rather than the inevitable outcome of decades of scientific and medical cover-ups and obfuscation. Heaven forbid that the power structures which permitted such abuses be formally challenged. Indeed, as we have seen, they will not be provided that returns on investment are maintained.

The authors of the American Constitution had a good notion of how to control executive power. Rather neatly, they divided power three ways – between the executive (the Presidency), the legislature (Congress) and the judiciary (the Courts). Such a division of power was originally advocated by John Locke and later, most enthusiastically by the late eighteenth century American republicans based on their experience of the corrupting influence and wasteful practices of the British crown.

If we are to have more accountability in business, and if we are to secure a better balance of the long-term interests of all stakeholders, then a formal division of powers and responsibilities at the top is required. In recent decades, two forms of power sharing have developed in North American and European board rooms. The first is the growth of nonexecutive directorships. Essentially these posts are to ensure the accountability of the executive to the investors. Nonexecutives do not necessarily disturb the simplistic model of owner control plus consumer sovereignty first articulated by Adam Smith. They are there mainly to stop executives dipping their hands too deeply into the corporate till. They do this with varying degrees of success.

The second form of formal power sharing, which most definitely does start to tilt the balance away from the shareholder control model is the development of supervisory councils – most notably in Germany.

Thomas Sheridan and Nigel Kendall[1] have characterized the difference between these two forms of power sharing:

> While British and US companies go out of their way to demonstrate the control nonexecutives are exercising on executives, pay and the financial controls on the company, perhaps taking their input into strategic matters for granted, with German and Dutch companies it is the other way around – they talk of strategic matters, perhaps taking the overview of matters such as executive remuneration for granted.

The continental European Supervisory Council model is made all the more powerful by including not just representatives of workers and trade unions, but also the banks. In the case of Scandinavian corporations, it is more likely that there will be a unitary board rather than a separation of executive and supervisory functions; but here worker directors sit on main boards alongside nonexecutives from outside the company. Where the state is formally involved, e.g. in France, it is commonplace to have directors representing the government.

Sheridan and Kendall contrast ownership and governance practice in English-speaking and non-English-speaking cultures (including Japan). In summary they result in the differences described in Table 12.1.

Table 12.1
Ownership and governance practice, English-speaking and non-English-speaking cultures[1]

	English-speaking boards	Non-English-speaking boards
Ownership	Dispersed	Concentrated
Control	Separated from ownership	Linked to ownership
Decision-making	Excludes outside stakeholders	Includes key stakeholders
Takeovers	Can be costly and antagonistic; can create monopoly	Hostile takeovers rare
Investor commitment	Low	Important in periods of difficulty

So the main issue in corporate governance is the strategic power structure: whether or not to have a unitary or dual structure and whether or not to embrace the wider constituency of stakeholders in either structure. But there is another important dimension of accountability in executive boards, and that is the question of concentration of power in the hands of individuals. At the beginning of the industrial revolution firms were often family-owned; thus stewardship and ownership were essentially the same things. However, as the executive managerial class rose in power and authority throughout the twentieth century, there was a tendency towards unaccountable autocracy, a trait which was firmly reinforced in the downsizing, delayering 1980s. At best, autocracy is associated with paternalism and philanthropy – one individual caring enough about his or her family of stakeholders to do the right thing by all of them. More frequently it is associated with individual aggrandizement, tough decisions and fabulous remuneration.

So this chapter is about power: who wields it, who controls it and who checks it. We take as our starting point the premise that a corporation will be run most effectively if all stakeholders have the appropriate level of empowerment and that executives will manage best provided that they recognize their accountability, in varying degrees, to all stakeholders.

That is not to say that companies have to operate like democracies. We are not arguing here for corporations to become cooperatives. But it is self-evident that numerous stakeholders invest resources, including money, time and energy, into companies. As resource investors, they have a right to call to account those who manage those resources.

The following stakeholders need to be taken into account in the governance and power structures of a corporation. They do not necessarily need to have seats on boards or supervisory councils, but their interests need to be reflected somewhere:

- investors (including banks) – for putting up the cash
- managers – to provide leadership, describe their plans and answer for their actions
- employees – to safeguard their security, livelihoods and well-being
- customers – to reflect their rights
- business partners (e.g. suppliers and subsidiaries) – to avoid them being squashed
- local communities – to safeguard their safety and economic interests
- civil society (including regulators and pressure groups) – because they represent the common good
- the natural environment/future generations/non-human species – unable to speak for themselves.

At this point, the reader who sees this list as a nightmare vision of extra responsibility may as well switch off. Stop reading now and pass the book to another colleague or the corporate library. The reader who sees the list as an opportunity to create a vibrant, inclusive and successful model of the corporation of the future should read on, for each of these stakeholders is capable of adding enormously to the resilience, creativity and commercial success of the company.

The process

Boardroom bliss or executive excitement – the strategic choice

Boards and senior executive groups are not always pleasant places. All too often behaviors are baronial rather than collaborative; individualist rather than team playing. Moreover, these are the fora where power is brokered and succession determined. Some companies are better than others in this respect. The most stakeholder friendly companies are often the ones where leaders are groomed from within, where collaboration across divisional boundaries is most encouraged and where bombast and individualism are least tolerated. Companies which have strong family interests with a long-term view which is complemented by structured senior management development programs often excel at this game.

If your company is not so fortunate, if internal politics and competition are frequent features of senior managerial behavior, if there are fundamental question marks over the effectiveness of the board, then some kind of fundamental review or "boardroom audit" of current structures and policies is probably necessary. It will be entertaining to say the very least. Without doubt, whoever first suggests such a measure will be perceived to have an ulterior motive. For this reason, it is best initiated either by the nonexecutive directors who have an obligation to ask difficult questions, or by the chairman, provided he or she is recognized to be reasonably neutral in the power games.

A fundamental review of the effectiveness of the board and senior management governance must include tests designed to check alignment of performance with business goals; whether there is serious discussion of financial and operational decisions; how the integrity of information for decision-taking is assured; and how effectively the company invests in R&D, human resources and market development. Sheridan and Kendall[1] recommend a boardroom audit process to check the overall effectiveness of company leaderships, along the lines of a strategic review. Their process is depicted in Figure 12.1.

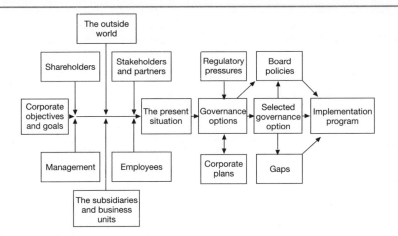

Figure 12.1
Sheridan and Kendall's boardroom audit[1]

The same authors identify ten key components for successful boards. We would suggest that these components also make for good relations with stakeholders (see Exhibit 12.1).

EXHIBIT 12.1

Ten key issues for boardroom governance (adapted from Sheridan and Kendall)

1 Defined roles for the chairman and chief executive.

2 If the two roles are combined in one person, the rationale for such an action.

3 The need for checks and balances in the board structure.

4 The importance of outsiders, i.e. nonexecutive directors.

5 The need to harness wisdom and experience to direction.

6 The importance of succession and board renewal: balancing experience with a fresh approach.

7 The importance of quality.

8 There has to be structure; without a defined structure there will be chaos.

9 The committee structure needs to be carefully defined; in particular the audit committee has to be looked at to ensure that control does not degenerate into second guessing and policing, and that the work of the committee does not duplicate that of the auditors or the internal accounting departments.

10 There has to be open and honest disclosure.

If you feel that your board or senior executive team fails to meet some of these vital criteria for effectiveness, then a full scale boardroom audit may be required. But be careful: the boardroom audit provides an opportunity to fundamentally reinvent the leadership of a company. Powerful forces will be unleashed. As Niccolo Machiavelli noted in *The Prince*: "There is nothing more difficult to execute, nor more dangerous to administer than to introduce a new order of things; for he who introduces it has all those who profit from the old order as his enemies, and he only has lukewarm allies in all those who might profit from the new." If you do not have a wholly dysfunctional leadership, and just want to enhance the quality of stakeholder inclusion in your business, then a stakeholder review and audit process is for you. The options are summarized in the flow chart in Figure 12.2.

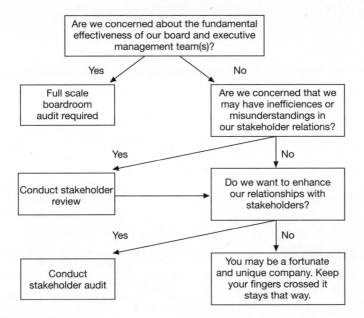

Figure 12.2
Boardroom audit, stakeholder review or stakeholder audit?[1]

Strategic stakeholder review and audit

As we have made clear throughout this book, we see governance as going well beyond its common interpretation, i.e. responsibility to shareholders. However, we are not going to forget owners and shareholders altogether, so in Chapter 14 you will find advice on how to consult effectively with shareholders and how to measure the quality of the corporation's relationships with its institutional and individual investors.

Figure 12.3 shows a cycle of governance for stakeholder review and audit which is based loosely on the model of continuous improvement much loved of advocates of quality management. It is a rational framework to help busy people establish where they are on the path to enlightened management and shared destiny and responsibility with stakeholders.

Leadership and commitment

In reaching this stage of the book, we assume that the reader already has a personal commitment and feels able to convince his or her colleagues of the benefits of stakeholder inclusion.

The starting point: assessing current structures and policies

Step 1 is to bring in an individual to assess structure; someone who is

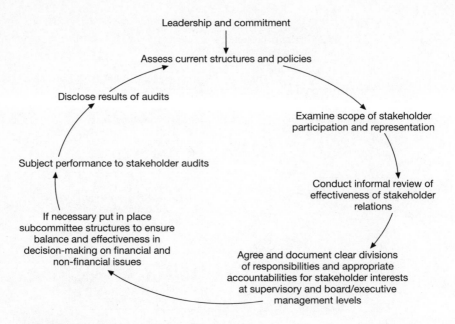

Figure 12.3
Cycle of governance: the strategic stakeholder review and audit process

trusted and independent and used to dealing with powerful egos – not a management consultant, but someone who knows a bit about decision making and leadership. This person should meet each member of the existing leadership individually and in private and ask the following questions:

1 List the stakeholders whose interests are important to the future of the business (if necessary prompt).

2 Record what works with current leadership and structures viewed from the perspective of the stakeholders.

3 What is clear about current direction and business planning?

4 What is unclear about current direction and business planning?

5 Which behaviors are contributing to the long-term success of the business and all its stakeholder interests?

6 Which behaviors are dragging the company into short-termism and expediency?

7 Which stakeholders' views are currently best captured in the power structure?

8 List the no-go areas of discussion for stakeholder relationships at senior management levels.

In any senior management forum the answers to these questions, if honestly given, will provide an excellent starting point for discussion. They are not intended to provide the basis for revolution or re-structuring – different questions would be needed for that (together with the engagement of a suitably expensive management consultancy to justify the effort). Rather, the purpose of the assessment of structures is to check whether there is space for all stakeholders views to be represented, one way or another, and if not what evolution is required so that they may be.

Step 2 is to commission an internal assessment of all existing documented and non-documented "policy" which may impact on stakeholders. It can be done by any senior manager, as it is a purely factual review – a legal department or other corporate department should be able to cope. In defining what is and what is not policy, the following definitions may assist:

- **A Policy** is a broad statement of principles (typically one page) which derives legitimacy from the Memorandum of Association or Mission Statement of the company.

- **Guidelines** explain the detail of the policy, expanding on individual components and leading the reader to specific procedures and work instructions which may be functionally and/or site specific.

- **Procedures** describe the specific steps which should be taken to ensure compliance with the general principles contained in the company policy and guidelines. They should be functionally and/or site specific.

Here is a non-exhaustive list of potential policy areas.

The shareholders/owners

- Directors' remuneration policy
- Dividends policy
- Mergers and acquisitions policy.

Employees and managers

- A general human resources policy covering remuneration, career development, grievance, equal opportunities consultation, representation, etc
- An occupational safety and health policy
- Code of ethics for individual rights and responsibilities (including the balance between confidentiality and rights to complain).

Customers

■ Complaints policy

■ Marketing and advertising policy.

The community

■ Volunteering policy

■ Donations policy.

Business partners, suppliers and small businesses

■ Code of ethics for purchasing staff

■ Payments policy

■ Code of ethics for behavior and gifts.

Global economy (relevant to transnationals and those sourcing overseas)

■ Ethical and human/civil rights policies for operations in developing countries.

The planet and future generations

■ Environmental policy.

The animal kingdom (relevant to agrochemicals, farming, pharmaceuticals and cosmetics and toiletries)

■ Animal welfare policy.

Government and civil society

■ List of legal and regulatory obligations in each jurisdiction

Of course it is possible to encapsulate basic notions of stakeholder inclusivity, corporate citizenship and social responsibility directly into company Mission Statements. Chris Marsden summarizes research conduction in 1990 which examined 200 company mission statements of which 25 included a specific commitment to social responsibility or corporate citizenship[2]. Included among these were giants like Ford: "The conduct of the company worldwide must be pursued in a manner that is socially responsible and commands respect for its integrity and for its positive contribution to society." And Du Pont: "We must conduct our business offering with the highest ethical standards and work diligently to be a respected corporate citizen worldwide."

The US Department of Commerce has issued a set of Model Business

Principles which attempt to encapsulate broad principles of social, environmental and ethical practice for US businesses and their worldwide operations (see Exhibit 12.2).

EXHIBIT 12.2

The US Government's Model Business Principles

Recognizing the positive role of US business in upholding and promoting adherence to universal standards of human rights, the Administration encourages all businesses to adopt and implement voluntary codes of conduct for doing business around the world that cover at least the following areas:

1 Provision of a safe and healthy workplace.

2 Fair employment practices, including avoidance of child and forced labor and avoidance of discrimination based on race, gender, national origin or religious beliefs; and respect for the right of association and the right to organize and bargain collectively.

3 Responsible environmental protection and practices.

4 Compliance with US and local laws promoting good business practices, including laws prohibiting illicit payments and ensuring fair competition.

5 Maintenance, through leadership at all levels, of a corporate culture that respects free expression consistent with legitimate business concerns, and does not condone political coercion in the workplace; that encourages good corporate citizenship and makes a positive contribution to the communities in which the company operates and where ethical conduct is recognized, valued and exemplified by all employees.

In adopting voluntary codes that reflect these principles, US companies should serve as models, encouraging similar behavior by their partners, suppliers and subcontractors.

Adoption of codes of conduct reflecting these principles is voluntary. Companies are encouraged to develop their own codes of conduct appropriate to their particular circumstances. Many companies already apply statements or codes that incorporate these principles. Companies should find appropriate means to inform their stakeholders and the public of actions undertaken in connection with these principles. Nothing in the principles is intended to require the company to act in violation of host or US law. This statement of principles is not intended for legislation.

Two good examples of corporate Mission Statements based on principles of social responsibility and stakeholder inclusion are those of Levi Strauss and the Co-operative Bank (see Exhibits 12.3 and 12.4).

EXHIBIT 12.3

The Levi Strauss Mission Statement

The mission of Levi Strauss & Co. is to sustain responsible commercial success as a global marketing company of branded casual apparel. We must balance goals of superior profitability and return on investment, leadership market positions, and superior products and service. We will conduct our business ethically and demonstrate leadership in satisfying our responsibilities to our communities and to society. Our work environment will be safe and productive and characterized by fair treatment, teamwork, open communications, personal accountability and opportunities for growth and development.

Aspiration Statement

We all want a Company that our people are proud of and committed to, where all employees have an opportunity to contribute, learn, grow and advance based on merit, not politics or background.

We want our people to feel respected, treated fairly, listened to and involved.

Above all, we want satisfaction from accomplishments and friendships, balanced personal and professional lives and to have fun in our endeavours. When we describe the kind of Levi Strauss & Co. we want in the future what we are talking about is building on the foundation we have inherited: affirming the best of our Company's traditions, closing gaps that may exist between principles and practices and updating some of our values to reflect contemporary circumstances.

What type of leadership is necessary to make our aspirations a reality?

New Behaviours

Leadership that exemplifies directness, openness to influence, commitment to the success of others, willingness to acknowledge our own contributions to problems, personal accountability, teamwork and trust. Not only must we model these behaviours, but we must coach others to adopt them.

Diversity

Leadership that values a diverse workforce (age, sex, ethnic group, etc.) at all levels of the organization, diversity in experience and diversity in perspectives. We have committed to taking full advantage of the rich backgrounds and abilities of all our people and to promote greater diversity in positions of influence. Differing points of view will be sought; diversity will be valued and honesty rewarded not suppressed.

Recognition

Leadership that provides greater recognition – both financial and psychic – for individuals and teams that contribute to our success. Recognition must be given to all who contribute: those who create and innovate and those who continually support the day-to-day business requirements.

Ethical Management Practices

Leadership that epitomises the stated standards of ethical behavior. We must provide clarity about our expectations and must enforce these standards throughout the corporation.

Communications

Leadership that is clear about Company, unit and individual goals and performance. People must know what is expected of them and receive timely, honest feedback on their performance and career aspirations.

Empowerment

Leadership that increases the authority and responsibility of those closest to our products and customers. By actively pushing responsibility, trust and recognition into the organization, we can harness and release the capabilities of all our people.

EXHIBIT 12.4

The Co-operative Bank Mission Statement

We, The Co-operative Bank Group, will continue to develop a successful and innovative financial institution by providing our customers with high quality financial and related services whilst promoting the underlying principles of co-operation which are …

Quality and Excellence

To offer all our customers consistent high quality and good value services and strive for excellence in all that we do.

Participation

To introduce and promote the concept of full participation by welcoming the views and concerns of our customers and by encouraging our staff to take an active role within the local community.

Freedom of Association

To be non-partisan in all social, political, racial and religious matters.

Education and Training

To act as a caring and responsible employer encouraging the development and training of all our staff and encouraging commitment and pride in each other and the Group.

Co-operation

To develop a close affinity with organizations which promote fellowship between workers, customers, members and employers.

Quality of Life

To be a responsible member of society by promoting an environment where the needs of local communities can be met now and in the future.

Retentions

To manage the business effectively and efficiently, attracting investment and maintaining sufficient surplus funds within the business to ensure the continued development of the Group.

Integrity

To act at all times with honesty and integrity and within legislative and regulatory requirements.

The Caux Round Table has also produced a set of principles for business which are based on concepts of stakeholder inclusivity and moral responsibility. The preamble to the code states explicitly: "Laws and market forces are necessary, but insufficient guides for conduct." The seven general principles advocated by Caux are:

■ The responsibilities of business: beyond shareholders, towards stakeholders.

■ The economic and social impact of business: towards innovation, justice and world community.

■ Business behavior: beyond the letter of the law towards a spirit of trust.

■ Respect the rules.

■ Support for multilateral trade.

■ Respect for the environment.

■ Avoidance of illicit operations.

In 1996 the UK Industrial Society surveyed 313 organizations to discover what aspects of ethical best practice were included in written company statements[3]. Many of these touched on important stakeholder relationships, especially those with employees. Regulatory compliance and relationships with customers, suppliers, the community and the environment were also included.

When the two reviews of structure and policies have been completed, the leadership of the company will need to consider the results carefully. Obviously it is important to depersonalize any issues which emerged from the structure and policy assessments and to make full play of the positives, but a skilled facilitator will be able to get the overall message across.

Examine scope of stakeholder participation and inclusion

Once the structure and policy assessments are complete, it is probably a good idea to take the leadership, including nonexecutives, away for a day or so to consider the results and whether omissions or dysfunctionalities present strategic problems or merely tactical, short-term ones.

This is also the opportunity to invite external experts to present on particular aspects of stakeholder inclusion, thereby allowing a little benchmarking. There are numerous businesses which have improved their stakeholder relations that will be only too pleased to pass on their experiences to a senior management team from a non-competing company. They may even do it for free. There are also many consultants who have expertise across the board on stakeholder relations. Our advice would be to avoid these (unless you already know and trust them) and go straight for the source of best practice in the areas you have gaps. Professional bodies like the Institute for Social and Ethical AccountAbility (UK), Institute for Environmental Assessment (UK), Business in the Community (UK), Businesses for Social Responsibility (USA), the Social Venture Network (USA and Europe), Institute for Business Ethics (UK), Council on Ethics and Economics (USA) and academic groups like the European Business Ethics Network are most likely to be able to identify sources of help for relatively low cost.

The main purpose of examining the scope of stakeholder participation and inclusion should be to spot any strengths and weaknesses which may impact on the long-term health of the company. In each case there could be opportunities and/or risks associated with

■ business efficiency

■ reputation and loyalty

■ liability and costs

■ market differentiation.

At its most basic, failure to understand customer motivation is likely to result in the launch of products and services customers do not want – a negative on all four criteria. Poor environmental management can lead to horrific costs and liabilities. Good environmental management can enhance reputation and stakeholder loyalty. Failure to understand supplier needs and constraints results in business inefficiency; getting it right improves efficiency and can reduce costs in warehousing and logistics.

A skilled facilitator with a good knowledge of your business and equipped with the results of the structural and policy assessments should have no difficulty assisting the leadership of the company with the analysis. A company might assess the risks and opportunities as strategic, tactical or non-applicable for each of its principal stakeholder relationships.

In brainstorming the risks and opportunities presented by current stakeholder relations, gaps will inevitably emerge. Some stakeholders may be very well catered for. Others may not. It will also become apparent that some are simply "floating" with no one taking absolute responsibility for nurturing the relationship. In each case relationships should be managed from the executive level, although parallel oversight from main board or supervisory board members is extremely valuable as well. The best option is a combination of board and executive responsibility for each stakeholder relationship. But before responsibilities can be allocated, an independent review of stakeholder relationships should be commissioned.

Conduct informal review of effectiveness of stakeholder relations

In the USA there has been a number of examples of companies commissioning independent reviews of the quality of their stakeholder relationships. Sometimes these reviews have been conducted following a spectacular breakdown in trust with one or another group of stakeholders. Occasionally, the reviews have been made public, either by way of atonement or simply as a means of demonstrating a commitment to corporate social responsibility. The best exponent of this latter art is most definitely Ben & Jerry's, the US ice cream manufacturer which between 1988 and 1994 invited in a succession of social responsibility experts to publish an independent commentary on the company's social performance.

In Britain, the term social audit has been applied to similar assessments conducted by individuals or groups totally independent of the organization.[4,5] In neither case are these activities true 'audits', because they are not conducted against defined measures or subject to an accounting process which can be independently verified. They are necessarily somewhat subjective because they tend to follow the individual professional judgement and values of the assessor as much as the policies and procedures of the organization under scrutiny. But this is not to understate the value of qualitative reviews. Indeed it is our recommendation that an informal, independent review of the quality of relationships is conducted before any formal accounting and audit process is embarked upon.

A review need not be onerous or exhaustive. Indeed for most companies which already measure and document employee attitudes, customer complaints and shareholder relations, it will be quite simple. The purpose of the informal review is to engage an independent outsider to produce a 10 to 20 page report summarizing the quality of current relationships based on existing information and some direct, confidential contact with representatives of key stakeholder groups. This may be done by a combination of documentation review, focus groups, telephone contact and face-to-face interviews. It should be undertaken in no more than a few working weeks, because a definitive assessment is not required. What is needed is a report to senior executives and the Board which allows them to decide whether a full process of stakeholder (social and environmental) auditing and reporting is appropriate to the organization. The reasons why the review should be undertaken by an independent person are twofold:

1 An insider may not be able to elicit honest responses to sensitive questions posed to business partners, employees, etc.

2 An insider may not be strong enough to put forward unpalatable conclusions to senior management; indeed they may have their own position to protect.

Selecting an individual to conduct an informal review is a tricky business. Academics may be seen as independent, but they can also be quirky and unreliable. Business ethics consultants are sometimes perceived to be more interested in the second, hoped for commission (to reinvent the culture of an organization) than the job in hand.

Our recommendation is to engage someone skilled in attitude surveys, market research and focus group work rather than a business ethics specialist. Market researchers have interview and telephone skills which enable them to get to the heart of individual concerns and issues quite rapidly. And it does not really matter to them if the interviewees are consumers or shareholders. Market researchers have professional codes of confidentiality and behavior which can usually be relied upon. They can be told that the exercise is a one off, not leading to further work, and they will not take it as an intellectual slight. Finally, they are good at presenting information in an accessible and intelligible manner before moving on to their next commission. For small businesses, a reliable MBA student may be able to do the job.

It will obviously assist the work of the reviewer if they are appointed and managed by a senior executive who can set up lists of representative contacts in each stakeholder category: shareholders, business partners, suppliers, etc. They will need direct support from the human resources department in gaining confidential access to employees and assistance from the marketing/sales department in contacting customers. Important elements of the brief for the reviewer are:

■ Do not give the reviewer the results of any previous senior management assessments (this might introduce a source of bias).

■ Keep the commission short and sweet.

■ Make clear the commission is a once only deal.

■ Satisfy yourself on confidentiality if you require it.

■ Manage the review via a senior officer who can mobilize internal administrative resources.

■ Make sure the review identifies both perceived strengths and weaknesses in the relationships with each stakeholder group.

It is one thing for the board or executive management to assess the strategic importance or otherwise of key stakeholder relationships. It is quite another looking at the relationship from the perspective of the stakeholders themselves. There are two ways to do this: informal and formal. Informal soundings can be taken by the researcher with a telephone and some contact numbers; it can also be done in face-to-face discussions. Formal assessments require fully designed questionnaire based surveys.

For most companies, an informal process of soundings will be enough for a review which is largely aimed at determining how responsibilities for governance and stakeholder relations should be distributed. In either case, the objective is to form an impressionistic picture of the performance of the company, and in particular its leadership, through the eyes of reasonably randomly selected representatives of its main stakeholders.

Telephone conversations or face-to-face interviews should follow a structured format to include the following elements:

1 Explanation of the purpose of the inquiry (i.e. the company is researching how it can improve its relationships with its stakeholders).

2 Reassurance on confidentiality.

3 Tests of general knowledge and understanding of key components of the company's mission and policies (to a member of staff: "Are you familiar with the company's Mission Statement? Yes/no." "Are you familiar with the company's health and safety policy? Yes/no.")

4 Tests of recognition of any policies especially relevant to that stakeholder group (to a supplier: "Are you aware that the company has a prompt payment policy?")

5 Queries of stakeholder perceptions of company performance against elements of the mission (to a customer: "How well do you think the company matches up to its stated belief in product quality: very well, quite well, moderately, not well?")

6 Queries of stakeholder perceptions of company performance against elements of policy particularly relevant to that stakeholder group (e.g. to a shareholder: "How do you feel about the company's dividend policy? Is it (a) excellent; (b) good; (c) average; (d) poor?")

The types of question to be asked will vary from company to company and stakeholder to stakeholder. The process should continue until a reasonably consistent feel emerges from those questioned. This review should not try to be statistically robust. But it should result in a brief report outlining impressions: identifying real positives and any significant negatives or omissions. As noted above, in most companies such impressionistic research should not take longer than a few weeks; for small companies it could be done in a matter of days.

The review report, when received can be made available to stakeholders if the leadership of the company believes that to be a good idea. However, this is not essential. We are strong advocates of transparency, but the best form of transparency is that based on thorough and comprehensive analysis, i.e. a systematic audit process. If the company leadership wishes to receive a confidential review report so they have an idea what they are likely to uncover before proceeding to full audit that is fine. If the leadership prefers to fix a few things on the basis of the review before moving to a systematic audit, that is fine too. What would be dangerous would be to receive the review report, smile at the good parts, wince at the bad parts, and quietly place it in the file marked "forget."

It is important that the board or executive management group understand that this review is not exhaustive and that care needs to be taken over interpretation. Nevertheless, if well done, the signposting to the next stage will be clear.

Agree and document responsibilities, including subcommittees and advisory councils

Accountability comes from having clearly defined roles, responsibilities and objectives. This is as true of a member of the board as it is an employee from the shop floor. It is as important for a subcommittee of the main board to have agreed terms of reference as it is for a quality circle in a manufacturing facility. From agreed definitions of roles and responsibilities flows clarity of purpose for the organization. If clarity is lacking then your company runs a severe risk of dysfunctional behaviors, e.g. exhibition of territorial ambitions and other forms of political game playing.

Sheridan and Kendall describe the current tendency of large companies to slim down corporate functions to the essentials in order to grant greater autonomy to wealth creating business units and divisions. They see a flattening of structure as an increasingly common model with divisions represented on executive committees based on technological and customer bases. In such decentralized structures, the corporate headquarters' role is more to do with maintaining standards and guidelines, for example, on finance, personnel and R&D issues, and not to interfere too deeply in wealth creation. Meanwhile, the main board, ideally with input from advisory councils of stakeholders, should play the strategic role. Sheridan and Kendall[1] cite organizations like Siemens and IBM as exemplars of this approach.

It seems to us that this is a good model for ensuring the effective inclusion of stakeholder views in corporate governance and the ideal separation of powers and responsibilities to ensure balance and stability in stakeholder relations. From a defined structure may emerge clear roles and responsibilities for all players. These should be documented and transparent to all stakeholders. Figure 12.4 shows our recommended general structure with suggestions for key divisions of responsibility.

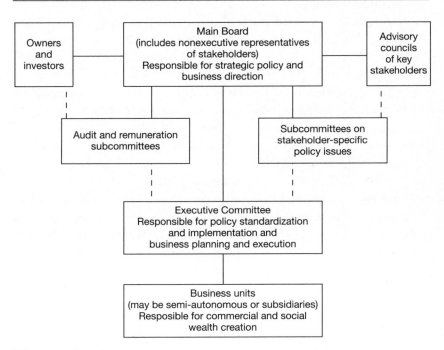

Figure 12.4
Idealized structure for the stakeholder-inclusive corporation

Undoubtedly, each of the directors and executives responsible for stakeholder groups will wish to rectify any deficiencies which have emerged from the review. That is natural and appropriate – it also ties in with any responsibilities they have accepted during the process. For some companies, addressing and allocating problems and responsibilities in a functional way like this may be enough. More imaginative companies will want to build on what they have done in the assessments and reviews so far. They will want to turn improvements of their stakeholder relations into positive virtues and broadcast the details in order to reinforce the participative and inclusive nature of their business. They will want to move to a formal cycle of stakeholder auditing. They will want to use processes of "continuous improvement" and disclosure to deliver enhanced relationships with all their stakeholders.

Subject performance to audit

In our view governance is about a lot more than accountability to owners and investors, although this tends to be the focus for much of the debate. In the UK, concerns about financial governance led first to the Cadbury Report on financial aspects of governance and then to the Greenbury Report on executive pay. These led, in turn, to new conventions on auditing and reporting on financial matters. These have been broadly helpful, and although financial accountability is not the subject of this book we would wish to recognize the positive contribution to shareholder rights which Cadbury and Greenbury have produced.

But when we talk of auditing stakeholder relationships, financial issues represent only one part of the equation. Stakeholding takes us into the territory of psychological contracts, trust, loyalty and inclusion.

There is growing interest in non-financial measures of corporate performance. It has been estimated that typically companies may have as much as 70 percent of their "value" tied up in reputational good will, know-how and the quality of their relationships with stakeholders. For a company in software design, advertising or biotechnology, the figure may be much higher. Skandia Life, the Swedish insurance firm, has developed a technique for assessing intellectual capital using nonfinancial measures which they believe to be far more relevant to their current and future performance as a business than the figures contained in their annual report and accounts.

The picture which is unfolding before us may be likened to cycles of interlocking processes. The first cycle reflects the recognition that the leadership can embrace the stakeholder agenda. The loops which engage with the main cycle may turn at different speeds, but they are all cycles of inclusion or "continuous improvement" for each stakeholder relationship. Pictorially it looks like Figure 12.5.

If Figure 12.5 looks complex, do not despair. You do not have to build

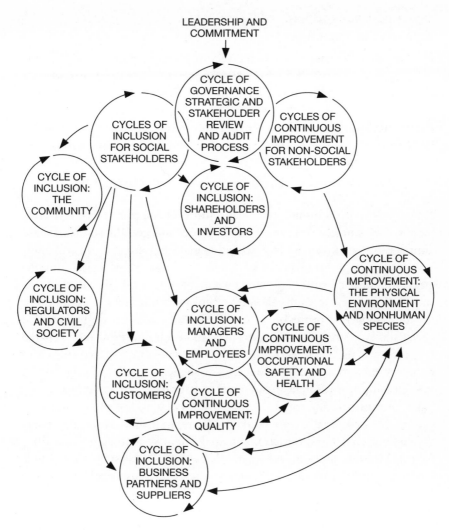

Figure 12.5
Cycles of stakeholder inclusion and continuous improvement

all of it at once. In all likelihood you will find several component parts already there, turning quite happily, but not necessarily linking directly to a central mechanism. The purpose of the rest of this book is to help you build the full picture. In the first part of this book we used the metaphor of the game to describe how stakeholders currently compete for attention in the modern free enterprise system. Now we are going to invite you to stop being game players and become designers of the social architecture of your organization instead.

Who takes responsibility for stakeholder relationship and audit and improvement?

It is worth exploring stakeholder relationships in both functional and cross-functional ways. So while it is important to have clearly defined board and executive level responsibilities for stakeholder relationships, it is also important to have a system for independent assessment of the quality of those relationships: discovering what works best so that it can be replicated as well as what needs improving. This avoids the poacher–gamekeeper phenomenon, where the individual ownership of a problem may act as an impediment to honest disclosure of the implications.

For large corporations – especially those in the public eye – it is no longer sufficient just to insert pious homilies and good news stories into annual reports and accounts. Statistics issued by companies on charitable donations, employee issues like health and safety at work, and the environment need to be 100 percent reliable and verifiable. In the same way that financial accounts should be subject to internal preparation following established professional standards and codes, so we believe that social and environmental accounts need to be administered and prepared by professionals. These accounts should be true and fair, and subject to independent verification by independent agencies, again meeting defined standards of professionalism and quality assurance. For small businesses, issues of transparency and accountability may be no less important[6].

Happily, in several areas of stakeholder relationships there are already defined national and international management systems standards which follow the continuous improvement philosophy. These standards include environmental management, quality as it relates to customers and suppliers, training and learning. In each case the principle is the same: the organization takes full responsibility for managing its own performance according to documented procedures and criteria; the organization also embraces communication feedback loops to enable it to learn from successes and failures in order to improve performance. Both the management system and the delivered performance are subject to periodic external accreditation or verification by a third party assessor.

We will now define some terms which we shall use throughout the rest of this book. They are terms which can be applied to the assessment of any type of stakeholder relationship.

Review   Informal, usually independent assessment based on largely qualitative and impressionistic information.

Accounts   Management information and data which reflect social and environmental performance, collected and presented in a systematic way.

Audit
Comprehensive, systematic, periodic and documented assessment of performance with respect to stakeholder interests, company policies and programs (equivalent to an internal audit of financial accounts).

Benchmark/ performance indicator
Qualitative or quantitative indicator of performance which can be compared within and between organizations.

Standard
A prescribed system of management which is not based on specific indicators, but rather on a process of continuous improvement which may be assessed both internally and externally.

Verification
A process of independent external validation to substantiate both the management process and the veracity of any accounts of social and environmental performance which are presented (equivalent to an external audit of financial accounts).

Accreditation
Process of certification against a management system standard leading to the award of an official seal of compliance.

Statement
A factual public statement of performance, ideally subject to verification (equivalent to the financial report and accounts).

With these building blocks in place, the question remains: who will drive the various processes necessary to measure and report on performance with respect to stakeholder relations? In our experience stakeholder audit functions should be independent of operational divisions and report directly to the main board and executive leadership of the company. This is the model that has developed successfully for financial accounting and reporting and which we have seen effectively replicated in social and environmental fields. We do not necessarily advocate integration of financial and nonfinancial accounting and auditing processes, although this may be appropriate in some organizations. But we do see the absolute importance of formally linking the outputs of stakeholder (social and environmental) auditing and inclusion to change management processes within the organization. To quote Michael Power "audits do as much to construct definitions of quality and performance as to measure them[7]."

The logic of this argument leads us to the conclusion that large companies should have professional units of stakeholder accounting and auditing. These units need to be operationally independent but report direct to the company leadership. They should embrace an appropriate array of professional disciplines and should aim their reports at those operational areas of the company which maintain direct relationships with stakeholders.

In this way, there is a gentle cyclical pressure which facilitates both dialogue and a desire for improvements in loyalty and inclusion in stakeholder relationships. It follows from this description of stakeholder auditing that it is not a process which can be effected by an outside agency. The company must take full ownership of its relationships and the processes by which the quality of those relationships is assured and enhanced. Anything less is lacking in seriousness.

CHAPTER 13

Developing inclusive relationships with stakeholders

a general approach

Who are the stakeholders?

Stakeholders are individuals and entities who can be influenced by, or can impact upon, an organization. We are going to define stakeholders in four ways:

- social
- non-social
- primary
- secondary.

Primary social stakeholders include:

- shareholders and investors
- employees and managers
- customers
- local communities
- suppliers and other business partners.

Secondary social stakeholders embrace government and civil society and include:

- government and regulators
- civic institutions
- social pressure groups, e.g. trade unions
- media and academic commentators

- trade bodies
- competitors.

Primary social stakeholders are those who have a direct stake in the organization and its success. Secondary social stakeholders may be extremely influential, especially in questions of reputation and public standing, but their stake is more representational than direct. Consequently, the level of moral accountability to a secondary stakeholder tends to be lower.

Primary non-social stakeholders include:

- the natural environment
- future generations
- nonhuman species.

Secondary non-social stakeholders include:

- environmental pressure groups
- animal welfare organizations.

Non-social stakeholders will be considered in Chapter 22.

Social stakeholders – the process

Broadly speaking, social stakeholders can be communicated with directly; nonsocial stakeholders cannot (for the purpose of this chapter we are discounting the possibility of communing effectively with generations as yet unborn, animals, rock crystals and trees). So, the quality of social stakeholder relationships can be measured in two ways:

- quantitative (based on benchmarks and performance indicators)
- qualitative (based on benchmarks and performance indicators plus investigations of the perceptions of stakeholders).

For each group, the generalized cycle of inclusion for ensuring participation of social stakeholders in the activities of the company can be set out as shown in Figure 13.1. This model will be reproduced in succeeding chapters in a specific form for each stakeholder group.

Small businesses may also wish to consult the New Economics Foundation workbook *Social Auditing for Small Organisations* which is wholly consistent with the model of stakeholder inclusion described here[1].

Let us now examine the common elements of relationship management and inclusion for social stakeholders.

Figure 13.1
Generalized cycle of inclusion for social stakeholders[1]

Leadership and commitment

It is assumed that in getting this far, the organization has legitimized the process from the top and has established an internal management audit team to drive the mechanics of the various cycles of inclusion and continuous improvement loops for stakeholder relationships.

Policy review

In the board/executive review process (Chapter 12) an assessment was made of existing formal policies with respect to stakeholder interests. Now, as we enter a more fundamental and comprehensive assessment of the quality of stakeholder relationships, a thorough examination of policies, guidelines and procedures is necessary. The stakeholder audit team will need to be very familiar with every current, documented and informal custom and practice which governs the relationship with each stakeholder. The audit process will involve testing compliance with each and every formal prescription issued by the company, so it is imperative that there is a full understanding of these within the audit team.

Determination of audit scope

There are two main dimensions to take into account in defining the scope of an audit of the relationship with a social stakeholder:

- geographic
- numerical.

Should employees in every facility and plant in every country be included in this or subsequent cycles? How many different stakeholder types can be accommodated in this cycle: one, two or ten? Should secondary stakeholders be included? Our advice on both of these points is to start small and build up. There is no harm in being cautious at first. A large corporation may decide to experiment with a single part of the organization first, e.g. a factory, and embrace a number of direct social stakeholders in the first instance, e.g. employees, suppliers, customers and the local community. A smaller company may decide it can assess its entire operation but restrict itself in the first cycle just to employees.

The important thing is simply to start somewhere and see how it goes. But there should be an intention at the outset to broaden and deepen the scope with each cycle, and there must be a commitment to full disclosure of the results of each cycle at the outset.

Agreement of benchmarks and performance indicators

Different cultures and geographical regions will have varying beliefs about what constitutes best practice in individual stakeholder relationships. This is an issue which causes endless headaches to ethical investment organizations and socially responsible business associations. The fact is that in North America affirmative action and large donations to charity are viewed as touchstones of corporate responsibility to stakeholders. In Europe and Japan they are not. In Europe, health and safety at work and employee representation is a high priority. In the USA public consciousness of these issues is weaker. In Japan loyalty and job security for the workforce are prized. In the USA there is more acceptance of the "hire and fire" culture.

The only guidance which can be provided in selecting benchmarks and indicators is to spend some time networking and establishing measures of best practice appropriate for your relationships. This can be done as a research exercise, seeking advice from trade associations, academics, ethical investors, rating agencies and other sources of socially responsible business advice. Or it can be done in focus group discussions with representatives of your stakeholders: what quantitative measures of your performance do they see as critical to the relationship? Your employees are likely to suggest pay, benefits, equal opportunities or the amount of time and money invested in their career development. Your shareholders will undoubtedly stress growth in share value and dividends.

It is not essential that you put in place comprehensive benchmarks and performance indicators for every stakeholder group in the first cycle. Inevitably you will discover that your own management information systems are inadequate to deliver statistics on every one of your ideal performance indicators anyway. Again, the important thing is to start somewhere and build up over time, establishing a successively more useful and comprehensive set of indicators with each cycle.

In succeeding chapters of this book, benchmarks and performance indicators will be highlighted by the following symbol

Stakeholder consultation

On the basis that what cannot be measured cannot be managed, quantitative indicators are very important. But just as important are the less tangible measures of performance which affect the relationships. In human interactions, perceptions are reality. If someone feels aggrieved because of a misunderstanding, the quality of the relationship suffers and loyalty declines, regardless of the reality behind the misunderstanding. The only way that the perceptions of stakeholders can be measured is by asking them how they feel. This is the territory of focus groups and attitude surveys, and these are precisely the kind of technique which should be used.

In our experience, a two stage process works best. Focus groups of stakeholder representatives should be convened to identify issues of relevance in the relationship. Care must be exercised to ensure that there is no inhibition to the dialogue and no bias in the process. So focus groups of employees should not include their supervisors or managers. Suppliers' focus groups should not be conducted in the presence of purchasing officers, and so on.

Focus groups should be facilitated either by the stakeholder audit team (provided they can create a truly safe space for dialogue) or by an external agency. In either case, the audit verifiers will need to be present on occasion to witness fair play (see also the section on Verification below).

A focus group should contain 10 to 20 people who are truly representative of their stakeholder group. For large and important groups of stakeholders a number of focus groups should be convened. They should take place in comfortable and pleasant surroundings and with maximum informality. The facilitator should be trained and the process should not extend beyond one and a half hours. The format should include:

1   A welcome and thanks for attendance.

2   An explanation of the purpose of the group, i.e. to explore what is important in the relationship between them and the company.

3   Clear reassurance on the confidentiality of the process.

4   An indication of how the results of the focus group will inform the rest of the audit process, to include more detailed questionnaires and publication of results.

5   An open invitation to focus group members to contribute:

- how the company is doing against its stated purpose
- what they feel is important in the relationship
- what they like best about the relationship
- what they like least or what worries them most about the relationship.

6   An invitation to contribute to how the quality of the relationship might be measured i.e what performance indicators might be adopted.

If it helps, the discussion can be stimulated by providing participants with a list of potential positive and negative propositions which they can rank according to their own perceptions and experiences.

At the end of the focus group, individuals are thanked for their contribution and reassured again about confidentiality. Their views and concerns are captured and listed as issues for further exploration in the next stage: the stakeholder surveys.

Stakeholder surveys

Surveys of opinion are very common in consumer research and they are used quite extensively by companies to ascertain employee attitudes. So there is no magic in extending the practice to other stakeholders, and there is no shortage of professional advice to ensure that questionnaires are designed and results analyzed in such a way as to eliminate bias.

There are organizations specializing in employee surveys that produce reasonably standard questionnaires and are able to generate comparisons between companies and even across nationalities[2]. This allows some degree of benchmarking and can provide a comparative health check on key questions. In our view this is interesting but of secondary importance because internal and external cultural influences are so diverse. The most important things to test in any stakeholder questionnaire are:

1 Is the company perceived to be delivering on its primary purpose (as described in its mission, policies and other public documents)?

2 Is the company perceived to be delivering on those issues considered most salient to individual stakeholders?

The most important comparisons are those between surveys: are the trends in percentage responses positive or negative from one cycle to the next?

Questionnaires are best administered by a third party: a market research organization or an academic institution skilled in social surveys and attitude studies[2,3]. For most stakeholder groups, a sufficiently large number of individuals in each group should be telephoned or direct mailed with prepaid reply envelopes to ensure that a statistically significant number of responses may be analyzed. Depending on stakeholder group, variations on this theme may be adopted. For example, local community responses may be captured by street interviews conducted by trained researchers. This will limit the number of questions which can be tested, but may prove more effective in ensuring a representative sample. For employees, a period should be provided within working time to complete the questionnaire in order to maximize response rate. In postal surveys response rates may be expected to vary, but do not be distressed if for certain groups it drops to well below 30 percent. Allowance should be made for this if numbers are not to fall short of statistically reliable totals.

Whatever method is chosen for questionnaire completion, it is essential that those completing it are reassured of confidentiality and anonymity: that the third party analyzing the results will not pass on information which will identify any respondent and their opinions. This point can be made in a covering letter attached to the questionnaire on behalf of the third party organization responsible for the analysis. It can also be repeated at the start of the questionnaire.

Self-completed questionnaires should be returned direct to the organization doing the analysis in sealed, prepaid envelopes. Similarly, questionnaires completed face to face in the street should be sealed and returned direct to the analyzing organization. Under no circumstances should any respondent fear that their responses will be read directly by the company.

In special cases it may not be possible to organize a questionnaire survey. For example, suppliers in foreign countries for whom English is not a first language, or business partners where numbers are so low as not to be able to provide a statistically reliable sample. In these cases it may be more appropriate to commission an independent interviewer who can visit the stakeholders personally, conduct structured interviews and then deliver a written commentary which avoids identifying the opinions of individuals while nevertheless conveying the important messages.

The internal audit

When benchmark and performance indicator data have been collected, questionnaires analyzed and results collated, then it is important to establish the integrity of the information and begin to explore more directly how well individual parts of the organization are equipped to handle their stakeholder relationships.

The best mechanism for this is the structured private interview with key staff in each department with direct responsibility for a stakeholder group. Internal audits are cross-sectional in nature and need to be handled with care. Departmental managers need to be involved in the process and convinced that it is a good idea for the audit team to come into their area and interview a number of staff to establish how well stakeholder interests are being handled. The one-on-one interviews will be confidential but some (including supervisors and managers) may find it threatening. So internal auditors need to be trained in diplomacy, tactful inquiry and careful presentation of their information needs.

Structured interviews for internal auditing purposes should cover at least the following categories of knowledge and competence with respect to the stakeholder relationships:

- management commitment
- compliance with company policies and goals
- clarity of roles and responsibilities
- effectiveness of communication
- adequacy of resources
- routine control procedures
- efficiency of emergency procedures
- robustness of documentation and data
- impact of training
- effectiveness of performance evaluation.

The results of interviews, together with any inspections of documentation and data, allow the audit team to build up a dynamic picture of the company's management system and compare this with the feedback coming in from the stakeholders. There is then an opportunity to identify positive findings for celebration and replication and any inefficiencies or misunderstandings in relationships so that appropriate recommendations can be made to management. We have found it essential in internal audits to ensure that internal recommendation reports remain confidential, i.e only disseminated within the relevant part of the organization. If this is not done, interviewees will be reluctant to speak their mind about the management of their own department. This is not a compromise on transparency, because overall performance against agreed quantitative indicators as well as perceptions of performance as judged by the stakeholders will be fully disclosed. Also, the reports will be made available to the external verifiers of the process. But there is little value in publishing a report listing good points and weaknesses of internal management systems which would mean almost nothing to an external audience: they are more interested in the performance of those systems.

Preparation of accounts

When the audit team has satisfied itself of the integrity of performance data and has a full picture of both internal management effectiveness and stakeholder perceptions it is possible to prepare the "account" of each relationship prior to independent verification.

A logical way to set out the accounts is to take a stakeholder by stakeholder approach following a common format:

1 The basis for the company's approach and aims for each group (with reference to relevant policies, etc.).
2 The methodology used for each consultation process (i.e. what combination of focus groups, surveys and discussions were used to capture stakeholder perceptions).
3 The results of stakeholder consultation with perception surveys described in as even-handed and neutral a way as possible so as to avoid premature interpretation, together with direct quotations from stakeholders, selected in an independent fashion.
4 Quantitative and qualitative indicators of performance where these exist.
5 A company response in the form of a quote from a main board member or senior executive setting out their reaction to the stake-

holder views and noting where progress is already being made and/or where improvements are clearly required.

Setting out the accounts in this way helps promote the dialogue process which is to follow and allows stakeholders who need the published accounts to take a view on the adequacy or otherwise of the company's response.

Agreement of strategic and local objectives

Naturally, it is not for the audit team or each stakeholder group to dictate the nature of the company response or the deadlines which it will impose for the execution of any improvements. This must be a matter for the company management taking into account any business constraints, and indeed the demands of other stakeholder groups. Shareholders cannot be given massive increases in dividends, however much they may want them, if this denies employees an annual pay rise. Customers cannot be given extended credit if this might lead to a cash flow crisis and the demise of the entire organization.

Moreover, in order to secure ownership of the process and its follow-up, it is essential that local managements, i.e. those responsible for individual stakeholder relations, commit to what they believe to be reasonable and achievable in the circumstances. An objective or target which is imposed from elsewhere is unlikely to be executed with enthusiasm or efficiency.

We have found that the best way to set local or stakeholder-specific objectives is for the audit team to engage senior managers in a dialogue and encourage them to come up with a reaction and some draft commitments, imagining themselves speaking on behalf of the entire organization. If they miss anything obvious, the audit team can point this out, and the senior managers may choose to accommodate this advice. Then, armed with a robust draft, the director or executive ultimately responsible can be asked to sign off on the commitments which the senior managers have worked up, together with any resource implications that may be involved.

Strategic company-wide objectives for stakeholder relations are more complex to arrive at. The process may start with the draft accounts, complete with all stakeholder-specific, local objectives being considered and agreed by the executive leadership of the company. They can then recommend any corporate objectives which seem to span stakeholder interests. Recommendations might include modifications to company structure, commitment of new resources to cross-company management systems, e.g. on quality or safety, alteration of company policies or the setting of more visionary objectives than departmental managements felt capable of delivering because of resource or policy constraints.

Strategic commitments of this nature being made by an executive group would normally require formal endorsement by a main board which includes nonexecutive representation. This way the future of stakeholder relationships may be kept consistent with strategic business goals and direction.

Objective setting must not be rushed. It is a sensitive and complex process which must allow adequate time for discussion, buy-in and genuine commitment to change. Carefully handled it can lead to large increases in motivation levels and consequent contribution to improvements in stakeholder relations.

Verification

Unlike verification or external auditing of financial or environmental accounts, where the process can be left towards the end of a reporting cycle, social stakeholder audit verification requires some engagement throughout the cycle. The main reason for this is that when verifying a process aimed at an audit of human relations, it is not enough simply to examine documentation, conduct interviews with key players and test the accuracy of data. The entire process of collecting views from stakeholders has to be witnessed as fair and open.

So social stakeholder verification has to engage in several elements of the cycle. Most importantly, the verifier should be involved in discussions around audit scope so that it can be demonstrated that key stakeholders have not been omitted through design, or if they have been omitted in the current cycle, how they will be dealt with in the future. It is also important that the verifier is satisfied that best endeavors have been exercised to agree, record and report on the most relevant performance indicators. The verifier should also satisfy themselves that focus groups and questionnaire research has been conducted in an unbiased and professional manner.

As with any external consultant, selection of a verifier of social stakeholder relationships is a delicate business. There are relatively few organizations with an established track record in this area, although through bodies like the Institute for Social and Ethical AccountAbility the number is increasing. The social stakeholder verifier will be getting very close to the heart and soul of your organization, so they need to have the highest standards of integrity and discretion: able to convey messages to senior management and to the outside world in a straightforward and fair manner at all times, pulling no punches, but avoiding gossip and post-commission mischief-making. Our advice for verifier selection is to use someone who comes with a recommendation as having done one before or who clearly and fully reflects an understanding of the state of the art and guarantees the right level of professional competence and integrity.

There is another interesting twist to social stakeholder verification which does not occur in financial and environmental auditing. Because the verifier has to engage in each part of the cycle, rather than just at the end, there is a danger, however slight, that they become a little compromised: too involved to be 100 percent objective. So it is necessary for the verifier to engage an advisory group or "verification panel" to review both the process and the draft accounts, and to probe and test the information presented for completeness and accuracy.

Verification panel members should reflect all of the various stakeholder interests included in the accounts. This is where the nongovernmental and pressure group sector can really help. While it may not necessarily be very easy to mobilize a representative individual consumer, it is certainly possible to invite a consumer advocacy group to join the panel and reflect the entire agenda of consumer rights. The general interests of workers can be reflected by a trade union or a professional organization in the human resources field. Ultimately, it is up to the verifier to appoint the panel to add the right degree of quality assurance. The company should agree the list but not control it, because the panel is there as much to provide the verifier with peer review as to check the accounts.

Once the panel has met a couple of times to review both processes and outputs, and they have had a chance to quiz everyone involved, the verifier is in a position to sign off on their part of the process. This should be done through addition of a verifier's statement to the stakeholder accounts. This statement should include commentary on the scope and constraints of the process and accounts, including notes of omissions and qualifications. Most importantly it should attest to the fact that the accounts are "true and fair" within the scope and constraints outlined. Reference should be made to the advisory role of the verification panel but responsibility for the verification statement must rest with the verifier, based on their professional reputation.

Publication of social statement

This is where the real fun starts. With a complete social statement based on independently verified assessments of social stakeholder relationships the challenge now is to communicate that information. Different stakeholders have different capacities and interest levels for absorbing information, so our advice is to use as many different vehicles as you need to convey what has been done and why. The dimension which is common and most important to all stakeholders and which you must not fail to communicate is your commitment to improvement. This is easier said than done. The strategy we advocate is to produce a comprehensive document detailing every statistic and measurement relating to stakeholder relationships, but not to rely on it. By all means send the full social statement to key opinion formers, public and college libraries, etc., and post it on the Internet. But also produce stakeholder-specific summary communications, e.g. broadsheets and leaflets for employees and customers; insert summaries of shareholder information into annual reports and accounts. Make it clear where stakeholders can get access to the comprehensive material if they want it, but do not destroy a forest in disseminating the unabridged version.

A decision has to be taken on how social statements should be positioned and timed regarding publication of annual reports and accounts, environmental statements, etc. So we will not go into more detail on publications and communications for social stakeholders here. We will save that for Chapter 23 where we describe a comprehensive strategy for social and non-social stakeholder reporting.

Dialogue

Armed with the right communication tools and support material, you now need to find out from your social stakeholders what they think of the process and whether they are convinced of your intentions to improve the quality of the relationship. This can be done in several ways:

- feedback forms attached to written communications
- focus groups
- workshops at stakeholder meetings (e.g. for shareholders at annual general meetings).

The questions which need to be posed, answered and recorded are:

- Do the stakeholders appreciate the process of auditing and reporting so far?
- What do they think of the information presented and does it ring true for them?

■ What do they think of the commitments made by the company to improve performance in the future?

This information should be captured and built into feedback loops for those executives and departments with direct responsibility for each stakeholder relationship.

Then take a deep breath, because the cycle starts all over again.

Postscript

In succeeding chapters we shall use two principal models for describing processes aimed at improving stakeholder inclusion and the overall performance of the company.

> **Cycles of inclusion** refer to processes of diagnosis, dialogue and audit aimed at securing the effective participation and active inclusion of stakeholders in the affairs of the company.
>
> **Cycles of continuous improvement** refer to more technical processes where diagnosis tends to be factually based. In this book these include processes for the optimal management of occupational safety and health, quality, environmental protection and animal welfare.

Naturally there are overlaps between cycles of inclusion and continuous improvement. So where appropriate we have twinned them for relevant stakeholder groups: i.e. occupational safety and health with employees and managers and quality with customers. Some companies elect to run the cycles of continuous improvement as combined systems, e.g. Total Quality Environmental Management or Health, Safety and Environmental Management.

For detailed case studies of companies which have embraced auditing and reporting of stakeholder relationships, the reader is referred to the work of Simon Zadek and colleagues: *Building Corporate Accountability*[3].

Before we move on to a stakeholder by stakeholder analysis of issues and priorities, Exhibit 13.1 presents seven key dos and don'ts for assessing the quality of relationships with social stakeholders.

EXHIBIT 13.1

Seven dos and don'ts of social stakeholder auditing and disclosure

Do start with quality or environmental auditing and disclosure if these are relevant to your organization. These audits are simpler to organize and conduct than social audits.

Do consider joining the Institute for Social and Ethical Accountability – an important source of independent advice and experience.

Do involve departments, managers and staff at every level, especially in deciding the scope for the audit. Key departments are those that have most to do with stakeholder groups, e.g. human resources, communications/PR, investor relations, etc.

Do set up an internal audit system or department and have them report to a main board director or senior executive.

Do exercise real care in selecting an independent verifier; they will have access to the very soul of the organization and their integrity is paramount. Always network to find verifiers with experience who are recommended by others.

Do allow plenty of time for drafting and finalizing the public statements of performance on stakeholder issues. Audited departments will be very keen to be involved in putting results in context and proposing priorities for improvement.

Do report: formally and informally, publicly and internally. Stakeholder understanding is crucial to progress, as are targets and objectives for the future.

Don't launch into a social audit without talking to someone who has done one. It is a long term commitment, so plan ahead at least two audit cycles.

Don't forget the importance of training for social auditing: for managers and auditors. In its current form it is a new science and the principles and pitfalls need to be understood.

Don't forget to focus on the benefits and business case for social performance measurement and disclosure for all stakeholders. Good stakeholder auditing should make an organization more responsive and efficient.

Don't omit to publicize the role of the audit team and its purpose; people may feel more threatened by a social performance audit than by an environmental audit.

Don't forget that you may also need other sources of expert advice, e.g. survey design and analysis.

Don't allow one stakeholder voice to outweigh others. Take into account minority views but don't let them take over; a good external verifier will act as wise counsel on the right balance to be struck.

Don't be afraid of including both good and bad aspects of social performance; better that you draw attention to any faults than your critics do.

CHAPTER 14

Cycle of inclusion

shareholders and investors

A global trend towards accountability

In 1992, consultants Oxford Analytica produced a report on trends in corporate governance in G7 countries for a group of US and UK firms concerned with investment and accounting standards[1]. Their report predicted a convergence between the "polar extremes" of governance in Japan and the USA, with a trend towards greater accountability, broader representation of stakeholder interests and enhanced roles for boards in strategy. They also noted that in a globalizing marketplace boards would have increasingly to demonstrate professionalism, ethical standards and familiarity with international markets. New forms of representation will be needed to reflect the pressures exerted by institutional investors, employees, local communities and environmentalists. "The direction of change in all countries," they concluded, "will be towards more accountability, even at the expense of managerial authority."

In this chapter and those succeeding that deal with specific stakeholders, we will describe both the process for shareholder and investor inclusion and two sets of measurements which will be crucial to how stakeholders will judge your social performance:

- Benchmarks and performance indicators (both qualitative and quantitative) denoted by the symbol
- Perception indicators.

The process

The process for ensuring shareholder and investor participation is that described in the generalized cycle of inclusion for social stakeholders (Chapter 13, pp. 168–80).

Figure 14.1
Cycle of inclusion for shareholders and investors

We will be giving you guidance on the kind of issues which it may be unwise to omit from your social accounting system and public statements of social performance (see Figure 14.1). Particularly on your first cycle, stakeholders should be sufficiently impressed by the exercise itself not to mind the odd omission from the list of ideal benchmark indicators. Nevertheless, you would need to explain why these omissions occurred, e.g. because of inadequacies in management information systems. And you would need to explain how you might present such information in the future. Also, as we discussed in Chapter 13, it is helpful to use focus groups to establish priorities both for benchmarks and other indicators. So the measurements set out in this chapter should not be taken as prescriptions – more as a starting point for discussion.

The benchmarks and performance indicators

In the USA it has long been considered good practice to separate executive and strategic decision-making and to rely on nonexecutive oversight of more strategic issues such as auditing and remuneration. In Britain, concerns over corporate governance have led to the publication of two landmark reports: the Cadbury Report on financial aspects of corporate governance and The Greenbury Report on directors' remuneration (see Case Studies 14.1 and 14.2).

CASE STUDY 14.1

The Cadbury Code: plenty to chew on, no soft centers

Published on 1 December 1992, the Cadbury Report on financial aspects of corporate governance followed in the wake of a series of spectacular corporate scandals in the UK: BCCI, Guinness, Maxwell, Polly Peck. The main prescription of Sir Adrian Cadbury and his committee took the form of a code of practice which could be used by any stakeholder to assess compliance with good governance. The principles underlying the code were made explicit:

The principles on which the Code is based are those of openness, integrity and accountability. They go together. Openness on the part of companies, within the limits set by their competitive position, is the basis for the confidence which needs to exist between business and all those who have a stake in its success. An open approach to the disclosure of information contributes to the efficient working of the market economy, prompts boards to take effective action and allows shareholders and others to scrutinize companies more thoroughly.

CASE STUDY 14.2

Executive pay – a necessary reform

In a series of interviews with 16 of the UK's leading companies in 1995, management accountants Coopers & Lybrand found somewhat grudging acceptance of the thrust of the Greenbury Committee report on executive pay. Some believed it to be too prescriptive on issues like remuneration and too much the product of "fat cat" scandals in the new privatized utilities. But with only one exception, the companies had all established remuneration committees comprising solely nonexecutive directors. There was some discomfort over allowing remuneration committees to establish a degree of autonomy, accounting directly to shareholders but several had already taken the step of including a report from the Remuneration Committee chairman in annual reports and accounts.

The practical implications of both of these reports have been summarized in a handbook[2]. The Cadbury and Greenbury Reports deal with rather narrowly defined aspects of governance. They are nonetheless helpful in setting out important basic principles for companies wishing to demonstrate proper levels of accountability to investors. Together with the requirements of the London Stock Exchange and the US Securities and Exchange Commission, these two reports provide up-to-date justification for many of the benchmarks which we would advocate for companies operating in English-speaking countries. To accommodate the different structures and best practice expectations of companies in continental Europe and the Far East, we shall also add a few benchmarks with more universal relevance.

It is important to recognize that some of the recommendations of Cadbury and Greenbury may be unwieldy and inappropriate for smaller companies, imposing burdens which add little to the principles of integrity and transparency which are most important from a stakeholder perspective. It should also be noted that superficial adoption of recommendations is not enough. For example, the mere appointment of nonexecutive directors provides no guarantees against fraud and incompetence, as the Maxwell case proved. To be effective, principles of good boardroom and executive governance must be deep rooted and subject to clear rules, procedures, audits and disclosure mechanisms.

As discussed in Chapter 12, there are compelling reasons to establish a clear separation of powers and accountabilities between ownership (board) and executive tiers. We also drew attention to the advantages of having supervisory, consultative or advisory councils comprising representatives of key stakeholders on the German model. Regardless of structure and how well it reflects the interests of other stakeholders, the most important benchmarks for shareholders and owners are likely to be similar.

Mission and policies

- Should be clear and freely available and include an executive remuneration policy linked to performance.

Structural and individual power

- Should be transparent and documented, i.e. no kitchen cabinetry.

- Should be balanced, e.g. in large companies chairman role separated from chief executive role. ✓

Boards, councils, committees and subcommittees

- ■ Should have written terms of reference (especially vital for remuneration and audit committees). ☑

- ■ Should all have formal agendas, minutes and clear lines of reporting. ☑

- ■ Should meet regularly and predictably. ☑

Directors and executives

- ■ Should have written selection procedures and formal training and induction programs (see Case Study 14.3). ☑

CASE STUDY 14.3

Ignorance is bliss

In a survey of board directors published by the UK Industrial Society in 1996, 21 percent of respondents admitted that new directors received no induction whatsoever. Just under half said it was the responsibility of the chief executive and just under one in five said it was up the chairman. Only 10 percent said that written guidance on the strategic nature of the board would be provided before appointment.

- ■ Should not decide their own remuneration. ☑
- ■ Should have clear job descriptions: especially essential for the chairman, chief executive and company secretary. ☑

Nonexecutive directors

- ■ Should have written selection procedures and formal training and induction programs. ☑

- ■ Should not be nominated and appointed solely by the chairman or chief executive. ☑

- ■ Should have fixed terms of office. ☑

Financial auditing

- ■ Should be quality assured by a subcommittee of the board, chaired and dominated by nonexecutive directors; executives may attend for information purposes (see Case Study 14.4). ☑

CASE STUDY 14.4

Audit committees after Cadbury

Guinness plc has had its share of controversy over executive ethics. But in its 1994 financial statement Guinness made its position on the independence and authority of its audit committee crystal clear:

> The Audit Committee comprises four non-executive Directors. The Chairman and Finance Director normally attend the meetings but the Committee also meets the external auditors without management present. The Committee operates under written terms of reference and its duties include the detailed review of financial statements prior to their recommendation to the Board for approval. The Group Internal Audit function formally reports to the Audit Committee which approves its plans in advance and reviews the conclusions of its work. Lessons learned are disseminated within the Group as appropriate. Audit plans are drawn up based on an assessment of the control risks in each operating unit and their materiality in a Group context. The Audit Committee has reviewed the system of internal controls and has reported to the Directors on the results of this review. Accordingly, the Directors are satisfied that the Group continues to have an effective system of internal controls.

- Should meet the most rigorous standards of probity in line with national laws and codes of professional accountancy.

Remuneration

- Should be determined by a subcommittee of the board, chaired and dominated by nonexecutive directors (independent expert advice can be commissioned).

- Should be absolutely transparent and described in detail in annual reports and accounts to include separate descriptions of basic salaries, bonuses, pension arrangements, benefits, share options and long term incentives (see Case Study 14.5).

CASE STUDY 14.5

Remuneration policy after Greenbury

In its 1995 Annual Report, retailer W H Smith welcomed the Greenbury Report and set out a very clear policy on executive remuneration:

> It is an objective of the W H Smith Group that it should attract and retain executives of high calibre and that they should be rewarded in a way which encourages the creation of value for shareholders. The remuneration of executive directors and the Chairman is determined by the Remuneration Committee of the Board, the members of which are all non-executive directors.

For executive directors and senior executives the three main elements in their remuneration package are a basic annual salary, an annual performance related bonus and long-term incentives in the form of share options and share awards. The intention is to ensure that the basic remuneration is at the mid-market rate for comparable jobs and that each year the achievement of clearly defined objectives will, through the bonus scheme, provide the opportunity to receive remuneration in the upper quartile for that year only. The executive directors and senior executives also receive health insurance and car benefits.

Reporting and communicating with investors

■ Annual reports and accounts must be credible, meeting the most rigorous standards of financial disclosure while providing sufficient commentary and real explanation to enable full understanding of the financial and nonfinancial health of the company (Management Discussion and Analysis in the USA, Operating and Financial Review in the UK).

■ Should include systems for periodic updates for individual and institutional investors on both financial and nonfinancial indicators of performance.

Quantitative performance indicators

■ Share price movement during current cycle.

■ Dividends during current cycles.

■ Spread of ownership (employees, individuals, institutions, etc.).

Perception indicators

As we described in Chapter 13, in human relationships perceptions are reality. That is why focus groups and surveys of opinion are so important if the quality of the relationships is to be properly tracked and, hopefully, improved (see Case Studies 14.6 and 14.7). See Chapter 13 for general advice on conducting focus groups and questionnaire design.

CASE STUDY 14.6

Something stirring in the state of Denmark

Danish regional bank Sparekassen Nordjylland (Sbn) has published "Ethical Accounting Statements" since 1990. They are based largely on telephone surveys of stakeholder opinion which feed into stakeholder "dialogue circles" and the management planning process. In 1993 shareholders were asked to comment on 21 propositions covering five main areas of interest to investors: Confidence and Trust; Communication; Financial Results; Quality and Competence; Commitment to the Community. Of respondents to the 1993 survey 81 percent either strongly agreed or slightly agreed that "Sbn bank enjoys the trust of the local community." But only 45 percent agreed with the proposition: "You are convinced that your shares in Sbn will yield satisfactory dividends in the long run." Some 96 percent agreed "You get friendly service" and 88 percent agreed "Your branch of Sbn stands for quality."

CASE STUDY 14.7

Shareholders of The Body Shop have their say

The Body Shop's first Social Statement was published in January 1996 as part of the Values Report – a four-volume document dealing with all aspects of the company's social, environmental and animal welfare commitments. Of shareholders surveyed, 371 returned questionnaires which covered a total of 28 aspects of The Body Shop's relationships with its institutional and individual investors. The company's share price has long been a roller coaster ride. Of shareholders responding, 90 percent either agreed or strongly agreed that "The Body Shop takes active steps to make its business more environmentally responsible" and 78 percent were satisfied with the information they received on the company's financial performance. But 29 percent either disagreed or strongly disagreed that "the company enjoys the trust of the financial community" and one third either had no opinion or disagreed that The Body Shop had a clear long-term business strategy. Ouch.

CHAPTER 15

Cycle of inclusion

employees and managers

Rebuilding the social and psychological contract

There is clear evidence from the USA that companies "built to last" do so because of a very strong focus on people and their ability to learn and exchange knowledge[1]. The 18 companies with 100-year track records examined by James Collins and Jerry Porras also outperformed the stock markets by a factor of 70. In stark contrast a Skills Audit published by the British Government in June 1996 showed Britain failing to keep pace with the USA, France, Germany and even Singapore on training and education. It should not escape anyone's attention that Britain's future competitive position is already being undermined by its skills deficit. Between 1979 and 1996, Britain slipped from thirteenth to eighteenth in the world league table of gross domestic product per head of population.

Japanese electronics magnate Konosuke Matsushita famously challenged the traditionalist model of western industrial capitalism[2] when he said:

> We are going to win and the industrial West is going to lose out; there's not much you can do about it because the reasons for your failure are within yourselves. Your firms are built on the Taylor model, and even worse, so are your heads. With your bosses doing the thinking while the workers wield screwdrivers, you're convinced deep down that this is the right way to run a business. For you the essence of management is getting ideas out of the heads of the managers and into the hands of labor. We have gone beyond the Taylor model. We realise that business has become so complex, the survival of firms so precarious, and our environment increasingly unpredictable, competitive and dangerous, that firms' continuing existence depends on their day to day mobilisation of every ounce of intelligence.

It is world views like this which underpin the increasingly urgent exhortations of management gurus to create learning and high performing organizations[3,4,5,6].

So as we described in Part 2, a new, more open style of working has emerged in many successful modern corporations. In summary it means less reliance on the male-dominated command and control model; less conformity; less bureaucracy; and certainly less hierarchy. Instead, as companies like Motorola, Microsoft and 3M have demonstrated, a vibrant, inclusive, team-based culture can be instilled which is far more conducive both to innovation and to commercial success[2]. This is especially true in knowledge-based industries where rapid sharing of ideas throughout the corporation is the most important source of competitive advantage.

In high technology endeavors, e.g. information technology, pharmaceuticals, auto-engineering, electronics, it is the organization which learns most rapidly – from evolving customer needs, from technological advances, from competitors – which succeeds. To learn fast, spread knowledge, innovate and reduce new product lead times requires a corporate "social architecture" that promotes rapid lateral communication, team-based working and an agreed set of values and behaviors which align individual aspirations to collective goals.

Another prescription from the East which reinforces the apparent attraction of less hierarchical and more participative forms of management is total quality management. American academics, most notably W. Edwards Deming, helped inspire an approach to product quality which took rapid and firm hold of Japanese industrial systems. The paternalistic, worker-inclusive and quasi-egalitarian nature of Japanese corporations was a perfect cultural match for notions of continuous improvement, quality circles, team-based problem solving, customer focus and just-in-time supply chain management. We will return to quality management in Chapter 18.

So if we accept that for many industries, business success will increasingly depend on knowledge and quality; and if we believe that both are best delivered by a more participative form of management; if we believe that the interests of management and employees must be aligned at corporate and individual levels in order best to deliver what customers and other stakeholders need, what are the special characteristics we should seek to discover and reinforce, and what are the constraints and barriers? We will start with the bad news.

Constraints and barriers

In Chapter 3 we explored some of the global economic realities facing business today. In a burst of realism in Chapter 7, we suggested that it is not a simple fix to engender the idealized energetic, creative and participative spirit in modern companies. This is especially relevant in an industry or company facing a collapse of sales because of cutthroat competition. We also argued in Chapter 6 that shareholder value is still a noose around the necks of many corporate leaderships in English-speaking countries. As we have seen, it can lead to short termism, autocratic managerial styles and lack of job security throughout the business. This is made much worse because of the shattering of psychological contracts caused by downsizing, delayering, outsourcing, etc. This in turn leads to organizational pathologies like long working hours and a general lowering of quality of life and spiritual contentment.[7] These phenomena are real and cannot be wished away.

Then there is the myth factor. Just because a total absence of hierarchy and job roles appears to work for Ricardo Semler's company (Semco) in Brazil, it does not mean it is the perfect organizational style for your firm. There are not many successful international companies with a total absence of structure, human resource procedures or job descriptions. Just because organizational fluidity and rapid knowledge transfer are vital for some companies (particularly those in high technology industries) it does not mean that clear roles and responsibilities and some degree of organizational structure is not helpful. No one would describe high performing Japanese and German companies as totally lacking in order or hierarchy. Just because creativity, rule breaking and innovation are often linked, it does not mean that companies need to abolish all formal rules and procedures. Safe and healthy working environments are characterized by shared vision and clarity of responsibilities, not by anarchy and indiscipline.

As we concluded in our parable of The Inclusive Magazine Company in Chapter 11, the real key to organizational effectiveness is integration of the science, art and spirit of management. It is not the replacement of one dogma by another. Each organization has to decide how it needs to respond to the external economic and knowledge environment if it wishes to achieve the optimum balance in its relationships with all stakeholders. Each organization has to decide for itself the right mix of social architecture, including structure, systems and style, in each case striking the right balance between flexibility and formality.

The process

In seeking the optimal outcome for the particular stakeholder group which is the subject of this chapter, the employees and managers, we will assume that the reader is not a management theory dogmatist, but a pragmatist. You will be aware of the danger of faddism but will be impressed by the empirical evidence from successful, employee empowering and high performing organizations both in the East and in the English-speaking world (see Case Study 15.1). Clearly, there is something to be said for addressing and improving certain aspects of traditional manager-worker relations.

CASE STUDY 15.1

Power to the people

In a survey of 580 UK businesses in 1994, the Industrial Society found that on almost every criterion empowering employees to take more control of their working lives led to expectations being exceeded. Better customer service, faster innovation and reaction to change, increases in productivity and increased competitiveness were all cited by companies as reasons for introducing empowerment programmes. In each case the number of firms witnessing these benefits exceeded the number citing them as original objectives. The Industrial Society experts concluded:

> It is becoming a competitive disadvantage not to be moving significantly towards empowerment, although there will always be organizations that manage to survive with the "command and control" approach. But you can only empower people when everyone shares a very strong vision of what the organization needs to be like. That usually means you have to be explicit about the organization's values.

As we stressed in Part 2, Michael Porter was right when he emphasized the importance of the external environment in formulating competitive strategy[8]. We simply argue that systematically understanding and including all stakeholder requirements (especially customers and employees) is the most effective way to process this.

Assuming you already have your corporate strategy in place and the core competitive competencies agreed, what are the key characteristics of participative, highly motivated employees and managers you should be looking for? What are the trends to be observed? In Table 15.1 we set out some pointers. We do not argue that the left-hand column is all wrong or that the right-hand column represents best practice or some kind of organizational nirvana. Our anti-dogmatism would not permit such simplistic analysis. We merely note the typical direction of high performance, employee inclusive enterprises.

Table 15.1
Trends to be observed

Employer directed companies	Usual —>— trend	Employee inclusive companies
Organizational goals emerge from leadership	—>—	Organizational goals are articulated through language of shared values and vision
Authority derives from position	—>—	Authority derives from behavior and intellect
Influence increases with seniority	—>—	Influence increases with knowledge
Organizational structure dictates work relationships	—>—	Organizational structure liberates and encourages team working
Work systems linear and technical	—>—	Work systems cyclical and organic
Style formal or uniform	—>—	Style informal or diverse
Responsibility devolved vertically	—>—	Responsibility shared laterally
Corporate objectives agreed by leadership and cascaded	—>—	Corporate, team and individual objectives aligned through dialogue

Each company and each industry needs to decide where it feels most comfortable with respect to each of these characteristics. It is perfectly possible to remain well to the left in certain respects and still maintain a highly participative and innovative culture. For example, in many Japanese companies authority often derives from position, and style and may be very formal, even uniform. This does not prevent the other characteristics compensating to generate effective worker inclusive environments.

The good news is that much of the above analysis is not new. Neither is it rocket science. As Tom Cannon has argued[2], despite the myth-making and the faddism there has been a good deal of consistency in management commentary from Frederick Winslow Taylor through Peter Drucker to Tom Peters today. But what is new, what has changed, and what needs to be held in clear view are the twin impacts of the knowledge explosion and economic globalization. These are the factors which will continue to drive up uncertainty and insecurity and will require both managers and employees to develop new attitudes and behaviors. These new ways of working do not just need to cope with the challenges and paradoxes, they need positively to embrace them. This will not be possible for everyone. Not every manager can be a leader or mentor and not every employee wants to be an energized participant.

The process we would advocate for systematizing optimal employee inclusion in determining the behaviours, ethics and culture of an organization is that of the cycle of inclusion for stakeholders described in Chapter 13 (pp. 168–80).

Figure 15.1
Cycle of inclusion for employees and managers

In following sections we deal with practical characteristics and benchmark performance indicators which can be measured in four key areas of management–worker relations (see Figure 15.1). They serve as indicators of progress towards more participative, inclusive and effective ways of working. We do not pretend that they are anything other than indicators. This chapter does not attempt to deal with methodologies for organizational development, the creation of learning organizations, high performance organizations or any other idealized form of organization. Important though these concepts are, they are outside the scope of this book.

Benchmarks and performance indicators

Roles, rights and responsibilities

In Chapter 12 we suggested that the following policies are of key importance for the administration of human resources:

■ A general human resources policy covering remuneration, career development, grievance, diversity, representation, etc.

■ A code of ethics for individual rights and responsibilities (including the balance between confidentiality and rights to complain).

■ An occupational safety and health policy.

It is no exaggeration to say that it is essential for every organization that basic frameworks and policies are in place to ensure consistency of approach to management–employee relations. Depending on the jurisdiction, some of this is driven by legal requirements, e.g. occupational safety and health and equality of opportunity. Sometimes it is simply good practice. But above all, it is vital to have clarity and consistency. The organization and the people within it need to know where they stand on basic rights and responsibilities whether it is sexual harassment or career development, representation or rewards.

We do not buy the argument that a *laissez-faire* attitude to policy is acceptable, because informal cultural norms and peer pressure are more important determinants of human behavior. Indeed they are, but formal policy is also vital. That is not to say that every single element of manager–employee relations should be prescribed in some compendium of rules and procedures. But a basic, written template is important, and training should be provided to everyone in the organization so that the codified cultural norms are fully understood. Beyond the formal generic policies, guidance should be available, e.g. in manuals and from service departments, and within the spirit of the organization, discretion and diversity should be encouraged. But a total absence of rules is both irresponsible and (potentially) illegal.

If workplace policies and codes are developed in the right way, with maximum consultation and engagement of all employees through focus groups and inclusive updating processes, they will be respected and honored in the spirit as well as the letter of the law.

Finally, it may be worthwhile noting that the UN Universal Declaration of Human Rights (1948) includes a number of basic employee rights which we would strongly encourage any aspiring stakeholder corporation to embrace within its human resource policies. In addition, the International Covenant on Economic, Social and Cultural Rights (1966) recognizes the right to work, free choice of employment, fair wages, and to form and join trade unions. So our checklist of good practice benchmarks in general human resources policy and systems includes:

■ The right to freedom of association. ☑

■ The right to freedom of opinion and expression. ☑

■ The right of representation. ☑

■ The right to a safe and healthy working environment. ☑

■ The right to equality of opportunity and freedom from discrimination. ☑

■ The right to equal pay for equal work. ☑

■ The right to basic skills training. ☑

■ Protection against unemployment. ☑

■ The right to information relevant to the job/company policies. ☑

■ The opportunity for personal learning and career development. ☑

■ Performance appraisal systems which are genuinely two-way and enhance dialogue, motivation and empowerment (see Case Study 15.2). ☑

■ Documented and transparent reward and remuneration systems. ☑

■ Documented benefits, entitlements and pensions, and leave arrangements. ☑

■ Documented and fair grievance and disciplinary procedures. ☑

CASE STUDY 15.2

Measuring human capital

Several years ago, Swedish insurance company Skandia realized that its conventional balance sheet was pretty well redundant when it came to measuring the real value of its business. As a knowledge-based organization Skandia recognized that the most important measures were nothing to do with physical assets – the true value of the group was locked up in its hidden assets of "intellectual capital." Since 1994 Skandia has produced indices of "empowerment" and "training expense per employee" for its employees linking them to more conventional business measures such as customer satisfaction, income and sales. President and CEO Björn Wolrath says "Within Skandia, processes that create value for customers, shareholders and the staff are carried out on a daily basis. Many of these are of an imaginary character – that is they are invisible. Nevertheless, they are innovative and they create value."

Telecommunications giant AT & T also tries to embrace alternative measures of value. The company captures management performance on three levels: economic value added (EVA), customer value added (CVA) and people value added (PVA). In the latter case the measure is based on their ability to manage and develop their direct reports.

Rewards, pay and benefits

Historically, the fairness of a company's approach to pay and benefits was the key determinant of the health or otherwise of its industrial relations. In unionized workplaces in the English-speaking world, the annual pay settlement was traditionally either the high point or the nadir of employee morale. Today it is not so simple.

In recent years a number of trends have cut across the equation of "a fair day's pay for a fair day's work." They are:

1 The increasing importance of job insecurity as a controlling influence on pay and benefits negotiations. According to *The Wall Street Journal*, corporate re-engineering may eliminate between 1 and 2.5 million jobs a year "for the foreseeable future[9]." According to the US Bureau of Labor Statistics the index of temporary employment increased fourfold between 1984 and 1994. A 1997 report by Mintel in the UK found that a third of 20–54 year olds were worried about losing their jobs in the next five years.

2 The tendency towards local level negotiations and performance-related pay based on business unit and individual performance rather than businesswide or national agreements.

3 The general decrease in workplace militancy around pay and corresponding increase in interest in quality of life gains, e.g. shorter working weeks, flexible working, etc.

4 Exchanges of commitments to productivity and flexibility by workers in return for security of tenure, participation, and performance-related rewards.

5 The general decline in influence of trade unions. For example, trade union membership in Britain fell from 12 million to 7 million between 1979, the year Margaret Thatcher came to power, and 1996. This represented a decline from 59 percent to 31 percent of the total workforce.

Reward systems say a lot about the culture of a company. Do they reinforce heroic, individualistic or team-playing behaviors? Do they encourage crisis-creators or crisis-preventers? Do they link to poor performance as well as good? Do managers and employees at all levels have an opportunity to build a financial stake in the organization? Are pay and benefits designed to match or exceed industry averages?

Organizational and geographical cultures vary a good deal, and it is not our intention here to dictate what specific benchmarks represent good and bad practice. For example in the USA, for workers in many industries health insurance and stock options might be considered "must haves." In Europe, a good basic salary and pension arrangements may be more important. Whatever the mix of rewards, important generic benchmarks are:

- **Transparency.** Does everyone know broadly what pay scale they and their colleagues are on and what they need to do to advance? ☑

- **Fairness.** Are anomalies addressed in a manner which allows for negotiation and appeal? ☑

- **Incentives.** Can everyone participate in the short-term financial success of the company? ☑

- **Financial participation.** Are all levels of staff encouraged to take a longer term, reasonably safe financial stake in the enterprise? ☑

- **Welfare.** Do insurances and pension arrangements take into account gaps in national welfare provision in order to safeguard the long-term wellbeing of the employee and his/her dependants? ☑

■ **Comparability.** Can employees judge how well their
rewards compare with industry and national standards? ✓

Of these benchmarks, transparency is probably the most important. Free
and active dissemination of information about rewards is the most important enabling right which makes sure that all of the other issues are up for
discussion (see Case Study 15.3).

Interesting quantitative indicators which some companies choose to
publish include:

■ Ratio of top salary to lowest salary. ✓

■ Ratio of top 10 percent pay to lowest 10 percent pay. ✓

■ Comparison of grades of basic pay with industry standards
(ideally broken down by gender and ethnic group). ✓

■ Value and percentage of options and actual ownership by
executives and employees. ✓

■ Spread of eligibility for benefits. ✓

CASE STUDY 15.3

Scooping the cream at Ben & Jerry's

Without a doubt, America's most radical and innovative socially responsible business is ice cream manufacturer Ben & Jerry's Homemade Inc.
Transparency and active public disclosure has long been a major strength.
The company's 1994 Social Performance Report was written by Paul
Hawken, former businessperson turned social commentator. Hawken's
report detailed how the salary and benefits ratio for the top 10 percent
earners to the bottom 10 percent shifted only very slightly from 3.2:1 in
1993 to 3.3:1 in 1994 – a commendably egalitarian level. However, the
arrival of a new CEO with a stock option of 180,000 shares – equal to
that of all employees combined – did raise an eyebrow or two. As
Hawken noted, "This would be insignificant in most companies, but at
Ben & Jerry's, where a low ratio of salaries from top to bottom has been
a prominent social goal, a stock option ratio of 500:1 from top to bottom
may pose some problems." In 1994 the company also dropped its famous
7:1 top to bottom salary ratio. The arrival of the new CEO pushed up the
ratio to 14.1:1 in 1995.

Communication: consultation, representation and participation

In Chapter 7 we discussed some of the history – good and bad – of employee involvement or non-involvement in companies. We also described some excellent examples of coownership of both cooperative ventures and publicly quoted companies which have resulted in highly inclusive and successful enterprises.

Before we set out the kind of qualitative benchmark indicators which are important here, some definitions are needed. Table 15.2 describes some key differences between the three main types of worker involvement.

Table 15.2
Three levels of employee involvement

	Consultation	Representation	Participation
Typical mode of communication	Presentation to focus group followed by discussion	Negotiating table	Discussion of cooperating partners
Likely impact on ultimate decision	Low	Medium	High
Level of employee empowerment	Low	Medium	High
Employee rights	Granted by company	Based on election	Based on coownership/ investment
Potential for dispute	Low	Medium	Low

The UK Industrial Society[10] firmly recommends separation of consultation, which it sees as an "upward communication" process from anything to do with negotiation, individual grievance or joint decision-making. This argument has some merit. But more important from our perspective is that whatever machinery is set up by a company to engage, involve and empower its employees, it must be clear as to its scope and honest as to its purpose.

In some jurisdictions, e.g. the European Union, it is a requirement to consult with employee representatives on Occupational Safety and Health and in business circumstances which might lead to significant redundancy, e.g. in takeovers and mergers. In most of the European Union (Britain still excepted in 1996), the Works Council Directive requires effective communication and consultation with representatives

of employees in properly constituted councils. And as we have also discussed, in Germany there are rights of codetermination for workers represented on supervisory councils.

A commitment to consultation does not necessarily empower employees. And it certainly does not disturb the traditional "right of managers to
manage" model. As the Industrial Society describes it, consultation
should be management initiated and business based, "not about welfare
or people's gripes and groans, but about quality, output, deadlines, costs
and customer service."

In traditionally unionized workplaces, new initiatives on consultation
may be perceived as a threat to established negotiating machinery. This
may be overcome by careful delineation of purpose as suggested above.
Also, if intentions are honorable, there is every reason to invite union representatives to play separate but dual roles in consultation and negotiation.
In Britain, the National Westminster Bank is an example of how relationships with trade unions can be turned from frosty to reasonably constructive and trusting – even when competitive pressures are mounting.

Our preference (though not prescription) is for the stakeholder corporation actively to transcend consultation and representation if it can, and
to move towards deeper participation wherever possible. Participation is
neither paternalistic nor confrontational; it implies a shared purpose and
stake at emotional, psychological and material levels. That is why we
prefer to talk of inclusion. For us, inclusion means participation to a level
which allows stakeholders to help steer the corporation in the right direction. So it may also mean, for example, employees coming to annual general meetings to ensure their interests are represented alongside other
owners, thereby helping to temper the short-termism of some investors.

But regardless of what may be possible or not in your organization
today, here are some of the benchmarks which would define a level of
serious commitment to employee involvement.

- Established procedures for involving employees and their
  representatives in significant business issues which may
  affect their interests. ☑

- Clear, written terms of reference for formal committees
  dealing with employee involvement. ☑

- Availability of training on participation for employee
  representatives and management. ☑

- Systems of independent representation, judgement and
  appeal for grievance and disciplinary issues. ☑

■ Systems for rapid, credible and engaging communications to employees.

Diversity and equality of opportunity

Permit us a small digression. As we argued in Part 2, it is a central tenet of ecology that diversity is a source of strength to a biological community. The fewer species in any habitat, the more likely the entire community is to collapse and die. Interdependency between diverse entities lies at the heart of much present day ecophilosophy and "systems thinking." Interestingly, such approaches have also generated powerful support among natural scientists like the physicist Fritjof Capra[11]. What contemporary ecophilosophers and systems thinkers are contributing to management theory is still reasonably novel. But the bottom line of the argument is that division of labor, duality of mind and spirit, and disconnectedness of decision-making from social and environmental effects is what has got the planet and its nearly six billion human inhabitants into their current mess. If humanity is to survive the twenty-first century it will be because it heals these false dichotomies, promotes cooperation and interdependency and maximizes the benefits of its own diversity. In short we need less analytical, mechanistic behavior and more holistic thinking, collaborative behavior and networking.

At a rather more parochial level it has not escaped the more enlightened corporation that their best chances of commercial success depend not just on team working and empowerment, but on maximizing the creative contribution of all employees: women, men, black, white, old, young, believers, nonbelievers, people with disabilities as well as the apparently able. Each human type brings a different set of strengths and qualities. Avoidance of discrimination is quite rightly an ethical issue for many people. Perhaps, just as important, the inclusion of all human types in an organization should be seen as a real source of real strength and resilience for the business.

Economic, technological, cultural and demographic factors are already having a massive impact on how people manage their careers and how organizations respond to diversity issues. According to Charles Jackson and coworkers, in Britain, by the year 2006 there will be 2.4 million more people aged between 35 and 54 in the workforce than there were in 1993[12]. There will be a corresponding drop of 1.6 million of people under 35. Women accounted for just 37 percent of the UK labor force in 1971; this is predicted to rise to 46 percent by 2006. Meanwhile unemployment hits older people and members of ethnic minorities hardest. In 1994 unemployment in the Pakistani/Bangladeshi group was 28 percent of the economically active population – more than three times the UK national average. Today just under half of the female workforce is working part-time. Just over half of women with children under 5 were working in 1994 compared with just 37 percent in 1984. Yet while there are nearly 4 million children under 5 in Britain, there are only 1.1 million places in childcare.

With 85 percent of the growth in the US labor force between 1985 and the year 2000 predicted to come from women and minorities[13], support for these groups has become a touchstone of corporate social responsibility in America. According to the US magazine *Personnel Journal*, the number of employer-sponsored childcare assistance programmes increased from 110 in 1978 to more than 4,000 in 1989[14]. This figure included more than 1,000 onsite or near-onsite centers, 200 sponsored by private companies, 777 by hospitals and 100 by government agencies. Johnson & Johnson's Balancing Work and Family program was rated best in the USA by the Families at Work Institute in 1991. It included an array of benefits for family-related leave, flexible working, up to $3,000 for adopting parents and a $5 million childcare center at the company's headquarters.

The US President Bill Clinton is in no doubt about the importance of diversity to the country's economic performance. According to a presidential campaign speech made in 1996, women-owned businesses in America contribute $2.3 trillion to the US national economy. One-third of all US businesses are women owned – about 8 million companies in all.

The situation is a little less rosy when one looks at who controls the major corporations. In 1996, American women made up 46 percent of the workforce but occupied only 10 percent of top executive positions in *Fortune 500* companies. In Britain, just 1 percent of executive directors in the top 200 companies are women. The first woman to become Chief Executive of a FTSE 100 company was Marjorie Scardino who was appointed CEO at the Pearson media group on 17 October 1996. City analysts signaled their support for this breakthrough by marking Pearson shares down 13 to 675p on the day.

So the case for diversity and equality of opportunity has a number of dimensions: philosophical, practical and political. From an organizational development perspective it is mostly about understanding the business arguments and benefits of policies that aim to promote equality of opportunity[15]. In part this means responding to continuing change and uncertainty in the world of work. But it also means recognizing that the business benefits of more flexible employment practices can, if introduced and managed in the right way, produce benefits for the people who work for the organization and from them to the community and other stakeholder groups to which the company is responsible. For individuals, the point which most concerns them is whether organizations create a culture that promotes equality and, in particular, what organizations are doing to promote flexible work options – that is work options that allow them to combine work and family life.

It is important to recognize that the interests of different groups vary. For some the primary concern is still to get access to any work at all, e.g. young people from ethnic minorities and people with disabilities. For others it is less about access to work and more about how to progress their work careers and benefit from genuine equality of opportunity, e.g. women working part-time.

In practice, organizations tend to approach equality of opportunity and diversity in a series of stages (see Figure 15.2). First of all they tend to develop a series of ad hoc programs to tackle particular issues. Second, these develop into a coherent set of programs before finally, and only in exceptional organizations, developing into a fully integrated part of the business strategy.

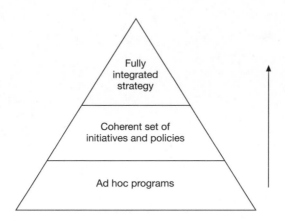

Figure 15.2
Stages of diversity programs[16]

Unfortunately, many organizations do not have a clear business rationale for promoting equality of opportunity. Without an argument to link diversity and equality of opportunity to the business, it may only be seen as something of a luxury which can be downgraded when other pressing issues arise. It is important therefore, to understand and develop arguments about the following:

1 Which types of business case arguments carry weight and with whom within the organization?

2 Is the business case undermined if it embraces wider ethical and societal issues rather than just financial issues?

3 How can the business case be most effectively articulated and communicated?

It is also important to see the linkages between organizational practice and overall business performance (see Figure 15.3). While it is commonplace to see direct links between issues such as recruitment, retention and motivation of employees and business performance, more companies are now realizing that how employees feel, how managers behave and how the company looks from the outside are just as crucial to business success.

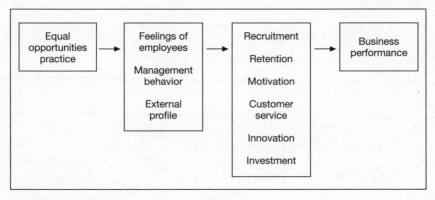

Figure 15.3
Linking diversity issues to the business case[17]

It is important for senior managers to realize that for strategic decision-making the following considerations should be made:

■ The "business case" is not a single argument but spans a range of ways in which diversity and equal opportunities can impact on the organization.

■ Care is needed in choosing those cases which are relevant to the business and its current concerns.

■ The business case need not be a detailed cost-benefit analysis for every aspect of equal opportunities policy and practice; however simple factual information, including costings, has high impact.

■ In communicating the business case it is important to think about the concerns of the particular audience, and help them reflect on how they have experienced the issues at first hand.

■ The equal opportunities performance of a company forms part of its external profile and this in turn will affect the behavior of key stakeholder groups – employees, suppliers, customers and investors (see Case Study 15.4).

CASE STUDY 15.4

A tale of two cultures at Texaco

Affirmative action on race and gender has long been a touchstone of corporate social responsibility in the USA. Surveys of good practice invariably focus on the number of women and black employees who make it into senior positions. Practices at oil giant Texaco illustrate why this is still an issue in America. In 1994, 1,500 present and former black employees filed a suit for more than half a billion dollars based on evidence of years of systematic discrimination on promotion and pay. The case blew wide open in late 1996 when secretly taped conversations revealed Texaco executives describing black employees unbelievably offensively as "black jelly beans." Following a boycott threat from leading human rights campaigner Jesse Jackson, Texaco caved in on the case. Shares rose $2\frac{3}{4}$ to $101\frac{1}{8}$ on the news. Meanwhile, Texaco UK has featured as one of six case studies in an Industrial Society report on Managing Best Practice on Diversity. Manager of equal opportunities and diversity Jennifer Malone identified three key elements of Texaco UK's approach to the subject: (i) board involvement and understanding of the need to change culture to a more coaching style; (ii) harnessing energy from employee involvement; and (iii) achieving early success with a popular policy. Quite so.

Even in companies which have been working on diversity for many years, there is a continuing need to communicate both the business case and practical information to managers and employees. All forms of communication (staff magazines, management briefings, annual reports) provide an opportunity to present both information and positive views. It is important that this communication goes both ways, so that there are opportunities to get feedback on how policies are working out in practice. Management information systems should take into consideration the following:

CASE STUDY 15.5

Diversity and public accountability

Vancouver-based credit union VanCity's 1995 Annual Report catalogs gender and length of service statistics for its workforce. In that year 56 percent of its Directors, 38 percent of its executives and 76 percent of its total workforce were women. Of staff 57 percent had a length of service greater than five years. Ben & Jerry's 1995 Social Report compared minorities and gender balance statistics for their own company versus the local Vermont population and national statistics. The total numbers of minorities employed at Ben & Jerry's was 3 percent compared with the Vermont figure of 1.8 percent. Three percent of professionals and managers were also from minority groups, including the CEO. The proportion of women in senior and professional positions was 40 percent and among operatives exactly the same. Compared with national statistics senior women at Ben & Jerry's were paid 37.5 percent more and operatives 51 percent more than median weekly wage rates.

1   Is the Board and senior management regularly briefed on equal opportunities progress and initiatives? (see Case Study 15.5)

2   Are there mechanisms for getting feedback on how policies are working?

3   Do the human resources functions practice what they preach?

4   Do line managers get regular information, training, and practical support?

5   Do networks exist which can act as a focus for sharing and learning from experience?

The most common approach to managing equal opportunities is concerned with creating employment opportunities for groups that have previously been disadvantaged. The expansion of part-time work opportunities has, for example, encouraged many women to go back to work. Similarly, opportunities to work some of the time from home have benefited both men and women.

All too often, however, people who take advantage of flexible working patterns are seen as reducing their commitment to the organization and as a consequence their chances of further promotion. Being confined to low skilled work is not a satisfactory solution and does not promote genuine equality of opportunity. And unless care is taken, affirmative action and antidiscrimination measures can cause suspicion and even backlash.

What is needed are ways of making sure that talented individuals of whatever background are identified and developed. It is especially important to ensure that the selection and assessment processes used to identify such people are not themselves biassed, perhaps because they are based on stereotypes of previous white male able-bodied job incumbents. So a more fundamental set of questions may need to be addressed by senior management:

1 Are processes for identifying people with potential and getting them considered for more senior jobs open to everyone?

2 Are processes for career management and appointment well understood and do they operate on merit?

3 Can all employees find out about possible job opportunities and register their interest in them?

4 Can employees get access to impartial advice on their careers?

5 Is the organizational culture antagonistic to people from minority groups?

Potential recruits, customers and investors are becoming more interested in how well organizations are run. The equal opportunities performance of a company feeds into its external profile and affects the behavior of all these stakeholders.

Of equal importance to direct stakeholder interests are the mechanisms which societies put in place to promote diversity in the workplace. In Britain there is a legislative framework (e.g. Sex and Race Discrimination Acts, Equal Pay Act) which has had considerable impact. Arguably voluntary initiatives, such as Opportunity 2000 (a Business in the Community program which aims to increase both the quality and quantity of women's participation in the workforce) and Race for Opportunity will have had at least as much impact.

In many other countries, there is a similar duality in approach with antidiscrimination legislation combined with voluntary codes of practice. In the USA discrimination against people diagnosed as HIV positive led the Citizens Commission on AIDS to develop in 1988 a ten-point statement of workplace principles which rapidly secured hundreds of commitments from US companies[18].

In their assessments of corporate social responsibility for *Shopping for a Better World*[18], the New York based Council on Economic Priorities rates companies in eight categories. No fewer than four categories relate to employee issues. One of these covers general workplace practices taking into account:

- medical and retirement cover
- labour relations
- safety (including regulatory violations)
- worker involvement and development (including profit-sharing, well-being, etc)
- assistance for displaced workers.

But even greater emphasis is placed on issues of diversity and equal opportunities, which are covered in three separate categories. Separate rankings are made for women's advancement (category A ratings going to companies which have 10 percent or greater representation of women at board or senior executive level) and advancement of minorities (more than 9 percent representation needed to achieve top marks).

Finally, on family friendliness, CEP examines companies' records on:

- leave (maternity, paternity, family and personal)
- flexible working
- daycare provision
- dependent care assistance
- education.

Bearing in mind the principles set out above, the following benchmarks and performance indicators are suggested for the aspiring stakeholder corporation.

Policy

- The company should have a clearly articulated policy on diversity, equality of opportunity and flexible working, ideally linked to company values and business goals (see Exhibit 15.1).

Volunteering codes

- Companies should participate enthusiastically in any local or national voluntary schemes aimed at raising awareness and promoting equality of opportunity in business.

Recruitment, promotion and retention

- The success of programs to promote diversity should be tracked and statistics regularly reviewed at senior executive levels.

EXHIBIT 15.1

The Procter & Gamble Policy on Diversity

What is Diversity?

Everyone at Procter & Gamble is united by the Company's values and goals. Diversity is the uniqueness each of us brings to fulfilling these values and to achieving these goals. Our differences are physical, such as race, sex and age. They also include less visible differences such as nationality, cultural heritage, personal background, functional experience and position in the organization. By building on our common values and goals, we are able to create advantages from our differences.

Why is Diversity important?

Developing and managing a strong, diverse organization is essential to achieving our business purpose and objectives.

- Our business opportunities are increasingly related to the entire world. And it is a diverse world. We must have the ability to deal with diverse consumers and customers in order to develop products and services of superior quality and value.

- Diversity provides for a broader, richer, more-fertile environment for creative thinking and innovation.

- Because we see diversity as an asset, we will attract and fully develop talent from the full range of the world's rich cultural base. It is from this increasingly diverse pool of talent that our future leadership will come.

We value the different perspectives that the diversity of Procter & Gamble people bring to the business. Our workplace environment encourages collaboration, which brings our different talents and experiences together to produce better ideas and superior services and products. At Procter & Gamble, we operate on the fundamental belief that individual differences are good and such differences will produce a genuine competitive advantage.

Training and communications

- Active programs on diversity, equal opportunities and prohibition of discrimination should be undertaken for all employees (especially those involved in recruitment and promotion).

Protection

■ Clear procedures should be in place to protect vulnerable workers from discrimination, harassment or other forms of workplace abuse.

Facilities

■ Daycare and other special care facilities should be supported, either through onsite facilities or provision of vouchers. Homeworking should be encouraged where appropriate.

Leave

■ Maternity, paternity and special personal leave for family difficulties should be flexible and generous.

Benefits

■ Should be provided equally to workers and dependants regardless of gender, ethnic origin or sexual orientation.

Goals

■ Should be set where women and minority representation in the workforce does not reflect local and national averages (including at senior executive levels).

Quantitative performance indicators

■ Proportions of women and minorities in each employee grade.

■ Average pay for women and minorities compared to average pay for all workers.

■ Numbers of employees trained in equal opportunities.

■ Costs of provision for daycare and other pro-diversity benefits.

Integrating individual, collective and corporate ethics

When the Sbn Bank published its first Ethical Accounting Statement[19], the two project designers, Professors Peter Pruzan and Ole Thyssen of Copenhagen University, wrote:

> Many people think of ethics as a personal matter that really cannot be discussed. Others regard ethics as some kind of checklist that can be used to determine right and wrong. We have a different perspective. The idea

behind the "Ethical Accounting Statement" is that ethics are socially constructive and that they can and should be discussed. A discussion of ethics does not elicit any unambiguous answers, but rather initiates a process in which the parties involved, each with their own values, must determine what they can agree is right and wrong. Ideally, a decision is ethical if all parties influenced by it agree. Therefore ethics deal with values which are strong enough to be shared, and with conflict resolution via attunement of these values.

Revolutionary vanguards through the ages have proven their credentials with the masses by giving them force of arms. From the *sans culottes* in France to the Sandinistas in Nicaragua, revolutionary leaders have demonstrated their ultimate trust in the people (or the "rabble" as Voltaire described them) by placing weapons in their hands. Happily, today's business leaders do not have to resort to quite such lengths to command respect and mobilize their followers. But in an increasingly competitive world, trust and shared values are possibly the most important tools which an executive can deploy.

Few people dispute the central importance of a core mission, a shared belief in basic values for running a successful enterprise. In Part 2 we reflected on some of the management theory which emphasizes the preeminent importance of unity around common values to commercial success. Sometimes core values are associated with company founders, but they do not need to be. The key point is whether the values have any consistent meaning and whether people feel able to live up to them. How is such a virtuous state of affairs achieved? The clues are in the two paragraphs above.

> **First:** Agreement and articulation of shared values is a process which can only evolve through dialogue. It is not a once only exercise of handing down Ten Corporate Commandments on tablets of stone. That has already been tried with only mixed results.
>
> **Second:** Leaderships have to place significant trust in their stakeholders, to the extent of allowing "their" values to be assimilated and contribute to the process of evolving and building "our ethics." Employees and managers in particular need to be part of their evolution.

A company which aspires to being a stakeholder corporation would almost certainly also aspire to being described as "ethical." Being ethical does not mean that the organization has to have detailed documentation prescribing the most desirable action for every conceivable circumstance which might emerge in the business. As we have already said mission statements, policies and guidelines including ethical codes are important for setting out basic assumptions and understandings. And specific, written work procedures may be essential to maintaining product quality, avoiding accidents at work and producing accurate financial accounts. But none of these will impact heavily on behavior. Mistakes will always be made. Supervision will not always work. Individual managers, employees and departments will occasionally go off the ethical rails. So the answer to achieving optimal ethical outcomes is exactly the same as many have argued for performance outcomes, that is: genuine involvement of the entire workforce in discussing and agreeing what represents best practice and then education programs to help make the shared values stick (see Case Study 15.6).

CASE STUDY 15.6

Education for shared values

The UK Co-operative Retail Society's first social report was published in 1988. It included details of social objectives for consumers, for the members, for the employees and for society. In each category, a commentary was provided which gave details of how the CRS engaged with its stakeholders and wider responsibilities. In the employee section greatest emphasis was placed on the need to ensure that the organization's 22,000 staff had a full understanding of the history and values of the Co-operative Movement.

Provided everyone recognizes that collective (team) and corporate (company) ethics are established via a two-way process, and that the individual has every opportunity to help shape the ethics of their working environment, problems will be minimized. At this point it is worth remembering that the ethics of other stakeholders also count. An employee or manager working in a company which manufactures land mines may be in perfect harmony with corporate goals and ethics. The mother of the Kampuchean child who has lost her leg will not be.

Integrating ethics: when it all goes spectacularly wrong

In consensual, social democratic societies such as exist in the Netherlands and in the Nordic countries, it is unsurprising that corporate, team and individual ethics are relatively simple to align. Equally, in well-ordered and (usually) well-behaved cultures like Germany and Japan societal norms also help underpin corporate alignment. In a litigious, individualistic society like the USA, or in a class-ridden nonconsensual country like the UK, life is not so simple.

Thus in the USA an entire profession has grown up around the need to reconcile individual and corporate ethics. The Association of Ethics Officers represents more than 200 corporate ethics officers – usually senior executives with a telephone hotline who can receive complaints and act on individual examples of disconnected values, corruption, undisclosed safety risks etc. Rather wonderfully, the psychologists refer to individual employees with a severe values-related problem as suffering from "cognitive dissonance."

US business literature contains many studies of the phenomenon of "whistle-blowing" – whether it is good or bad for the corporation or society, how it should be handled, and (of course), what are the legal and regulatory implications. Miceli and Near[20] describe the costs and benefits of whistle-blowing and the failure to whistle-blow in the USA. Using examples like the Challenger Space Shuttle disaster, the My Lai massacre in Vietnam, and the infamous General Motors Corvair safety cover-up, they demonstrate both the massive organizational pressures on individuals not to disclose wrongdoing for fear of being disloyal and the horrendous costs to external stakeholders if a culture of nondisclosure is allowed to prevail.

In Britain, Public Concern at Work campaigns for the rights of workers with a conscience and Freedom to Care provides a counseling and information service to prospective whistle-blowers. Many of the most celebrated cases in the UK have involved the financial services industry (see Case Study 15.7).

CASE STUDY 15.7

Collapse of ethics in investment and insurance

The financial services industry has had its fair share of scandals in recent years: rogue traders, banking collapses, insider dealing. The Barings and Morgan Grenfell disasters both represented a total failure of internal compliance systems. But the industry does itself no favors whatsoever in cultivating a culture of secrecy and punishment for those who do speak out. In 1996 Kleinwort Benson and Colonial Mutual were reported as having fired employees for speaking out against impropriety in dealings with clients. Apparently Kleinwort sacked high-flying fund manager Mark Horn for a breach of his "duty of confidentiality." According to *The Guardian* Horn had been concerned that pressure from other parts of the Kleinwort business were in danger of compromising his legal fiduciary duties to clients.

Others have involved public servants, e.g. in education, the health service and local government whose personal commitment to standards of public ethics were undermined by organizational cost-cutting, or more commercially driven colleagues[21]. Freedom to Care has produced Ten Principles of Accountability for raising concerns at the workplace (see Exhibit 15.2).

All too often the individual whistle-blower may believe they have support from peers and from senior colleagues at work, only to find they end

---

EXHIBIT 15.2

- **Transparency:** a procedure for raising concerns which is recognized by all and accessible to all.

- **Openness:** a culture in which it is safe to raise concerns and discuss them with any relevant and appropriate person, and in which the presumption is in favor of openness rather than secrecy. Employers should not use "confidentiality" as a means of gagging staff.

- **Fairness:** a procedure which is fair and is seen to be fair, which does not discriminate in terms of sex, race, conscience, status or position.

- **A hearing:** people who have concerns they wish to express should be heard, preferably in person, by those who have the power to change things for the better.

- **Independence:** conscientious employees should be able to raise a concern with some person or body who/which is independent and impartial, i.e. has no interests to defend in the matter being complained of.

- **Knowledge:** employers and managers should have working knowledge of nationally accepted rules on discipline, relevant codes of professional conduct, regulatory instruments, rights of staff under employment law and relevant antidiscrimination statutes on sex, race and disability, and civil rights.

- **Participation:** employers/managers should participate with employees/professionals in setting standards, and in drawing up and monitoring procedures for the raising of concerns.

- **Promptness:** concerns should be dealt with as efficiently and quickly as possible.

- **Support:** staff who raise concerns should be supported in doing so, e.g. being allowed to have the time and the resources to make their case, the appropriate access to evidence, and witnesses/observers/representatives at relevant hearings.

- **Appeal:** staff should have the opportunity to appeal and be given guidance on appropriate channels of pursuing their concern to the highest level.

up very alone and very exposed. Stories of personal tragedy are not uncommon. The example of Stanley Adams was especially tragic. Having blown the whistle on his employer, drugs giant Hoffman La Roche, to the European Commission for illegal trading he was exposed for breaking Swiss laws on commercial confidentiality. Threatened with twenty years imprisonment and his career ruined, Adams' persecution was complete when his wife took her own life.

Integrating ethics: getting it right

There are a couple of handy guides for aligning the personal ethics of managers with those of their organization: *Good Business*[22] and *Honest Business*[23]. They are written respectively from a British and American perspective and both use plenty of anecdotes and tips to illustrate how managers can recognize and address stakeholder concerns in the context of their business responsibilities. *Honest Business* has more of a small enterprise focus. Both guides lay maximum stress on the importance of transparency and integrity.

As far as the firm–manager–team–employee equation goes, the fundamental solution lies in promoting dialogue to establish and evolve a common ethic. Companies must ensure that dialogue processes are genuinely participative. Ethical and values related discussions must allow all managers and employees to express their views about what they believe the company stands for, how it falls short, and how collective values and behaviors may be improved and reinforced. There should be total protection for the expression of critical as well as positive views, and no fear of comeback, however uncomfortable the issue. IBM UK maintain a "Speak Up!" program for staff to request clarification from management on any aspect of the company's business. The process is centrally administered and confidential. In 1992, 529 letters were received from the 15,000 employees. The most frequently raised issues were company cars, office systems and company policies. The previous year's top scoring issue of pay slipped to seventh place.

Features of a healthy organizational culture which will maximize ethical values alignment and minimize the risks of cognitive dissonance (i.e. employees feeling fed up and powerless) include the following:

- Values statements and ethical codes for personal behavior related to two-way responsibilities with the company and other stakeholders.

- Education and training to reinforce values awareness and ethical codes of behavior.

- Explicit company commitments to the protection of those who speak out against wrong doing.

- Formal mechanisms for channeling private complaints to senior level and then acting on them.

- Use of audit and survey systems (e.g. attitude surveys) to test employee and manager attitudes to core values.

- Use of focus groups and other modes of communication to create opportunities for employees and managers to help shape and evolve statements of core values and ethical codes.

- Formal contracts of work which reinforce ethical behaviors.

In our experience, the subjection of organizational values to critical assessment by employees and managers is quite straightforward. Core components of mission and values statements, even quotations from founders, can be built into staff questionnaires and "approval rated." Confidential telephone surveys and questionnaires can also be used successfully to test the degree to which an organization walks its talk on sensitive issues like harassment, tolerance of differences in sexual orientation and race discrimination.

Armed with the results of systematic surveys of this nature, focus groups can be convened to explore new visions and new models for enhancing the integration of corporate, team and individual ethics (see Case Study 15.8).

CASE STUDY 15.8

Testing the reality of shared values

In Sbn Bank's 1993 Ethical Accounting process, researchers tested employee opinions on how well the bank's Code of Values was implemented. Some 47 percent agreed that the code was used in conflict resolution, 32 percent disagreed. Some 50 percent believed their head of department made the code "visible" through their action, 35 percent did not. Happily 86 percent agreed they could be "honest and open at work," up from 83 percent the previous year.

Perception indicators: the employee survey

In Chapter 13 we described a generic model for social (stakeholder) auditing and reporting which made use of two types of indicator: **quan-**

titative (based on benchmarks and performance indicators) and **qualitative** (based on benchmarks and performance indicators and investigations of the perceptions of stakeholders). We also advocated testing of perceptions by focus groups, questionnaires and telephone surveys.

In preceding sections of this chapter we have suggested a wide variety of benchmark indicators. We have also given examples of how questionnaires can be used to test the level of "values fit" between individuals, teams and corporations.

In this section, we list ten key points for conducting employee surveys. Further guidance can be found in the Industrial Society's best practice guide on the subject[24].

1 Our first and most important recommendation is to use a professional agency with a demonstrated track record in the area. University-based research units may provide best value for money.

2 Use professionally facilitated focus groups to make sure all relevant issues are included.

3 Integrate issues which emerged in employee focus groups with "standard" questions in the following categories (your professional survey advisors will assist in producing a questionnaire format that will work and avoid bias or confusion):

- demographics and personal details
- corporate values/mission (including founders' values if relevant)
- learning and personal development
- diversity and equal opportunities
- communications
- work satisfaction
- occupational safety and well-being.

4 Use mostly positive assertions in questionnaires and invite agreement or disagreement. Allow plenty of space for extra commentary.

5 Pilot test the questionnaire with groups of employees chosen to represent the range of views and types of people in the organization.

6 Ensure middle management is fully involved in briefing team members on the purpose of the survey and that they make adequate time available during working hours for all employees to complete the questionnaire.

7 Ensure absolute anonymity and confidentiality in collecting questionnaires, sending them for analysis and presenting results.

8 Put at least as much effort into analyzing and communicating results, ideally department by department, with full supporting documentation, summaries, etc., as you did into organizing the survey itself.

9 Put at least as much effort again into ensuring that departments get opportunities to discuss and debate the results and formulate positive action plans, recommendations for change.

10 Don't repeat surveys too frequently. It is demotivating for annual or more frequent surveys to show little progress on key findings. A two-year cycle may be optimal.

International Survey Research recommend up to eighteen categories of question for inclusion in surveys; they are: work organization and efficiency; quality; customer service; management style and effectiveness; supervision; employee involvement; working relationships; communication; performance management and appraisal; training; employee development; pay and benefits; safety and working conditions; job priorities and satisfaction; employment security; employee commitment; company image and company change (see Case Study 15.9).

CASE STUDY 15.9

International comparisons of employee morale

Employee surveys are now commonplace throughout industry and commerce. International Survey Research is one company which has specialized in workplace attitude surveys around the world. Their clients include giants such as AT&T, Du Pont, General Motors, Grand Metropolitan, IBM, Shell, Sony and 3M. Operating across more than 60 countries they are able to provide cultural and industrial sector specific comparisons. For example, in 1995–6 they found that in Europe the countries with the highest level of employee satisfaction were Switzerland, Denmark, Norway and Austria – the four countries with the highest GDP per head of population. In contrast employees in the UK were "the most negative in Europe" ranking in the lowest quartile on most dimensions of employee satisfaction. They found that high technology companies tended to have the highest morale, with financial services and telecommunications companies tending to fare worst.

Categories of question can be grouped and developed to embrace specific tests of stakeholder identification and inclusion e.g. with respect to the company's mission and purpose (see Case Studies 15.10–15.12).

CASE STUDY 15.10

Honesty and total transparency reinforce hope – even when the going gets tough

Ben & Jerry's 1995 Social Report made public the results of staff focus groups conducted in early 1996 and compared them with the results of staff surveys going back to 1990. After what had clearly been a couple of very difficult years for the company, the picture which emerged was mixed. Between 1990 and 1994 the proportion of staff agreeing that "things run smoothly" slumped from 58 to 29 percent. A financial loss in 1994 led to significant changes in management and internal culture, including the dropping of the company's famous 7:1 top to bottom maximum salary ratio. What was not in doubt was the pride that most employees felt in the company's history and social mission. The 1995 report said, "At virtually all sites, focus groups spoke at length about internal management issues that remain difficult and confusing for many of Ben & Jerry's staff. At the same time, there was in these groups a solid core of pride in and loyalty to Ben & Jerry's, most commonly expressed as appreciation for the strength and goodwill of their fellow employees."

CASE STUDY 15.11

Employees endorse company values but express concerns about day-to-day realities

The Body Shop International Social Statement 95 devoted 37 pages to a detailed analysis of the company's relationship with its 2,200 direct employees in the UK. The results of the employee survey provided a reassuringly high vote of confidence for the company's mission and the beliefs of its founders, Anita and Gordon Roddick. Of employees 93 percent either agreed or strongly agreed that "The Body Shop lives up to its mission" on the issues of environmental responsibility and animal testing. Some 83 percent identified with the founders' statement that "our success depends on the commitment, skill, creativity and good humour of our employees." Some 75 percent said they were proud to tell others they were part of The Body Shop, and 71 percent enjoyed their job. On the less than positive side, 53 percent either disagreed or strongly disagreed that the behavior and decision-making of managers was consistent and 26 percent could not recall ever having had a job appraisal; 23 percent felt the best way for them to develop their career was to change companies. Just under half agreed that "the company's commitment to being a caring company is apparent on a day-to-day basis."

CASE STUDY 15.12

Support for community involvement by employees

One aspect of corporate social responsibility which is especially relevant to explore in an employee survey is the question of community involvement. NatWest Bank and American Express regularly include questions testing support for the company's community program in their staff attitude surveys. In 1994, 93 percent of NatWest's employees agreed that working in a community initiative was good for personal development. In 1993, 35 percent of American Express UK staff responded favorably to the proposition that "The Company encourages good citizenship" (15 percent unfavorable) and 48 percent agreed "The Company contributes to overall welfare of the community" (13 percent disagreed).

Postscript: organizational development

Earlier in this chapter we have touched on some key indicators for the stakeholder corporation which wishes to measure its progress on employment and management issues. What we are unable to do is to recommend an ideal organizational development strategy to take your company forwards in terms of improved performance.

In our experience, simply identifying issues may be enough to spur relevant parts of the organization to improve their performance or the levels of stakeholder inclusion. On employee issues this may well include the corporate human resources department, the internal communications department and the occupational safety and health department. With luck these departments will use the results of the diagnosis to legitimize and accelerate their own programs of change.

But some elements of the assessment may have wider cultural and organizational significance. There may be more generalized problems, e.g. morale or effectiveness which cannot be addressed except in a strategic way.

CHAPTER 16

Cycle of continuous improvement

occupational safety and health

Moving from compliance to a high performance, high commitment culture

Occupational safety and health is one of the most comprehensively legislated and well regulated elements of good stakeholder management. Because it involves direct threats to the well-being of employees and contractors, and because mistakes can result in significant liabilities for companies and their executive officers (including fines and imprisonment), it is one aspect of management which many companies see as a simple issue of compliance and liability control.

Every week, tens of thousands of Americans are injured at work. Around a hundred die. Between 1970 and 1990 workplace fatalities in the USA dropped but injuries trebled in number[1].

According the US National Safety Council, the costs of workplace related injury in 1995 were just under $120 billion – equivalent to the combined profits of the 50 largest companies in the USA. In 1995, 3.6 million Americans suffered a disabling injury at work and 6,210 people died. In a 1996 survey conducted by the Dublin-based European Foundation for the Improvement of Living and Working Conditions, it was found that of Europe's 147 million workers 18 percent were absent from work for at least five days during the previous year for occupational health reasons. The British Health and Safety Executive estimate that the costs attributable to work-related ill-health and accidents at work in Britain equate to up to £16 billion or 10 percent of company profits.

The vast majority of accidents at work are due to human error, not the failure of physical controls. So the best companies try to go beyond compliance; beyond the minimization of direct risks. They try to make safety a proactive, culturally important element of day-to-day management[2,3]. This means that training and education should focus as much on motivational messages as on regulatory issues. Monitoring should be as much about the physical and psychological well-being of individuals as about accident statistics and costs.

Occupational safety and health is managed in different ways in different industries. It is increasingly common for the issues to be managed in an integrated way with environmental protection – particularly in higher risk operations like chemicals and oil. Thus Health, Safety and Environment (HSE) management systems are strongly advocated by the Chemical Industries Association under their Responsible Care program. In these industries the responsibility for implementation is invariably a line management function and auditing is an offline, semi-independent technical activity. The well-being elements of workplace health provision then devolve to medically qualified units with more of a human resources mandate.

In lower risk operations occupational safety and health may be run in parallel with environmental and even quality management programs. But it is equally likely to be run as an isolated, stand-alone function established for compliance reasons but typically under-resourced and organizationally disempowered. In these circumstances, the welfare dimension is usually nonexistent and safety is wrongly perceived as a boring subject with little to contribute to organizational goals. Until, that is, something goes wrong, or until an enlightened senior manager recognizes that promoting health and well-being in the workplace is actually a morale boosting and cost-saving opportunity.

The process

In this section a number of sources of best practice have been identified[4,5,6]. The following pages synthesize key points from these sources of best practice and put them into an easy-to-follow navigational tool for managers.

In each jurisdiction there will be numerous specific regulatory and standards based requirements for best practice. In the USA these are available from the Federal Occupational Safety and Health Administration (part of the Department of Labor), from their state equivalents and from professional bodies such as the National Institute for Occupational Safety and Health, the American Society for Testing and Materials, the American National Standards Institute and the National Fire Protection Association.

In the UK, the national and regional offices of Health and Safety Executive, national bodies such as the Royal Society for the Prevention of Accidents, and the local authorities are the best sources of standards relevant to your company. Each company will also have to take into account the framework of basic law. In the USA the Williams–Steiger Occupational Safety and Health Act of 1970 was a landmark, as was the 1974 Health and Safety at Work Act in Britain. Today much of the momentum on new safety and health regulations in the UK comes from the European Union. At international level, the International Labor Organization and the International Confederation of Free Trade Unions are at the forefront of pressing for the highest standards of worker safety. Let us now consider why it is important that you should try to achieve best practice.

Why do it?

Here are the main benefits and risks associated with the management of occupational safety and health – just in case you need a checklist to convince your colleagues of the need to do this properly. For real skeptics, the prosecution and imprisonment point usually secures buy-in.

1 Benefits to business of managing occupational safety and health effectively

- positive contribution to a culture of shared responsibility
- maintenance of a caring reputation
- preservation of individual health
- enhancement of general well-being and morale
- contribution to continuous improvement of efficiency, productivity and business success.

2 Risks to business of failure to manage occupational safety and health effectively

- increased insurance costs
- fatal and serious injuries to employees, contractors and clients incurring serious liabilities
- negative impacts on morale, stakeholder loyalty and commitment
- prosecution and imprisonment
- loss of reputation
- temporary or permanent closure of business activities (see Case Study 16.1)

CASE STUDY 16.1

The price of catastrophe

In 1990 M&M Protection reviewed 100 major incidents in the oil, gas and petrochemical industries over a thirty-year period. Just under half (44) resulted from explosions caused by vapor cloud escapes. The eight major incidents in 1989 had an average property damage and clean-up cost of $13 million dollars. These figures excluded costs of business interruption, employee injuries and other liabilities. The largest explosion of all occurred at the Phillips Petrochemical polyethylene plant in Pasadena, Texas on 23 October 1989. Within a minute of its escape, a mixture of ethylene and isobutane ignited with the force of 10 tons of TNT. The accident resulted in 18 months lost production and property damage estimated at between half and three quarters of a billion dollars. Scores of employees were killed or injured.

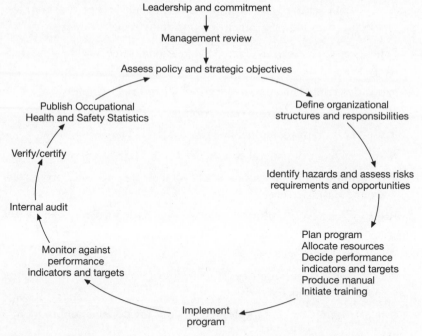

Figure 16.1
Cycle of continuous improvement for effective management of occupational safety and health

Convinced? Now proceed. The management system illustrated in Figure 16.1 is consistent with the continuous improvement cycles used throughout this book. It also reflects the recommendations of best practice guides cited in the references. There is currently no accepted international management systems standard for occupational safety and health. However, the British Standards Institution has produced a scheme consistent with environmental management standard ISO 14001 (see Chapter 22). The BSI standard is not necessarily designed for certification but is listed as BS 8800.

Leadership and commitment

Very few CEOs ever made it to the top on the basis of their expertise and skills in safety management. But even fewer got to the top and stayed there by ignoring the issue (see Case Study 16.2).

CASE STUDY 16.2

A well-motivated business is a safe business

There was an engine remanufacturing operation which was faced with closure after a string of commercial and management errors. When no white knight appeared on the horizon, the managers and workers pulled themselves up by their bootstraps, introduced a very financially transparent and participative style of management and totally revolutionized the company. Today it represents a major success story, highly focussed on customer needs and efficiency and the subject of an inspirational text on how to turn defeat into commercial success for workers, managers, customers and the community. The company's CEO had this to say about safety: "Safety is basic. It's the first thing that can turn people against you. It can undermine everything else you try to do. We'd be sunk if people started thinking, 'They say they care about us, but they're not concerned whether we get hurt or not.' And if that were true, they'd be right."

Here are seven tips for a CEO or senior executive who wishes to be a leader and an individual example on occupational safety and health.

1   **Tour and talk:** schedule regular visits to the facilities, always wear correct safety apparel and ask people about their safety and how accidents and near misses should be prevented.

2   **Encourage honesty:** ensure no-blame communications on hazard and incident identification. Better that people report minor mistakes, accidents and near misses than they hide them.

3   **Reward success:** give awards and commendations; create a culture of reward and recognition for excellence in safety management and for creativity in individual behavior and ideas.

4   **Take a stand:** use disciplinary procedures and when necessary dismiss managers or staff for willful failures.

5   **Be transparent:** include safety and health statistics in annual reports and other communications from the CEO's office; make sure safety communications are always two-way.

6   **Make it stick:** ensure that occupational health and safety features in appraisals and job performance systems.

7   **Be visionary:** integrate safety goals with commercial and business objectives.

A CEO or director prepared to follow these seven tips will have the moral authority to drive a high performing OHS management program. Whether he or she is new in the role, or simply recognizes the need to stay on top of the issue, occasional management reviews are essential.

The management review

It is surprising how few top managements deal with safety risks in a planned and systematic way. Crisis management can be seductive; it is where entrepreneurial leaders thrive. And this is how many top managers operate: routine safety risks are forgotten about until something awful happens. Then, depending on the size of the disaster (usually the number of people killed or injured), a process of upward scapegoating occurs until the buck stops with the senior management team. Just having the requisite insurance cover in place is not an ethically sound approach to safety risk management (see Case Study 16.3).

CASE STUDY 16.3

Death by management incompetence

A report published by the Human Factors in Reliability Group in 1995 noted that human error is a major contributing factor in 90 percent of accidents and that 70 percent of accidents could have been prevented by management action. They quote the findings of the *Herald of Free Enterprise* Inquiry where a P&O passenger ferry sank off Zeebrugge with the loss of 187 lives: "All concerned in management, from the members of the board of directors down to the junior superintendents, were guilty of fault in that all must be regarded as sharing responsibility for the failure of management. From the top to the bottom the corporate body was infected with the disease of sloppiness."

To avoid being part of a senior management team that has to deal with a public scandal and multiple deaths, it is a good idea to have occasional senior management reviews of the occupational safety and health management system. If it is an initial review it is advisable to bring in an independent consultant to assist. The local regulatory agency should be able to advise on suitable organizations and the manager responsible simply goes out to tender. But whether you use an external organization or an established and trustworthy inhouse team to assist in the process, here are ten of the key issues to address in a review:

1 Is there a list of safety legislation which has to be complied with in our business?

2 Is there a list of hazards in this business categorized by activity and prioritized according to likelihood of occurrence and severity?

3 Are the structures of accountability for occupational safety and health clear and generally understood?

4 Do line managers and safety managers have adequate financial and human resources to discharge their responsibilities?

5 Do we have adequate emergency plans and are people practised in their execution?

6 Do we have adequate competence and understanding at all levels, supported by an energetic program of training and awareness for all managers, staff and contractors?

7 Do we have a transparent system of safety performance measurement and is communication on performance active and two-way?

8 Are there clear objectives and targets to generate continuous improvement in performance?

9 Are safety policies, guidelines and workplace procedures properly documented and distributed?

10 Do we have access to adequate internal and external safety expertise to enable us to meet best practice now and in the future?

Policy and strategic objectives

In many jurisdictions it is a legal requirement to have a written statement of policy for occupational safety and health and to ensure that all employees have access to it. But whether it is a legal requirement or not, it is clearly good practice to make it clear to employees and the community at large exactly where the organization stands on their well-being and safety.

There is a number of strategic issues which need to be addressed with respect to the scope of an occupational safety and health policy. These include:

1 Should the OSH policy be integrated with the environmental policy?
2 Should the OSH policy be integrated with the quality policy?
3 Should the OSH policy embrace health promotion and the enhancement of well-being as well as safety and the protection of health?
4 Which stakeholders are covered: employees, contractors, customers, the local community?

The best statements of OSH policy share the ideal characteristics of all pronouncements on the stance of the organization towards its stakeholders. They should be:

■ general (ideally fitting on one page)
■ easily understood
■ based on line management responsibility
■ committed to best practice
■ endorsed by the CEO
■ public
■ subject to audit
■ subject to periodic updating
■ linked to processes of objective and target setting
■ supported by general guidance and specific procedures/rules for each workplace.

Your occupational safety and health policy should include as a minimum, commitments to

■ legal and regulatory compliance
■ communication and training
■ relevant industry standards and benchmarks
■ continuous improvement.

As noted above, for a statement of policy to come alive, it must be linked to objectives and targets, and it must be supported by general guidance and workplace specific procedures.

In the chemical industry a policy is a general statement of principles whereas an objective is considered to be a goal of medium term significance and a target something of shorter term relevance. Both objectives and targets should be quantifiable and subject to clear timescales for implementation. Objectives and targets should be documented and well communicated.

Definition of organizational structures and responsibilities

For organizations used to managing in a hierarchical way, it is a relatively simple task to ensure that line managers have job descriptions that reflect their responsibilities for safeguarding the health of those for whom they are responsible. Supervisors and operatives can also be made contractually and operationally accountable through a combination of written agreement, training support and good management. The only threat to this is rapid organizational change, e.g. in middle management, due to downsizing and high levels of employee turnover or short term working (see Case Study 16.4).

CASE STUDY 16.4

Stability is the key to clear responsibility and authority

Alan Reder investigated the safety record of Du Pont for the US Social Venture Network's guide to best business practices. He found a high level of senior management commitment, with CEO Edgar Woollard requiring every lost-time injury at any of the company's worldwide facilities to be reported to him in writing within 24 hours. As a result of this level of leadership, Du Pont's injury record is 10 times better than the chemical industry average. There was a correlation between low injury plants and workforces with less absenteeism and low turnover. However, one long term employee and former head of the union's health and safety committee drew attention to the risks of middle management insecurity: "They're shuffled in and out too fast"; and downsizing: "Some people tend to be really overloaded and how people work through that I don't know."

Matters are even less simple in nonformal environments. Indeed it is one of life's little ironies that ethical ideals often thrive best in nonhierarchical, creative, participative organizations. These are often the sorts of businesses which adapt least well to rules, procedures and written instructions on safety.

The trick which unlocks this particular conundrum is that of communication style. In a high risk industry with a typically hierarchical structure such as is found in the chemicals, power or engineering sectors, issuing sets of documented job descriptions will almost certainly be appropriate and effective.

In lower risk or less hierarchical working environments, other systems may also be necessary to reinforce standard written descriptions of management responsibility, e.g. morally pitched, visible management charters, wallet cards, special training sessions, etc. We will not present here detailed specifications of the numerous sorts of job roles and appropriate safety responsibilities which might be found in a "typical" business. This is precisely the kind of detail which has to be painstakingly worked out company by company, division by division, manager by manager and job role by job role. It is a laborious effort but an essential one if safety risks are to be managed in an effective way.

We will limit ourselves to seven tips for successful managers. These should be read in conjunction with the tips for senior executives on pages 227 and 228.

1 **Lead and delegate:** make the management system work by ensuring that the line responsibilities laid on you by the organization are properly cascaded through your division with well-understood and documented expectations and accountabilities (but don't forget, the manager remains *responsible*).

2 **Empower:** everyone in your part of the company should have the financial resources and freedom to act on safety *regardless of other constraints*.

3 **Educate:** make training programs on safety energetic, targeted and mandatory; ensure that there is sufficient access to qualified, experienced safety professionals both within and outside the organization.

4 **Communicate:** use every available communication forum and medium to generate two-way dialogue on safety; include progress on safety targets and objectives in newsletters, meetings, events, etc.

5 **Motivate:** maximize employee inclusion via safety committees; reward good practice (see Case Study 16.5).

6 **Integrate:** generate cooperative behavior across the organization through cross-departmental participation in problem-solving task groups.

7 **Evaluate:** act on audit reports, measure and report regularly on safety performance, set local targets and objectives consistent with organizational policies and strategic goals.

CASE STUDY 16.5

Incentives at Du Pont

Du Pont places special emphasis on rewarding teams rather than individuals for good safety performance. A high performing team with a good record on avoiding lost time injuries is recognized by a Du Pont Board of Directors Safety Award which entitles every member of the group to select a $20–85 prize from a catalog. Just as important is the linkage of good safety performance to the career prospects of managers. "If a supervisor or manager has difficulty managing safety in the Du Pont culture – then it is likely that he or she is experiencing performance problems in other areas," explains safety manager Jeffrey Wilson. "Du Pont uses safety performance as a critical yardstick for measuring management potential when evaluating the future promotion and progression of an employee. This kind of accountability – where safety performance is a significant part of overall performance – provides a real incentive for achieving safety excellence."

Underpinning all all these procedures and recommendations is the need for documentation. Policy documents and manuals of guidance and procedure represent the collective safety wisdom of an organization. Training is vital in order to bring policies and procedures alive. Manuals can be as dull as dishwater. The trick is to make procedures user friendly and match the level of detail to the level of risk. The next section deals with one of the greatest challenges to good safety management: how to identify hazards and quantify risks.

Hazard identification and the assessment of risks and opportunities

Deciding on how to prioritize controls on occupational safety and health requires: (i) an understanding of the range of hazards which are faced by the business; and (ii) assessments of the likelihood and consequence (the risks) of each type of incident occurring.

In some jurisdictions, risk assessment is a regulatory requirement. For example, in the European Union certain types of high-risk industry are subject to the Control of Industrial Major Hazards Regulations (CIMAH) which require the provision of information to the public and extensive emergency planning both onsite and offsite. Also, in the EU, there are specific mandatory directives dealing with requirements for workplace risk assessments on manual handling, visual display screens and hazardous substances. In the USA, the Occupational Safety and Health Administration (OSHA) requires hazard assessments of specific activities in all industries. Trade associations may also maintain best practice guidance on risk assessment. Failures in risk assessment are potentially catastrophic (see Case Study 16.6).

CASE STUDY 16.6

Twenty minutes to doomsday

In the UK in February 1994, a release of liquefied flammable and toxic gases occurred at the Ellesmere Port plant of the Associated Octel Company Ltd. Two hours later the vapors ignited, leading to extensive damage and significant risks of environmental and health impacts on the local community. In an area of numerous chemical plants and high-risk facilities, the press described the accident as "20 minutes to Doomsday." The official report of the incident concluded that the principal contributing factor to the accident was a failure of risk assessment procedures. A major hazard review ten years earlier had failed. "The incident might have been prevented or its severity greatly reduced if a more detailed assessment of the inherent hazards and risks of the plant had been carried out by the company beforehand."

The management review should have identified all generic regulatory and best practice requirements for hazard identification in your particular business. It is now the role of individual line managers to translate the businesswide inventory of hazards into a divisional or departmental list and systematically to assess the risks in their parts of the business.

The process of hazard identification and risk assessment should be done in conjunction with stakeholders – in particular employees, contractors and in some cases the local community too. It should not be confined to a discussion between the senior manager and his or her safety advisor. The manager and the safety advisor do, though, have a responsibility to set out a framework for the identification and assessment of risk. The chemical industry does risk analysis taking into account:

- controlled versus uncontrolled events
- routine versus nonroutine hazards
- past, present and future activities
- direct and indirect effects.

Then, a matrix for screening risks can be compiled according to the likelihood of the event and the severity of the consequence (see Figure 16.3).

Using a pictorial, matrix-based approach to risk assessment, it is possible to get representatives of staff, managers, contractors and (where

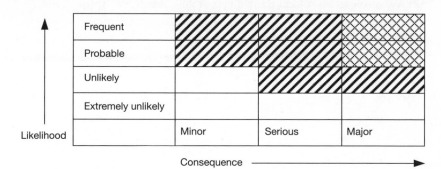

Figure 16.2
Chemical Industries Association matrix for screening hazards according to risk[4]

appropriate) the local community to brainstorm priorities. They will undoubtedly use their own knowledge and experience and take into account recent history from their perspective. They should also have access to records and technical assessments based on audits, surveys and hazard analyses. These should be presented by the safety advisor acting in an independent capacity.

A final note on risks and opportunities

Risk management should not always be seen as a defensive issue requiring controls over hazards associated with hardware, plant, procedures and people. Undoubtedly, risk reduction can be achieved through controls: consequences can be mitigated and the likelihood of accidents reduced. But good risk management can also be seen as an opportunity to examine human factor issues to totally eliminate certain risks and to build trust and confidence with key stakeholders. This type of thinking is characteristic of the best type of senior line manager.

From this process should emerge the priorities which will form the basis of an operational plan, complete with performance measures and targets.

Planning, resourcing and targeting performance

As we noted earlier, corporate goals and strategic objectives will have emerged from the management review and will be tied very closely to business goals and policy. They will necessarily be long term and quite general. But now we are in the realm of operational planning and targeting, where senior managers are able to set in place meaningful and motivational game plans which their direct stakeholders will appreciate.

A plan need not be complex. Indeed, it helps communication and execution of the plan if it is as simple as possible. The familiar acronym SMART is as good a guide as any. Plans and targets should be SMART.

S   Specific
M   Measurable
A   Agreed
R   Realistic
T   Timetabled

Performance indicators

Communication of progress on any plan is contingent on there being indicators of performance which are meaningful. So whether the indicators are based on achievement of targets or on other aspects of the plan, they must make sense and create a culture of common interest and achievement. Projects need to be fully owned by the individuals and teams charged with their execution. Some examples of quantitative performance indicators are listed below:

- Numbers of failures to comply with regulations per plant or facility.

- Numbers of regulatory infringements or improvement notices per plant or facility.

- Frequency of accidents by category (total accidents of differing severity expressed as levels or ratio of hours worked).

- Incidence of accidents by category (total accidents of differing levels of severity expressed as a ratio of the number of people employed).

- Costs of accidents expressed as a ratio of budget or turnover (to include lost time, compensation, liability, physical damage).

- Investments in accident prevention (including training) as a ratio of budget or turnover.

- Numbers of inspections and audits.

- Levels of employee involvement in safety committees and improvement teams.

- Compliance with occupational exposure limits based on technical monitoring (e.g. noise, chemicals, radiation). ✓

- Reporting levels of near misses and incidents expressed as ratios of time worked, units of production or output or people employed. ✓

- Proportion of employees screened on occupational risk. ✓

- Statistics on employee well-being. ✓

It is especially important here to have a good understanding of any external benchmarks for your business, for example, on accident rates or costs of accidents. Meeting or exceeding best practice in your sector is the best motivator of all.

Implementation of program

In our seven tips for senior operational managers we stressed the importance of both leadership and delegation. We also talked of the importance of adequate resourcing.

Whatever the type of business, there are several resource management priorities which are crucial to driving effective implementation throughout the operating division or department. These are:

- management of people
- management of processes
- management of equipment
- management of externally sourced equipment and services (e.g. purchasing, contracting)
- management of the physical environment (routine housekeeping and emergency controls).

Much of the above is common sense. But in managing resources for effective implementation of a safety plan, some special factors need to be recognized. For example, management of processes will depend on employees having free access to information on chemical and physical hazards. Typically information on such hazards is included in Materials Safety Data Sheets (MSDS) obtained from suppliers. Management of people has to take special account of organizational change: if individuals are transferred, seconded or promoted they will need a fresh assessment of competency to ensure that appropriate safety training is given. Management of contractors will require special systems of onsite inspection, supervision and training. Management of equipment may require physical guards and locks to prevent unauthorized operation. It will most certainly require ensuring the adequacy of equipment provision. It is worthwhile remembering that when the *Titanic* sank on 15 April 1912, it carried lifeboats for less than half its 2,200 passengers. The death toll for that tragedy was 1,523.

Monitoring performance

Unlike audits and management reviews which are periodic, performance measurement is a continuous process. Assuming that the correct indicators have been selected, the collection and distribution of performance data is mostly a question of effective communication.

A comprehensive safety performance report is likely to include incident and accident statistics, financial and human resource costs of occupational illness, health surveillance and exposure records, as well as performance indicators related to local targets and objectives.

It is essential that key performance indicators are presented regularly to executive management. These might include statistics on numbers of serious accidents, lost working time and costs of accidents, together with trends and plant-by-plant comparisons. On a more local level, "near miss" statistics, results of regular workplace inspections and more detailed breakdowns of accidents and incidents would be appropriate. Reward and incentive schemes must not undermine incident reporting. Safety committees and local managements should examine these statistics on a continuous basis and ensure that risk assessments, remediation measures and training are all focussed on achieving the correct trends in safety performance.

Internal audit and verification

Technical audits of occupational safety and health management systems developed several decades ago based largely on the experience of US companies in high risk activities like oil refining and petrochemicals. In the last twenty years, consulting consulting companies like Arthur D. Little and Environmental Resources Management have developed multinational global businesses on the strength of their abilities to provide external assessments of the effectiveness of health, safety and environmental management systems. Today there are authoritative guides on HSE auditing[7] backed by numerous software-based systems to support inspections and risk assessments.

Audits of safety management are often driven by issues of compliance and liability prevention. In this context it is worth remembering that the costs of the Bhopal and Chernobyl disasters ran into hundreds of millions of dollars, as did the Seveso disaster in Italy which was estimated to have incurred expenditure 15,000 times what the incident would have cost to prevent[8]. So unsurprisingly, investment banks and lending institutions are especially fond of commissioning independent audits prior to acquisition and loans.

Currently there is growing interest in the "softer" side of safety auditing – examining the human factor questions: employee morale and motivation, as well as whether procedures are documented and accountabilities assigned. Issues like long working hours and stress at work are especially relevant here (see Case Study 16.7).

CASE STUDY 16.7

People being worked to death

The Workers' Health International Newsletter regularly catalogs examples of death through overwork. They cite cases such as that of a woman worker in a Spotec factory in Indonesia producing sports shoes for a well-known American brand who died after being refused permission to take sick leave. The husband of the 28-year-old mother of two said his wife was often forced to work 11-hour shifts, overtime could not be refused and there was compulsory Sunday working. In Japan, the labor ministry registered more than 60 deaths through overwork in 1995. In 1996, major advertising agency Dentsu was ordered to pay more than $1 million in compensation to the family of a junior copywriter, Ichino Oshima, who committed suicide after completing a project. He had worked 17 months without a day off, surviving on as little as half an hour sleep per night. In awarding the damages, the judge said: "The employee was totally tired and depressed. He was relieved when his project was finished. But when he thought of the extremely long hours of work he had to face again the next day he fell into depression."

Our advice on internal safety audits and external audit verification is to be guided by best practice in your industry as advised by your local regulator. There are important linkages between employee well-being, corporate culture and safety performance. And effective occupational safety and health audits need to reflect this, examining issues like how people relate to rules and procedures, training and working conditions as well as the physical elements of worker protection.

If you do not already have an internal safety audit system in place, an external expert should be consulted in order to design one for you.

CHAPTER 17

Cycle of inclusion

customers

Knowledge is power

Ever since the time of Adam Smith, the customer has been assumed to be sovereign. The individual making his or her consumer purchasing decisions or the business deciding on which vendor to choose exercises preferences in a market of competing suppliers, goods and services. Subject only to limitations of cash and legislative constraints, the customer behaves according to the principles of freedom of choice. All the customer needs to make those choices is full access to relevant information. So goes the theory.

The theory works well in markets where there are diverse, competing suppliers and an absence of monopolistic behavior[1]. It works provided information is freely available and the customer is not subject to distorted messages and misleading advertising. But there is the rub. In many markets these conditions do not prevail. In 1758, Samuel Johnson said, "Advertisements are now so numerous that they are very negligently perused, and it is therefore become necessary to gain attention by magnificence of promises and by eloquence sometimes sublime and sometimes pathetick. Promise – large promise – is the soul of advertising."

There are few areas of governance and stakeholder inclusion which are as ambiguous and complex as the relationship between a company and its customers. Putting goods and services into a marketplace and selling them involves numerous important commercial and ethical choices. Markets are not values free zones. Monetary factors govern pricing, i.e. costs of production, distribution and margins versus the ability of the customer to pay. But product quality, brand strength and many other intangibles may actually drive the final purchasing decision.

This is why branding is taken so seriously. The importance of investments in brand equity (often reinforced by fabulous advertising budgets) is illustrated by the significant attention paid to protecting brands and their value by large corporations. Supermarket chains provide occasional entertainment when they tread on the toes of heavyweight players in highly branded markets. In 1995, Grand Met took grave exception to UK supermarket chain Asda producing lookalike products. They claimed that the "Deep South" bottle and label looked suspiciously similar to those of Southern Comfort; and "Windward Caribbean" white rum with coconut bore an uncanny resemblance to Malibu Caribbean white rum with coconut. Cola companies are renowned for their touchiness in defense of their brands and trademarks. By 1926, forty years after the invention of Coca-Cola, its owners had resorted to litigation no fewer than 7,000 times to protect its trademark[2].

Rather more seriously, bodies like the World Trade Organization and the International Chamber of Commerce get quite agitated by examples of theft of intellectual property, abuse of trademarks, counterfeiting and bootlegging (e.g. of music and software) and are likely to give companies and governments who condone it a very hard time indeed[3].

In Chapter 15 we argued that it is absolutely vital to the competitive success of the enterprise that employees' values "fit" with those of the company. So how important is it that customers are aligned too? How important is it that companies engage their customers in dialogue to discover not just what they need, but why they feel they need it?

In our view, genuine processes of customer inclusion and participation are probably the only sure way to retain long term market share in an increasingly competitive world. Superficial loyalty and incentive schemes may provide quick fixes to build or retain customer bases. Anyone can provide those. High levels of product quality and service are now required from virtually every provider – even in monopolies and public utilities. In the future, enduring competitive advantage will not come from these areas. This is especially true in price sensitive Western markets which experience serious intrusion from Far Eastern producers with massive labor cost advantages. In the global marketplace of the future, it is a deepening of the psychological contract between the company and the customer which will matter most. It is easier to retain a loyal customer than to gain a new one.

This observation provides both hope and a significant challenge to the aspiring stakeholder corporation. Hope comes from the fact that understanding the customer and connecting with him or her at a deeper level is not difficult; it is the main subject of this chapter. The challenge is to do this in a morally respectable way. If the company's motives are short term and superficial that will become apparent. If the company's objectives are to share values and allow genuine inclusion of customers in the objectives and purpose of the company, then it will work.

Unhappily, the temptation for companies to market their firm or their products and services in the most favorable light is almost overwhelming. Adam Smith may have prescribed full access to information for customers to be able to exercise their sovereign choices. But when was the last time you saw a jar of premium brand coffee bearing the label, "This coffee was picked by Colombian peasants routinely exposed to unacceptable levels of agrochemicals"? When did you ever see a cosmetics label qualified with the information "We commission safety tests on rabbits"? When did you see a pair of exclusive athletic shoes marketed with the words "Made in China by teenagers working seventy-five hours per week for less than a dollar an hour"? The resistance to labeling unpalatable truths is enormous (see Case Study 17.1).

CASE STUDY 17.1

The arrival of the superbean

In Europe and North America there is mounting concern over the lack of labeling of food products derived from genetically modified plants like tomatoes, maize and soyabeans. Monsanto developed a soyabean specially engineered to resist its herbicide Roundup in order to increase yields. But the company was not particularly interested in the demands of consumer groups and environmentalists that the modified beans be subject to special labeling. The Pure Food Campaign in the USA and the Genetics Forum in the UK drew attention to the concerns of the general public and the potential environmental dangers of herbicide resistance transferring in nature to "superweeds." With scant regard to issues of transparency and consumer rights, Monsanto bleated, "The beans are the same beans. They are indistinguishable. You cannot tell them apart. There is no reason for the beans to be labeled."

Instead, it is left to marketeers and advertisers to use positive attributes to reinforce the values behind their brand. On matters of price and service, this leaves little room for debate. The customer experiences both directly and is in a direct position to judge both. But even on issues of functional quality (washes whiter, lasts longer, etc) the customer may have to buy on trust. When it comes to implications for life style, when anything from a soft drink to a sports car says something important about the drinker or driver, then we really do enter complex territory (see Case Study 17.2).

CASE STUDY 17.2

Sexual ambiguity in advertising standards

Print advertisements depicting women and men in their underwear clearly cause confusion for the UK Advertising Standards Authority. Having passed the Wonderbra advertisement depicting model Eva Herzigova in a provocative pose over the phrase "Hello Boys", it rejected a similar advertisement from male underwear firm Brass Monkeys entitled "The Loin King" and "Full Metal Packet." The male model was as conspicuously well endowed as Ms Herzigova. Brass Monkeys' founder Kevin Higgs was perplexed: "If we were a female underwear brand there would have been no problem. If you use a nice female model with her boobs hanging out that is not a difficulty. We were advised to reshoot the poster with a very small man."

In recent years, environmental and ethical claims have been a real battleground. Publications like *Shopping for a Better World*[4], *The Green Consumer Guide*[5] and *Shopping with a Conscience*[6] sought to bring fact rather than fiction into play, only to be overtaken by a burgeoning plethora of ethical claims. These include: (i) self-asserted claims (environmentally friendly, dolphin-safe, recyclable, not tested on animals, etc); (ii) private and sometimes competing third party labeling schemes (e.g. the various European fair trade marks, Green Seal versus Green Cross in the USA); (iii) official, government sponsored schemes (the European Union Ecolabel, the Japanese Ecomark, and the German Blue Angel). Today, this area is a confusing mess for consumers. Nevertheless, despite all odds, the socially conscious, green or ethical consumer appears to be alive and well in most parts of the world.

According to a 1993 Cone/Roper Benchmark Survey on Cause-Related Marketing, more than 60 percent of Americans would switch brands or stores to purchase from companies which support particular social causes[4]. Some 48 percent would support companies that "donate money to a cause through a foundation or non profit agency," and 29 percent applauded firms that "allow employees time off to volunteer for a cause." The opportunities this creates for US environmental marketeers have been explored in some detail by Walter Coddington[7].

A survey by Mintel in 1994 found that 40 percent of UK consumers make a positive effort to buy environmentally friendly products and services and a further 20 percent will do so if they see them. In 1995, the UK Co-operative Wholesale Society published a report based on the UK's "largest ever independent survey of ethical concerns": *Responsible Retail-*

ing. They found that 57 percent of the public are more worried about the "ethical history" of the products they buy than five years previously. A third claimed to have boycotted a shop or product on ethical grounds. Three-quarters wanted the food industry to provide more information about the products they sell. Some 71 percent said retailers had a responsibility to animals, 66 percent believed it was important for the food industry to make sure animals are treated humanely. A MORI poll conducted in late 1995 showed that 23 percent of the British public claim to avoid using products or services which have a poor environmental record and 40 percent claim to choose environmentally friendly products.

Research commissioned by the Institut für Markt-Umwelt in Hannover, Germany, in 1993[8] found that 58 percent of consumers in the German market prefer to buy products from socially responsible companies. Of these, the most frequently mentioned influences on purchasing behavior were: strong environmental commitment (63 percent), not animal testing (55 percent), engagement in the former East German states (44 percent), consumer protection (40 percent) and the interests of employees (40 percent).

Although consumer concerns about environmental, social and ethical issues are increasing, there are clearly important national characteristics to consider – even within Europe. A Eurobarometer survey in 1992 found that an average of 46 percent of consumers in the European Union claimed to buy an "environmentally friendly" product "even if it is more expensive." Most fastidious in this respect were the Luxembourgeoise (66 percent), the UK (57 percent), the Germans and the Danes (both 54 percent). Lowest commitment was expressed by the Greeks (28 percent) and Spanish (30 percent).

To complete our world tour of global ethical consumerism, in 1993 a study by the Office of the Prime Minister in Japan found that 69.8 percent of women and 58.1 percent of men expressed a concern about environmental issues related to everyday life[9]; 34.4 percent of women and 20.5 percent of men claimed to buy ecologically conscious products, e.g. recycled paper.

A deeper approach to shared ethics

Moving beyond the hype of claims and labels and seeking to engage customers on a deeper level can bring its own dilemmas. A number of companies has projected their sincerely held ethical values through public campaigns. In the USA, three shoe companies have vied for moral leadership on social issues: Ryka Inc, a women's sports shoe supplier pioneered campaigns against violence towards women; Reebok has promoted awareness of human rights abuses; Timberland has taken on racism through mass advertising[10]. In each case, significant amounts of money were spent on campaigns which seemed to go beyond the tokenism and superficiality of cause-related marketing. On an even more innovative level, embracing product offerings as well as campaigns, Ben & Jerry's produced Peace Pops ices during the Gulf War as a protest against militarism. In 1995 Patagonia declared it would ensure all of its cotton clothing would be organically sourced within two years. Also connected to products, in Britain The Co-operative Bank has launched an overt policy of differentiation from its competitors based on ethical lending. The Body Shop has tweaked the tails of the cosmetics industry giants for ten years with its Against Animal Testing campaigns.

Such stances bring their own risks as several of the companies listed above could attest. However popular they may be with customers, and however genuine the motivation, an ethically based approach to stakeholder engagement can lead to cynicism and controversy.

Happily for the stakeholder corporation, the lesson for those who wish to engage stakeholders in an overtly ethical way is encouraging. No one is perfect and no company is invulnerable to challenge on its imperfections. But years of building up trust and customer loyalty through a genuine commitment to stakeholder inclusion are not easily deflected, even by the most savage attacks.

Ethical disengagement can be just as powerful as ethical engagement. There are those who argue that some companies and their products are so morally dubious that they should not be allowed to promote their goods or advertise at all. We have a good deal of sympathy with this view. Arms sales to Third World despots and cigarette sales to vulnerable groups are good examples. In these cases, promotion can be corrupting, subtle and pernicious. It frequently involves a diabolical pact between companies and governments which need revenues from sales and the jobs which depend on them (see Case Study 17.3).

CASE STUDY 17.3

Tobacco marketing – a dance with death, jobs and governments

In the USA annual tobacco sponsorship of sports and other activities of special interest to the young totals $5 billion, compared with only $500 million for direct advertising. It is estimated that smoking hastens the death of about half of those who take up the habit in their youth. As a

▶ result of extremely heavy promotion in developing countries, sales of British American Tobacco brands to Latin America and the Caribbean are now higher than in both North America and Europe. In 1995 BAT's worldwide profits increased by 18 percent to $1.5 billion. With sales to Western adults dropping year by year, it appears that the tobacco industry now depends on new addictions being created among the young and in countries of the developing world for its future growth. Meanwhile, the European Commission spends £700 million per annum subsidizing tobacco production in southern Europe. In comparison it invests just £10 million per annum trying to combat the 500,000 deaths attributable to tobacco consumption in the EU. The tobacco companies lobby hard to protect their interests – and their subsidies. Pointing out that 120,000 EU jobs depend on tobacco, the cigarette companies rely on sympathetic governments like the UK to block any tightening of advertising guidelines.

Readers may have an interest in the ethics of marketing and production of morally dubious goods. Or they may simply wish to wade through the case studies of consumer boycotts ranging from Dow Chemicals (supplying napalm for antipersonnel use in Vietnam), through Nestlé (baby formula to the developing world) to Barclays Bank and others in South Africa. These cases provide salutary reading for anyone interested in corporate reputation and trust[10]. There are also one or two honorable examples of companies that have done the right thing by withdrawing products and services which may be abused by children and teenagers, e.g. solvent-based household products and telephone chat lines. Very occasionally a company will make a moral judgement even when the customer and their clients are quite happy in exotic but relatively harmless forms of abuse (see Case Study 17.4).

CASE STUDY 17.4

Services withdrawn

Just occasionally, a business may consider it the appropriate ethical course of action to remove services from customers altogether. Anyone who visited a London public telephone kiosk in the mid-1990s could not fail to have been impressed by the array of business cards encouraging people to telephone for every form of sexual service imaginable. At the height of the epidemic, BT contractors were removing 150,000 cards per week from its kiosks. Eventually, BT decided that corrective action of its own was called for, and set up a system for warning the offending subscribers not to misuse their telephone numbers for "unauthorized advertising." Failure to comply with a series of warnings would lead to complete withdrawal of their services.

In coming years the consumer movement will probably focus on services more than products – financial services, leisure services and the like where quality and value for money may differ significantly. Another increasing focus will be the services offered by public and privatized utilities and the role consumers have in monitoring their actions. Providing not just price and quality information, but information about environmental and ethical implications of products and services also will be part of the consumer education process of the future.

Like biotechnology, the information superhighway will have a potentially enormous impact on consumers. Issues of privacy, pornography, and availability of information will undoubtedly be tackled by consumer organizations in coming years. As we have already argued, the future will be a world where trading blocs – such as the European Union and the North American Free Trade Agreement area – and transnational corporations play a larger and larger role. In response, consumer organizations will be increasingly effective in challenging developments and policies that undermine the best interests of consumers.

The process

In order to ensure inclusion and participation of customers in the affairs of a company we again advocate the generalized cycle of inclusion for social stakeholders (Chapter 13, pp. 168–80).

Special challenges exist for companies in fast moving consumer markets. They may be dealing with millions or tens of millions of customers of all ages, in many diverse cultures and across numerous languages. Small businesses and companies producing very expensive products and services, e.g. airplanes or infrastructure, may have only a handful of key customers. In both cases the principles are the same. Two-way dialogue and open communication leads to alignment of values, mutual understanding and loyalty (see Case Study 17.5).

CASE STUDY 17.5

You're never too young to wear Levis

Many companies conduct systematic market research with their adult customers. Companies like Microsoft and Levi Strauss go one better, employing America's teenagers in creative focus groups for cash. American teenagers spend $100 billion a year, so it makes sense for companies to tap their ideas on future products and fashion trends. Thirteen-year-old Joshua Koplewicz received between $100 and $120 for 20 hours

> work with Levi Strauss over a period of three years but was under no illusions about his job prospects when he was asked to provide some names of younger contemporaries: "I haven't been officially fired or downgraded or whatever, but they haven't really given me a call in a while. I think I'm too old."

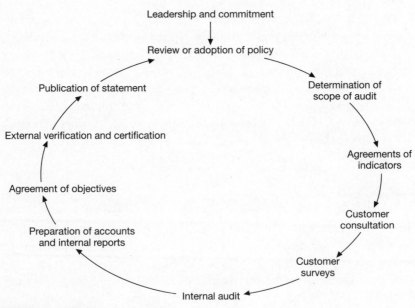

Figure 17.1
Cycle of inclusion for customers

General principles

Happily, market researchers are more skilled in promoting genuine two-way communications with customers than with any other stakeholder group. Moreover, their profession is governed by quite strict national and international codes of conduct with respect to confidentiality, integrity and objectivity, e.g. the ICC/ESOMAR Code of 1986 (revised 1995). Rather less happily, the advertising profession sometimes comes under extreme pressure to undermine the long-term integrity of the relationship for short-term expedience or even worse, resorting to saturation sales pitches to current and future customers. It is estimated that by the age of 18 American children have been exposed to 350,000 TV commercials[2].

To compensate for the absence of absolute standards in consumer relationships, we propose the following ten general principles of consumer communication and inclusion for the stakeholder corporation. Most of the principles deal with honesty in one form or another.

1 **Truth:** information provided to customers should be clear, unambiguous and relevant, not misleading, out of date or exaggerated (see Case Study 17.6).

CASE STUDY 17.6

What price security in old age?

In the late 1980s around half a million people in Britain were misleadingly sold pensions which would leave them worse off in retirement than their existing arrangements. It was all part of a free-for-all which was stimulated by government-backed incentives for private pension schemes. When the scale of the problem became known – compensation could run into billions of pounds – the regulators started to apply pressure to the offending pension and insurance firms. Some of these firms were the City's finest. But after three years, only 1 percent of the most urgent cases had been settled and only £50 million paid out in compensation. Sir Andrew Large, Chairman of the Securities and Investment Board, the City's most senior watchdog, was not impressed. He chided firms with a "sense of responsibility" to get on with it: "Investors who were mis-sold personal pensions and suffered loss are entitled to redress and we are determined they will get it."

---

2 **Transparency:** no relevant information should be withheld by omission, particularly where the rights or sensibilities of the customer may be offended, e.g. on environmental, human or animal welfare impacts in sourcing and procurement. Absence of knowledge is no defense.

3 **Active disclosure:** sellers should disclose through effective labeling and accessible customer literature all relevant characteristics of the product or service, i.e. price, performance and quality (including ethical quality where relevant).

4 **Dialogue:** customers should have the ability to question and comment upon all aspects of the company, its products and its services, positive and negative, thereby contributing to improvements in performance.

5 **Protection:** customers should be protected against known and unknown risks, e.g. to safety and health; children and vulnerable groups may need special arrangements in this regard.

6 **Fairness:** pricing should be nonexploitative and clear; market domi-

nation where it has been allowed to develop must not lead to extortion, especially in essential goods and services.

7 **Autonomy:** customers should be treated as individuals or entities with rights. Their purchasing decisions should be informed but not forced through aggressive advertising or coercion; vulnerable groups and dependent small businesses, e.g. franchisees, need to maintain their sovereignty and a level of independence in the relationship.

8 **Integrity:** customers should not be bribed or deceived into buying stolen or counterfeited goods or services, whatever the apparent direct advantage to the purchaser.

9 **Respect:** poor taste should be avoided and children should be protected; stereotypes and assumptions about customers' preferences and self-images must not lead to offense either in customers or noncustomers, e.g. exploitative images of women aimed at male customers (see Case Study 17.7).

CASE STUDY 17.7

Bad taste, bad examples and bad language in advertising

In a study commissioned by the UK Advertising Standards Authority in 1996, a quarter of the British public claimed to have seen misleading or offensive advertising in the previous 12 months. The top three causes of offence were: (1) a bad example to children (16 percent); (2) unsuitability for children (14 percent); (3) bad language (13 percent). Some 12 percent were concerned about misleading or sexually explicit advertising. When asked about which words should not be allowed on posters or in press advertising, less than a third were concerned about the use of the world "damn." About half said they would take a dim view of the word "bugger" and about two thirds would be decidedly unimpressed to see "bollocks" included in printed advertisements.

---

10 **Redress:** customers must retain rights to obtain prompt compensation for faulty goods and services.

Benchmarks and performance indicators

In Chapter 12 we suggested that as a minimum, companies should maintain two policies with respect to their customers. We would consider both of these to represent best practice benchmarks:

- general policy on marketing and advertising ☑

- customer care and complaints policy. ☑

Examples of charters and policies which may have some relevance to the formulation of your policies are: International Chamber of Commerce International Codes of Advertising Practice, Sales Promotion, Direct Marketing, Environmental Advertising and Sponsorship, and the ICC/ESOMAR International Code of Marketing and Social Research Practice[11]. In 1995, Consumers International launched a Consumer Charter for Global Business.

Relevant national codes and guidelines are issued by regulatory authorities, professional bodies and standards organizations (e.g. the US Federal Trade Commission's 1992 guidelines on environmental marketing claims).

In addition to policies and guidelines which the company may adopt, there is a number of qualitative and quantitative benchmarks which will be relevant in most cases:

- Provision of full information on finished products, ingredients/component sourcing and performance (on product labels or packaging or in store). ☑

- Customer communications as a proportion of total transactions expressed as complaints, compliments, requests for information, educational material, etc. ☑

- Number of guarantees or warranties redeemed because of product/service failure as a proportion of total transactions. ☑

- Market share by product range. ☑

- Number and nature of contract cancellations. ☑

- Number and nature of product withdrawals. ☑

- Number and nature of violations of product safety, consumer and/or competition law. ☑

- Number and nature of breaches and/or actions on labeling or advertising standards. ☑

- Number of quality awards. ☑

Perception indicators

Market research through customer focus groups and opinion surveys is perhaps the best developed of the arts of stakeholder auditing. Most customer research is focussed quite understandably on questions of product or service quality, pricing and value for money. However, as we have argued, it is becoming increasingly important for companies to try and secure competitive advantage through alignment of values between themselves and their customers via their products and services and how they are marketed. Because there is great diversity in lifestyle issues and values which a company may wish to explore with its customers, it would not be especially helpful for us to list candidate propositions for customers in this book.

Companies are somewhat reluctant to publish details of market research into customer satisfaction and motivation. This may be for reasons of commercial sensitivity or sheer embarrassment. One honorable exception to this rule is the Sbn Bank in Denmark (see Case Study 17.8).

CASE STUDY 17.8

Customers bank on quality and service in Jutland

In 1993, the Sbn Bank's Ethical Accounting Statement included results from 22 propositions posed to their customers. The four main categories of question were quality and competence, confidence and respect, communication and commitment to the community in North Jutland. Of the bank's customers 83 percent agreed, either slightly or strongly, that "your branch of Sbn Bank stands for quality" and 80 percent agreed that the bank "provides the sort of special offers and services you need;" 96 percent agreed they received friendly service and 90 percent fast service. On community issues 79 percent of customers believed that "the local community trusts Sbn bank" but only 53 percent agreed that the bank "expresses it opinion on important local and societal matters."

CHAPTER 18

Cycle of continuous improvement

quality

Delivering quality and value for money

This section of the book could have followed any one of three chapters: Employees and Managers, Customers or Suppliers. We have chosen to place quality management after the chapter on customers because the majority of definitions of quality speak to issues of fitness for use or meeting the requirements of customers. In this respect, quality is not some predetermined set of physical criteria; it is a reflection of products and processes which satisfy, and ideally delight the customer's needs and desires. Those needs and desires may in turn be economic, social, physiological or psychological.

In earlier chapters we referred to the quality revolution which was spurred by academic theorists like W. Edwards Deming and enthusiastically embraced by Japanese companies well placed to capitalize on disciplined but participative ways of working. We also described how companies in Europe and North America have successfully reproduced Japanese innovations like "just in time" manufacturing and "zero defects" approaches through worker inclusive and empowering approaches to management. According to Frederick Reichheld, employee loyalty and customer loyalty are closely related[1]. US companies lose 50 percent of their customers every five years, 50 percent of their employees every four years and 50 percent of their investors every year. The most successful companies in the USA hold on to their employees and customers longer.

Today there are well-established national and international standards which businesses may use as templates for introducing processes of quality management. They include the International Standards Organization ISO 9000 series[2], British Standard BS 5750, the European Foundation for Quality Management European Quality Award (EQA) and the US

Malcolm Baldridge National Quality Award (MBNQA) and Deming Prize. The strengths of the EQA and Baldridge criteria lie in their linkage of strategic business objectives with human resource development, customer satisfaction and even (in the case of EQA) impact on society. This approach is usually referred to as Total Quality Management (TQM).

John Oakland describes a model for TQM which links quality directly to competitive performance by optimizing processes and relationships (interfaces) between customers and providers (suppliers)[3]. To do this requires "soft" mechanisms: commitment, communication and culture and "hard" management processes: systems, tools and teams (see Figure 18.1).

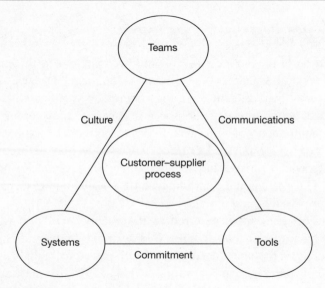

Figure 18.1
Total quality management (TQM) model

In this chapter, we shall not explore TQM in exhaustive detail. This is partly because most companies (probably including yours) already have strong views on quality management, but mostly because there are lots of manuals and even more experts out there describing how to do it. However, we will stress two key principles for the aspiring stakeholder corporation before taking a quick skim around the subject. These are:

1 Quality and perceived value can only be established through effective dialogue with customers (and thereafter with other stakeholders, most especially suppliers).

2 Quality must transcend simply functional issues of fitness for use and should embrace psychological and emotional components of customer needs and desires (see Case Study 18.1).

CASE STUDY 18.1

Redefining the value equation at IKEA

IKEA has a worldwide network of stores selling simple, low cost, high quality furnishings made to Scandinavian design but globally sourced. The key to IKEA's success is a redefinition of the value equation between the company and its customers and suppliers. The company's stores are convenient to use and provide family friendly facilities. Their products are largely flatpacked for self-assembly at home. So the customer is mobilized to add their own value in return for a lower cost product. IKEA's suppliers are also embraced in the innovative values equation: provided they also keep costs down, they receive access to global markets, technical support and even help with equipment leasing. Thus the company has been described as "more than a link on a value chain. It is the center of a constellation of services, goods and design."

The process

Figure 18.2 depicts a generic cycle of improvement for quality management that embraces the two principles noted above and is consistent with most quality and TQM standards. The observant reader will recognize that it is not dissimilar to the cycles of continuous improvement advocated for occupational safety and health (Chapter 16) and environmental protection (Chapter 22). This is intentional because, as we have noted, many companies are now integrating environmental management with either quality or safety or both.

Leadership and commitment

The European Quality Award makes explicit the connections between leadership, processes and business results (see Figure 18.3).

The enlightened reader will already have worked out why a quality or total quality management program is important to his or her business. There are few successful people in business today who do not recognize the importance of quality as a strategic business issue. The really sharp reader will have also spotted how all this talk of stakeholder inclusion is just another way of describing how value can be established through a process of dialogue and sharing of ethics in order to establish what quality actually means to a customer. When Ross Perot was at General Motors

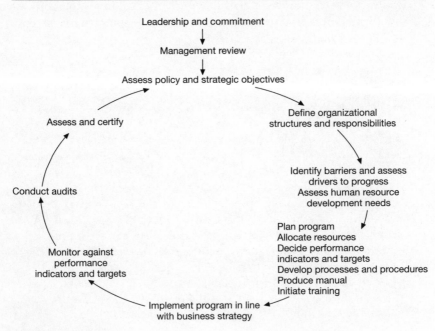

Figure 18.2
Cycle of continuous improvement for effective management and audit of quality

he had no difficulty in identifying the linkages between leadership, strategy, customer care, people management and future prosperity. In a typically direct memorandum to GM executives he wrote, "You hate your customers, you hate your dealers, you hate your workers and your shareholders, you even hate each other – how can you have a bright future?"[4]

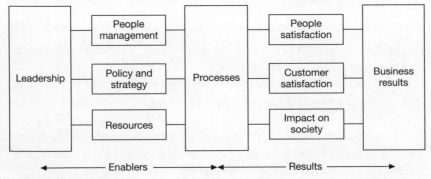

Figure 18.3
Connections between leadership, processes and business results (EQA)

Oakland suggests ten key characteristics for leadership in implementing TQM:

1 The organization needs long-term commitment to constant improvement.

2 Adopt the philosophy of zero errors/defects to change the culture to right first time.

3 Train the people to understand the customer–supplier relationships.

4 Do not buy products or services on price alone – look at the total cost.

5 Recognize that improvement of the system needs to be managed.

6 Adopt modern methods of supervision and training – eliminate fear.

7 Eliminate barriers between departments by managing the process – improve communications and teamwork.

8 Eliminate arbitrary goals, standards based only on numbers, barriers to pride of workmanship, fiction.

9 Constantly educate and retrain – develop the "experts" in the business.

10 Develop a systematic approach to manage the implementation of TQM.

The only extra component we would add to the list is vision. CEOs who have a clear long-term view of where they want their customer relationships to be in five to ten years' time can revolutionize the commercial prospects of their business.

Management review and assessment of policy and strategic objectives

Senior management should regularly review its strategy on quality – at least annually, and ideally more often. In addition, measures of quality performance should feature on a continuous basis in all management information systems designed to assess the health of the business.

Where such systems do not already exist and a quality policy has yet to be formalized, a company might usefully engage a consultant to undertake a rapid review of the current status of quality management in the business. This review might encompass an assessment of existing "contracts" (formal and informal) with customers and suppliers, direct interviews with customers and other stakeholders on their perceptions of quality management, inspections of records of complaints and an analysis of any trends in communications between the company and its customers.

If the customer perception and inclusion activities described in the first part of this chapter have been undertaken, the management review will benefit enormously.

As noted above, a number of options exists for setting strategic objectives and policy. Achieving accreditation to one of the national or international quality management systems standards is a logical goal for most companies. This may be done as a stand-alone exercise or alongside human resource development (for TQM) or environmental management or both (for TQEM). Philips is one company which has successfully put quality at the center of its business strategy (see Case Study 18.2).

CASE STUDY 18.2

Philips: the total quality approach

Philips, the Dutch-based electronics group is famed for its successful refocussing on quality as the route to correcting declining sales performance. When the company decided to introduce a formalized process of environmental management and audit, it was natural to extend their inhouse Philips Quality Standard PQA-90, adding 12 specific criteria to the 153 assessment elements of the existing standard. In this way, the four pillars of their "total quality" approach became quality, environment, people and finance. In addition, certification to European (EQA) or US (Baldridge) quality awards could be supported by both ISO 9000 and ISO 14001 systems.

The quality policy should be drawn up in such a way as to reflect the vision of the company and its purpose as a business. Indeed many companies ensure that customer satisfaction is part of their overall company mission. In assessing current policy and strategy, the following seven questions may be posed.

1 Has the company defined its commitments towards its customers?
2 Are suppliers formally embraced in the quality policy?
3 Is quality a declared responsibility of senior management?
4 Is employee participation in quality improvement explicit and understood?
5 Does the company have a stated commitment to training and awareness-raising or quality?

6 Is the reporting of progress on quality a mandatory part of management communications in all parts of the business?

7 Has the company specifically stated the priority of designing quality into products and services (rather than inspecting it in *ex post facto*)?

When a policy or strategy is being announced for the first time, or if it is being relaunched following significant amendment, maximum efforts must be devoted to its communication. Pledges from the CEO, mass meetings, videos and bulletins should all be used to maximum effect to energize workers and set the tone for their inclusion in the process. The articulation of quality goals alongside other business objectives ensures they are seen as central to the long-term future of the company.

Define structures and responsibilities

As with all aspects of governance and continuous improvement, responsibility for quality cannot be devolved to a specialist director or department. It must be shared by all managers and reflected in the job descriptions of all relevant employees. Nevertheless, the internal expertise must be developed and led. So a senior executive should answer directly to the leadership of the company on all matters of quality improvement and he or she should be supported in turn by the specialists, assessors and auditors necessary to oversee and encourage implementation of the program.

Identify barriers and drivers: assess human resource development needs

Employee morale is a critical success factor in the implementation of a quality program. Effective communications at the supplier and customer interfaces are equally vital. Morale and communications are both reflections of the culture of the organization. Some of the best examples of cultural revolutions achieved in the UK come from the automotive industry. Traditionally a bastion of conflict and noncooperation, the British motor industry has witnessed several complete reinventions of company culture based on a quality led, employee inclusive approach (see Case Study 18.3).

We touched briefly on organizational development in Chapter 16. Before introducing TQM, a fundamental appraisal of human resource strategy may be needed. Any dysfunctionality or barriers in the organization which might lead to disruption of teamworking or disempowerment need to be eliminated or ringfenced. Behaviors and values need to be aligned and positive attributes reinforced. Questions of diversity and equal opportunities may be especially relevant here[5]. Business success and a commitment to quality must be shared throughout the company. If this cannot be done, you may as well abandon all hopes of achieving a high standard of quality management.

CASE STUDY 18.3

A revolution at Rover

Spurred on by their first employee attitude survey in 1986 and their association with Honda, Rover launched a Total Quality Improvement program with the objective of promoting "company-wide awareness of Total Quality principles and the involvement of all employees in quality improvement activities, focusing in particular on process change to contribute to the delivery of Extraordinary Customer Satisfaction." Underpinning the transition was a commitment to job security, top level leadership and extensive training and development. The management style which emerged was more based on optimizing processes and culture, less on structure and hierarchy. Team working and corporate learning became key features of Rover's "New Deal" culture.

Plan program

In our cycle of continuous improvement on page 256 we identified five factors which need to be embraced as a minimum in the quality program:

1 **Resources:** must be adequate both with respect to time and money; real investments need to be made before they can be recouped in improved efficiencies and enhanced business performance.

2 **Performance indicators:** may include results of safety testing, production failure/success rates, costs/benefits, supplier and customer service levels, productivity measures, inventory, results of supplier rating, staff morale/turnover, customer complaints and satisfaction statistics, etc. They may be corporate or local, but they must be understood and agreed by everyone and everyone must feel they can make a difference in driving the indicators in the right direction; they should also be linked to the reward and recognition system.

3 **Processes and procedures:** may include flow charts, work instructions, terms of reference for employee quality circles and problem-solving teams.

4 **A quality manual:** hard work to compile and update but essential to link overall policies/goals with processes and procedures; also, you cannot get accreditation without one.

5 **Training:** a TQM program will need a significant investment in training, especially with respect to teamworking, team leadership and problem-solving; training needs to impact at every level of the organization (including executives). It should be inspiring, motivational and should start with the first day induction; training must be recorded and itself subject to continuous improvement.

None of the above can be omitted from a TQM program, but the key factor linking everything together and driving employee inclusion is training. One company which has successfully balanced all of the key factors and placed training at the heart of its quality program is Unipart (see Case Study 18.4).

CASE STUDY 18.4

A deep commitment to learning

In 1987 John Neill led automotive parts manufacturer Unipart in a management buyout. In eight years, share value increased 40,000 percent and turnover to £864 million. At the center of Neill's approach is the Spirit of Unipart – a stakeholder inclusive "people culture" based on group philosophy which is "to understand the real and perceived needs of its customers better than anyone else, and to serve them better than anyone else." At the group headquarters, the learning culture is emphasized by the space and effort devoted to vibrant internal communications and to the "Learning Curve", part of the Unipart University – a facility opened in 1993 "to develop, train and inspire people to achieve World Class performance within UGC companies and amongst its stakeholders." John Neill participates personally in the induction program of every new employee.

Implement program in line with business strategy and monitor performance

We have stressed the linkage of the quality program to business strategy because there is no point in making quality an academic or second order activity. These days customers treat quality as a nonnegotiable. Consequently, if quality (in its broadest sense) is not delivered, customers will be lost to competitors. Even where there is only one source of supply, customers will not be slow to exercise their rights and incur costs for a sloppy provider by lodging complaints, warranty claims, and even claiming liabilities for product or service failure.

There is no substitute for total alignment of the quality program with business performance goals. This must, in turn, be underpinned by continuous monitoring and reporting of those key performance indicators of quality relevant to senior management and the rest of the business (see Case Study 18.5).

CASE STUDY 18.5

Measuring the impact of quality improvements in Britain

In a survey of quality management in Britain published by the Industrial Society in 1996, 90 percent of responding companies claimed to have some kind of quality initiative in place. About a quarter were pursuing ISO 9000, 16 percent total quality management and 8 percent the business excellence model of the European Foundation for Quality Management. The majority of companies (59 percent) was able to identify cost savings arising from a quality drive, only 5 percent said it cost more to implement than it saved. For those involved in quality programs, the top three ways of measuring quality improvements were: number of customer complaints (82 percent), delivery performance (68 percent) and customer surveys (63 percent).

Conduct audits, assess and certify

John Oakland[3] draws a distinction between first party audits carried out by an internal quality assurance assessor, second party audits, i.e. where a customer audits a supplier, and third party audits where an independent assessor provides certification against an external standard. Most external standards require an internal audit to have been carried out as part of the "feedback loop" of continuous improvement. So the auditing process can be thought of as something of a continuum.

In our experience, it is possible to embrace all aspects of quality in an audit: physical and psychological. A company with defined "values" can audit its suppliers to establish "goodness of fit" with those values and the basis of ongoing dialogue about alignment. A number of companies has done this on environmental and safety issues, and some (including Levi Strauss and Reebok) on human welfare and social issues. In Chapter 19 we shall explore this in more detail.

International Standards Organization standard ISO 10011 is intended to provide general guidance on auditing and how to provide for independence between the assessor and the client. As we noted for occupational safety and health auditing and shall do again for environmental auditing, the skills of an auditor are manifold and there is no substitute for professional training and expertise. Auditors need to be diplomatic, courteous, firm and persistent. They need to have a high level of integrity and be able to maintain confidentiality of individuals who bring problems to their attention. Auditors need to be well organized and able to frame recommendations in a constructive and motivational way. They need to be able to communicate effectively at all levels and generate confidence and trust quickly. Auditors must have a good eye for documentation and "corroborating evidence" for their judgements on the effectiveness of management systems, but they should not behave like police inspectors. They are there to help. An effective internal quality audit team will ensure that external assessment and certification brings no surprises to the organization.

CHAPTER 19

Cycle of inclusion

suppliers and business partners

Partners as a source of competitive advantage

In Chapters 17 and 18 we stressed the importance of linking the needs of customers with the aspirations of employees in order to help facilitate the delivery of value and quality. We also stressed that for total quality management to work there needs to be a strong thread of shared values between customers, employees and suppliers. According to British academic David Farmer:

> We buy things to add value to them in some way and then to sell. Thus, effective purchasing is an "enabler" for effective marketing. Indeed I would argue that many western companies which were seemingly effective in marketing their products, failed because their purchasing was not good enough to give their products competitive advantage in their end markets. However, the marketing-production-purchasing relationship is not simply linear, it is iterative[1].

In their handbook, *Strategic Supply Management*, Tom Chadwick and Shan Rajagopal describe a study of eight UK-based multinationals which had entered into strategic partnerships with key suppliers based on information sharing and trust. The companies included IBM, Philips and Motorola. Seven key potential benefits of partnership purchasing were identified.

- contribution to improvements in the quality of inputs and to the final product
- contribution to reducing the total cost of the relationship to the buyer
- contribution to enhancing customer service

- significant reduction in risks involved in procurement
- contribution to technological superiority
- contribution to reduction of time to market for the buyer's products
- contribution to competitive position.

In all eight case studies and across all seven areas of potential benefit there were very few examples of detrimental impact or failure to improve from a partnership approach. In the majority of cases improvements were either "significant" or "considerable."

The history of supply chain management has been profoundly affected by the Japanese approach to managing industrial relationships[2,3,4]. We have already seen how the UK and US automotive industries were revolutionized by their adoption of principles of continuous improvement and just-in-time manufacturing. The impact of the philosophy of Japanese car makers like Nissan, Toyota and Honda on parts suppliers has been no less significant (see Case Study 19.1).

CASE STUDY 19.1

Supplier partnership at Honda of America

At Honda of America 800 people are dedicated to supporting more than 200 supplier relationships. Honda has a strategy which it calls "BP": Best Position, Best Product, Best Productivity, Best Partner and Best Price. The impact of the program on more than 50 suppliers in the USA was an overall improvement in productivity of nearly 50 percent. The kind of assistance available to suppliers goes beyond quality management. Honda technical experts on environmental management, safety, finance and tax and even personnel issues may be made available to suppliers who need it. As Dave Nelson, vice president of purchasing at Honda of America says: "We buy from suppliers who help us to satisfy our customers' needs. We believe Honda suppliers are not simply selling their parts to Honda, they are selling their parts to our customers through Honda. We expect every supplier to develop the same care and dedication to customer satisfaction as we have."

Exactly the same phenomena have been witnessed in electronics, computing and telecommunications.

The shift in psychology between buyers and suppliers mirrors that between managers and employees and between companies and customers. There is an ever-increasing blurring of the traditional boundaries. Twenty years ago large companies would treat their relationships with suppliers as purely transactional: clear specifications were laid down and the supplier with the best service and keenest prices would win. Suppliers would be picked up and dropped at will. Ten years ago there was a recognition that in an increasingly competitive global economy, common interests such as efficiency and quality depend on more loyal relationships. Now we are in the era of mutuality and transparency, where retailers and manufacturers see suppliers of goods and services as extensions of their own operations, the upstream ownership structure being largely irrelevant to the end customer.

Of course suppliers are not the only important business partners. Key partners also include subsidiaries, distributors, franchisees and other organizations which may have complementary marketing and promotional strategies.

Chadwick and Rajagopal summarize their concept of factors which go to making a successful supplier partnership in Figure 19.1.

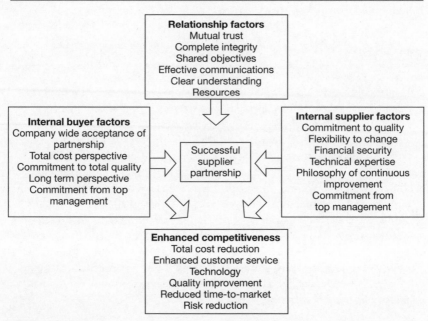

Figure 19.1
Summary of factors for a successful partnership[1]

On close examination of the model, it is evident that two-way communication and a shared understanding of customer needs are of paramount importance to a successful business partnership. Product design, quality and costings are important and obvious elements of the relationship which require mutual agreement. The UK Department of Trade and Industry guide *Getting the Best from Your Supply Partners* includes a list of easily measured supplier qualities:

- on time delivery
- number delivered against number ordered
- rejects on delivery and in process
- complaints by customers
- price stability.

The guide also suggests other, less measurable, but nevertheless very important indicators:

- after sales service
- willingness to get involved in design, cost reduction, etc
- investment programs
- good communication
- flexibility and good ideas
- efficient paperwork.

But as we noted in Chapter 16, there is more to quality than meets the eye. There are dimensions of "shared values" between companies and their customers which must also be mirrored between companies, their suppliers and their other business partners.

In recent years there has been growing interest in the ethics of the supply chain. In the USA considerable pressure has been exerted on retailers of footwear and garments to ensure that abuses of human rights, e.g. companies employing child or bonded labor or unsafe working conditions, were avoided. As a result, companies like Levi Strauss, The Gap and Reebok have developed inhouse monitoring and audit systems for verifying the standards of their suppliers. In effect they are checking that the values of their suppliers are consistent with those of their customers[6]. This kind of scrutiny is not reserved for Third World suppliers. In 1996 the US Department of Labor issued a monitoring guide entitled *No Sweat – Protecting America's Garment Workers*. The US National Minority Supplier Development Council lobbies to ensure that large companies give smaller and minority-owned vendors a fair chance of competing for business.

Outside the USA there is growing interest in human and civil rights issues in the supply chain. This is often manifested via third party inspection and labeling schemes. Examples include the Rugmark Foundation in India and the various fair trademarks in Europe: Transfair in Germany, the Fair Trade Mark in Britain and Max Havelaar in the Netherlands.

There has been just as much interest in the environmental credentials of suppliers. In 1993, Business in the Environment produced detailed guidelines for "integrating the environment into purchasing and supply" entitled *Buying into the Environment*[7]. The fact that these guidelines were endorsed both by the Prince of Wales and the Chartered Institute of Purchasing and Supply (the largest organization of its kind in Europe) demonstrated the mainstream applicability of the "greening" of supply chains. Organizations like BT, IBM UK, The Body Shop and home products retailer B&Q all provided case study material based on inhouse monitoring and assessment systems.

External certification of supplier environmental performance has also been developing – especially in the context of sustainable agriculture and forestry. The Smart Wood scheme of the Rainforest Alliance and the Forest Certification program of the multimember Forest Stewardship Council are two recent developments which now sit alongside the longer established systems for organic certification of food stuffs.

The process

For suppliers and business partners we will follow the same general process for stakeholder inclusion and participation as we advocated in Chapter 13 (pp. 168–80). The cycle depicted in Figure 19.2 gives step-by-step guidance on how to stimulate the kind of dialogue between companies which is necessary for aligning values and pursuing a common purpose.

When a large company first presents its agenda to potential suppliers and business partners, there is considerable scope for misunderstanding. This is especially the case where issues of ethical performance are raised, e.g. environmental and social practices. It is one thing sending details of required physical quality or technical specification to a potential supplier; this is unlikely to be deemed coercive or impertinent. It is quite another to request information concerning employment practices, pay rates and details of safety or environmental management. Suppliers who are keen to secure work may not feel offended, but they may well feel challenged. So style is everything.

Our recommendation for companies initiating dialogue on deeper partnership with potential suppliers and other business partners is to

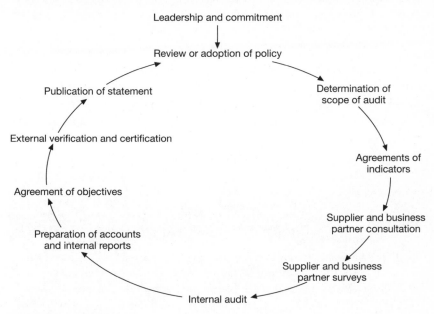

Figure 19.2
Cycle of inclusion for suppliers and business partners

avoid paternalism, eschew coercion and instead start with the following ground rules:

- the long-term objective is the alignment of values from end-customer to purchaser to supplier
- everyone can improve their performance, including the purchaser
- transparency is a two-way process.

Dialogue can be initiated via supplier seminars and conferences, one-to-one meetings, through questionnaires, via site visits and (more formally) through quality or ethical audits of one sort or another. Our advice is to consider carefully which method is most likely to satisfy the three rules listed above. Optimal progress will not be achieved through aggressive policing of standards backed by onerous contractual obligations. A flexible approach to continuous improvement supported by sharing of technical expertise and experience will generate a sense of unity of purpose and common understanding. Rewards and awards for improved performance may also help, as may common commitments to certification via quality systems standards (ISO 9000 series), environmental management standards (EMAS or ISO 14000 series) or total quality management approaches (e.g. European Quality Award, Baldridge or Deming prizes).

Aligning ethical values

According to research conducted for Business in the Environment in 1993, the majority of business customers (65 percent) and suppliers (71 percent) in the UK found that addressing issues of environmental performance led to improvements in relationships. A good example of a flexible, audit led approach to enhancing relationships with suppliers is that of Levi Strauss (see Case Study 19.2).

CASE STUDY 19.2

Levi Strauss reconcile corporate idealism with Third World reality

In 1992 Levi Strauss put in place sourcing guidelines to cover its worldwide manufacturing and procurement activities. The guidelines cover the 50-plus factories which the company operates around the world as well as its 600 plus primary contractors. The guidelines focus especially on social welfare and environmental protection. Many of the contractors are in the developing world where Western standards cannot be assumed. The guidelines deal with country specific issues and contractor level terms of engagement. The first round of audits led to 35 contractors being dropped and 175 needing to make improvements, mostly on occupational safety and health grounds. Audits are conducted by staff familiar with the trading relationship. This ensures that the results may be used constructively as part of an ongoing development of the commercial relationship rather than as a formalized pass/fail test. Vice president of community affairs Judy Belk says: "We're a consumer-driven company. Outside of our values, our brand and reputation are our most valued possessions. We were hearing from consumers that they were beginning to be much more concerned about where their products were being manufactured and under what circumstances. We wanted to be responsive and we wanted to do the right thing."

A UK-based group of nongovernmental organizations, The Independent Monitoring Working Group, has described how different parties may need to be involved in values-related dialogue beyond the customer–supplier relationship[6]. They consulted a number of key stakeholders in the debate around how to verify compliance with ethical codes of conduct dealing with social and environmental grades and produced the summary of stakeholder interests depicted below. It is important to note here that especially in developing world situations, local and international nongovernmental organizations may have strong points of view which it would be unwise to ignore. Moreover, the need for external assessment and verification is paramount.

Table 19.1
Summary matrix of stakeholder needs and requirements for improving social and environmental standards in supply chains[6] (southern in this context means being based in the Third or developing world)

Stakeholder	Main needs	Requirements
Workers	Improved working conditions	Reliable grievance procedures for workers and their representatives, feeding into process of gradual improvement of existing contractors
		Protection of workers' anonymity/confidentiality. Assessment of impact of pilot monitoring/verification experiences
Consumers	Reliable information	Cost effective, external verification of monitoring to back up promotional claims
Companies	Reliable information	Internal or external monitoring capacity (need for training and information)
	Protection	Verification by a trusted external verifier who guarantees company's confidentiality
Verifiers	Capacity to verify	An auditable code, background information
Contractors	Ability to meet codes of conduct	Built-in process of gradual improvement for contractors and companies within long-term relationships
Trade unions	Ability to represent workers	Input into grievance procedures, input into developing verification processes (e.g. in accrediting verifiers)
Southern non-governmental organizations	A voice in the process	Input into grievance procedures, input into developing verification process (e.g. in accrediting verifiers or in acting as verifiers themselves)
Northern non-governmental organizations	Reliable information	External verification of monitoring of companies codes of conduct by a trusted (accredited?) verifier. Assessment of impact of pilot monitoring/verification experiences.

Benchmarks and performance indicators

For conventional trading relationships, some basic criteria which may need to be agreed prior to contract are:

- specification and quality (including the broader, values based definition where appropriate)
- service and delivery
- pricing
- payment schedule
- ownership of know-how
- freedom and competition.

Tom Sorrell and John Hendry quote a 1993 survey of 5,200 small–medium sized businesses in the European Union where it was found that the average delay on payments to suppliers was 65 days[8]. A survey of 700 UK firms in 1992 showed that whereas companies with a turnover in excess of £50 million were paid an average of 15 days late, small firms with a turnover of less than £2.5 million were paid on average 29 days late.

Using suppliers and business partners and especially small businesses as an inexpensive form of credit is clearly morally dubious. At best it adds to costs, thereby reducing productivity and efficiency. At worst it may precipitate cash flow crises and bankruptcy. Other ethically suspect practices would include the creation of dependency, i.e. monopolizing a supplier's or business partner's output to the extent that they could not successfully compete elsewhere in the marketplace. It has been suggested that as a rule of thumb no more than 50 percent of a supplier's output should be taken by a single customer. However, this may not be realistic in some industries – especially where there is a high level of partnership being established. So our recommendation is simply to keep the dangers of dependency in mind when developing deeper relationships.

Finally, we are assuming that customer–supplier relationships should not be built on bribery and corruption. Our proposed benchmarks for assessing the quality of business–business relationships are detailed below.

Policy

- Should include a prompt payment policy, ethical codes for purchasing staff and agents, and standards against which business relationships will be measured e.g. safety and environmental standards and human and civil rights policies covering operations in countries where such rights may be denied. ☑

Contracts

■ Should include reference to ethical standards as well as conventional quality specifications and service requirements. ☑

Speed of payment

■ Should be tracked and reported. ☑

Pricing and margins

■ Should be transparent to both parties. ☑

Support and partnership arrangements

■ Should be documented and negotiated on a case-by-case basis. ☑

Trade with marginalized groups

■ Should be tracked and reported as a percentage of total purchasing, e.g. trade with ethnic minority suppliers, trade with small producers in developing countries, etc. ☑

Perception indicators

See Chapter 13 for general advice on conducting focus groups and questionnaire design.

Several companies have reported on their relationships with business partners and suppliers. In the case of Ben & Jerry's and The Body Shop this has included franchisees who act as important channels for distributing product. Traidcraft, the UK-based fair trade organization, has been especially keen to track the strength of its relationships with suppliers based in the developing world (see Case Studies 19.3 and 19.4).

CASE STUDY 19.3

How fair is fair trade with the developing world?

Traidcraft has a fair trading mission "to establish a just trading system which expresses principles of love and justice fundamental to the Christtian faith." In 1994–5 Traidcraft sourced goods from more than 100 producer organizations in 26 countries, to a total value of £2.2 million. The organization's social accounts for 1994–5 captured many of the joys and some of the frustrations of their trading partners. The report noted, "All producers [in Bangladesh] identified continuity of their relationship with the company and continuity of orders as the key factor in assessing Traidcraft's performance." However "producers were not generally aware of Traidcraft's longer term marketing plans and none had been given forecasts to indicate what continuity of business might mean for them." This conclusion echoed a similar comment from one of The Body Shop's fair trade partners: "Someone from The Body Shop has told us how much they will buy this year, but we cannot trust this since they have never before been right."

CASE STUDY 19.4

Franchisee options split on core values and business performance

The complex nature of relationships with business partners operating franchisees was revealed in the 1995 social reports of both Ben & Jerry's and The Body Shop. In both cases franchisees provided strong endorsement for their franchisor's mission. Of Ben & Jerry's franchisees 75 percent agreed or strongly agreed that the company's social mission was "vital to franchisees". The same percentage agreed that Ben & Jerry's maintains high ethical standards. Similarly 96 percent of The Body Shop's international franchisees said that the company's mission of dedicating its business to the pursuit of social and environmental change was important to them. Some 78 percent agreed that The Body Shop's reasoning for campaigns "is usually well communicated and thoughtful." On business relationships there was a little further to go. For example, 61 percent of Ben & Jerry's franchisees felt that the company's commitment to them "is sometimes inconsistent". Of The Body Shop's international franchisees 43 percent were dissatisfied with "the efficiency of communications on things that affect their market."

CHAPTER 20

Cycle of inclusion

the local community

Community involvement – a practical and ethical imperative

According to the Conference Board, in 1993 more than 90 percent of large companies in the USA had a community volunteer program, more than two-thirds allowed time off during work for volunteering and 63 percent had a community involvement fund[1]. In the UK, the commitment of business to community involvement is somewhat lower. A survey by the Charities Aid Foundation in 1995 found that only a third of large British companies had a volunteer program and in only 44 percent of those was time off work granted. Some 60 percent provided financial support and 70 percent offered matched funding. According to a 1996 MORI poll, 82 percent of people in Britain believe that a company's activities in society are fairly or very important in forming an opinion about the company.

In North America, it has been common practice for many years for firms involved in high risk activities to pay a great deal of attention to local community relations. Following the Union Carbide disaster in Bhopal, India, the US Congress enacted sweeping legislation to improve the rights of people living in close proximity to chemical plants. The Emergency Planning and Community Right to Know Act (EPCRA) required the US Environmental Protection Agency to develop regulations mandating business which manufactured hazardous substances to report details to local emergency planning committees, state agencies and local fire departments.

Oil refineries, chemical plants, nuclear stations and waste incineration facilities do not tend to inspire the trust of the local community if there is an atmosphere of secrecy and noncommunication. And if something goes wrong, the cost of poor community relations in terms of litigation and liability can be very great indeed. There is often a delicate interplay between the psychology of workers employed in the plant and the community where the plant is sited. The nuclear and waste industries provide some especially fascinating case studies in this area.

In the USA, the phenomena of NIMBY (not in my back yard), BANANA (build absolutely nothing anywhere near anyone) and the rather more hard line NOPE (not on planet earth) are well known to the nuclear and waste industries. In recent decades scores of nuclear power plants and incinerators for domestic and toxic wastes have been cancelled or blocked because of the refusal of local communities to live with the perceived risks. In Japan, opposition to nuclear power is so intense that only two new reactor sites have been approved since the accident at Three Mile Island in the USA in 1979[2].

In France, a rather more centralized planning system allows local communities to benefit from the reduction and even elimination of local taxation in exchange for the imposition of nuclear plants. This form of direct compensation (or bribe, depending on one's point of view) has proven rather effective, and nuclear expansion continues in that country. But elsewhere in Europe the industry is in retreat. Not a single new reactor was commissioned in Europe in 1995.

Whatever the local regulatory and planning system, and whether it is for environmental, safety, or wider ethical and social reasons, there is now general understanding of the need to maintain good community relations – particularly where companies are a major, or indeed the main local employer.

There have been different approaches to this over the years. There was the paternalism of the early industrial era, with local magnates like the Pilkingtons distributing wealth locally both through wages and direct community investment, e.g. in education and infrastructure. There has been the size factor with large enterprises like Du Pont in Wilmington, Delaware, Dow in Midland, Michigan, General Motors in Detroit, which simply become a *de facto* component part of the local civic scene. There has been the community investment approach, with largesse distributed to community, cultural and sporting groups wherever the company has head offices or local operations. IBM, S. C. Johnson, Levi Strauss, McDonald's, Shell UK and BT are well known for this approach (see Case Study 20.1).

CASE STUDY 20.1

Enlightened self-interest in investing in the community

David Logan has cataloged case studies of giving by transnational companies such as American Express, IBM, Royal Dutch Shell and Allied Dunbar. He describes the main motivations of Trans National Companies for community involvement as:

- to demonstrate moral and social responsibility
- to influence the social and political environment, i.e. social investment to enhance long term self-interest
- to promote direct self-interest through donations and sponsorship.

He quotes IBM's objectives in the USA: "Our philanthropic activities are founded in the corporation's self-interest. We endeavor to be responsive to community efforts, within the limits of financial ability, in all locations where we operate."

There is the consultation approach – particularly favored by higher risk operations like oil refining and petrochemicals, where channels of formal communication and information provision are established to avert legitimate concerns of the community turning into outright suspicion and hostility. And finally there is the mutual development approach, where companies see community involvement through community volunteering in company time as an effective way of developing both the community and the employees. Procter & Gamble, IBM (again), Grand Metropolitan and BP have made this an overt part of their approach to corporate citizenship (see Case Studies 20.2 and 20.3).

CASE STUDY 20.2

The Grand Metropolitan Kapow program

A Gallup poll sponsored by Grand Met in the USA in 1991 discovered that only 23 percent of 8 to 12 year olds believed that education would lead to a successful career. So Kids and the Power of Work was codesigned by Grand Met and the National Child Labor Committee to connect company volunteering with classroom activities, visits to sponsoring businesses and a professionally designed curriculum. The object is to teach team working, good behavior and decision-making skills while combating gender, age and race stereotypes. By 1994, the program was operating in 16 US states and was benefitting 4,500 students via a network of 400 volunteers and 200 educators.

CASE STUDY 20.3

British Petroleum - an overt commitment to education

Like Grand Metropolitan, in 1994 BP produced a detailed (if unaudited) report of its investments in the community. *BP in the Community* described BP's corporate citizenship activities in community development, education, the environment and the arts. Support for educational activities absorbed 41 percent of the $29 million committed by the company in 1994. In the BP UK Schools Link Scheme 200 schools (more than 100,000 pupils) were linked to 22 BP sites which provided teacher and student placement opportunities and other sources of educational support. Although unaudited and largely written from a noncritical public relations perspective, BP did attempt to list the benefits and impacts of each of its programs around the world.

For some companies, community volunteering has major spin-offs for employee and management development. In a report on Employees and the Community prepared by Prima Europe on behalf of seven blue chip companies, including IBM and Grand Met, the business benefits of volunteering were made quite explicit. There was no doubt that from US and UK experience, individuals volunteering in the community improved specific competencies, particularly people skills, e.g. customer focus, communication, collaboration and influencing. Evidence from both the UK and USA showed that volunteering was generally good for morale and the retention of valued employees. Grand Metropolitan has a matrix which allows employees to match opportunities for personal development, e.g. mentoring, internal individual assignments and volunteering in the community with skills such as influencing, problem-solving and interpersonal behaviors. Companies like BT assess the success of community volunteering programs in staff attitude surveys.

Each of these approaches has its merits, depending on the particular circumstances of your company. It is unlikely you will be able to excel at all of them. For example, in the USA, companies like Tom's of Maine and Ben & Jerry's have devoted regular, quite high percentages of pretax profits to charitable causes, i.e. 10 and 7.5 percent respectively (see Case Study 20.4).

S. C. Johnson devotes 5 percent in the USA (approximately 3 percent elsewhere). Rates of 1 to 5 percent are not uncommon in the USA. During the 1980s, companies like Polaroid, Hewlett-Packard, H. B. Fuller, Cummins Engine Company and Stride Rite regularly gave sums in the upper part of this range. In Britain Wellcome set up a charitable trust to absorb

CASE STUDY 20.4

A well-developed sense of local philanthropy in Vermont

In 1995 Ben & Jerry's gave 7.5 percent of pretax profits to charity. This compares with around 1 percent for the US food and manufacturing sectors as a whole. The policy is to allocate 50 percent to the Ben & Jerry's foundation, 35 percent to employee community action teams and the remainder to corporate donations. In addition, the company gave away tens of thousands of gallons of ice cream.

all of the profits of its drugs sales. It is not easy to match examples such as these.

In Britain, in 1986, the Per Cent Club was launched by the Prince of Wales; today members are committed to contributing no less than half a percent of pretax profits or one percent of dividends to the community[3]. Although some members comfortably exceed this target, it would be seen as somewhat undemanding in corporate social responsibility circles in the USA. In their assessments of corporate philanthropy, The Council on Economic Priorities accords a category A ranking only to companies donating more than 1.6 percent of pretax profits to charitable causes.

The process

The process for ensuring local community participation is that described in the generalized cycle of inclusion for social stakeholders (Chapter 13, pp. 168–80). It is worthwhile remembering that community consultation and participation can be done directly or via local voluntary organizations. So focus groups and surveys can embrace ordinary members of the local community, local authority, civic bodies, voluntary and welfare agencies, conservation groups, residents' and tenants' associations and so on.

Business in the Community recommends a six point approach with the acronym ACTION: Assess, Commit, Tell, Integrate, Organize and Nurture. These components fit well with the cycle of inclusion shown in Figure 20.1.

Below we set out some benchmarks for community involvement which embrace the multiplicity of options available. Our belief is that companies which maintain the support and involvement of communities where they operate will help create a more vibrant local economy from which they will inevitably derive some benefit. But we would also suggest two basic ground rules:

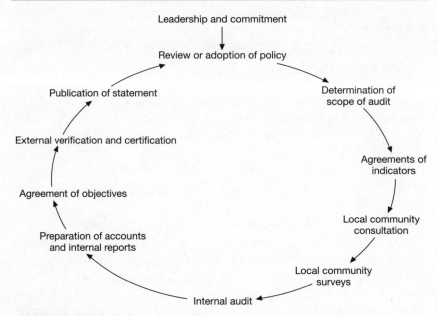

Leadership and commitment

Review or adoption of policy

Publication of statement

Determination of
scope of audit

External verification and certification

Agreements of
indicators

Agreement of objectives

Local community
consultation

Preparation of accounts
and internal reports

Local community
surveys

Internal audit

Figure 20.1
Cycle of inclusion: the local community

1 Community involvement has to be real. It must be a genuine, two-way, participative and inclusive deal. It should not be based on a paternalistic "gift" mentality. The community has to be able to engage with the company to articulate their needs and develop joint initiatives on social, environmental and economic questions from a position of genuine empowerment. This can be formal, through elected local representatives and politicians, or it can be through creative and energized forums to which the local private sector contributes.

2 There must be full transparency on how community engagement happens and how it is measured both in quantitative and qualitative terms. In kind donations, volunteering, secondments, use of company facilities are all of potentially immense practical value to the community. But their cash value should not be overstated for the purposes of public relations.

Just occasionally, a company will have to withdraw its support or involvement in a community, for unavoidable economic reasons. In other cases, the investment is by its nature transient, e.g. in construction or infrastructural development (see Case Study 20.5).

CASE STUDY 20.5

Nuclear energy expansion: a very mixed blessing for one community

The small English community of Leiston in Suffolk became a boom town during the construction of a second nuclear power plant at Sizewell. The 4,000 construction workers on pay rates five times the local average brought wealth, prostitution and drug abuse. After their departure Leiston was left with bankruptcy and dereliction. Local butcher Michael Day said, "Our reputation has gone and no one will invest in the town. No one wants to live here either; and those who could get out have already done so."

A company which has observed the rules of participation and transparency while it was involved will be respected a lot more than one that sprays cash around for PR reasons when the going is good, but disappears in the dead of night with no consultation with the community when times are hard. A good example has been set in the European Union by the the European Business Network for Social Cohesion. This group was set up in 1995 to counteract the negative social impacts of an increasingly competitive global economy. Companies like Philips, Kellogg's and British Telecom are part of a coalition of more than 300 European businesses examining ways to avert redundancies, improve training and reintroduction of workers into the labor market and to protect vulnerable groups in the community.

Benchmarks and performance indicators

Donations

- Straight financial donations should be separately administered, accounted and reported as a percentage of pretax profits. This may include administration costs, separately accounted.

- If employee fund-raising is encouraged or matched by the company, this should be recorded and reported, but the distinction between company and employee contributions made clear.

■ Donations policies should be clear to avoid time-wasting ☑

■ Foundations, where established, should operate to formal terms of reference, observing all relevant legal and moral duties for financial stewardship and respecting the rights and needs of recipients of grants at all times. ☑

Volunteering and secondment

■ The volunteering policy should be clear and well communicated. ☑

■ Time volunteered by individuals should be recorded and reported, but not necessarily costed. This is because there is an ambiguity over the real value of the individual's time. If it is in part for personal development, the activity is not a straight financial gift. ☑

■ There should be a high level of devolvement of decision-making around community involvement. Where appropriate, employees should be given the opportunity as an established right, but not coerced into it for career development or other reasons. ☑

■ Where appropriate, community volunteering should be enhanced and reinforced by parallel activities, e.g. human resource development and direct charitable donations. ☑

Investment and disinvestment

■ Companies must treat local public opinion and local democratically elected representatives with the utmost respect. Where a company is a dominant economic influence in a community there should be formal and regular channels of communication. ☑

■ Planning law must be respected at all times. ☑

■ Where disinvestment or complete withdrawal is contemplated, full collaboration with other local economic entities should be undertaken to mitigate the impacts of unemployment and to maximize opportunities for reskilling and re-employment. ☑

Training and education

■ Companies with expertise to share with small businesses in their local community should do so. This might include

general business skills, marketing, environmental and
safety management.

■ Businesses with a genuine commitment to local education
(rather than product marketing) will devote resources to
schools and colleges in the form of materials and support.

Perception indicators

Community surveys and questionnaires should be designed following
focus groups to identify all relevant issues. See Chapter 13 for general
advice on conducting focus groups and questionnaire design (see Case
Study 20.6).

CASE STUDY 20.6

Testing the temperature of local opinion

In 1991 IBM conducted a worldwide study of attitudes of the general
public, opinion leaders and employees towards the company's record on
corporate social responsibility. Respondents were asked to rate the company on a number of issues relating to engagement with the community,
including IBM's support for education, charitable donations and
employee volunteering.

In its telephone survey of local people in 1993, Sbn Bank asked eight
questions designed to explore the quality of its relationships with the
local community: 53 percent agreed either strongly or slightly that "Sbn
Bank takes an active part in developing the region of North Jutland" (23
percent had no opinion); but only 18 percent agreed that the bank
involves citizens "in evaluating how it should contribute to developing
the local community" (39 percent disagreed and 42 percent expressed no
opinion).

CHAPTER 21

Cycle of inclusion

government and civil society

Globalization spells the end of the simple life

In a recent publication endorsed by the World Bank and the United Nations Development Program[1], the Prince of Wales Business Leaders Forum identified four "Rs" as foundations of corporate wealth:

- Reputation management
- Relationship management
- Responsiveness to systems and service needs
- Resource efficiency and enhancement.

The authors concluded that partnerships between the community, governmental and nongovernmental organizations and businesses are going to become the most important drivers for wealth creation, sustainable development and good governance in the future.

But today, business has been cast adrift from many of its former political certainties. Instead it has inherited a Pandora's box of political opportunities and pressures which have placed it in a state of confusion for much of the last twenty years. Companies are only now beginning to emerge from this period and to work out how to forge relationships with those groups in society and on the international scene which vie with business and with other economic actors for political space.

The last two decades have witnessed seismic shifts in the position of business within British society. The relatively cordial if ineffectual relationships which prevailed between government, employers' organizations and trade unions in the immediate post-war decades have been rendered superfluous. The corporatist state was well and truly buried during the

Thatcher years, being seen as anticompetitive and wholly antithetical to the operation of the free market[2]. Privatization of state industries (which had previously enjoyed a relatively comfortable sociopolitical role) and the elimination of the industry sponsoring functions of the Department of Trade and Industry were just two obvious manifestations of the single-minded pursuit of free market nostrums in 1980s Britain.

Meanwhile, because of privatization there has been massive growth in the power of regulatory agencies in the UK, with Oftel, Offer, Ofgas and Ofwat now responsible for the telecommunications, electricity, gas and water industries. And there has been an explosion in the power and resources of quasi-autonomous nongovernmental organizations (quangos). According to Democratic Audit, in 1994–5 more than 6,000 quangos run by more than 60,000 government or self-appointed individuals spent more than £60 billion of public funds – one-third of all government spending. These bodies are responsible for a wide variety of public service provision from housing to hospitals and from education to economic development. Neither the regulatory agencies nor the quangos are directly accountable to the democratic process.

Partly as a result of the political and accountability vacuum created by the withdrawal of the state from important aspects of social and environmental policy, the memberships of single issue pressure groups soared in Britain during the Thatcher years. Environmental pressure groups now number around 3 million members. Nearly one million of those simply wish to see birds properly looked after. These people give a massive £30 million per annum to the Royal Society for the Protection of Birds. At the other end of the spectrum more confrontational groups like Greenpeace and Friends of the Earth command memberships of several hundred thousand – easily on a par with the memberships of the major political parties. This phenomenon has occurred at a time when more traditional institutions like trade unions, professional bodies and even the churches have stagnated or declined in power and influence. So for British business, the map of regulatory and civil responsibility is now unrecognizable compared with twenty years ago.

In the USA, which invented the word "lobby" political influence has always been something of a free market free for all[3]. For American corporations, access to the legislature has always been direct and pluralistic (see Case Studies 21.1 and 21.2).

In the USA, industries, unions and pressure groups form competing Political Action Committees (PACs) to exert leverage and invest heavily in the re-election of favorably disposed political representatives. It was once possible for a presidential nominee for the post of Secretary of

CASE STUDY 21.1

Silas Deane and the French connection

In March 1776, a wealthy merchant and Connecticut politician was despatched by Congress to France to procure supplies for the American war against Britain. Silas Deane was to receive a commission of 5 percent on everything purchased from the French government. Anxious not to irritate the British monarchy too much, the French secretly gave large amounts of guns and ammunition to Deane and his French counterpart, Pierre Augustin Caron de Beaumarchais, without expecting payment. This did not stop the two *bon viveurs* presenting a massive bill to Congress for their efforts. Despite a huge public outcry, fermented in typically controversial fashion by the Secretary to the Committee for Foreign Affairs, Tom Paine, Deane mobilized numerous political supporters for whom public virtue and war profiteering were not incompatible. Robert Morris, a congressman from Philadelphia, was not averse to making a little on the side himself. He summed up the philosophy of the merchant supporters of Deane: "It is inconsistent with the principles of liberty to prevent a man from the free disposal of his property on such terms as he may think fit."

CASE STUDY 21.2

Empires more powerful than governments

A number of US multinational corporations overreached themselves when they tried to intervene in international politics in the 1970s. Anthony Sampson relates how arch autocrat Harold Geneen used unprecedented methods to exert IT&T's political muscle around the world. Geneen offered $1 million to help stop Salvadore Allende's election in Chile, fearing that the local telephone system would be nationalized. A subsequent Securities and Exchange Commission investigation of the company revealed spending of $8.7 million dollars on illegal activities in countries like Indonesia, Iran, the Philippines, Algeria, Mexico, Italy and Turkey. The abuses at IT&T, the short-sightedness of oil companies in the Middle East and the bribery scandals at Northrop and Lockhead led to robust investigations by a Senate subcommittee on multinational corporations chaired by Senator Frank Church (Idaho). It was only after the Church Committee decided to take on the international banks that it was wound up.

Defense to claim publicly and unabashed that "what was good for our country was good for General Motors, and vice versa[4]." David Korten traces the recent more subtle mobilization of US industrial political

muscle to the early 1970s[5]. He describes how in 1970 very few top companies retained public affairs offices in Washington; by 1980 more than
80 percent of the Fortune 500 did. In 1974 unions funded about half of
the activities of PACs; by 1980 this declined to less than a quarter. By the
mid-1980s, companies like Lockhead, Boeing and General Dynamics
were giving hundreds of thousands of dollars a year to PACs[6]. Most of
this money went to support incumbent politicians, and about half was
directly defence related.

Korten gives examples of how business interests have set up powerful
links with academia and developed worthy-sounding front organizations
to capture the moral highground and disguise their lobbying intent, e.g.
the National Wetlands Coalition, Consumer Alert, Keep America Beautiful. Networks of think tanks like the Heritage Foundation, the Competitive Enterprise Institute and the Institute for Educational Affairs link to
advocate the moral superiority and efficiency of the free market. Sometimes the methods employed by these coalitions appear quite sinister[7] (see
Case Study 21.3).

CASE STUDY 21.3

Scapegoating and subverting the greens

Andrew Rowell describes how some right-wing think tanks continue to
fight the old battles against environmentalists. Ron Arnold, the intellectual force behind Wise Use, the US coalition of industrialists, miners, log-
gers and property rights activists says, "Our goal is to destroy, to
eradicate the environmental movement." The PR agencies advising Wise
Use and their think tank fellow travellers advise scapegoating and dema-
goguery against environmentalists; so terms like "fascists," "terrorists"
and "communists" are routinely applied to activists. This language is
even parroted by politicians. Chip Berlet of Boston-based Political
Research Associates concludes "Ultimately, some people persuaded by
these scapegoating arguments conclude that the swiftest solution is to
eliminate the scapegoat."

The passage of the North American Free Trade Agreement provided an
insight into the sheer power of corporate America to drive through a
measure which may yet pose potential harm to ordinary people in the
USA. The Business Roundtable comprises about 200 CEOs of top companies. To mobilize support for the free trade case, the Roundtable set up
a broad-based coalition called USA*NAFTA to represent its interests and
propagandize the theoretical benefits to jobs and the environment of
North American free trade. But as the Inter-Hemispheric Resource

Center pointed out, the companies behind USA*NAFTA included businesses like General Electric, General Motors, Allied Signal, AT&T and IBM which had played their part in exporting nearly 200,000 jobs to Mexico in the preceding twelve years.

In 1991, the top 50 public relations firms in the USA had a turnover of $17 billion. Today there are more people employed in the US PR industry than there are news reporters[5]. Democracy is a harder game to play. In the 1996 presidential race, Green Party candidate Ralph Nader polled nearly half a million votes, coming fourth in the race. In Oregon Nader scored 4 percent of the popular vote and in some west coast districts and counties he polled nearer 10 percent. After the race, the Federal Election Commission unanimously declined to accord the Green Party the status of a national party because unlike the somewhat exotic Natural Law and Libertarian parties, they had not spent enough on their campaign.

The power of US industrial anti-environmental lobby groups like Wise Use has stimulated the environmental movement to join forces and put money into the League of Conservation Voters; a mechanism for targeting anti-environmental politicians and securing the election of their greener challengers. But the resources mobilized by LCV are just a fraction of those being deployed by their adversaries. The USA also has a long tradition of active citizenship on consumer and environmental issues. Ralph Nader has spearheaded much of this movement. The nonpartisan Citizens Action has built a network of 3 million activists ready to be switched on to local political issues ranging from environmental protests to civic mobilization. But again these groups have nothing like the money to play with that is mobilized by corporate America.

The more established political strength of business associations in Germany and the historically influential Ministry of International Trade and Industry in Japan illustrate that some countries retain machinery for perpetuating strategic national alliances between business and government. But even these are weakening against the pressures of economic globalization. Today the goodwill of the international banking and capital market systems and the politics of the trading blocs are proving much more of a lure to Japanese and German multinational businesses than their traditional avenues of power and influence.

All of these struggles are now moving supranational. The global warming debate is one that touches all of us. The threat to the planet and its ecosystems of a significant worldwide rise in ambient temperature is now well recognized. The financial costs are probably incalculable. As a result, some interesting alliances have sprung up to exert pressure on governments and international bodes. And for the first time, the US energy industry has split with the Edison Electric Institute (a trade association representing 600 US utilities) distancing itself from the relative complacency of the Global Climate Coalition sponsored by Chevron, General Motors and others.

So much for the macroeconomic and political issues of the day and the changing patterns of confrontations and alliances in business–government relationships. What of the day to day relationships of business with civil society? What of the behaviors and norms of companies conducting their everyday business? What standards should they aspire to? We believe that for most companies there are four key relationships to address:

1 Relationships with governments and regulators.

2 Relationships with civic bodies within local communities covered in Chapter 20.

3 Relationships with national and international nongovernmental organizations which represent relevant constituencies.

4 Relationships with opinion formers and reputation-makers, e.g. academics and media commentators.

Some of this takes us back into the territory of corporate giving, so in the following pages we will touch on that subject again.

The process

By now, it will not surprise you to learn that for the four principal stakeholder relationships listed above, we advocate a separate but similar process of inclusion and participation in the affairs of the company following the generalized model from Chapter 13 (pp. 168–80).

Where there is a history of suspicion and antagonism, e.g. with pressure groups, special care needs to be taken. In these cases intervention or mediation by third parties may be essential (see Figure 21.1). In recent years fora have evolved which allow former antagonists to meet and exchange views and develop some level of mutual understanding without losing their independence. European Partners for the Environment (EPE) is a group which was inspired by industrialist Claude Fussler of Dow to create some safe space for dialogue. Biotechnology company Novo Nordisk was advised by pro-environmental consultancy SustainAbility in their strategy of open dialogue with environmentalists suspicious of genetic engineering. But for industries involved in mining and logging there is a very long way to go before environmental groups express anything other than outright hostility to their operations (see Case Study 21.4).

CASE STUDY 21.4

Logging: pressure groups and industry in opposite camps

Logging is one of the most contentious issues between business interests and pressure groups. In September 1996, the Environmental Investigation Agency issued a report to coincide with UN Inter-Governmental Panel conference on forests. The EIA report, entitled Corporate Power, Corruption and the Destruction of the World's Forests, accused the $100 billion timber industry of "running out of control." The Report accused two firms of corruption and illegality and identified companies like Mitsubishi (Japan), Hyundai (South Korea) and Georgia Pacific (US) of "permanent degradation" of native forests, "clear cutting" and "double-speak." According to EIA, among the environmental threats exacerbated by logging companies and their activities are soil erosion, flooding, global warming and species extinction.

Many pressure groups now recognize the preeminent and increasing power of business and industry and are modifying their own approaches accordingly. Thus even Greenpeace has engaged directly with industrial interests to promote technologies in the refrigeration and automotive industries which generate benefits for the environment. The Council on Economic Priorities, Human Rights Watch and Amnesty International have established dialogue with corporations sourcing in countries with poor human rights records in order to avoid abuses such as forced labor and the employment of children. Christian Aid has worked with UK supermarket groups to develop charters which protect the interests of workers in developing countries.

As pressure groups engage with business in this way, the potential for boycotts and confrontation recedes. But the threat always remains if things go wrong. And the antics of ideologues on the far right of the political spectrum may yet precipitate a return to more confrontational relations. The main issue for a company wishing to deepen its relationships with civil society is to decide how it wishes to be positioned.

Tom Cannon has proposed a "matrix of enlightenment" which may be helpful[8]. We have modified it a little for our purpose, which is to explain options for engagement in civil society (see Figure 21.2).

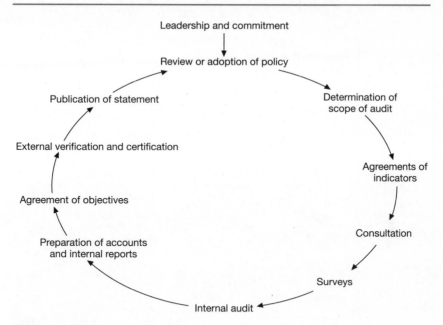

Figure 21.1
Cycle of inclusion for government and civil society

In the social mission category we might place companies with a very strong ethic, perhaps based on religious or social beliefs, where achievement of the mission is by its very nature intimately linked with the philanthropic behavior of the company. Here we might place alternative trade organizations like Traidcraft, the cooperative movement, Ben & Jerry's and The Body Shop. Pure philanthropists might include companies which bequeath cash to foundations without any direct requirement for publicity or control over how the money is spent. Some of the largest philanthropic donors in the USA today are foundations whose original source of cash came from decidedly nonphilanthropic activities. For example, in 1990, the combined assets of the Carnegie and Rockefeller foundations were more than $2 billion. Some of the most important recipients of the largesse of these and other industrial foundations have been the American universities. The Rockefeller foundation has contributed £180 million to the University of Chicago and Columbia University alone[8].

It is perfectly possible to make a strong conventional business case for philanthropic behavior[9]. Socially responsible companies are those which combine moderate–high levels of philanthropic behavior with a clear

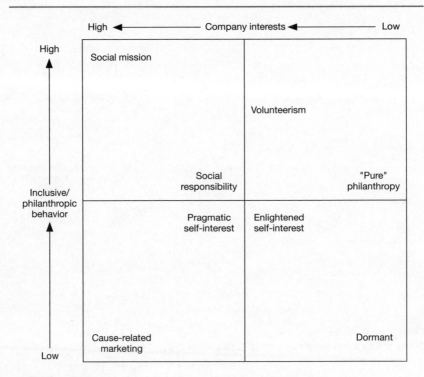

Figure 21.2
Matrix of enlightenment for engagement in civil society

recognition of the need to behave accountably and of the benefits which should accrue by way of reputation, customer loyalty and cohesiveness. Into this category we may place exemplar companies like Levi Strauss. Quite close to this group are those following a strategy of enlightened self-interest. Apart from the "dormant" group, this is probably the largest single category of all. Companies like IBM, Ford, S. C. Johnson, Grand Met and BT are mainstream examples which would probably say that moderate philanthropic behavior is good for business reputation and corporate legitimacy.

Globalization means that many multinational companies are now aligning their philanthropic activities with a strategic view of corporate citizenship[10]. This type of approach we may characterize as pragmatic self interest. In contrast to Asian companies where philanthropy is expected but relatively discrete, large US corporations like Coca-Cola, Merck, Philip Morris and Du Pont have reorientated their philanthropy to reflect "a broad view of their own self interest" and quite public programs of community engagement where they operate around the world.

Rather more volatile is the group which embrace cause-related marketing, using sponsorship of popular issues much more for corporate image making and sales promotion than for reasons of straight philanthropy. Walter Coddington has summarized a number of green cause-related marketing deals which were made in the USA in 1991[11]. The largest ranged from $300,000 from Procter & Gamble to Keep America Beautiful to $500,000 each from Conoco and Citicorp to the National Parks Foundation. In Europe, Benetton is possibly the best known exponent of this art, but Boots' sponsorship of cancer research linked to sales of its sun care products was a classic example[12]. In 1993 an undisclosed six-figure sum was raised for the Cancer Research Campaign by Boots' Play Safe in the Sun campaign which "built considerable traffic in-store for the Boots Company." On a lower level we may include all those companies which have paid for the use of the Worldwide Fund for Nature's panda logo on their products over the years.

As the reader may imagine, our advice to the mainstream stakeholder corporation is to pitch for a position somewhere between enlightened self-interest and the socially responsible position. More daring companies will trek a little further towards the social missionary position.

Companies in the upper left hand segment of Figure 21.2 need to have especially productive and inclusive relations with organizations representing civil society. And having decided upon strategic positioning, the next challenge is to encapsulate that positioning in a policy statement.

Our advice on policy statements is to cover positioning on at least the following topics:

- compliance with the law (especially consumer, safety, environmental and anti-trust law)
- political engagement, lobbying and payments to political parties and politicians
- government relations in countries with nondemocratic regimes
- bribery and corruption in business practice
- honesty in external communications
- sponsorship, donations and partnership arrangements with not-for-profit groups.

Procter & Gamble have a statement on Honesty and Integrity in Business which includes the following: "The Company's basic policy is that P&G funds or resources may not be used to make a political contribution to any political candidate or political party anywhere in the world."

According to a survey of international business people by Transparency International, Italy is one of the most corrupt countries in the world for business deals. On a scale of 0–10 (all deals corrupt – all deals clean), Italy scored just 2.99. On the same scale, the USA scored 7.79 and the UK 8.57. One of the cleanest countries was Singapore, with an impressive 9.26. Historically, corruption has been so endemic in Korea that until recently it was perfectly legal for individuals to maintain bank accounts under false names. A number of Korean companies has now adopted public codes of noncorruptibility to ensure that employees and officers of companies are not tempted to obtain business advantage through the accepting or giving of gifts (see Case Study 21.5).

CASE STUDY 21.5

Bribery and corruption: that'll be the Daewoo

In August 1996, a South Korean court took the rather novel if draconian step of sentencing a former president to death for accepting bribes and leading a military coup. In his term as president, Chun Doo-Lwan accepted millions of dollars of bribes from leading Korean firms like Daewoo and Samsung. Kim Woo-Choong, founder and chairman of Daewoo received a two year jail sentence. The Seoul Stock Exchange dropped 15 points on the day of the convictions. Happily for Mr Kim, the Federation of Korean Industries and the investment community in Seoul rallied round, fearing that his removal from the business scene could undermine confidence in the entire Korean economy. The local head of research at BZW securities was horrified by Kim's sentence and those dished out to eight other corrupt industrialists: "The consequences of imprisoning the business leaders are so awful for the economy that the market is hoping that they will receive suspended jail terms on appeal."

When strategic positioning and company policy is in place, then it is possible to complete the cycle of focus groups, surveys and audits of stakeholder opinion. In principle, there is no reason why politicians, not-for-profit organizations, academics and media commentators should not be asked for their opinion of a company.

Benchmarks and performance indicators

There are no standard lists of benchmarks in this area, so we will offer some:

Corporate policy

■ There should be a clear published statement of engagement with governments and civil society, including charitable, volunteering and other philanthropic activities described in Chapter 18.

Transparency

■ Companies should conduct public policy initiatives in the open without resort to disguised intermediaries and front organizations.

Political fairness

■ Companies should not distort party political processes by excessive donations.

Engagement with issues

■ Companies should contribute to the work of agencies in civil society which promote charitable, underrepresented or underfunded causes, and encourage employees to do the same e.g. via matched payroll giving, time off for volunteering, etc.

Perception indicators

There are examples of organizations which have undertaken research via focus groups to determine their reputation with civil society. Issues captured in this process have then been applied successfully in questionnaire surveys of civil society, i.e. organizations in the not-for-profit and charitable sectors (see Case Study 21.6).

CASE STUDY 21.6

Testing the water with campaign groups

In 1995, The Body Shop conducted a survey of 137 UK-based, non-governmental and campaigning groups. There was a low response rate (31 percent), but the overall message which came back was very clear. As with other stakeholder surveys conducted that year, there was strong support expressed for the company's ideals: more than four out of five agreed or strongly agreed that "The Body Shop takes active steps to make its business environmentally responsible" and three-quarters were satisfied with the "dedication to issues" of individuals they dealt with. How- ▶

▶ ever, there was room for improvement in how the relationships were managed. More than a third of the NGOs were dissatisfied with The Body Shop's delivery on commitments in "a timely and effective manner." Only around a third agreed it was easy to find the right decision-makers in the company.

We do not suggest that you issue questionnaires to politicians and regulators unless you are a very large and well-established corporation. For most companies, particularly those with track records in volunteering and donations, it will be perfectly possible to convene focus groups prior to questionnaire design and issue. See Chapter 13 for general advice on how to do this.

CHAPTER 22

Cycle of continuous improvement

the physical environment and nonhuman species

According to surveys commissioned by the UK Department of the Environment, between 1986 and 1989 the number of people in Britain spontaneously mentioning pollution of the environment as "one of the most important issues the Government should be dealing with" increased from 8 percent to 30 percent. By 1993, the effects of economic recession pushed the figure back down to 22 percent, behind unemployment (46 percent) and health/social services (29 percent). These figures compared with only 3 percent expressing concerns about income tax and a similar percentage on defense or nuclear weapons. According to an NDP survey in 1993, 44 percent of British people claimed to use bottle banks "on a regular basis"; 28 percent bought products because they were "environment friendly" and 16 percent used low energy light bulbs in the home. In the same year, a study by the Office of the Prime Minister in Japan found that 68.0 percent of women and 51.4 percent of men claimed to cooperate with waste separation and recycling systems; 39.2 percent of Japanese women and 33.4 percent of men tried to conserve electricity and water on a daily basis. There is little doubt that environmental protection has arrived as an issue of major significance both for individuals and for governments around the world.

As we have seen, the "business and environment" agenda is one of great complexity which is subject to significant and sometimes unpredictable political, economic and social influences. As a topic area of business ethics and good stakeholder relations, more is written about the environment than almost any other single subject (the main exceptions, perhaps being employment practice and quality management). The main advantage of this state of affairs is that there is no lack of written advice and punditry, no shortage of consultants willing and able to help, and certainly no chance of ignoring the issue. The downside is that much of the advice is conflicting and some of the initiatives coming from the business sector are divisive, defensive or downright disingenuous. Meanwhile many people are trying to make a fast buck out of the genuine concerns of ordinary citizens about the state of the planet.

Animal welfare and conservation is another issue – in this case involving nonhuman species – which any stakeholder inclusive company would be unwise to ignore. In 1996, the International Fund for Animal Welfare (IFAW) commissioned MORI to explore British attitudes to a range of animal welfare issues. Eighty-eight percent were concerned about seal killing and 83 percent about animal testing by the cosmetics industry. Sixty-nine percent were concerned about the transportation of live animals before slaughter and 67 percent about factory farming.

It would appear that these concerns are based on deeply held beliefs about the rights of animals. IFAW also found that in 1996, just under half the British people agreed with the proposition "Animals have rights which should be respected as much as human rights." Half agreed that animals have rights but secondary rights to humans. Less than 3 percent said animals have no rights.

The retail sector is especially sensitive to the growing interest of consumers in animal-friendly produce. According to research conducted in Britain by MORI, the number of people who claimed to have bought household or toiletry products which had not been tested on animals increased from 43 percent in 1990 to 52 percent in 1994. In the same period, the number of people buying free range eggs or chickens increased from 44 to 49 percent. Those claiming to buy organic produce in the previous twelve months remained relatively stable at around a quarter of the population.

Consumer concerns over unnecessary testing of consumer products on animals are not just confined to Britain. In 1996, The Body Shop International commissioned MORI to explore public attitudes to animal testing in the cosmetics industry in six European countries. Respondents were asked how strongly they supported or opposed a ban by the European Commission on the sale of cosmetic products ccontaining ingredients tested on animals. Opposition to animal testing was strongest in Britain where 73 percent strongly supported or tended to support a ban (with 18 percent undecided or offering no opinion). Figures for other countries in the EU were: Sweden, 68 percent in favour of a ban; Holland, 66 percent; Germany, 61 percent; France, 54 percent; and Italy, 46 percent (33 percent undecided or no opinion). Those opposed to a ban on animal testing ranged from just 8 percent in Holland to 21 percent in Italy.

Whatever your personal views about the importance of environmental or animal welfare issues to your business, they are both topics which should be approached with care and some humility. Undoubtedly you will have individual stakeholders – employees, customers and investors – for whom such issues are central to their personal belief system. Taking a responsible attitude to the environment and the protection of nonhuman species is therefore high on our list of priorities for stakeholder inclusion.

PART I – The physical environment

It is the somewhat ambitious goal of this section to guide you through the maze of environmental philosophy, policy, regulation, standards, management tools and audit systems. To do this we will offer an entirely pragmatic analysis and leave you to follow up on the detail. We will give you a routemap – everything a senior manager might need to steer a suitable course whether your business is large or small. Our only premise is that the issue is not a fad and is not likely to go away. Indeed the pace of regulatory activity now can only be superseded by the extent of fiscal and economic interventions in the future. So as a business person, you should now be considering what will be the implications for your company of significantly increased costs for energy and raw materials. What will be your approach when your company is made totally responsible for the costs and liabilities of all of its waste products, even when those wastes are incurred by consumers? You need to know how your business will approach future mandatory requirements for disclosure of all environmental impacts.

In order to help navigate this chapter, let alone the much tougher terrain beyond it, we are going to have to start with some definitions (see Exhibit 22.1). Our advice is to read these definitions three times and hand the book to the nearest teenager to test your powers of recall. If you score six out of ten or more, proceed to the next section.

EXHIBIT 22.1

The bluffer's guide to environmental terms

The environment. There is no single definition; it means different things to different people. Always check the definition of the person you are talking to before proceeding with the conversation. It will range from the technical (resources, energy, wastes, pollution) through the ecological (embracing humans, plants, animals and every other living creature), to the positively spiritual and philosophical (conservation, esthetics, and rights of human and other species).

Sustainable development. Economic development which meets the needs of the present while not compromising the rights of future generations to meet their own needs. Sounds simple, but extends the issue from environmental protection to social and economic fairness (equity) and the long term survival of humanity (futurity).

Environmental Management System (EMS). Like a quality management system, but in this case based on continuous improvement of environmental performance.

Environmental audit. A systematic, objective, periodic and documented assessment of a company's overall environmental performance (needs to be part of an EMS).

Environmental impact assessment. A thorough review of the environmental effects of a particular activity or new development (mandatory in some jurisdictions for planning purposes).

Environmental Statement. Objective, publicly available, and ideally independently verified statement of all relevant environmental impacts together with information on how those impacts will be controlled and minimized in the future.

Product stewardship. How products and services are sourced, produced and used, making sure that environmental/ecological/social effects are minimized and benefits maximized. Includes tools like Life Cycle Assessment (LCA)/ecobalances, vendor screening and accreditation, Design for the Environment (DfE)/eco-efficiency in manufacturing, "takeback" for recycling, consumer recovery, reuse and recycling.

Environmental effects register. A list of significant environmental effects incurred by your business, ideally linked to wider environmental issues such as contribution to global warming and resource depletion. Will tend to focus on issues of energy, raw materials, pollution and waste.

Global warming. The process by which fossil fuels (coal, oil, natural gas, gasoline) are burned producing carbon dioxide (CO_2) which in turn enters the atmosphere and causes a rise in temperature by helping trap energy from the sun (the greenhouse effect). Now accepted as a real effect by scientists and politicians – will lead to significant climate change and unpredictability, more hurricanes, floods and natural disasters.

Ozone depletion. The process whereby ozone in the upper atmosphere gets knocked out by chlorine atoms liberated by manmade chemicals like CFCs (chlorofluorocarbons) – now tightly controlled by international protocols, but the resulting excess penetration of harmful radiation from the sun will cause hundreds of thousands of extra skin cancers before things return to normal in the late twenty-first century.

The process

As we have noted, sources of information on environmental issues are multitudinous. There are numerous examples of best practice guidance we would recommend as consistent with the advice given here. They are listed at the end of the book. Each jurisdiction will also have its plethora of national and local enforcement agencies, environmental laws, regulations and standards which should be complied with, and ideally exceeded.

Why do it?

The risks and benefits associated with environmental management may be worthy of consideration by the company leadership before a commitment is made to a full-scale environmental management and audit system. With luck, your colleagues will find them compelling. Those colleagues with schoolage children or who are especially worried about financial liabilities may be your best allies. The costs of the Exxon Valdez oil spill in Alaska totalled $2.5 billion.

1   Benefits to business of effective environmental management

- positive contribution to corporate culture of shared responsibilities and values
- enhanced reputation with all stakeholders, leading to
- improved morale and greater loyalty
- cost savings – especially on energy and raw materials
- market opportunities
- contribution to efficiency, productivity and business success.

2   Risks to business of failure to manage environment effectively

- public embarrassment through accidents, spillages, and obvious waste (see Case Study 22.1)
- negative impacts on morale, stakeholder loyalty and commitment
- loss of business from environmentally aware clients and customers
- loss of money through wastage
- prosecution and imprisonment
- temporary or permanent closure of business activities.

CASE STUDY 22.1

The legacy of Bhopal

In 1984, the Union Carbide chemical company suffered a disaster of enormous proportions. A subsidiary plant in Bhopal, India manufacturing agrochemical products released hundreds of tonnes of highly toxic methyl isocyanate into the atmosphere, precipitating the deaths of 2,000–3,000 people in the local community and contributing to long-term health effects in tens of thousands more. The incident forced a fundamental rethink of Union Carbide's health, safety and environmental strategy. The vice president of HSE was made directly accountable to the CEO and to a new Health, Safety and Environmental Affairs Committee of the Board, chaired by a former head of the US Environmental Protection Agency. The audit program was completely revamped and policies streamlined and clarified. The corporate culture quickly embraced a new concern for the environment. Chairman and CEO Robert D. Kennedy confirmed in 1994, "As CEO, I have tried to strengthen that culture of concern. Our employees know that I spend a great deal of time on health, safety and environmental affairs. They know that I insist on being informed immediately about any serious incident. And top management as a whole continues to make it plain that we expect concern for health, safety and the environment to be part of everyday decision making."

How to start: leadership and commitment

The environment is a subject in which industrial leaders can still excel, demonstrating vision and depth of thinking. Frank Popoff of Dow Chemicals, Percy Barnevik of ABB and Sam Johnson of S. C. Johnson are just three examples of business leaders who have demonstrated a commitment to environmental issues which resonated strongly with stakeholders, especially their employees. A genuine commitment to the future of the planet and the well-being of generations as yet unborn is a vision which most people will happily share. It transcends the everyday and raises employees' aspirations and sense of self-worth if they believe that their company has long-term, environmentally responsible leadership. In our experience the best corporate environmental leaders exhibit most of the following traits:

1 **Vision** to deal with the larger social and economic issues which link environmental protection to sustainable development.

2 **Confidence** to speak out publicly in print or via speeches on the environmental and social challenges facing the planet and business.

3 **Energy** to sponsor internal "hard work" initiatives on environmental training, objective setting, auditing, rewards for success, etc.

4 **Humility** to encourage constructive criticism and challenges to the status quo and never to claim environmental excellence.

5 **Innovation** to imagine their business in 20, 30 or 50 years with a revolutionized product offering to meet the environmental and social needs of future generations.

6 **Integrity** to ensure transparency on environmental performance with all stakeholders.

7 **Humanity** to recognize that improved environmental performance can only be delivered if all stakeholders are enthused and committed to the vision from the grassroots upwards.

On the happy assumption that your CEO or company leadership is prepared to go along with at least some of the above, then you have a chance.

The next thing to consider is how the vision can be delivered. As with stakeholder reviews and social audits, where continuous improvement is the key to success, good environmental management is also delivered by a cyclical program. The cycle depicted in Figure 22.1 is consistent with the sources of best practice listed in the *References and further reading* section. It is also consistent with the European Union Eco Management and Audit Scheme (EMAS) – the most exacting international environmental standard available. For small companies or those looking for a less challenging route to environmental excellence, the verification and reporting steps may be omitted on the first cycle. This still provides you with a process consistent with International Standards Organization standard ISO 14001.

It is not essential to decide at the outset whether your organization is going to seek external accreditation against a particular international standard. You could just make a start on the cycle and decide at each stage how to implement the next element. However, this could be interpreted by some within the organization as a lack of seriousness on the part of the company leadership. A better approach, therefore, is to take a look at what is happening in your industry sector and decide whether you are aiming for best, good or just average practice. Japanese industry has been especially quick off the mark on ISO 14001 (see Case Study 22.2).

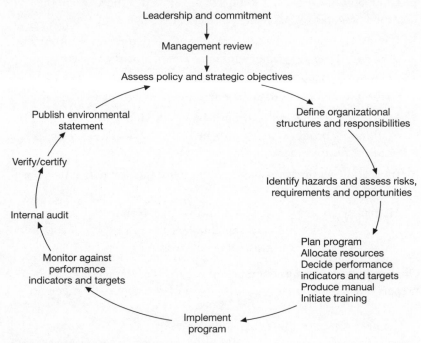

Figure 22.1
Matrix of enlightenment for engagement in civil society

CASE STUDY 22.2

The Japanese electronics industry moves fast on ISO 14001

When International Standards Organization quality management standards in the ISO 9000 series were first published, they were largely ignored by Japanese companies. Their belief that their reputation for quality would be enough proved ill-founded and in order not to lose out in international markets Japanese companies were forced to catch up. By 1995 nearly 100,000 companies and factories achieved the ISO 9000 standard. Japanese industry was not to repeat the error on environmental management standards in the ISO 14000 series. Even before finalization of the standards ten electronics manufacturers set up the Japan Audit and Certification Organization for the Environment JACO. By the time the ISO 14000 series started to take shape, the NEC Corporation already had eight sites accredited for environmental management system standard ISO 14001 and was committed to having all worldwide locations in compliance by the year 2000.

Table 22.1
Comparison of environmental management system standards (adapted from Environmental Resources Management)

System component	Management system						
	ISO 14001	EMAS	BS 7750	ICC	PERI	CEFIC	Keidanren
Company policy	XXX	XXX	XXX	XX	X	X	X
Senior management commitment	XXX	XXX	XXX	XX	X		X
Initial review of impacts	XXX	XXX	X	X	X	X	X
Register of regulations	1	XXX	XXX	2			
Allocated responsibilities	XXX	XXX	XXX	XX	X		X
Objectives and targets	XXX	XXX	XXX	XX	X	X	X
Management program	XXX	XXX	XXX	XX	X	XX	X
Manual	XXX	XXX	XXX				
Operational control	XXX	XXX	XXX	XX		X	
Records	XXX	XXX	XXX				
Training	XXX	XXX	XXX	XX	X	X	X
Audits (internal)	XXX	XXX	XXX	XX	X	X	X
Public statement/reporting	X	XXX		XX	XX	X	X
System verification	XXX	XXX	XXX		X		
Commitment to continuous improvement of system	XXX	XXX	XXX	XX		XX	

Key

XXX A requirement of the standard
XX Principle
X Guideline/good practice
1 Review regulations/impacts
2 Assess compliance

ISO: International Standards Organization
EMAS: EU Eco-Management and Audit Scheme
BS: British Standard
ICC: International Chamber of Commerce
PERI: Public Environmental Reporting Initiative
CEFIC: European Chemical Industry Federation
Keidanren: Japanese business and environment charter

For most industries, and for most large companies today, best practice requires driving the cycle in Figure 22.1 to full environmental audit and disclosure with external verification. For smaller companies or those in sectors where environmental impacts are exceptionally low, best practice may not require external verification. But our strong recommendation to any business person who wishes to be seen as a leader in this area is to push for the "accredited standard plus full disclosure" option. In stakeholder terms, this objective is unassailable. It demonstrates a level of vision and commitment to transparency that should impress all but the most jaundiced stakeholder. The various requirements of seven environmental management systems standards from around the world are summarized in Table 22.1.

Having identified the level of aspiration of the organization and established leadership on the issues, the sensible CEO or management team will identify a trustworthy independent consultant or individual to conduct an initial management review.

Management review

The purpose of an initial review is to do a rapid assessment of the main issues facing the business and to prepare a report to the company leadership. Depending on the style of the company, this initial report can either be confidential to the management team or freely shared with employees and other stakeholders. If you are in a sensitive industry where legal or reputational liabilities are significant, you should not consider yourselves stakeholder unfriendly for commissioning a confidential initial review. The important thing is to generate momentum. So if your more nervous colleagues feel that a modicum of confidentiality is important at this stage that is fine. However, a clear commitment should be made to full disclosure of environmental performance in the future. A management review should take no more than a week or two of one person's time. A small business may employ a university student studying environmental management or business administration, and receive a perfectly sensible report. A larger company will want to employ a trusted external consultant or an environmental specialist from a different geographical and organizational location of the group.

Methodologies for initial reviews are now so standardized that it is unnecessary to provide a detailed brief for the exercise here[1]. But key elements of a good initial review will include:

1 Engagement of a trustworthy and competent independent reviewer.

2 Agreement of scope of review to include at least:
   - management systems (roles and responsibilities)
   - policies
   - significant environmental effects and risks
   - legislative and regulatory obligations
   - records and documentation
   - targets and objectives
   - resources
   - emergency arrangements.

3 Agreement of methodology to include:
- questionnaires
- checklists
- structured interviews
- inspections
- examination of documentation.

4 Drafting and finalizing report.

5 Presentation of report to company leadership.

6 Delivery of clear response to report from company leadership, followed by implementation of an action plan.

The types of questions you should expect the independent reviewer to cover via questionnaires, inspections, etc. will be similar to those we suggested be posed for occupational safety and health. They include:

1 Is there a list of environmental legislation which has to be complied with in our business?

2 Is there a list of environmental hazards in our business categorized by type and prioritized according to likelihood and severity?

3 Are the structures of accountability for environmental management clear and generally understood?

4 Do our line managers and environmental managers understand their responsibilities and have adequate financial and human resources to discharge them?

5 Do we have adequate environmental emergency plans and are people practised in their execution?

6 Do we have adequate competence and understanding of our environmental obligations at all levels, supported by an energetic program of training for all managers, staff and contractors?

7 Do we have a transparent system of environmental performance measurement (e.g. on energy efficiency and waste) and is communication on performance active and two-way?

8 Are there clear objectives and targets to generate continuous improvement in performance?

9 Are environmental policies, guidelines and workplace procedures properly documented and distributed?

10 Do we have access to adequate internal and external environmental expertise to enable us to meet best practice now and in the future?

Policy and strategic objectives

Armed with its management review, the senior management team or board is in a position to make some decisions. The first decision to make is whether the environmental policy, if it already exists, is adequate for the organization or whether, in the light of stakeholder aspirations and the direction of the global economy, it needs to be updated and made more visionary. One of the most frequently cited business charters in this field is the International Chamber of Commerce Business Charter for Sustainable Development (see Exhibit 22.2).

EXHIBIT 22.2

ICC Business Charter for Sustainable Development

1 *Corporate priority:* To recognise environmental management as among the highest corporate priorities and as a key determinant to sustainable development; to establish policies, programs, and practices for conducting operations in an environmentally sustainable manner.

2 *Integrated management:* To integrate these policies, programs, and practices fully into each business as an essential element of management in all its functions.

3 *Process of improvement:* To continue to improve corporate policies, programs, and environmental performance, taking into account technological developments, scientific understanding, consumer needs, and community expectations, with legal regulations as a starting point; and to apply the same environmental criteria internationally.

4 *Employee education:* To educate, train, and motivate employees to conduct their activities in an environmentally responsible manner.

5 *Prior assessment:* To assess environmental impacts before starting a new activity or project and before decommissioning a facility or leaving a site.

6 *Products and services:* To develop and provide products or services that have no undue environmental impacts and are safe in their intended use, that are efficient in their consumption of energy and natural resources, and that can be recycled, reused, or disposed of safely.

7 *Customer advice:* To advise, and where relevant educate customers, distributors, and the public in the safe use, transportation, storage, and disposal of products provided; and to apply similar considerations to the provision of services.

8 *Facilities and operations:* To develop, design, and operate facilities and conduct activities, taking into consideration the efficient use of energy and materials, the sustainable use of renewable resources, the minimization of adverse environmental impacts and waste generation, and the safe and responsible disposal of residual waste.

---

9 *Research:* To conduct or support research on the environmental impacts of raw materials, products, processes, emissions, and wastes associated with the enterprise and on the means of minimising such adverse impacts.

10 *Precautionary approach:* To modify the manufacture, marketing, or use of products or services or the conduct of activities, consistent with scientific and technical understanding, to prevent serious and irreversible environmental degradation.

11 *Contractors and suppliers:* To promote the adoption of these principles by contractors acting on behalf of the enterprise, encouraging and where appropriate requiring improvements in their practices to make them consistent with those of the enterprise; and to encourage wider adoption of these principles by suppliers.

12 *Emergency preparedness:* To develop and maintain, where significant hazards exist, emergency preparedness plans in conjunction with the emergency services, relevant authorities, and the local community, recognising potential boundary impacts.

13 *Transfer of technology:* To contribute to the transfer of environmentally sound technology and management methods throughout the industrial and public sectors.

14 *Contributing to the common effort:* To contribute to the development of public policy and to business, government, and inter-governmental programs and educational initiatives that will enhance environmental awareness and protection.

15 *Openness to concerns:* To foster openness and dialogue with employees and the public, anticipating and responding to their concerns about the potential hazards and impacts of operations, products, wastes, or services, including those of trans-boundary or global significance.

16 *Compliance and reporting:* To measure environmental performance; to conduct regular environmental audits and assessments of compliance with company requirements, legal requirements, and these principles; and periodically to provide appropriate information to the board of directors, shareholders, employees, the authorities, and the public.

ICC Business Charter for Sustainable Development, ICC Publication No. 210/356A. Published by the International Chamber of Commerce, Paris. Copyright © 1991 International Chamber of Commerce (ICC).

The ICC Charter is not especially visionary because, although it covers most of the ground on environmental protection, it completely omits the social and economic agenda, and thus has almost nothing to do with sustainable development. It is an environmental management charter which does not mandate full disclosure of environmental performance; it merely talks about providing "appropriate information" to the board of directors and other stakeholders.

Many companies base their environmental policies on the ICC Charter. The Charter has also spawned the Global Environmental Management Initiative designed to assess compliance with the principles contained in the Charter. Companies like Allied Signal, Boeing, Procter & Gamble and Union Carbide have been involved with GEMI program, developing checklists and other schemes to demonstrate their commitment to improved environmental performance.

Whatever starting point your business takes for its environmental policy, there is a number of factors which must be taken into account:

- The development of a new or updated policy should include some element of stakeholder consultation. Policy drafts should ideally be tested in focus groups with employees, customers and other important groups.

- The policy should cover all significant environmental impacts and risks, including those which arise in unplanned or emergency situations and which may affect local communities.

- Reference should be made to continuous improvement and meeting or exceeding all regulatory requirements.

- There should be a commitment to publication and active communication of both the environmental policy and details of environmental performance.

- Business decisions, including those involving products and processes, should formally take into account environmental implications.

- There should be a commitment to training and awareness-raising, at least for employees, customers and suppliers.

- There should be explicit references to resource conservation and waste minimization and a clear statement of principle on the company's attitude to pollution (see Exhibit 22.4 for options).

More visionary "sustainable development" policies might also include references to:

- social and economic fairness today and for future generations
- minimising unnecessary consumption
- fair trade with developing countries and marginalized communities.

However comprehensive and visionary the policy, it is important that it is formally endorsed by the leadership of the company and enthusiastically communicated. It is not necessary for the policy to include specific objectives, or targets with time scales. This would date it too quickly. A

EXHIBIT 22.4

Pollution: which principles will you embrace?

Basic: Integrated Pollution Control – agreeing that it is stupid to treat each discharge to the environment (air, land or water) as a separate problem, potentially transferring a pollutant from one medium to another where there are fewer controls. Conspicuous successes: incinerator emission standards in Europe and North America. Conspicuous failures: contamination of domestic sewage sludge with industrial pollutants, preventing its use as a fertilizer.

Best Practice: Polluter Pays Principle – accepting the need for license fees, liability legislation, market mechanisms and taxation to ensure that companies do not leave the real costs of environmental clean-up to society at large or to future generations. Conspicuous successes: introduction of special fees for land filling in the USA and Europe. Conspicuous failures: the inability of governments to introduce international taxes on fossil fuels (a carbon tax).

Visionary: Precautionary Principle – avoiding the discharge of pollutants or the introduction of processes which have unknown consequences for the environment or human health, now and in the future. Conspicuous successes: none. Reasonable wins: the convening of the Inter Governmental Panel on Climate Change, controls placed on nutrients like phosphates entering sensitive aquatic ecosystems. Conspicuous failures: too numerous to mention, but the list would include the nuclear industry, chlorinated pesticides, ozone-depleting chemicals.

---

good policy is one which lasts for a few years before needing updating but which will give continuing legitimacy to plans, objectives and targets as they are updated and strengthened over time.

Strategic questions which need to be addressed at the same time as the environmental policy is signed off are:

1 What will be the linkages of environmental policy and management with quality and occupational safety and health management? This is as likely to be a cultural decision as a technical one (see Case Study 22.3).

2 To what extent can environmental performance improvement contribute to other strategic business goals, e.g. cost reduction, product innovation, business performance?

3 Can training, learning and motivational programs benefit from enrichment by environmental values?

4 What opportunities will improved environmental management create

for enhanced stakeholder relations, especially with customers, employees and suppliers?

CASE STUDY 22.3

Pollution prevention pays – 3P approach at 3M

Minnesota Mining and Manufacturing (3M) is a conglomerate which makes tens of thousands of products: from Post-it notes to X-ray films, from fiber-optics to dental fillings. They have a highly decentralized structure with around 100 plants spread across the USA and a similar number overseas. Employees are encouraged to spend 15 percent of their time on unauthorized projects with colleagues. As a result, 3M has a highly energized, creative organizational culture. 3M is often quoted as a prime exemplar of the integration of total quality and environmental management (TQEM). Health and safety is managed and audited separately. TQEM at 3M is twinned with the enthusiasm of its employees for problem solving. Since the company introduced its companywide Pollution Prevention Pays program in 1975, 3M estimates its employees have undertaken more than 3,000 3P projects, preventing 600,000 tonnes of pollution and saving more than $600 million (cumulative first year savings).

Environmental policies, indeed any policy of relevance to a wide range of stakeholders, should be clear and concise, ideally filling no more than a single side of paper. The policy should legitimize medium-term objectives and shorter term targets but not include them (see also our advice on occupational safety and health policies in Chapter 16).

Once the policy is settled the organization is ready to move on to the next step of the cycle which is the agreement of roles and responsibilities within the organization. But first, the new policy should be launched with all the internal communications energy which the company can mobilize including formal endorsement by the CEO and exhortations by all members of the company leadership. This is the opportunity to create a real sense of vision and forward momentum. Every employee, the local community and indeed other stakeholders should be left in no doubt that the policy is meaningful and will lead to real action.

Organizational structures and responsibilities

Driving environmental performance usually requires continuous sponsorship from the board and senior management team. The most effective environmental management systems are those which are led from the top but which: (i) promote interest and engagement throughout the organization; and (ii) are intimately linked to business strategy (see Case Study 22.4).

CASE STUDY 22.4

Environmental management as a competitive issue in Japanese industry

In a survey conducted by Nikkei in 1993, 89.7 percent of Japanese companies with more than 3,000 employees had established an environmental department, 58.7 percent had appointed senior executives to oversee their environmental programs. This strategy, together with strategic intervention from Japan's Ministry of Trade and Industry was closely linked to Japanese industry's renowned drive towards efficiency and market advantage. According to a survey of Japanese companies conducted by the Japan Environmentally Conscious Products (ECP) Committee in 1995, 89 percent had developed and marketed "ecoproducts." The 210 companies polled embraced sectors as diverse as metals, chemicals, electronics, cars and paper. In most cases, ECPs were so classified because of production improvements, e.g. minimization of energy and wastes and material recycling.

As with any important management function, it is vital that top management cascades responsibility and authority through the line managers. Responsibilities should be documented, included in job descriptions, and subject to periodic performance review. Inclusion of environmental performance in reward and compensation schemes is also a powerful driver for progress. There is nothing quite like the prospect of losing 50 percent of one's annual salary bonus because of an environmental infringement to concentrate the mind of a plant manager.

It would not be especially useful here to provide lists of potential job description supplements for plant managers, personnel officers, lawyers, accountants, site engineers and facilities managers, procurement officers, factory and office workers. All might reasonably have a couple of lines in their contracts to reinforce their responsibilities for environmental best practice. These are the details which need to be explored and agreed painstakingly, step by step throughout the organization. It will take several turns of the cycle of continuous improvement to get this delegation of responsibilities absolutely right.

The best starting point is to identify who within the organization at the most senior level will drive the process and what authority they will have within the structure.

We have already suggested that a powerful combination of a board sponsor plus a dedicated executive manager is optimal to enhance any stakeholder relationship. In small companies it may not make sense to have a full-time environmental manager sitting on the principal executive management group. In such cases it could be a part-time activity, possibly twinned with an operational role.

Some companies have successfully employed the device of a sub-committee of the senior management group providing multidisciplinary guidance to a more technical environmental manager. This manager then champions the cause with his or her senior colleagues and throughout the organization.

Other companies have run decentralized networks of departmental and divisional environmental representatives to supplement the authority of line managers and to act as an extra channel of communication and peer motivation.

Whichever structure is chosen and whatever combination of line management, cross functional networks and supervisory teams is used, it will be essential to have one central person or department responsible for strategic coordination and sponsorship of the environmental management system.

This person's authority should allow them to transfer to management colleagues responsibilities and departmentally specific objectives that make sense for the organization and which connect the environmental policy to real life. Senior managers who receive "agreed" extra environmental responsibilities have, in turn, to exhibit the following characteristics:

1 **Lead and delegate:** make the environmental management system work by ensuring that the line responsibilities laid on you by the organization are properly cascaded through your division with well-understood and documented expectations and accountabilities (but don't forget, the manager remains *responsible*).

2 **Empower:** everyone in your part of the company should have the financial resources and freedom to act on environmental protection issues swiftly and effectively.

3 **Educate:** make training programs on the environment energetic, targeted and mandatory; ensure that there is sufficient access to qualified, experienced environmental experts both within and outside the organization.

4 **Communicate:** use every available communication forum and medium to generate two-way dialogue on environmental protection; include progress on targets and objectives in newsletters, meetings, events, etc.

5 **Motivate:** maximize employee inclusion via environmental commit-tees; reward good practice.

6 **Integrate:** generate cooperative behavior across the organization through cross-departmental participation in problem-solving task groups.

7 **Evaluate:** act on audit reports, measure and report regularly on envi-ronmental performance, set local targets and objectives consistent with organizational policies and strategic goals.

Underpinning all of the above is the need for documentation. As for occu-pational safety and health, environmental policy documents and manuals of guidance and procedure represent the collective environmental wisdom of an organization. Training is vital in order to bring policies and procedures alive. The trick is to make procedures relevant to every single manager and employee. The next section deals with one of the greatest challenges to good environmental management: how to identify hazards and quantify risks.

Identify hazards and assess risks, requirements and opportunities

There is a whole industry developing around environmental risk man-agement. It has its expert consultants, specialist magazines and a jargon all of its own. It is driven by the insurance industry and the legal profes-sion and consequently tends to look on life a little pessimistically.

The problem with risk management as a stand-alone activity or even as an umbrella for aspects of stakeholder relations is that it is by definition focussed on liabilities. It does not speak to vision and opportunity. Some companies have successfully integrated environmental and safety risk audit and control with other business risk areas, for example fraud, infor-mation technology and security. This provides an opportunity to deal with management systems in a strategic way while putting in place the right training elements necessary to establish employee involvement. But this is a difficult hand to play in any organization: it tends to squash the motivational opportunities. For this reason, we would not advocate a straight "risk management" approach to any aspect of business behavior and stakeholder relations. Rather, risk assessment should fit within an environmental or safety management program alongside the positive dimensions of SWOT analysis (Strengths, Weaknesses, Opportunities and Threats).

An environmental SWOT analysis is ideally based on the following building blocks:

- Register of environmental effects
- Register of legislation and regulations
- Assessment of strengths, weaknesses, opportunities and threats associated with products and processes.

Register of environmental effects

Compiling a register of environmental effects is not usually an exciting activity. Many companies leave it to an expert – perhaps the same consultant who conducted the environmental review – or assume that the person responsible for coordinating the environmental management system will do it. Either approach is perfectly acceptable, it simply involves having eyes and ears and the technical knowledge to match what the company does to what impacts it may have on the environment. A more forward-thinking company will extend the boundaries of its environmental effects register to include the potential environmental impacts of suppliers and customers, taking a "life cycle" approach. In these days of outsourcing and increasing liability to consumers, this is not a bad strategy: just because you close a factory and switch supply to a subcontractor does not mean that your environmental impacts have been eliminated. A visionary company would include potential impacts on social and economic questions, and on future generations in a "sustainability effects" register.

But for most companies, and to satisfy the current demands of environmental management systems standards like ISO 14001 and EMAS, direct impacts on the natural environment (atmosphere, water and land) are the obvious things to include. Air pollutants, including acidic and volatile emissions, steam, dust, smoke and noise, all have local relevance. Global warming gases like carbon dioxide, methane and other hydrocarbons, and ozone depleting chemicals in refrigeration and firefighting systems have global relevance. Direct industrial discharges to the sewage system, rivers and seas tend to have local rather than international implications, unless of course they are radioactive or spectacularly and persistently toxic. Solid wastes which cannot be reused or recycled may be buried in the ground (landfilled) or incinerated. In each case there may be local nuisances through toxin release to water or air and contributions to global problems: methane from landfills and carbon dioxide from incineration both contributing the greenhouse effect. If these are the types of direct effect which should appear on the register, what about indirect impacts on the natural environment?

The consumption and combustion of nonrenewable resources like oil, coal and natural gas is an obvious double whammy from a sustainability perspective: these resources are being depleted and denied to future generations at the same time helping warm up the planet and thereby contributing to future mayhem for millions. Step forward all users of road transport and energy (and do not forget – in most countries the majority of electricity for business comes originally from fossil fuels like coal, oil or natural gas). Road transport also has one or two local impacts too: choking the atmospheres of cities and giving kids asthma. You can see how this exercise gets a bit depressing.

The important point to bear in mind is that by putting both direct and indirect effects on the register, by defining them as primarily local or global, you can start to do something about them. If you leave them off the register, they may as well not exist.

This provides another clue to how to pep up the register and make it more of a dynamic, stakeholder inclusive and motivational tool. Why not get employees and even focus groups of the local community to come up with their own registers? Facilitated discussions starting with some obvious, visible impacts and broadening into consideration of more global concerns can provide a great educational opportunity as well as demonstrating the ability of the company to deal with a usually dry, technical activity in a more innovative and participative way (see Case Study 22.5).

CASE STUDY 22.5

Participation as a strategic opportunity in environmental impact studies

In 1990 the Norwegian aluminum industry launched a $2.5 million study into the ecological impacts of its activities. The five year study involved more than 30 scientists in 13 research institutions. Midway through the study the steering committee for the project adopted an innovative strategy of stakeholder inclusion setting up Neighbor Contact Groups of community representatives around each aluminum plant to help inform the direction of the research. Environmentalists and regulators were also invited to participate as observers. As research findings were gathered, they were circulated openly and immediately to the stakeholder groups. Trust and engagement strengthened. When the study closed in 1995, the principle of "participative dialogue" was well established in the future business strategy of the Norwegian aluminum industry.

It also allows for some discussion of risks and opportunities to minimize those risks. How would we as a department, a division, a plant or a community eliminate or minimize an environmental effect? What opportunities are there to turn an effect into a benefit? Can we envisage using renewable energy to help preserve fossil fuels? Can we recycle cooling water to avoid depleting local sources of water? Can we recycle a solid waste to avoid it being incinerated? Can we plant some trees to "soak up" some of our carbon dioxide emissions (trees use CO_2, water and sunlight to grow)? In short, how would we get this issue off the register?

Register of legislation and regulations

Now this one is a real challenge to make stakeholder inclusive. There is not much chance of turning a workshop on regulatory compliance into a fun event.

Our advice on compiling a register of legislative obligations is to use it as the opportunity to make your legal department or advisor feel loved and part of the vision – and to improve relations with local regulators. Like accountants, many lawyers are bursting to be loved. They hate being seen as dry and dusty merchants of doom: the part of the business which loves to say no. So, if it is not asking for too great a stretch of the stereotype, give your legal department a copy of the environmental effects register, hand them a reputable environmental management manual which lists all relevant local, national and international laws and ask them to project manage the deal.

One piece of advice. In stakeholder relationship terms, it is important to take the draft legal register and show it to the local regulatory agencies for their input. Invite them over; they will be delighted to be asked. They too want to be treated as part of the human race. For some company lawyers this will cause a psychological problem. They are usually trained to snarl at regulators, not to engage them in pleasantries. So this step, valuable as it is, may need some counseling in advance. The best lawyers will cope.

Assessment of strengths, weaknesses, threats and opportunities associated with products and processes

Earlier we discussed the opportunities for company leaderships to show real vision. There can be nothing more visionary than examining one's product and service offerings and working out what consumers of the next generation may actually want from an environmental and social perspective.

Before the Business Council for Sustainable Development was taken over by the International Chamber of Commerce it did some quite useful work on the question of ecoefficiency. Taking models of population growth and extrapolating for the likely implications of industrialization in the Third World, the BCSD came up with some rather alarming conclusions. And coming from a group of business people, rather than the usual sources of doom and despondency, these conclusions have to be taken seriously.

The ecoefficiency argument goes like this. For the next thirty years or so, the world's population will grow by 85 to 90 million per annum.[2] In a world where population is set to nearly double in the next 50 years and where industrialization and globalization of the world economy is inevitable, the demand for consumer goods will rocket. More televisions, refrigerators, cars and more raw materials and infrastructure to support and transport them: metals, plastics, energy, roads, trucks, airplanes. Between 1950 and 1995, the gross world product increased fivefold in real terms[2]. No one is betting against a similar increase in the next 50 years.

The result of all this extra industrial activity and consumption is that basic materials and energy will have to flow through the economic system ever faster. But as any schoolage student will tell you, there are limits to the speed with which materials can be consumed and not replaced, and there are constraints on how effectively wastes can be recovered, reused and recycled. Most importantly, for political reasons, the consumption of fossil fuels simply will not be allowed to accelerate in step with the growth of the global economy.

In addressing this scenario, and backed by calculations from influential research organizations like the Wuppertal Institute in Germany, the BCSD suggested that huge increases in ecoefficiency would be required. Incremental improvements, e.g. 20 percent more fuel efficient cars, 30 percent lighter weight packaging on consumer goods, will be almost irrelevant. Instead, the BCSD talked about fourfold, eightfold, tenfold and in some cases even twentyfold increases in efficiency being required for key products and services. This would mean, for example, vehicles relying on a fraction of current locomotive energy requirements and lasting for perhaps two million miles rather than one or two hundred thousand. And all of this has to happen in the space of one or two generations.

What are the practical implications of this analysis? In our view it is inevitable that as economic globalization progresses, it will become increasingly difficult to manufacture goods competitively in the older, more mature economies where social standards are high but where basic skills and educational standards are beginning to slip behind those of the tiger economies. Not impossible, but more difficult. Equally, there will be increased pressure for ecotaxation to penalize overconsumption of raw materials and energy (and, by the way, provide a politically more expedient alternative to income tax). This will further inhibit the ability of the mature industrial economies to manufacture goods efficiently and competitively.

So for mature economies this is all heading in one of two directions: either the protectionist backlash, or the conversion of wealth creation to more service intensive and less resource consuming activities. Taking the more optimistic of these scenarios, business people have to recognize that the goods which will sell best are those which are accompanied by service value-added and do not simply represent material value-added. In ten years time, a supermarket which provides leisure and entertainment for the children while the adults choose their options and punch their requirements into a computer screen for immediate home delivery will do better than one which asks it customers to push trolleys around with bawling kids in tow. A skin and hair care company which provides expert hairdressing, stress relief and aromatherapy services will do better than one which simply sells shampoo in bottles. A car manufacturer which leases low energy vehicles and supplies zero maintenance freedom to travel, taking back the vehicle for refurbishment every few years, will do better than one simply selling the hardware. These companies will be providing more attractive services, more efficiently to the consumer of the twenty-first century. Consequently they will outcompete their local rivals and will avoid getting into unwinnable, lowest cost per product scraps with the Philippines, Indonesia or Malaysia (see Case Study 22.6).

CASE STUDY 22.6

Designing for zero waste

One company which has taken a serious look at its product offering and decided to "design for the environment" is Rank Xerox. Faced with fierce competition from Canon and other Japanese photocopier manufacturers in the 1980s, Rank Xerox embarked on an award-winning quality program. In 1990 it launched its Environmental Leadership Program. The strategy included recovery, reuse and recycling of copiers. By 1995 approximately two-thirds of the company's 120,000 copiers discarded in Western Europe were recovered. The return rate for copier cartridges was more than 50 percent and its packaging rationalization program was estimated to have saved £4 million between 1990 and 1995. The company's long-term aim is "waste-free products from waste-free facilities," with "zero landfill" machines operating in "waste-free" factories and offices.

This is the background against which the long-term risk and opportunity profile of your company's products and services should be assessed. Of course there are short-term cost and efficiency gains which can be generated in your current product profiles: increased energy efficiency, less packaging, more efficient logistics. But do not be seduced by these short-term opportunities into believing that they will secure the long-term future of your company, still less the long-term loyalty of your customers. A more fundamental strategy will be needed for that.

So our advice is to put this one in the hands of your marketing director and encourage them to work with the most visionary futurologists and researchers they can identify. Be automatically suspicious of anyone in the marketing field who overuses any of the following terms:

Life cycle assessment (LCA) – a technical tool for ecoefficiency which currently completely overlooks the wider stakeholder and social perspective.
Ecolabel – transient marketing fix usually based on lowest common denominator standards.
Environmental cause-related marketing – faddish attempt to enlist short-term support of cash-strapped, not-for-profit groups in the hope that the image will rub off.

These three activities all have their place: LCA in your technical department; ecolabels in the hands of your more gullible competitors (the ones who do not mind paying a premium to self-appointed experts in order to carry a meaningless seal of approval); and cause-related marketing somewhere in the late 1980s.

Do encourage dialogue with people who:

- understand macroeconomic and demographic trends and how this will impact on consumer behavior in the twenty-first century
- recognize the need to provide service value-added as well as product value-added in mature markets of the future
- understand the importance of providing full information on the environmental and social impacts of products, their procurement and their use (the total transparency approach)
- recognize the overriding need to build deep customer and stakeholder loyalty based on trust and understanding rather than hype and quick fixes.

The companies which recognize that consumers of the future will want leisure not chores, freedom not commitments, social and environmental value-added not liabilities, transparency not hype, are the ones who will come up with the right answers in their review of products and services. It is not overstating the case to say that companies which fail to embrace this kind of serious analysis in their environmental management system and make it an item of strategic importance are taking a big gamble on the future – namely their survival as a business.

Plan program

If you have reached this far – well done. We are now entering territory where strategic influence is less important and where functional responsibilities start to dominate. The moral support must continue to flow from the top, but most of the hard work is now the responsibility of line managers and specialists.

The results of the risks and opportunities analysis should first be collated by the individual charged with coordinating the environmental management system. The task then becomes one of working with functional management painstakingly to put in place the following:

1 Guidelines and procedures to control, minimize or eliminate risks and to maximize the opportunities for improvement.

2 Job descriptions which reflect line management responsibilities to ensure best practice.

3 Departmental, divisional and facility based objectives and targets consistent with overall policy and direction.

4 Performance indicators and management information systems to measure progress against objectives and targets.

5 Resource plans to ensure availability of money and people to carry through improvements.

6 Communication and training plans to raise awareness and motivate stakeholders (especially employees).

It is highly desirable, if not essential, that all of the above is captured in some form of manual so that people have access to the comprehensive detail of how to implement the environmental program. Most environmental policy and procedures manuals are unwieldy and deadly boring. So it is vital to ensure that the most relevant parts of the main manual for each individual are best understood on a specific functional level and that the overall approach and fundamental sentiments of policy are understood and supported on a general level. Whatever communication and educational opportunities can be engineered to deliver these two levels of understanding should be seized upon. Below is a list of the kind of specific environmental management responsibilities which would require written procedures and plans to be fully understood by everyone in that area. We will follow a life cycle or "cradle to grave" approach starting with product specifications and procurement:

Marketing

■ Strategy for specifying and sourcing portfolio of environmental and social value-added products and services.

■ Procedures for honest labeling and ensuring full access to product information by consumers.

Purchasing departments

■ Buying guidelines and procedures to avoid purchasing environmentally and socially inappropriate products, packaging, raw materials and services.

■ Systems to rate the overall environmental and social performance of suppliers and contractors.

Technical

■ Quality control and assurance procedures to minimize waste.

■ Environmental design guidelines, procedures for life cycle assessment, etc.

■ Procedures for controlling hazardous chemical use.

■ Monitoring systems for measuring the quality of environmental emissions.

Manufacturing

■ Procedures to eliminate or minimize airborne, solid and liquid wastes and control emissions.

■ Spillage and emergency pollution control systems.

■ Energy efficiency procedures.

Warehousing

■ Spillage and emergency pollution control (including especially fire preventions) systems.

■ Energy efficiency procedures.

■ Secondary packaging reuse and recycling procedures.

Distribution

■ Procedures for minimizing freight inefficiency, use of air and road transport etc.

■ Systems for standardizing transport packaging.

■ Driver and vehicle efficiency guidelines.

Engineering/facilities management

■ Environmental guidelines for contractors.

■ Procedures for energy and waste minimization.

■ Systems for encouraging recycling and re-use.

■ Emergency plan.

Sales

■ Procedures for dealing with customer enquires on environmental and related issues.

■ Systems for dealing with post-consumer waste.

Accounts

■ Systems to catch and measure expenditures and liabilities on environmental management.

In an ideal world, each guideline, procedure and system will be fully "owned" and reflected in job descriptions and work instructions. They will be the subject of performance indicators, local objectives and targets. And most importantly, they will be underpinned by energetic and entertaining job-specific training for everyone in each area of the company and the continuous generation of inspirational and motivational messages from the company leadership and middle management. This is best driven by a combination of environmental management or audit departments, communications and training departments and the office of the CEO.

There is also a need to pay attention to how these guidelines, procedures and systems are working.

Implementation and monitoring

The likelihood is that you the reader are not starting out with a company which has no environmental policy, program or procedures whatsoever. Indeed you may be working in an organization that has put in place such programs decades ago and where they are already comprehensive, fine tuned and effective. But regardless of how environmentally well developed your company is, it is almost inevitable that improvements can be made to stakeholder understanding and commitment, and hence to performance in the implementation of your program.

Many companies are excellent in raising awareness among employees and liaising with the local community on environmental risks. But there are several areas where almost all companies have a lot more to contribute. These are:

- supplier performance
- customer understanding
- investor understanding.

Promoting environmental best practice among your suppliers can have a significant multiplier effect in improving your environmental profile. As we noted in Chapter 19, a number of British companies have devoted a good deal of systematic effort into greening their supply chains[3].

Educating consumers about careful use and disposal of products and packaging, including reuse and recycling constitutes a real contribution to minimizing the environmental impact of consumer goods.

Including investors in your environmental awareness and improvement strategy, ensuring they understand how you measure your environmental performance, how you cut down on waste, how you maximize efficiency, may prompt them to ask other companies whether they match your approach. Again, a multiplier effect can be generated. So it is a mistake to see the implementation of an environmental management system solely in terms of gains to be made within the organization.

Equally, it is a mistake to believe that success internally or externally can be driven without performance indicators and management information systems which allow progress to be tracked by management and employees. The best performance indicators relate to established objectives and targets and provide meaningful comparisons, facility by facility, month on month, year after year.

In the early 1990s a huge debate started about indicators of sustainability. The debate continues to engage academics, commentators and politicians in a good deal of brain-stretching discussion. Sustainability indicators for business would require environmental measures to be linked with economic or social factors to be meaningful. Some very useful work has been done[4], including the linkage of environmental impacts like CO_2 emissions to the creation of economic value. But the subject is something of a holy grail. In the meanwhile, until such indicators prove themselves, here is a list of the kind of indicator which every business could usefully include in their monthly management information reports, public environmental statements and annual reports and accounts.

Benchmarks and performance indicators

Electricity per unit of production/service ☑

Other fuels per unit of production/service ☑

Water consumed per unit of production/service ☑

Waste water discharged per unit of production/service ☑

Solid wastes disposed per unit of production/service ☑

Airborne emissions per unit of production/service ☑

Electricity costs per employee ☑

Other fuel costs per employee ☑

Water costs per employee ☑

Waste water costs per employee ☑

Solid waste costs per employee ☑

Environmental permitting costs per employee ☑

Environmental permitting costs per unit of production/service ☑

Proportion of total energy consumed from renewable sources ☑

Proportion of solid wastes recovered and reused/recycled ☑

Proportion of liquid wastes recovered and reused/recycled ☑

Quantity of hazardous wastes discharged to the environment per unit of production/service ☑

Numbers of community complaints per facility ☑

Numbers of failures to comply with permits or regulations per plant or facility ☑

Numbers of regulatory infringements or improvement notices per plant or facility ☑

Investments in environmental protection (including training)
as a ratio of budget or turnover ☑

Numbers of inspections and audits ☑

Guidelines for measuring environmental performance have been produced by Business in the Environment[5]. The document provides a useful
summary of the arguments for environmental performance measurement
and includes case studies from a number of companies including BT, Ford
Motor Company, IBM (UK), Kodak, National Power and National
Westminster Bank.

Auditing

There are numerous textbooks on environmental auditing[6,7]. An environmental audit is a systematic, objective, periodic and documented assessment of environmental performance. Environmental auditing is now a
profession with professional registration schemes, codes of practice,
international standards to audit against (e.g. ISO 14001 and EMAS) and
a well-developed jargon all of its own[8,9].

Audits can be subject specific (e.g. energy and waste audits); they can
be restricted to legal compliance and liability control (e.g. in advance of
a takeover or major loan) or they can be generic – to test an entire environmental management system against internal and external standards.

All the evidence is that whatever the size of your business, audits are
almost always "no lose" deals. Any investment you make in energy and
waste audits is likely to repay itself several times over. In a US study of
181 waste prevention activities at 29 chemical plants, only one resulted
in a net cost increase in production. In a study of 33 major process
changes at ten printed circuit board manufacturers, 13 were initiated for
pollution control reasons. Of these 13, 12 resulted in cost reduction, 8 in
quality improvements and 5 in improved product capability[10]. The potential for environmental cost savings has also been emphasized in a recent
study by the World Resources Institute[11]. Environmental costs in case
studies of products manufactured by five major US corporations ranged
from 2.4 percent of net sales (a consumer product from S C Johnson) to
nearly 22 percent of operating costs (excluding feed stock) at an Amoco
refinery. An agricultural pesticide from Du Pont incurred more than 19
percent of its manufacturing spend in environmental costs. There are
consultants who make a real specialism of exercises in environmental cost
saving.

If you are a bank or a company about to invest in another you will not want to gamble on that company having significant hidden environmental liabilities. In 1991, the average cost of a contaminated land clean up in the US Superfund program was $80 million – not the kind of liability anyone wants to inherit. Due diligence audits prior to investment are now absolutely essential prior to the acquisition of any company. The World Bank has developed a powerful environmental assessment capacity to guard against investment mistakes in the former Soviet bloc. For both specialist and due diligence audits it is best to bring in an expert consultant. Professional bodies can help you find the right one, but always ask for and follow up on references with former clients to ensure you are going to get quality and value for money. In Britain, ENDS produces an extremely helpful guide to environmental consultancies[12].

When it comes to comprehensive audits of the effectiveness of management systems, our strong recommendation is to do this yourself. Appoint your own full-time or part-time environmental auditor, make that person independent of any operational and line management responsibilities for environment, safety or quality, and have them report direct to the senior management team. There is simply no point having an outsider spend weeks or months getting to know your operation before conducting a thorough audit of the management system and all the documentation and data that generates. So, if you have got as far as implementing an environmental program without a centralized audit function to provide expertise and help guide progress you have done extremely well. But now is the time when if you do not already have an environmental auditor on the payroll you should probably get one.

Good young auditors are not necessarily expensive. If they are not to have an executive role, or get too deeply involved in strategic questions or publicly representing a company, you can probably pick one up for the same cost as a midranking management accountant. The more public and strategic this role the more expensive environmental auditors and managers become. The main point is, if you are appointing one of these, you do not need to know any more about audits except:

- always to read audit reports when your receive them (especially the bits about liability and legal compliance)
- to celebrate and reward every example of good performance
- to home in on any deficiencies and recommendations for improvement and require line managements to give you a response
- to ensure that the environmental auditor gets opportunities to present six monthly or annual round-up reports to senior management

■ always to back the auditor if they experience resistance in the organization; they are often all that stands between the executive team and prosecution for environmental offences, liabilities and failures to cut down on waste

■ to support the auditor in taking the environmental performance of the company into the public domain, ideally via verification.

Verification

The term verification came into vogue in the early 1990s when it was used in the European Union Eco management and Audit regulation to describe the process whereby an external accredited agent comes into the company to check that the requirements of the European standard are being met. The term carries a pleasant ring about it, implying that the whole truth and nothing but the truth will emerge from the process (see Case Study 22.7).

CASE STUDY 22.7

Benchmarking and environmental glasnost at Norsk Hydro

Norsk Hydro employs more than 30,000 people in Europe, around half in Norway. The company is involved in a variety of sectors: oil, petrochemicals, fertilizers, light metals, i.e. magnesium and aluminum, pharmaceuticals, and fish farming. Following many assaults on its reputation by environmental groups during the 1980s, Norsk Hydro entered into a collaborative benchmarking exercise with Du Pont in order to help change attitudes, motivate employees and embrace a culture of continuous improvement.

The three cornerstones of Norsk Hydro's new approach were: (i) a shift from a reactive to a proactive strategic approach; (ii) a reinforcement of line management responsibilities; and (iii) a commitment to transparency. The third element was to prove the most interesting and externally influential. In 1989 and 1990 the company published three reports on its environmental performance: for Norway, for the UK and groupwide. The UK report was externally validated, thereby creating a new benchmark for the entire chemical industry. When the European Union published its draft Eco-audit regulation in 1991, external "verification" was firmly established as a key component of best practice in environmental auditing and reporting.

In the context of EMAS and especially the publication of environmental statements, it is important to establish credibility. Sadly, in these days of mistrust and cynicism, stakeholders may not trust a company left to its own devices to produce a full set of accounts on its environmental impacts. Surely, companies would include the good things and omit the bad. This is where the verifier comes in. A company seeking work as an independent verifier of environmental management systems and public statements of environmental performance has to fulfil criteria to gain accreditation under EMAS. The verifier must demonstrate its competence to a national certification body and show that it has appropriate quality assurance procedures in place.

In our experience, even with a well developed environmental management system and audit process, an external verifier adds real value. Because they have a professional reputation to lose and a clear protocol to follow, they cannot ignore any instance of nonconformity with best practice or fail to point out any gaps in an environmental statement. Verification provides a fresh look and an opportunity for an independent person to challenge assumptions and priorities and comment on whether enough effort is being put into meeting best practice. In short it is an invigorating and healthy addition to the management system. Most importantly, the addition of a verifier's statement at the end of a published environmental statement gives a level of confidence in the integrity of that statement to stakeholders which could not be established by the company alone. It is the equivalent of a financial auditor signing off on the annual accounts as a "true and fair" picture.

The main rule for appointing a verifier is to find someone who has done it before and comes with good word of mouth references. Our advice is to change your verifier every three or four cycles to avoid them (and you) getting stale. A good verifier will require you to submit a good deal of documentation (policies, programs, responsibilities, organizational charts, etc.) in advance of their site visits. And they will want to scrutinize your draft environmental statement in great detail. When they visit they will not replicate the audit process but will test data for integrity, sample documentation and interview a range of managers and employees to satisfy themselves of the completeness of the environmental policy and its implementation. After their visit they will provide a statement for inclusion in the published report and a more detailed report to management which adds more recommendations and further urgency (if that is needed) to any areas of noncompliance with best practice or nonconformity with standards. For a typical manufacturing site employing around 1,000 people, verification might take four to five days' consultancy time on site and a similar number of days preparing and reporting.

Even under less stringent standards like ISO 14001, external assessment and certification should be just as rigorous; the main difference being that without a published environmental statement the stakes are much lower.

Publishing your environmental statement

Congratulations. You have got as far as the really interesting part. Everything up to now has been really hard work. There have been opportunities to engage external stakeholders in policy formulation (e.g. nongovernmental organizations), risk and opportunity identification (e.g. the local community) and even the environmental program (e.g. suppliers). But most of the effort has been put in by internal stakeholders, most especially the employees and the company's managers. But now, after all that effort you are ready to engage all your key stakeholder groups in a really big way. In Chapter 8 we discussed the evolution of environmental reporting and we reproduced the United Nations Environment Program five-stage model of sustainable development reporting. Today there is a number of benchmarks and award schemes which allow companies to compare best practice in this vital area of stakeholder communications. Chapter 23 provides guidance on environmental and sustainability reporting.

Ultimately, the responsibility for the style and scope of an environmental or sustainable development report rests with the senior management team, but it is inevitable that the environmental audit/management department, the corporate public relations department and the office of the CEO will play key roles.

PART II – Nonhuman Species

The philosophical discourse on man's relationship with animals goes back centuries[13]. Leonardo da Vinci wrote, "I have from an early age abjured the use of meat, and the time will come when men such as I will look upon the murder of animals as they now look upon the murder of men." Writers Jonathan Swift and George Bernard Shaw were keen advocates of animal rights as were philosophers Jean-Jacques Rousseau and Jeremy Bentham.

In 1976, Australian academic Peter Singer published an influential work entitled *Animal Liberation*[14]. The book accomplished for animal rights what Rachel Carson's *Silent Spring* did for the early environmental movement. It provided a compelling and intellectually coherent critique of prevailing social attitudes to the suffering of animals. As Singer made clear, business had its responsibilities too.

In the mid 1970s, agricultural enterprises in the USA were responsible for the raising and killing of hundreds of millions of cattle, pigs and sheep and no less than 3 billion chickens. Just twelve corporations controlled 40 percent of this total. Little attention was paid to the conditions of battery hens used for egg-laying. Singer quoted the head of a Georgia-based poultry firm with 225,000 laying hens: "The object of producing eggs is to make money. When we forget this objective, we have forgotten what it is about."

Unhappily, in the last two decades the behavior of small groups of extremists on the fringes of the animal rights movement has caused a good deal of resentment and suspicion in business sectors such as agriculture and pharmaceuticals. But this should not distract us from the deepening concern which ordinary citizens express about the welfare of animals in farms and in the laboratory[15].

As a business person, and especially if you and your suppliers are involved directly in the care of animals, it would be unwise to adopt a dismissive attitude on issues of animal rights and animal welfare. It is unlikely that your other stakeholders will.

Agriculture is one area where the treatment of animals plays through directly into public attitudes. Just as direct action environmental protests seem to embrace all ages and sectors of society, so do obvious breaches of good animal welfare practice. Protests against the live exportation of animals from the UK to continental Europe caused uproar in British ports in 1995 and 1996. Conservative politician and historian Alan Clark joined middle-class ladies and young radicals on the picket lines attempting to block the export trade in live farm animals.

In Britain at least some of the growing high levels of consumer concern expressed about agricultural practices relate to the perceived risks of infection with Creutzfeldt Jakob disease from consumption of cattle afflicted by Bovine Spongiform Encephalopathy (BSE); see Case Study 22.8.

A parallel set of consumer concerns relates to the conservation of wild animals and the importance of what we now refer to as biodiversity. Here, if one's business is logging or mining in biodiverse environments, or if one is an agrochemical producer accused of poisoning wildlife in farming areas, or a pharmaceutical company accused of plundering and patenting commercially valuable genetic material from the rainforest, one should expect lively intervention from pressure groups and possible consumer action.

It is worth noting here that there are strong overlaps between welfarism, conservationism and environmentalism, but one should not

CASE STUDY 22.8

Mad Cow Disease: British farmers pay the price and consumers vote with their wallets

BSE first appeared in British cattle in 1986. Controls on infected materials entering cattle feed and the human food chain were introduced in 1988 and 1989 but they were riven with loopholes and poorly enforced. Low levels of compensation for farmers and fierce competition between abattoirs combined to undermine and outwit an under-resourced and ineffectual inspection system. Spot checks by the State Veterinary Service in 1995 showed that 48 percent of abattoirs were failing on aspects of the Specified Bovine Offal (SBO) regulations. Following a government announcement that there may be a link between BSE and a virulent new form of Creutzfeldt Jakob disease in humans, 10 percent of the red meat inspection service were disciplined or dismissed for failure to adhere to regulations. Meanwhile, food retailers were ahead of the game. Fast food outlets like McDonald's imposed a total ban on procurement of British beef, and supermarkets like Tesco introduced quality control schemes of their own to provide consumers with reassurance. And not surprisingly, sales of organic meat soared. Organic farmer Helen Browning concluded that the BSE scare "was a pretty crucial warning of the world. It produced a rise not just in organic meat sales but in all organic sales because people have realised that you can't just forget about where food comes from."

assume that they necessarily come from the same philosophical or political space. Whaling can be opposed on either welfare or conservationist grounds (or both). The shooting and hunting lobby may put conservation high on its list of political priorities but is less concerned about the rights of the birds and animals they kill for sporting purposes. Hunting and fishing bodies may strike up productive strategic alliances with environmental conservation groups but be despised by animal welfare organizations. The oceans' fish may be protected for welfare, conservation or environmental reasons: to protect their rights to exist, to eat them or to marvel at them.

So it is important for business people whose enterprises may impact or depend upon animals that they understand the forces at play, the philosophical and emotional factors which influence stakeholders and most crucially the importance of dialogue to resolve misunderstanding of motives.

The role of the law and standards

According to Francione[16], "as far as the law is concerned, an animal is the personal property, or chattel, of the animal's owner and cannot possess rights." This underlying assumption is something of a handicap to animal rights campaigners, but nevertheless, animal welfare law has been enacted around the world.

In Britain, legislation dates back to 1822 with "Martin's Act" designed to protect the welfare of horses, later extended (1835) to cover all domestic animals. In 1876, the Cruelty to Animals Act sought to control animal experimentation expected to cause pain. Today, welfare legislation operates at both national and regional levels[17]. So, for example, the Council of Europe has five animal welfare conventions covering farm animals, transport, slaughter, animal experimentation and pets. The European Union has, in turn, adopted legislation covering each of these areas and supplemented it with specific measures on hens, calves and pigs, drift net fishing, seals, fur-trapping and wild birds. Some of the strictest national legislation on animal welfare has been developed in Denmark and Switzerland.

In most jurisdictions the law is underpinned by sector-specific guidelines and codes of practice, usually based on the minimization of suffering. For example, a well-established handbook on laboratory experimentation neatly restates the assumptions of the law, i.e. that the experimenter "owns" the animals, but ties this to the needs of the experimenter to generate good science through minimizing stress: "Animal welfare goes hand in hand with good science. Everyone concerned has a duty towards his experimental animals, to ensure that their treatment is in accordance with the best contemporary practice[18]."

In the travel industry, trade associations including the International Air Transport Association (IATA) have adopted minimum standards for air transportation of animals; individual airlines have gone further eliminating live transportation altogether. And enlightened tour companies now include routine advice to tourists on avoiding purchases of souvenirs made from the body parts of endangered species.

The impact on industry and commerce of growing international concerns about the conservation of wild animals has been widespread[17]. There are now four major international conventions on conservation of wild animals: the Convention on International Trade in Endangered Species of Wild Fauna and Flora (CITES 1973), the Convention on Wetlands of International Importance (Ramsar 1971), the Convention Concerning the Protection of the World Cultural and Natural Heritage

(World Heritage Convention, 1972) and the Convention on the Conservation of Migratory Species of Wild Animals (Bonn Convention 1979).

The role of pressure groups

Pressure groups have done their best to drive higher standards for animal protection into business. The fashion industry has long been a target for animal rights activists. In the mid-1990s, the US group People for the Ethical Treatment of Animals (PETA) famously persuaded a number of "super models" to pose (very tastefully) without clothing saying they would "rather go naked" than wear fur. Since the mid-1980s, the cosmetics and toiletries industry has seen successive campaigns against animal testing targeted against some of the major manufacturers and retailers. Much to the irritation of trade associations, animal welfare groups have combined with progressive companies in the sector to produce positive lists of approved companies which avoid animal testing. And in 1996, five US animal welfare groups adopted a strict common standard for the industry.

By far the most bitter disputes have focussed on animal testing in the pharmaceutical industry and in medical research institutes. Here campaigners have targeted the companies and researchers concerned with highly emotive and sometimes daring interventions, releasing laboratory animals, disrupting research programs and picketing annual meetings of companies involved.

But perhaps the greatest area of animal welfare activism where issues of well-being (rather than conservation) impact most on business behavior is in the agricultural and agrochemical sector. Increasingly this plays through consumer and food retailing as people become more concerned about the negative implications for both human and animal health of intensive farming practices. The International Federation of Organic Agriculture Movements (IFOAM) is one of the longest established international forums for promoting humane farming practices. Together with national organic associations around the world, e.g. the US Organic Trade Association, IFOAM sets comprehensive standards which impact on policy-makers, food retailers and consumers alike. Then there are the vegetarian societies that advocate avoidance of meat, and the vegan organizations which would outlaw meat and dairy produce altogether.

In order to provide frameworks for improving animal welfare in agriculture, Compassion in World Farming has produced a Farm Animal Welfare Charter (see Exhibit 22.5).

<hr>

EXHIBIT 22.5

Compassion in World Farming
Farm Animal Welfare Charter

Housing

- Positive encouragement of systems which allow daily access to the out-doors
- Comfortable bedding
- Natural light and ventilation where possible
- Space allowances to permit natural movement and exercise

Physiology

- A planned move away from fast growing strains in e.g. chickens
- Use of slower-growing, more sustainable animals
- Adequate and appropriate feed for each species
- Access to clean water at all times
- No non-therapeutic mutilations, operations or invasive procedures
- Ability to perform natural behaviours, e.g. rooting, dust-bathing, grazing

Psychology

- Companionship of own kind
- No isolation or overcrowding
- Natural weaning periods
- Prohibition of electric goads and rough handling

General welfare

- Live exports for further fattening or slaughter should be brought to an end
- Minimum transport, with a maximum total journey time of 8 hours
- Urgent reform of livestock markets
- Encouragement of alternatives to markets such as direct sales and electronic marketing
- Licensing of all livestock handlers
- Compulsory minimum stunning currents in slaughterhouses

<hr>

Meanwhile in 1994 the UK Royal Society for the Prevention of Cruelty to Animals (RSPCA) launched the Freedom Food labeling scheme which inspects, accredits and trademarks farms, hauliers and abattoirs which abide by five freedoms:

■ freedom from fear and distress

■ freedom from pain, injury and disease

■ freedom from hunger and thirst

■ freedom from discomfort

■ freedom to express normal behavior.

In Britain, retailers like Tesco and the Co-operative Wholesale and Retail Services were quick to adopt the Freedom Food labeling scheme. By the end of 1996, a million of the UK's 750 million farm animals and 1200 farms, hauliers and processors were covered by the scheme. Between 1994 and 1996 the number of eggs sold within the scheme grew from 100,000 to 35 million. Nevertheless, according to Compassion in World Farming, 86 percent of Britain's 33 million egg-laying hens still eke out a miserable existence in battery cages and have urged an immediate phase out of the practice on a Europewide basis[19].

The process

Systems for minimizing or eliminating negative impacts on animals will depend a great deal on which industry you are in and what philosophical stance is most appropriate for your company and stakeholders. In some industries, e.g. pharmaceuticals, testing products on animals may be a legal prerequisite for obtaining a product license and you may have no choice but to continue to test. If one is involved in agriculture, a deeply held belief in animal *welfare* might imply a commitment to organic meat production, whereas a commitment to animal *rights* might necessitate a vegetarian stance.

Our strong recommendation therefore is to pay significant attention to an initial review of policy and strategic objectives before introducing a process of continuous improvement. Secure the best sources of advice on what represents best practice in your industry and using processes described in Chapter 19 enter into close dialogue with well-established animal protection groups and other stakeholders in order to determine expectations and your ability to deliver.

In many cases, animal protection will turn into a supply chain issue in which case the cycle of continuous improvement advocated for quality management in Chapter 18 may prove the best vehicle. For example, we have found that prohibiting animal testing of cosmetics ingredients is best delivered by auditing and external assessment to ISO 9002, an international quality management standard linked to the quality assurance of suppliers. Such an approach would, we believe, lend itself to any consumer or retail driven strategy embracing agricultural and animal products.

Figure 22.2 demonstrates the cycle of continuous improvement used by The Body Shop for ensuring compliance with ISO 9002 for its Against Animal Testing policy.

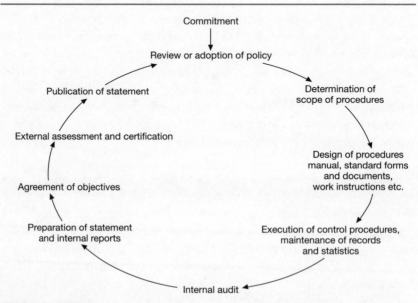

Figure 22.2
Framework for Against Animal Testing auditing and disclosure at The Body Shop[20]

Benchmarks and performance indicators

Below we set out a number of general standards and indicators which a stakeholder-inclusive company could embrace to demonstrate its commitment to animal welfare.

Legal compliance

■ The company should be able to demonstrate compliance with all relevant industry standards and codes of practice, national regulations and licences and international conventions relating to animal welfare and the conservation of wild animals.

Policy

- The company should have clear policies relating to the elimination or minimization of negative welfare impacts on animals, the conservation and protection of endangered species (including fisheries), the promotion of biodiversity wherever the company operates, and to the avoidance of negative impacts of genetic manipulation or bioengineering.

Practices

- Where a company is reliant on animal experimentation it should seek to avoid such experiments except where legally prescribed and should promote the use of humane alternatives to animal testing for all possible applications.

- Where a company is reliant on animal by-products or other agricultural activities involving animals it should seek accreditation wherever feasible to the highest possible standards of welfare.

- Animals should not be used for entertainment, as prizes or as decorations.

- Animals should not be transported long distances except under conditions of strict supervision.

Training

- Company staff responsible for implementation of policy and caring for animals must be competent and ideally licensed or otherwise certified as such.

Auditing and disclosure

- Where relevant, supervisory ethics committees and suitable inspection and auditing schemes should be established to ensure compliance with company policies and procedures; information relating to compliance and details of external assessments and certification should be communicated routinely to stakeholders.

- Where appropriate, animal derived products should be labeled according to best practice standards; labels should be independently granted and certified.

Sponsorship, education and awareness raising

- Where appropriate, the protection of animals should be promoted but only in concert with established conservation and welfare organizations.

CHAPTER 23

Cycle of continuous improvement

transparency and public reporting

The pressure for disclosure

In 1901 Theodore Roosevelt said, "Great corporations exist only because they are created and safe-guarded by our institutions; and it is our right and our duty to see that they work in harmony with these institutions.... The first requisite is knowledge, full and complete; knowledge which may be made public to the world."

Sadly, annual financial reports and accounts are often deadly dull and completely ineffective in holding the attention of stakeholders – even investors. They are required by law, but many are a complete waste of paper and money. Some companies have tried radical departures from convention to stimulate more interest. Dutch consulting firm BSO Origins used its 1991 annual report to raise some fundamental philosophical issues, converting its apparently healthy financial result into a rather more questionable ecological performance by subjecting all of its activities to full environmental costing. Sharing the real costs of global warming would probably dent the balance sheet of most companies.

In 1995, US ice cream manufacturer Ben & Jerry's turned its annual accounts into a colour-in cartoon book – complete with crayons. This was the latest in a long line of sparky ideas to try to add interest and value to the company's reports. Rather more seriously, Ben & Jerry's had for many years been pioneers of social disclosure – including independent commentaries of their social performance in their reports to shareholders.

There have been numerous attempts by more conventional companies to include information about their social and environmental performance in annual reports. Rob Gray and colleagues[1] have described the history of social and environmental accounting and reporting. The work of David Linowes and Abt Associates in the USA in the 1970s was based largely on capturing the cost-benefit impacts of corporate social engagement. Companies like Eastern Gas and Fuel (US), and Atlantic Richfield (US) attempted "total impact" assessments and published the results. In Europe there was less interest in internally driven assessments, although a number of externally commissioned reports were published.

Despite sporadic activity in Europe, e.g. Migros in Switzerland, Fortia in Sweden and Shell in Germany, the social accounting trend declined in the 1980s. Happily it was replaced in the 1990s by a much stronger level of enthusiasm for environmental auditing and reporting and the continuing desire of large companies to include some social commentary in their corporate literature. Today the extent to which environmental and social information is reflected in annual reports still varies very significantly.

Statistics relating to community involvement, charitable giving, human resources and safety are relatively common in the annual reports of top US companies. The Securities and Exchange Commission also has clear environmental disclosure requirements relating to liabilities and future investment commitments. These are often covered in specific sections dealing with regulation. Companies like Grand Metropolitan have made a virtue of their community volunteering and have included plenty of detail in annual reports. In Germany, BMW has included safety statistics in its reports while RWE has included general employment statistics, e.g. on diversity, employee turnover and length of service. Gray and colleagues note that in Europe, German companies are the top reporters for employee-related issues, averaging 3.4 pages per annual report, followed by the UK (2.0 pages), with Swiss, Swedish, Dutch and French companies a little lower. Japanese companies tend to be less forthcoming.

As we have seen from some of the case studies referred to already in this book, the mid-1990s have also seen significantly renewed interest in serious social reporting, both of the audited and nonaudited variety. Cooperatives like the UK Co-operative Retail Services and the Swedish Kooperative Förbundet retail society have been active in nonaudited disclosure, as have credit unions like Vancouver-based VanCity. Sbn Bank and Ben & Jerry's developed a degree of systemization to their public reporting in the early 1990s. Traidcraft, Ben & Jerry's and The Body Shop have now embraced both systemization and external verification.

In 1991 it was estimated that only 8 percent of UK companies outside the chemical sector were engaged in environmental audits of any description. According to management consultancy KPMG, by 1994, more than one third of the FTSE 100 companies were producing stand-alone environmental statements and around two thirds included some environmental information in their annual reports. By 1996, UK-based consultancy SustainAbility estimated that 300 to 400 companies worldwide were producing environmental statements; 27 companies had environmental reporting sites on the Internet, from ABB in Switzerland to Sony in Japan and Xerox in the USA, from Bank America via Ben & Jerry's to BT and The Body Shop[2].

There is an increasingly mainstream understanding of the necessity for credible, appropriate and independently verifiable information on the financial, social and environmental performance of companies. As we have already noted, national regulatory bodies are requiring more and more financial disclosure around issues of governance and liability.

On an international level, one of the most important documents emerging from the UN Conference on Environment and Development in 1992 was Agenda 21[3]. This compendium of prescriptions for every sector of the global economy to achieve sustainable development included a chapter for business and industry. The important point to note about Agenda 21 is that it was not a radical document; it was mainstream. Indeed it had to be drafted by countless international bureaucrats and endorsed by 178 governments. So when the document encourages business and industry "to report annually on their environmental records," it must be taken seriously.

The European Union is not always noted for its vision on social and environmental issues, often moving at the speed of the slowest member state. But its *Fifth Environmental Action Programme: Towards Sustainability* requires that "the public must have access to environmentally relevant data to enable them to monitor the performance of industry and regulators alike[4]." In the UK, the government-appointed Advisory Committee on Business and the Environment Financial Sector working group has argued that environmental disclosure should be one of the listings particulars on the London Stock Exchange. The group has also issued draft environmental accounting and reporting guidelines.

These initiatives are in turn supported by more urgent calls from groups like the Coalition on Environmentally Responsible Economies (CERES) which lobbies for routine disclosure of environmental and safety statistics by US companies.

But perhaps the most telling arguments for corporate environmental disclosure come from within mainstream industry itself. In 1993, management consultants Deloitte Touche Tohmatsu International conducted a survey of industrialists in North America, Europe and Japan to discover attitudes to corporate environmental reporting[5]. Two thirds of survey respondents agreed that companies "hardly ever" release disadvantageous information. More than 60 percent accepted that voluntary reporting will "never be adequate" and that stricter legislation will be necessary.

With increasing demands for coverage of corporate governance issues in annual reports and the unstoppable trend for more social and environmental disclosure, it is inevitable that something has to give. It is simply not practical to include everything in a single report.

It is our belief that companies will increasingly produce consistent but tailored summaries of relevant financial, social and environmental information for each stakeholder group. The trend towards summary financial statements for individual shareholders is already well established. The British Airports Authority found that when given the option, 86 percent of their private investors chose a summary financial statement rather than the full report and accounts; BAA calculates this saves them half a million pounds a year. Around one-third of FTSE companies now produce summary financial reports. Many companies have produced separate corporate marketing statements in addition to their annual reports and accounts. Happily, where early marketing statements dealt primarily with environmental issues (the infamous "green glossies"), they tended to graduate in the direction of properly constituted environmental reports later.

So the overall direction is clear. Companies which have an increasing amount of information to disclose are struggling to do it in one corporate report for all stakeholders. And with the number of stories to tell and the amount of data being generated, it is even more difficult to incorporate the public relations spin (i.e. glossy photographs of chief executives or products) without the whole thing becoming a self-indulgent waste of space.

So our prediction is that stakeholder corporations of the future will produce limited numbers of comprehensive reports, detailing all business-related financial, environmental and social information. Some full reports may be necessary for analysts, institutional investors and a minority of individual shareholders. And some may be needed for general distribution to business partners, trade bodies and academic institutions. But the smart company will put the whole thing on the Internet and save paper. It will also produce targeted, stakeholder-specific summaries according to demand and need.

The process

As with most processes advocated in this book, a cycle of continuous improvement is the best way to approach corporate reporting to stakeholders. The model in Figure 23.1 is as applicable to financial reporting as it is to social and environmental reporting.

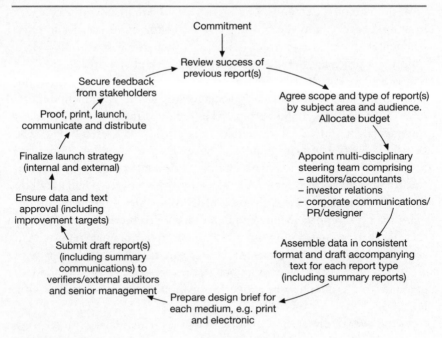

Figure 23.1
Cycle of continuous improvement for public reporting

Each of the steps shown in Figure 23.1 needs little clarification. Most companies will have sufficient experience in communicating with investors, employees and customers to be able to judge these audiences appropriately.

Many companies quite rightly put special emphasis on internal audiences, i.e. managers and employees. These are arguably the people who most need to be convinced that the process is an authentic part of improving the business and who need to get behind corporate and business unit targets. In our experience, there is no substitute for vibrant internal communications, face-to-face meetings between senior executives and shop floor workers to convey the seriousness of the message of financial, social and environmental performance. Senior managers must motivate and enthuse employees and line managers. They should do internal roadshows, not just send out summary reports with covering memos or rely on corporate videos – helpful though both these may be by way of reinforcement. There must be a genuine desire to generate feedback on the reports themselves.

Benchmarks and performance indicators

As noted in Chapter 8, coming from a declared sustainable development perspective, the UN Environment Programme published their five-stage plan for environmental and social/economic reporting in 1994. Two years later the scale was expanded, with 50 quantitative indices ("reporting ingredients") based on four point scales. Suddenly, stakeholder inclusion had arrived in a big way. No longer could companies argue that systematic disclosure of social information was impossible or that indicators of sustainability were too diffuse. Here was a set of measures which any company could use to benchmark the quality of its environmental and social disclosure. From UNEP's perspective, accountability to stakeholders should not be restricted to good public consultation on a company's environmental report, as IBM and Dow Chemicals in Europe had pioneered[6]. The UNEP rating required systematic and active engagement with stakeholders on the full range of environmental, social and economic questions – the triple bottom line.

SustainAbility describe ten transitions on corporate environmental and social reporting for the future (see Table 23.1).

These ten transitions, together with the fifty quantitative indicators (reporting ingredients) which are used for the UNEP rating, are the benchmarks we recommend for stakeholder corporations wishing to build a reputation for transparency and integrity. For benchmarks on each stakeholder relationship, please refer to the relevant chapters.

Table 23.1
Ten transitions

Established focus on		Emerging focus on:
1 One-way, passive communication	➡	Multi-way, active dialogue
2 Verification as option	➡	Verification as standard
3 Single company progress reporting	➡	Benchmarkability
4 Management systems	➡	Life cycles, business design, strategy
5 Inputs and outputs	➡	Impacts and outcomes
6 Ad hoc operating standards	➡	Global operating standards
7 Public relations	➡	Corporate governance
8 Voluntary reporting	➡	Mandatory reporting
9 Company determines reporting boundaries	➡	Boundaries set through stakeholder dialogue
10 Environmental performance	➡	Triple bottom line – economic, environmental and social – performance

We conclude with seven dos and don'ts for public reporting – tips to bear in mind throughout the process[7] (see Exhibit 23.1).

Seven dos and don'ts of public reporting

Do put internal monitoring systems in place and ensure that senior management and staff are committed to regular monitoring, auditing and reporting.

Do consider who your key stakeholders are and design your communications appropriately.

Do agree what your objectives are – not only for ethical management but also for reporting. Ensure that these relate to overall company goals.

Do concentrate on priority issues and report on them in depth while keeping reports simple, clear and user friendly.

Do represent raw data clearly in diagram or table format to allow reader interpretation.

Do be honest. Report on the problems as well as the progress. Your performance should be transparent and accountable.

Do ask for feedback. You need to understand whether you are meeting the needs of your stakeholders by offering questionnaires or discussion forums for completion.

Don't attempt to publish an ethical statement without having the infrastructure in place and support of management and employees for systematic auditing.

Don't attempt to meet the needs of all stakeholders in one communication vehicle; a report designed to meet everybody's needs could end up serving nobody's.

Don't decide to report without a clear direction for your ethical management. Reporting is easier to start than it is to stop.

Don't be tempted to report on every aspect of ethical issues in exhaustive detail.

Don't detract from the information by overuse of graphics or photographs.

Don't attempt to overhype information. PR will be seen for what it is and judged accordingly.

Don't underestimate the importance of stakeholder feedback. You are not just reporting on what you want to say but also what you think your stakeholders want to know.

Epilogue

We hope you have enjoyed this book. We have tried to advance an optimistic vision of free enterprise based on a socially responsible approach to business which fosters commercial resilience and rejects conflict and unnecessary distress.

Those business people, and there are many, who believe that companies have a higher purpose than simply the creation of financial wealth will have no difficulty accepting the central idea of stakeholder inclusion which we advocate in the book. We hope they will use the best practice examples and techniques described in the later chapters as a source of ideas for their own work. Business people who have a more traditional perspective may take issue with some of the historic and economic analyses in the earlier parts of the book. But we trust they too will recognize the overwhelming evidence which suggests that stakeholder inclusive behavior is also good for business: good for customer loyalty, good for employee empowerment and good for the bottom line. Whether one looks to North America, Europe or the Far East, this conclusion is inescapable.

Stakeholder inclusion is no longer restricted to the fringes of the socially responsible business sector. The most successful companies in the world are active on most, if not all, fronts: through community programmes, charitable donations, investments in training and career development of employees, promotion of diversity in the workplace, quality management, and environmental and safety management. A growing number of companies, east and west, foster active partnerships with suppliers, government agencies, voluntary organizations and trade unions.

Looked at from this perspective, stakeholder inclusion ceases to look like a soft option or some kind of philanthropic add-on. It means complying with the law and seeking to meet best practice in one's own business sector. It means being open and transparent in one's dealings with investors, employees and customers. It means engaging with the local community and with civil society in a constructive and mutually beneficial way.

We believe that in the future, stakeholder inclusion will be the key to long term commercial viability. In coming years, the most successful businesses will draw on all of the best traditions of free enterprise. They will combine innovation with stability, match flexibility with security, and balance short term entrepreneurship with long term planning. They will learn from different business cultures around the world and leave behind them the sterile debates of yesteryear. They will recognize that in deepening relationships, increasing levels of trust and sharing ideas they will maximize their commercial opportunities.

In an ever more complex and competitive global economy, those companies which fail to connect with their customers, fail to harness the creative energy of their employees and suppliers, and fail to respond to the needs of the wider community, will lose out. Companies which do communicate, which do engage and which build lasting commitment based on genuine involvement, will succeed.

If you would like to take the ideas and suggestions in the book further, we would invite you to join the growing networks of practitioners in this field by filling out and returning the form opposite. We will undertake to connect you into the right network.

Are you seriously interested in becoming a stakeholder inclusive corporation?

Please return to:

New Academy of Business Centre for Stakeholding & Sustainable Enterprise
The Business School
Kingston University
Kingston Hill
Kingston Upon Thames
Surrey KT2 7LB
UK

Mr/Mrs/Miss/Ms/Dr/Prof

Name _____

Department _____

Job Title _____

Organization _____

Address _____

_____

E-Mail _____ Fax No. _____

Areas of special interest _____

Audits   ❏

Surveys   ❏

Quality management and stakeholding   ❏

Environmental management   ❏

Ethical issues   ❏

Management training   ❏

Other   ❏

Any comments on *The Stakeholder Corporation*?

_____

_____

References and further reading

Introduction
1   Plender, J. (1997) *A Stake in the Future: The Stakeholding Solution*. London: Nicholas Brealey.
2   Kay, J. (1995) *Foundations of Corporate Success: How Business Strategies Add Value*. Oxford: Oxford University Press.

Chapter 1
1   Carmichael, S. (1995) "Business ethics: the new bottom line." Paper No. 16. London: Demos.
2   Handy, C. (1995) *The Empty Raincoat. Making Sense of the Future*. London: Arrow.
3   Galbraith, J. K. (1992) *The Culture of Contentment*. London: Sinclair-Stevenson.
4   Hutton, W. (1996) *The State We're In*. London: Vintage.
5   Hamilton, N. (1992) *JFK. Reckless Youth*. London: Random House.
6   Anonymous (1996) *Primary Colors. A Novel of Politics*. London: Chatto & Windus.
7   Power, M. (1994) "The audit explosion." Paper No. 7. London: Demos.
8   Nalebuff, B. J. and Brandenburger, A. M. (1996) *Co-opetition*. London: HarperCollins.

Case study
1.1   Based on Achar, R., Nitkin, D., Otto, K., Pellizzani, P. and EthicScan Canada (1996) *Shopping with a Conscience*. Toronto: John Wiley and Sons.

Chapter 2
1   Trevelyan, G. M. (1978) *English Social History*. London: Longman.
2   Galbraith, J. K. (1977) *The Age of Uncertainty*. London: BBC/André Deutsch.
3   Keane, J. (1995) *Tom Paine, A Political Life*. London: Bloomsbury.
4   Reilly, R. (1978) *Pitt the Younger. 1759–1806*. London: Cassell.
5   Ehrman, J. (1969) *The Younger Pitt*. London: Constable.
6   Ayling, S. (1991) *Fox. The Life of Charles James Fox*. London: John Murray.
7   Gregg, P. (1973) *A Social and Economic History of Britain 1760–1972*. London: George G. Harrap.
8   Moscowitz, M., Levering, R. and Katz, M. (1990) *Everybody's Business. A Field Guide to the 400 Leading Companies in America*. New York: Doubleday.
9   Jacobs, M. (1991) *The Green Economy*. London: Pluto.

Case study
2.1   Based on Keane, J. (1995), ibid.

Chapter 3
1   Bryan, L. and Farrell, D. (1996) *Market Unbound. Unleashing Global Capitalism*. New York: John Wiley and Sons.
2   Worldwatch Institute (1996) *Vital Signs*. New York: W. W. Norton.
3   Bennett, R. (1996) *International Business*. London: Pitman Publishing.
4   MacShane, D. (1996) "Global Business, Global Rights." Pamphlet No. 575.

London: Fabian Society.

5 Charkham, J. (1995) *Keeping Good Company. A Study of Corporate Governance in Five Countries.* Oxford: Oxford University Press.

Case study

3.1 Based on an article in the *Financial Times*, 25 October 1996.

Chapter 4

1 Hobsbawm, E. J. (1990) *Industry and Empire.* London: Penguin.
2 Hobsbawm, E. J. (1995) *The Age of Capital 1848–1875.* London: Weidenfeld and Nicolson.
3 Goyder, G. (1993) *The Just Enterprise. A Blueprint for the Responsible Company.* London: Adamantine Press.
4 Bryson, B. (1995) *Made in America.* London: Minerva.
5 Cannon, T. (1992) *Corporate Responsibility.* London: FT/Pitman Publishing.
6 Anon (undated) *Outline of American History.* Washington: US Information Service.
7 Estes, R. (1996) *The Tyranny of the Bottom Line. Why Corporations Make Good People Do Bad Things.* San Francisco: Berrett-Koehler.
8 Korten, D. C. (1995) *When Corporations Rule the World.* West Hartford, Conn: Kumarian Press Inc. and Berrett-Koehler Publishers.
9 Anderson, S. and Cavanagh, J. (1996) *The Top 200. The rise of global corporate power.* Washington: Institute for Policy Studies.
10 Rifkin, J. (1996) *The End of Work. The Decline of the Global Labor Force and the Dawn of the Post-market Era.* New York: G. P. Putnam's Sons.

Case study

4.1 Based on an article in *The Observer*, 27 October 1996.

Chapter 5

1 Friedman, M. (1962) *Capitalism and Freedom.* Chicago: University of Chicago.
2 Baumhart, R. S. J. (1968) *Ethics in Business.* New York: Holt, Rinehart and Wilson.
3 Velasquez, M. G. (1982) *Business Ethics.* Englewood Cliffs, New Jersey: Prentice-Hall.
4 Donaldson, T. (1982) *Corporations and Morality.* Englewood Cliffs, New Jersey: Prentice-Hall.
5 de George, R. T. (1986) *Business Ethics.* London: Macmillan.
6 Donaldson, T. (1989) *The Ethics of International Business.* Oxford: Oxford University Press.
7 Donaldson, T. (1992) *Business Ethics: A European Case Book.* London: Academic.
8 Sutton, B. (ed.) (1993) *The Legitimate Corporation. Essential Readings in Business Ethics and Corporate Governance.* Cambridge, Mass: Blackwell.
9 Sorrell, T. and Hendry, J. (1995) *Business Ethics.* Oxford: Butterworth-Heinemann.
10 Kitson, A. and Campbell, R. (1996) *The Ethical Organisation.* Basingstoke: Macmillan.
11 Galbraith, J. K. (1977) *The Age of Uncertainty.* London: BBC/André Deutsch.
12 Galbraith, J. K. (1974) *Economics and the Public Purpose.* London: André Deutsch.
13 Hutton, W. (1996) *The State We're In.* London: Vintage.
14 Sheridan, T. and Kendall, N. (1992) *Corporate Governance. An Action Plan for Profitability and Business Success.* London: Pitman Publishing.
15 Bain, N. and Band, D. (1996) *Winning Ways Through Corporate Governance.*

London: Macmillan Business Press.
16   Hennessy, P. (1992) *Never Again. Britain 1945–51*. London: Jonathan Cape.
17   Shuman, M. H. (1994) "GATTzilla v Communities". *Cornell International Law Journal*, 27 (3): 527–52.
18   Lang, T. and Hines, C. (1994) *The New Protectionism*. London: Earthscan.

Case studies
5.1   Based on Korten, D. C. (1995) *When Corporations Rule the World*. West Hartford, Conn: Kumarian Press Inc. and Berrett-Koehler Publishers.
5.2   Based on a personal communication from Ed Mayo of the New Economics Foundation.
5.3   Based on VanCity (1995) *Annual Report*.
5.4   Based on an article in *The Observer*, 3 November 1996.
5.5   Based on an article in *The Guardian*, 27 August, 1996.
5.6   Based on an article in *The Observer*, 3 November 1996.
5.7   Based mostly on Pilger, J. (1989) *A Secret Country*. London: Jonathan Cape.

Chapter 6
1   Goyder, G. (1993) *The Just Enterprise. A Blueprint for the Responsible Company*. London: Adamantine Press.
2   Cannon, T. (1992) *Corporate Responsibility*. London: FT/Pitman Publishing.
3   Galbraith, J. K. (1977) *The Age of Uncertainty*. London: BBC/André Deutsch.
4   Galbraith, J. K. (1974) *Economics and the Public Purpose*. London: André Deutsch.
5   Sampson, A. (1995) *Company Man. The Rise and Fall of Corporate Life*. London: HarperCollins.
6   Moskowitz, M., Levering, R. and Katz, M. (1990) *Everybody's Business. A Field Guide to the 400 Leading Companies in America*. New York: Doubleday.
7   Peters, T. (1992) *Liberation Management. Necessary Disorganisation for the Nanosecond Nineties*. New York: Alfred A. Knopf.
8   Handy, C. (1995) *The Empty Raincoat. Making Sense of the Future*. London: Arrow.
9   Sheridan, T. and Kendall, N. (1992) *Corporate Governance. An Action Plan for Profitability and Business Success*. London: Pitman Publishing.
10   DuPree, M. (1989) *Leadership is an Art*. New York: Doubleday.
11   Liebig, J. (1994) *Merchants of Vision*. San Francisco: Berrett-Koehler.
12   White, R. P., Hodgson, P. and Crainer, S. (1996) *The Future of Leadership. A Whitewater Revolution*. London: Pitman Publishing.
13   Cannon, T. (1996) *Welcome to the Revolution. Managing Paradox in the 21st Century*. London: Pitman Publishing.

Case studies
6.1   Based on an article in *The Guardian*, 15 November 1996.
6.2   Based on Nunan, R. (1988) "The libertarian conception of corporate property: a critique of Milton Friedman's views on the social responsibility of business." *Journal of Business Ethics*, 7:891–906.

Chapter 7
1   Gregg, P. (1973) *A Social and Economic History of Britain 1760–1972*. London: George G. Harrap.
2   Trevelyan, G. M. (1978) *English Social History*. London: Longman.
3   Reed, J. (1926) *Ten Days That Shook The World*. London: Communist Party of Great Britain.
4   Snow, E. (1937) *Red Star Over China*. London: Left Book Club.
5   Radice, E. A. and Radice, G. H. (1974) *Will Thorne. Constructive Militant*.

London: George Allen and Unwin.

6   Jones, J. (1986) *Union Man*. London: Collins.
7   Moldea, D. E. (1978) *The Hoffa Wars*. New York: Paddington Press.
8   MacShane, D. (1996) "Global business, global rights." Pamphlet No. 575. London: Fabian Society.
9   Cannon, T. (1992) *Corporate Responsibility*. London: FT/Pitman Publishing.
10 Galbraith, J. K. (1977) *The Age of Uncertainty*. London: BBC/André Deutsch.
11 Birchall, J. (1994) *Co-op. The People's Business*. Manchester: Manchester University Press.
12 Goyder, G. (1993) *The Just Enterprise. A Blueprint for the Responsible Company*. London: Adamantine Press.
13 Fingleton, E. (1996) *Blindside: Why Japan is Still on Track to Overtake the US by the Year 2000*. London: Simon and Schuster.
14 Gold, M. (ed.) (1996) "Direct participation in organisational change." *European Participation Monitor*. Issue No. 12. Dublin: European Foundation for the Improvement of Living and Working Conditions.
15 Rifkin, J. (1996) *The End of Work. The Decline of the Global Labor Force and the Dawn of the Post Market Era*. New York: G. P. Putnam's Sons.
16 Roberts, E. (1966) *Consumers*. London: New Thinker's Library.
17 Mayer, R. N. (1989) *The Consumer Movement. Guardians of the Marketplace*. Boston: Twayne.
18 Bollier, D. (1989) *Citizen Action and Other Big Ideas: A History of Ralph Nader and the Modern Consumer Movement*. Washington: Center for Study of Responsive Law.
19 Sim, F. G. (1991) *IOCU on Record: A Documentary History of the International Organisation of Consumers' Unions 1960–1990*. New York: Consumers Union.
20 John, R. (1994) *The Consumer Revolution: Redressing the Balance*. London: Consumers' Association.

Case studies
7.1 Based on articles in *The Observer*, 1 September 1996 and *The Guardian*, 16 November 1996.
7.2 Based on Reder, A. (1995) *75 Best Business Practice for Socially Responsible Companies*. New York: G. P. Putnam's Sons.
7.3 Based on an article in the *Financial Times*, 25 October 1996.

Chapter 8

1   Welford, R. and Starkey, R. (1996) *Business and the Environment*. London: Earthscan.
2   Taylor, A. (1992) *Choosing Our Future. A Practical Politics of the Environment*. London: Routledge.
3   US Environmental Protection Agency (1991). *Environmental Stewardship*. Washington: USEPA.
4   World Commission on Environment and Development (1987). *Our Common Future*. Oxford: Oxford University Press.
5   United Nations (1992) *Agenda 21*. Geneva: UN.
6   Schmidheiny, S. with The Business Council on Sustainable Development (1992) *Changing Course*. Cambridge Mass: MIT Press.
7   Hawken, P. (1993) *The Ecology of Commerce. A Declaration of Sustainability*. New York: HarperCollins.
8   Gore, A. (1992) *Earth in the Balance*. New York: Houghton Mifflin.
9   UNEP (1994) *Company Environmental Reporting: A Measure of the Progress of Business and Industry towards Sustainable Development*. Technical Report 24. Paris: United Nations Programme.

10   Pepper, D. (1993) *Eco-socialism. From Deep Ecology to Social Justice*. London: Routledge.

Case study
8.1   Based on MacCarthy, F. (1994) *William Morris*. London: Faber and Faber.
8.2   Based on Taylor, A. (1992) *Choosing our Future*. ibid.

Part Two
1   Hutton, W. (1996) *The State We're In*. London: Vintage.
2   Royal Society for the Encouragement of Arts, Commerce and Manufactures (1995) *Tomorrow's Company*. London: RSA.
3   Freeman, E. (1984) *Strategic Management: A Stakeholder Approach*. Marshfield, MA: Pitman Publishing.
4   Carroll, A. and Näsi, J. (1997) 'Understanding Stakeholder Thinking: Themes from a Finnish Conference,' *Business Ethics: A European Review*, 6(1), pp. 46–51.

Chapter 9
1   Friedman, M. (1962) *Capitalism and Freedom*. Chicago: University of Chicago Press.
2   Hayek, F. (1944) *The Road to Serfdom*. Chicago: University of Chicago Press.
3   Sternberg, E. (1994) *Just Business: Business Ethics in Action*. London: Little, Brown and Company.
4   Fayol, H. (1949) *General and Industrial Management*. London: Pitman Publishing (first published 1916).
5   Berkeley-Thomas, A. (1993) *Controversies in Management*. London: Routledge.
6   Taylor, F. (1911) *Principles of Scientific Management*. New York: Harper & Row.
7   Crainer, S. (1996) *Key Management Ideas: Thinking that Changed the Management World*. London: Pitman Publishing.
8   Gilbert, D., Hartman, E., Mauriel, J. and Freeman, E. (1988) *A Logic for Strategy*. Cambridge, MA: Ballinger Publishing.
9   Kennedy, C. (1996) *Managing with the Gurus: Top Level Guidance on 20 Management Techniques*. London: Random House.
10   Ansoff, I. (1965) *Corporate Strategy: Business Policy for Growth and Expansion*. New York: McGraw-Hill.
11   Chandler, A. (1962) *Strategy and Structure: Chapters in the History of American Industrial Enterprise*. Cambridge, MA: MIT Press.
12   Sloan, A. (1964) *My Years with General Motors*. New York: Doubleday.
13   Andrews, K. (1987) *The Concept of Corporate Strategy*. Homewood, Ill: Richard D. Irwin.
14   Steiner, G. (1969) *Top Management Planning*. New York: Macmillan Press.
15   Higgins, J. (1979) *Organizational Policy and Strategic Management*. Hinsdale, Ill.
16   Lorange, P. (1982) *Implementation of Strategic Planning*. Englewood-Cliffs, NJ: Prentice-Hall.
17   Levitt, T. (1960) "Marketing myopia." *Harvard Business Review*, July–August: 45–56.
18   Markowitz, H. (1959) *Portfolio Selection: Efficient Diversification of Investments*. New York: John Wiley.
19   Abell, D. (1977) "Using PIMS and portfolio analysis in strategic market planning – a comparative analysis. Harvard Business School Case: 578–617.
20   Ohmae, K. (1982) *The Mind of the Strategist*. New York: McGraw-Hill.
21   Ouchi, W. (1981) *Theory Z: How American Business Can Meet the Japanese Challenge*. Reading, MA: Addison-Wesley.

22   Porter, M. (1980) *Competitive Strategy: Techniques for Analysing Industries and Competitors*. New York: Free Press.

23   Porter, M. (1985) *Competitive Advantage: Creating and Sustaining Superior Performance*. New York: Free Press.

24   Porter, M. (1990) *The Competitive Advantage of Nations*. London: Macmillan Press.

25   Stalk, G. and Hout, T. (1990) *Competing Against Time*. New York: The Free Press.

Chapter 10

1   Ansoff, I. (1979) "The changing shape of the strategic problem". In: Schendel, D. and Hofer, C. (eds) *Strategic Management: A New View of Business Policy and Planning*. Boston: Little, Brown and Company.

2   Morgan, G. (1986) *Images of Organization*. Beverly Hills: Sage Publications.

3   Kanter, R. (1983) *The Change Masters*. New York: Simon & Schuster.

4   Mayo, E. (1933) *The Human Problems of an Industrial Civilisation*. New York: Macmillan.

5   Drucker, P. (1954) *The Practice of Management*. New York: Harper & Row.

6   Drucker, P. (1969) *The Age of Discontinuity: Guidelines to Our Changing Society*. New York: Harper & Row.

7   Maslow, A. (1954) *Motivation and Personality*. New York: Harper & Row.

8   McGregor, D. (1960) *The Human Side of Enterprise*. New York: McGraw-Hill.

9   Herzberg, F., Mauser, B. and Snyderman, B. (1959) *The Motivation to Work*. New York: John Wiley.

10   Herzberg, F. (1966) *Work and the Nature of Man*. World Publishing.

11   Heilbronner, R. (1964) "The view from the top: reflections on a changing business ideology." In: Cheit, E. (ed.) *The Business Establishment*. New York: John Wiley.

12   Jacoby, N. (1973) *Corporate Power and Social Responsibility: A Blueprint for the Future*. New York: Macmillan.

13   David, K. and Bloström, R. (1975) *Business and Society: Environment and Responsibility*. New York: McGraw-Hill.

14   Capra, F. (1996) *The Web of Life: A New Synthesis of Mind and Matter*. London: HarperCollins.

15   Burrell, G. and Morgan, G. (1979) *Sociological Paradigms and Organizational Analysis*. London: Heinemann Educational Books.

16   Kast, F. and Rosenzweig, J. (1970) *Organization and Management: A Systems Approach*. New York: McGraw-Hill.

17   Dill, W. (1975) "Public participation in corporate planning: strategic management in Kibitzer's world." *Long Range Planning*, 8(1): 57–63.

18   Brenner, S. and Molander, E. (1977). "Is the ethics of business changing?", *Harvard Business Review*, 58: 54–65.

19   Freeman, E. (1984) *Strategic Management: A Stakeholder Approach*. Marshfield, MA: Pitman Publishing.

20   Freeman, E. and Gilbert, D. (1988) *Corporate Strategy and the Search for Ethics*. Englewood Cliffs, NJ: Prentice-Hall.

21   Mintzberg, H. (1976) "Planning on the left side and managing on the right." *Harvard Business Review*, July–August: 49–58.

22   Minztberg, H. (1989). *Mintzberg on Management: Inside Our Strange World of Organizations*. New York: The Free Press.

23   Andrews, K. (1987) *The Concept of Corporate Strategy*. Homewood, Ill: Richard D. Irwin.

24   Aldrich, H. (1979) *Organizations and Environments*. Englewood Cliffs, NJ: Prentice-Hall.

Chapter 11

1 Ouchi, W. (1981) *Theory Z*. Reading, MA: Addison-Wesley.
2 Trist, L. (1982) "The evolution of socio-technical systems as a conceptual framework and as an action research programme." In: Van de Ven, H. and Joyce, W. (eds) *Perspectives on Organization Design and Behaviour*. New York: John Wiley.
3 Trist, E., Higgin, G., Murray, H. and Pollok, A. (1963) *Organizational Choice*. London: Tavistock.
4 Trist, E. (1976) "A concept of organisational ecology." *Australian Journal of Management*, 2.
5 Shein, E. (1985) *Organisational Culture and Leadership*. San Francisco: Jossey-Bass.
6 Handy, C. (1977) *Understanding Organisations*. London: Penguin.
7 Handy, C. (1978) *The Gods of Management*. London: Pan Books.
8 Parcale, R. and Athos, A. (1981) *The Art of Japanese Management*. New York: Simon & Schuster.
9 Peters, T. and Waterman, R. (1982) *In Search of Excellence*. New York: Harper & Row.
10 Deal, T. and Kennedy, A. (1982) *Corporate Cultures*. Reading. MA: Addison-Wesley.
11 Capra, F. (1996) *The Web of Life: A New Synthesis of Mind and Matter*. London: HarperCollins.
12 Argyris, C. and Schon, D. (1978) *Organizational Learning: A Theory of Action Perspective*. Wokingham: Addison-Wesley.
13 State, R. (1989) "Organizational learning: the key to management innovation." *Sloan Management Review*, Spring.
14 Argyris, C. (1990) *Overcoming Organisational Defences*. Boston, MA: Allyn & Bacon.
15 Stacey, R. (1992) *Managing Chaos: Dynamic Strategies in an Unpredictable World*. London: Kogan Page.
16 Morgan, G. (1986) *Images of Organisation*. Beverly Hills: Sage Publications.
17 Bateson, G. (1979) *Mind and Nature*. New York: Bantam Books.
18 Senge, P. (1990) *The Fifth Discipline: The Art & Practice of The Learning Organisation*. New York: Doubleday.
19 Stacey, R. (1993) "Strategy as order emerging from chaos." *Long Range Planning* 26(1).
20 Nonaka, I. (1991) "The knowledge-creating company." *Harvard Business Review,* November–December.
21 Garvin, D. (1993) "Building a learning organisation." *Harvard Business Review,* July–August.
22 Nonaka, I. and Takeuchi, H. (1995) *The Knowledge-Creating Company: How Japanese Companies Create the Dynamics of Innovation*. New York: Oxford University Press.
23 Hammer, M. and Champy, J. (1993) *Re-engineering the Corporation: A Manifesto for Business Revolution*. London: Nicholas Brealey.
24 Gilbert, D. (1995) "Management and four stakeholder politics." *Business & Society*, April.
25 Rifkin, J. (1996) *The End of Work: The Decline of the Global Labour Force and the Dawn of the Post-Market Era*. New York: G. P. Putman's Sons.
26 Micklethwait, J. and Woolridge, A. (1996) *The Witch Doctors: What the Management Gurus Are Saying, Why It Matters and How to Make Sense of It*. London: Heinemann.

Chapter 12

1   Sheridan, T. and Kendall, N. (1992) *Corporate Governance. An Action Plan for Profitability and Business Success*. London: Pitman Publishing.
2   Marsden, C. (1996) *Corporate Citizenship*. Warwick University Business School.
3   Industrial Society (1996) *Managing Ethics*. Managing Best Practice 26. London: Industrial Society.
4   Goyder, G. (1993) *The Just Enterprise. A Blueprint for the Responsible Company*. London: Adamantine Press.
5   Gray, R., Owen, D. and Adams C. (1996) *Accounting and Accountability. Changes and Challenges in Corporate Social and Environmental Reporting*. London: Prentice Hall.
6   New Economics Foundation (1996) *Social Auditing for Small Organizations. The Workbook*. London: NEF.
7   Power, M. (1994) "The audit explosion." Paper No. 7. London: Demos.

Case study
12.1 Based on authors' experience.

Chapter 13

1   New Economics Foundation (1996) *Social Auditing for Small Organisations. The Workbook*. London: NEF.
2   International Survey Research (1996) *Understanding Employee Survey Results: Managers' Guidelines*. London: ISR.
3   Zadek, S., Pruzan, P. and Evans, R. (1997) *Building Corporate Accountability. Emerging Practice in Social and Ethical Accounting and Auditing*. London: Earthscan.

Chapter 14

1   Oxford Analytica (1992) *Board Directors and Corporate Governance. Trends in the G7 Countries over the Next Ten Years*. Oxford: Oxford Analytica.
2   Gee Publishing (1996) *The Corporate Governance Handbook* (Executive Editor Richard A. Derwent, Consultant Editor Martyn E. Jones). London: Gee Publishing.

Case studies
14.1 Based on Gee Publishing (1996) *The Corporate Governance Handbook*. (Executive Editor Richard A. Derwent, Consultant Editor Martyn E. Jones). London: Gee Publishing.
14.2 Based on Coopers & Lybrand (1995) *The Greenbury Effect. Company Reactions to the Greenbury Report on Directors' Remuneration*. London: Coopers & Lybrand.
14.3 Based on Industrial Society (1996) *Director Development*. Managing Best Practice 23. London: Industrial Society.
14.4 Based on Gee Publishing (1996). ibid.
14.5 Based on Gee Publishing (1996). ibid.
14.6 Based on Sbn Bank (1993) *The Ethical Accounting Statement*.
14.7 Based on The Body Shop (1996) *Social Statement 95*.

Chapter 15

1   Collins, J. C. and Porras, J. I. (1995) *Built to Last. Successful Habits of Visionary Companies*. London: Century, Random House.
2   Cannon, T. (1996) *Welcome to the Revolution. Managing Paradox in the 21st Century*. London: Pitman Publishing.
3   Senge, P. (1990) *The Fifth Discipline*. New York: Doubleday.

4   Garvin, D. A. (1993) "Building a learning organization." *Harvard Business Review*. July–August; 78–91.

5   Senge, P., Kleiner, A., Roberts, C., Ross, R. B. and Smith, B. J. (1996) *The Fifth Discipline Fieldbook. Strategies and Tools for Building a Learning Organization*. London: Nicholas Brealey.

6   Joyce, M. E. (1995) *How to Lead Your Business Beyond TQM. Making World Class Performance a Reality*. London: Pitman Publishing.

7   Fox, M. (1994) *The Re-invention of Work: A New Vision Of Livelihoods For Our Time*. San Francisco: Harper San Francisco.

8   Porter, M. (1980) *Competitive Strategy*. New York: The Free Press.

9   Rifkin, J. (1996) *The End of Work. The Decline of the Global Labor Force and the Dawn of the Post-market Era*. New York: G. P. Putnam's Sons.

10   Industrial Society (1995) *Employee Consultation*. Managing Best Practice 7. London: Industrial Society.

11   Capra, F. (1996) *The Web of Life. A New Synthesis of Mind and Matter*. London: HarperCollins.

12   Jackson, C., Arnold, J., Nicholson, N. and Watts, A. G. (1996) *Managing Careers in 2000 and Beyond*. Institute for Employment Studies Report No. 304. Brighton: IES.

13   Vince, R. (1996) *Managing Change. Reflections on Equality and Management Learning*. Bristol: The Policy Press.

14   Reder, A. (1995) *75 Best Business Practices for Socially Responsible Companies*. New York: G. P. Putnam's Sons.

15   Ross, R. and Schneider, R. (1992) *From Equality to Diversity: A Business Case for Equal Opportunity*. London: Pitman Publishing.

16   Court, G. (1995) "Creating a culture for equality." In: *Towards 2000: A Workplace Agenda for the Next Half Decade*. London: Opportunity 2000/GHN Ltd.

17   Hirsh, W. (1995). "The business case". In: *Towards 2000: A Workplace Agenda for the Next Half Decade*. London: Opportunity 2000/GHN Ltd.

18   Council on Economic Priorities and Hollister, B., Will, R., Tepper Marlin, A. and Dyott, S., Kovacs, S. and Richardson, L. (1994) *Shopping for a Better World*. San Francisco: Sierra Club Books.

19   Sbn Bank (1993) *Ethical Accounting Statement 1993*.

20   Miceli, M. P. and Near, J. P. (1992). *Blowing the Whistle. The Organizational and Legal Implications for Companies and Employees*. New York: Lexington.

21   Hunt, G. (ed.) (1995) *Whistleblowing in the Health Service. Accountability, Law and Professional Practice*. London: Edward Arnold.

22   Carmichael, S. and Drummond, J. (1989) *Good Business. A Guide to Corporate Responsibility and Business Ethics*. London: Century Hutchinson.

23   Phillips, M. and Rasberry, S. (1996) *Honest Business. A Superior Strategy for Starting and Managing Your Own Business*. Boston US: Shambhala.

24   Industrial Society (1994) *Employee Surveys*. Managing Best Practice 5. London: Industrial Society.

Case studies

15.1 Based on Industrial Society (1995) *Empowerment*. Managing Best Practice 8. London: Industrial Society.

15.2 Based on Skandia (1995) *Value-Creating Processes*, and Collins, J. and Porras, J. ibid.

15.3 Based on Ben & Jerry's Homemade Inc (1994) *Annual Report*, and Ben & Jerry's (1996) *1995 Social Report*.

15.4 Based on an article in *The Guardian*, 18 November 1996, and Industrial Society (1995) *Managing Diversity*. Managing Best Practice 14. London: Industrial Society.

15.5 Based on VanCity (1995) *Annual Report*, and Ben & Jerry's (1996) *1995 Social Report*.

15.6 Based on Co-operative Retail Services (1988) *Social Report*.

15.7 Based in part on an article in *The Guardian*, 18 October 1996.

15.8 Based on Sbn Bank (1993) *Ethical Accounting Statement 1993*.

15.9 Based on International Survey Research (1996) *Understanding Employee Survey Results: Managers' Guidelines*. London: ISR.

15.10 Based on Ben & Jerry's Homemade Inc (1996) *1995 Social Report*.

15.11 Based on The Body Shop International (1996) *Social Statement 95*.

15.12 Based on Tuffrey, M. (1995) *Employees and the Community*. London: PRIMA Europe.

Chapter 16

1   Council on Economic Priorities and Hollister, B., Will, R., Tepper Marlin, A. and Dyott, S., Kovacs, S. and Richardson, L. (1994) *Shopping for a Better World*. San Francisco. Sierra Club Books.

2   Saunders, R. and Wheeler, T. (1991). *Handbook of Safety Management*. London: Pitman Publishing.

3   Krause, T. R., Hidley, J. H. and Hodson, S. J. (1990) *The Behavior-based Safety Process-Managing Involvement for an Injury-free Culture*. New York: Van Nostrand.

4   Chemical Industries Association (1995) *Responsible Care Management Systems for Health, Safety and Environment*. London: CIA.

5   Health and Safety Executive (1991) *Successful Health and Safety Management* (HS (G) 65). Sudbury: HSE.

6   Croner (regularly updated) *Health and Safety at Work*. Kingston Upon Thames: Croner.

7   Harrison, L. (ed.) (1995) *Environmental, Health, and Safety Auditing Handbook*. New York: McGraw-Hill.

8   Wheeler, D. (1994) "Auditing for sustainability." In: Harrison, L. (ed.) (1995). ibid.

Case studies

16.1 Based on M&M Protection Consultants (1990) *Large Property Damage Losses in the Hydrocarbon Chemical Industries. A Thirty Year Review*. New York: M&M.

16.2 Based on Stack, J. (1992) *The Great Game of Business. The Only Sensible Way to Run a Business*. New York: Doubleday.

16.3 Based on Human Factors in Reliability Group (1995) *Improving Compliance with Safety Procedures. Reducing Industrial Violations*. Sudbury: Health and Safety Executive.

16.4 Based on Reder, A. (1995) *75 Best Practices for Socially Responsible Companies*. New York: G. P. Putnam's Sons.

16.5 Based on an article in *Occupational Health and Safety*, October 1996.

16.6 Based on Health and Safety Executive (1996) *The Chemical Release and Fire at Associated Octel Company Ltd*. Sudbury: HSE.

16.7 Based on *Workers Health International Newsletter*, Issue 47/48. Summer 1996.

Chapter 17

1   Galbraith, J. K. (1974) *Economics and the Public Purpose*. London: André Deutsch.

2   Bryson, B. (1995) *Made in America*. London: Minerva.

3   Kraus, J. (1994) *The GATT Negotiations*. Paris: ICC.

4   Council on Economic Priorities and Hollister, B., Will, R., Tepper Marlin, A.,

   and Dyatt, S., Kovacs, S. and Richardson, L. (1994) *Shopping for a Better World*. San Francisco: Sierra Club Books.

5   Elkington, J. and Hailes, J. (1988) *The Green Consumer Guide*. London: Victor Gollancz.

6   Achar, R., Nitkin, D., Otto, K., Pellizani, P. and EthicScan Canada (1996) *Shopping with a Conscience*. Toronto: John Wiley and Sons.

7   Coddington, W. (1993) *Environmental Marketing. Positive Strategies for Reaching the Green Consumer*. New York: McGraw-Hill.

8   Lübke V., Schoenheit, I., Wilhelm, A. and Winter, W. (1995) *Der Unternehmens-tester. Die Lebensmittel-branche. Ein ratgeber für den verantwortlichen einkauf*. Hamburg: Rowohlt.

9   Ohashi, T. (1995) "Economic efficiency and environment in Japan – how green are the Japanese consumers, companies and government from the viewpoint of green marketing." *Journal of Economic Studies (Reitakin International)* 3 (1): 59–81.

10   Smith, N. C. (1990) *Morality and the Market. Consumer Pressure for Corporate Accountability*. London: Routledge.

11   International Chamber of Commerce (1995) *ICC International Codes of Marketing and Advertising Practice*. Paris: ICC.

Case studies

17.1 Based on an article in *The Observer*, 6 October 1996.

17.2 Based on an article in *The Guardian*, 13 November 1996.

17.3 Based on an article in *The Guardian*, 23 August 1996.

17.4 Based on an article in *The Guardian*, 11 September 1996.

17.5 Based on an article in *The Guardian*, 17 August 1996.

17.6 Based on an article in *The Times,* 14 November 1996.

17.7 Based on Paul Winstone Research (1996) *Drawing the Line. A Survey into the Prevailing Standards of Taste and Decency in Non-broadcast Advertising*. London: Advertising Standards Authority.

17.8 Based on Sbn Bank (1993) *The Ethical Accounting Statement*.

Chapter 18

1   Reichheld, F. (1996) *The Loyalty Effect*. Harvard, Mass: Harvard Business School Press.

2   Hall, T. J. (1995) *The Quality Systems Manual. The Definitive Guide to the ISO 9000 Family and TickIT*. Chichester: John Wiley.

3   Oakland, J. S. (1996) *Total Quality Management. Text with Cases*. Oxford: Butterworth-Heinemann.

4   Moskowitz, M., Levering, R. and Katz, M. (1990) *Everybody's Business. A Field Guide to the 400 Leading Companies in America*. New York: Doubleday.

5   The Equality Foundation (1995) *Equal Opportunities Quality Framework*. Bristol: The Equality Foundation.

Case studies

18.1 Based on Normann, R. and Ramírez, R. (1993) "From value chain to value constellation: designing interactive strategy." *Harvard Business Review*, July–August: 65–77.

18.2 Based on information provided by Philips.

18.3 Based on Harfield, T. (1996) "The Rover experience." *European Participation Monitor*, 12: 37–41.

18.4 Based on information provided by Unipart.

18.5 Based on Industrial Society (1996) *Business Excellence*. Managing Best Practice 25. London: Industrial Society.

Chapter 19

1   Chadwick, T. and Rajagopal, S. (1995) *Strategic Supply Management. An implementation toolkit.* Oxford: Butterworth-Heinemann.
2   Hines, P. (1994) *Creating World Class Suppliers.* London: Pitman Publishing.
3   Lamming, R. (1993) *Beyond Partnership – Strategies for Innovation and Loan Supply.* Englewood Cliffs, New Jersey: Prentice Hall.
4   Womack, J. P., Jones, D. T. and Roos, D. (1990) *The Machine that Changed the World.* New York: Rawson.
5   Department of Trade and Industry (1995) *Getting the Best from Your Supply Partners. A management overview.* London: HMSO.
6   Independent Monitoring Working Group (1996) *Open Trading: Monitoring Working Conditions Against Corporate Codes of Conduct.* Draft Discussion Paper. London: New Economics Foundation.
7   Business in the Environment (1993) *Buying into the Environment.* London: BiE.
8   Sorrell, T. and Hendry, J. (1994) *Business Ethics.* Oxford: Butterworth-Heinemann.

Case studies
19.1   Based on Chadwick, T. and Rajagopal, S. (1995). ibid.
19.2   Based on Independent Monitoring Group (1996). ibid; and Reder, A. (1995) *75 Best Business Practices for Socially Responsible Companies.* New York: G. P. Putnam's Sons.
19.3   Based on Traidcraft plc (1995) *Social Accounts 1994–1995*; and The Body Shop International (1996) *Social Statement 95.*
19.4   Based on Ben & Jerry's Homemade Inc (1996) *1995 Social Report*; and The Body Shop International (1996) *Social Statement 95.*

Chapter 20

1   Tuffrey, M. (1995) *Employees and the Community. How Successful Companies Meet Human Resource Needs Through Community Involvement.* London: PRIMA Europe.
2   Brown, L. R., Flavin, C. and Kane, H. (1996) *Vital Signs 1996. The Trends that are Shaping our Future.* New York: W. W. Norton.
3   Business in the Community (1994) *The Per Cent Club.* London: Business in the Community.

Case studies
20.1   Based on Logan, D. (1993) *Transnational Giving. An introduction to the corporate citizenship of international companies operating in Europe.* London: The Directory of Social Change.
20.2   Based on Grand Metropolitan (1994) *Community Involvement.*
20.3   Based on British Petroleum (1994) *BP in the Community. International Report.*
20.4   Based on Ben & Jerry's (1996) *1995 Social Report.*
20.5   Based on an article in *The Guardian,* 15 June 1996.
20.6   Based on Tuffrey, M. (1995) *Employees in the Community,* ibid; and Sbn Bank (1993) *The Ethical Accounting Statement.*

Chapter 21

1   Nelson, J. (1996) *Business as Partners in Development.* London: Prince of Wales Business Leaders Forum
2   Grant, W. (1993) *Business and Politics in Britain.* Basingstoke: Macmillan
3   Epstein, E. M. (1969) *The Corporation in American Politics.* Englewood Cliffs, New Jersey: Prentice Hall.
4   Moskowitz, M., Levering, R. and Katz, M. (1990) *Everybody's Business. A Field Guide to the 400 Leading Companies in America.* New York: Doubleday.

5   Korten, D. C. (1995) *When Corporations Rule The World*. West Hartford, Conn: Kumarian Press Inc. and Berrett-Koehler Publishers.

6   Council on Economic Priorities and Alperson, M, Tepper Marlin, A., Scorsch, J. and Will, R. (1991) *The Better World Investment Guide*. New York: Prentice-Hall.

7   Rowell, A. (1996) *Global Subversion of the Environmental Movement*. London: Routledge.

8   Cannon, T. (1992) *Corporate Responsibility*. London: Pitman Publishing.

9   Burlinghame, D. F. and Young, D. (eds) (1996) *Corporate Philanthropy at the Crossroads*. Indiana University Press.

10 Marsden, C. (1996) *Corporate Citizenship*. Warwick University Business School.

11 Coddington, W. (1993) *Environmental Marketing. Positive Strategies for Reaching the Green Consumer*. New York: McGraw-Hill.

12 Business in the Community (1994) *Managing for Success. A Study of Community Involvement Management*. London: BiTC.

Case studies
21.1 Based on Keane, J. (1995) *Tom Paine. A Political Life*. London: Bloomsbury.
21.2 Based on Sampson, A. (1996) *Company Man. The Rise and Fall of Corporate Life*. London: HarperCollins.
21.3 Based on an article in *The Guardian*, 18 September 1996.
21.4 Based on an article in *The Observer*, 8 September 1996.
21.5 Based on an article in the *Financial Times*, 27 August 1996.
21.6 Based on The Body Shop International (1996) *Social Statement 95*.

Chapter 22

1   Croner (regularly updated) *Environmental Management, Policies and Procedures*. Kingston Upon Thames: Croner.

2   Worldwatch Institute (1996) *Vital Signs*. New York: W. W. Norton.

3   Business in the Environment (1993) *Buying into the Environment. Guidelines for Integrating the Environment into Purchasing and Supply*. London: BiTC.

4   MacGillivray, A. and Zadek, S. (1995) *Accounting for Change*. London: New Economics Foundation.

5   Business in the Environment (1992) *A Measure of Commitment*. London: BiTC.

6   Harrison, L. (ed.) (1995) *Environmental, Health, and Safety Auditing Handbook*. New York: McGraw-Hill.

7   Greeno, J. L., Hedstrom, G. S. and Di Berto, M. (1986) *Environmental Auditing. Fundamentals and Techniques*. Cambridge, Mass: Arthur D. Little.

8   Sayre, D. (1996) *Inside ISO 14001. The competitive advantage of environmental management*. Delray Beach FL: St Lucie Press.

9   Business in the Environment (1995) *EC Eco-Management and Audit Scheme (EMAS) – Positioning Your Business*. London: BiTC.

10 Porter, M. and van der Linde, C. (1996) "Green and competitive: ending the stalemate". In: Welford, R. and Starkey, R. (eds) (1996). *Business and the Environment*. London: Earthscan.

11 Ditz, D., Ranganathan, J. and Banks, R. D. (eds) (1995) *Green Ledgers: Case Studies in Corporate Environmental Accounting*. Washington: World Resources Institute.

12 ENDS (1995) *Directory of Environmental Consultants*. London: Environmental Data Services.

13 Magel, C. R. (1989) *Animal Rights*. London: Mansell.

14 Singer, P. (1976) *Animal Liberation: Towards an End to Man's Inhumanity to*

Animals. London: Jonathan Cape.

15   Ryder, R. D. (1975) *Victims of Science: The Use of Animals in Research*. London: Dennis-Poynter.

16   Francione, G. L. (1995) *Animals, Property and the Law*. Philadelphia: Temple University Press.

17   World Society for the Protection of Animals (1995) *Animal Protection Legislation. Guidance Notes and Suggested Provisions*. London: WSPA.

18   Poole, T. B. (ed) (1987) *The UFAW Handbook on the Care of Laboratory Animals*. Harlow: Longman.

19   Compassion in World Farming (1996) *A Welfare Charter for Laying Hens*. Petersfield: CIWF.

20   The Body Shop International (1996) *The Body Shop Approach to Ethical Auditing*. Littlehampton: The Body Shop.

Case studies

22.1   Based on Kennedy, R. D. (1994) "Have Laptop, Will Travel". In: Harrison, L. (1995) *Environmental, Health, and Safety Auditing Handbook*, ibid.

22.2   Based on an article in *The Japan Times*, 8 October 1996.

22.3   Moskowitz, M., Levering, R. and Katz, M. (1990) *Everybody's Business. A Field Guide to the 400 Leading Companies in America*. New York: Doubleday; and Dressler, A. and Schmid, D. (1994) "Manufacturing: Environmental Auditing at 3M." In: Harrison, L. (1995) ibid.

22.4   Based on *Network News* (1995) The Environmental Network Newsletter by Working Group of Japan ECP Committee. Issue 2.

22.5   Based on von Welzier Høvik, H. (1996) *Taking Anticipatory Ethics Seriously in Strategic Management: A Case Study*. Oslo: Norwegian School of Management.

22.6   Based on an article in the *ENDS Report*, 261, October 1996.

22.7   Based on Aarasether, S-I. (1994) "Environmental, health, and safety auditing at Norsk Hydro." In: Harrison, L. (1995). ibid.

22.8   Based on articles in *The Observer*, 22 December 1996; and *The Guardian*, 8 January 1997.

Chapter 23

1   Gray, R., Owen, D. and Adams C. (1996) *Accounting and Accountability. Changes and Challenges in Corporate Social and Environmental Reporting*. London: Prentice Hall.

2   SustainAbility and United Nations Environment Programme (1996) *Engaging Stakeholders. Engaging Stakeholders 1: The Benchmark Survey. The second international progress report on company environmental reporting*. Paris: United Nations Environment Programme.

3   United Nations (1992) *Agenda 21*. Geneva: UN.

4   European Community (1992) *5th Environmental Action Programme: Towards Sustainability*. Brussels: Commission of the European Communities.

5   Deloitte Touche Tohmatsu International, International Institute for Sustainable Development and SustainAbility (1993) *Coming Clean*. London: Touche Ross.

6   IBM (1995) *Consulting the Stakeholder*.

7   The Body Shop International (1996) *The Body Shop Approach to Ethical Auditing*. Littlehampton: The Body Shop.

Index